THE MAKING OF MODERN THEOLOGY

NINETEENTH- AND TWENTIETH-CENTURY TEXTS

This major series of theological texts is designed to introduce a new generation of readers—theological students, students of religion, professionals in ministry, and the interested general reader—to the writings of those Christian theologians who, since the beginning of the nineteenth century, have had a formative influence on the development of Christian theology.

Each volume in the series is intended to introduce the theologian, to trace the emergence of key or seminal ideas and insights, particularly within their social and historical context, and to show how they have contributed to the making of modern theology. The primary way in which this is done is by allowing the theologians chosen to address us in their own words.

There are three sections to each volume. The Introduction includes a short bibliography of the theologian, and an overview of his or her theology in relation to the texts which have been selected for study. The Selected Texts, the bulk of each volume, consist largely of substantial edited selections from the theologian's writings. Each text is also introduced with information about its origin and its significance. The guiding rule in making the selection of texts has been the question: in what way has this particular theologian contributed to the shaping of contemporary theology? A Select Bibliography provides guidance for those who wish to read further both in the primary literature and in secondary sources.

Series editor John W. de Gruchy is Professor of Christian Studies at the University of Cape Town, South Africa. He is the author of many works, including *Church Struggle in South Africa*, and *Theology and Ministry in Context and Crisis*.

Volumes in this series

1. Friedrich Schleiermacher: Pioneer of Modern Theology
2. Rudolf Bultmann: Interpreting Faith for the Modern Era
3. Paul Tillich: Theologian of the Boundaries
4. Dietrich Bonhoeffer: Witness to Jesus Christ
5. Karl Barth: Theologian of Freedom
6. Adolf von Harnack: Liberal Theology at Its Height
7. Reinhold Niebuhr: Theologian of Public Life

D0911201

Adolf von Harnack, 1851–1930

THE MAKING OF MODERN THEOLOGY

Nineteenth- and Twentieth-Century Texts
General Editor: John W. de Gruchy

ADOLF VON HARNACK

Liberal Theology at Its Height

MARTIN RUMSCHEIDT
Editor

Fortress Press
Minneapolis

ADOLF VON HARNACK:
Liberal Theology at Its Height
The Making of Modern Theology series

First Fortress Press edition, 1991. Copyright © 1988, assigned 1991 Augsburg Fortress.

Internal design: Colin Reed
Cover design: Neil Churcher
Cover photo: from an oil on canvas painted by Hans Kowatzki, 1901, in the private collection of Dr. Margarete von Zahn, Berlin, and used with her kind permission.

Library of Congress Cataloging-in-Publication Data

Harnack, Adolf von, 1851–1930.
    [Selections. English. 1991]
    Adolf von Harnack : liberal theology at its height / ed. Martin
Rumscheidt.
       p.   cm.
    Reprint. Originally published: London : Collins ; San Francisco :
Harper & Row, 1989. (The Making of modern theology).
    Includes bibliographical references and indexes.
    ISBN 0-8006-3406-3
    1. Theology. 2. Dogma, Development of. 3. Christianity—Essence,
genius, nature. I. Rumscheidt, Martin. II. Title. III. Series:
Making of modern theology.
    [BR85.H24 1991]
    230'.092—dc20   91-14238
                                                   CIP

Manufactured in the U.S.A.   AF 1-3406

---

95   94   93   92   91   1   2   3   4   5   6   7   8   9   10

CONTENTS

EDITOR'S NOTE

However much one may welcome the invitation to prepare an anthology of texts which are to introduce others to a significant theologian's person and work, the final product reveals how much such an introduction bears the individual editor's personality. I do not conceal that, ever since the time of working on my dissertation, the person of Adolf von Harnack has deeply fascinated me. I experienced how much he had touched me in a poignant way in 1982 when, on a visit to Berlin, I went to Grünewald, where the Harnacks had lived for so long, only to find that in the course of through-way construction the house had been demolished. Disappointment became anger; fortunately, my host that afternoon, Dr. von Zahn, took me to a number of other places in the city where the long and significant career of Harnack had left its "spirits."

The anthology also shows the editor's theological perspective. As an historical theologian, I am attracted to Harnack's work; his pursuit of development and change, his search for the reasons of the changes was so sharp and discerning. In that he became and remains my teacher. But I try not to share the theological liberalism of his which I find today far too bound by the privileged position he held, with so many others of those who influenced the thinking of the time, in European society. Instead, I like to be able to see, with eyes as sharp as his, how theological liberalism itself needs to be reformed, if it is even capable of reform, in order to be able to speak of the gospel with a clarity like his.

The translations of Harnack, found in this volume, are not of a piece; at least six different hands are at work here. Some of them are my own, others I had prepared by a colleague, the Revd. Nancy Price. I owe her much for that labor and thank her here for it. There has been no attempt to coordinate all the texts in the diversity of translation nor to make the language inclusive. Suffice it to say, it has become clear to modern readers that the German *Mensch* and *Menschheit* would have to be rendered consistently into English by inclusive terms, such as human being and humanity. But just as one can train oneself in writing to use inclusive language, so one can train oneself to read a text as if it were written in such language.

It would be remiss of me not to express my thanks to John W. de Gruchy for his invitation to return, once again, to one of my "old flames" and produce a Harnack reader. I am grateful to the staff of the Library of Atlantic School of Theology in Halifax and to the Librarian of Yale Divinity School in New Haven, Stephen L. Peterson, for their help in securing texts for selection. Finally, I wish to declare publicly my ongoing appreciation of the contribution made to my studies of Adolf von Harnack by dedicating this volume to my host in Grünewald in 1982, Harnack's grand-daughter, still residing in Berlin, Frau Dr. Margarete von Zahn.

Martin Rumscheidt
Atlantic School of Theology
May 1988

ABBREVIATIONS

C   *What is Christianity?*

CA   *Confessions of St. Augustine*

CH   *Christianity and History*

CL   *Constitution and Law of the Church in the First Two Centuries*

HD   *History of Dogma*

OHD   *Outlines of the History of Dogma*

PSR   *The Present State of Research in Early Church History*

SG   *Essays on the Social Gospel*

TfG   *The Two-fold Gospel in the New Testament*

INTRODUCTION
HARNACK'S LIBERALISM IN THEOLOGY: A STRUGGLE FOR THE FREEDOM OF THEOLOGY

What kind of people are they who live lives in which it is possible to produce a literary legacy of over sixteen hundred titles, while they are full professors at an illustrious university, presidents for lengthy periods of international congresses, general directors of Royal Libraries in their nation's capital and, by an imperial decree, first president of a Royal Society — and all of those positions overlapping one with another? Since this is Harnack of whom we speak, the question is: what kind of person was Harnack? When he was elected president of the Evangelical-Social Congress, he was fifty-two years old; two years later he took on the Royal Library position; these two he held concurrently for six years. At the age of sixty, laying down the Congress' presidency, he assumed that of his monarch's Royal Society, whilst still retaining his position as general director of the Library and full professor at the University of Berlin. These two positions, not counting the university job, overlapped by ten years. Only at the age of seventy did he allow himself to hold only one of them — the Royal Society; he was still its president when he died in his 80th year, during the 18th annual meeting of that Society, at which he was presiding.

Who are such people who, in addition, also manage to combine all that with a rich personal life? Who was Adolf von Harnack, the man, academician, theologian and Christian? And what was his theology?

I

"I was born on the 7th of May 1851 in the school of veterinary medicine at Dorpat and was one of the 'superfluous'" — this is how Adolf Harnack used to reply when asked about his origins. "'Superfluous' was the appellation given the people who lived across the Embach, that is, in that part of town which was reached by crossing the stone bridge across the little river Embach."[1]* "Superfluous" — the word is a play on the two Latin

---

*For numbered footnotes see pp. 321ff.

words *super* and *fluvius*, in German *überflüssig*, over or across the river. He was the older of the twins Adolf and Axel, the second and third of the five children of theologian Theodosius Andreas Harnack and Anna Carolina Maria Ewers, whose residence at the time of the twins' birth was in a wing of the veterinary school. Dorpat, now known as Tartu, is in what used to be called East Prussia, today part of the Soviet Socialist Republic of Estonskaja. The Harnacks were Lutheran and belonged, by education, social position and, by a strong degree too of conscious-ness-reinforcement, to the ruling minority of Prussians who main-tained the language and customs of Germany in this far outpost of German ecclesial and commercial missionary work. The Lutheran uni-versity in the city had been founded in the 17th century; here Theo-dosius Harnack taught church-history and homiletics and was, in addition, the university preacher.

Adolf Harnack's early childhood was spent in Erlangen, the ortho-dox Lutheran university-town in Bavaria; the family had moved there in 1853 when Professor Harnack had received a call there. Four years after the move from Dorpat Harnack's mother died in childbirth, aged only twenty-nine. His father took the upbringing of the five children entirely into his own hands. He was a man of very serious disposition who seldom laughed (AZH 17). When Adolf Harnack was in his mid-teens, at a time when changes are difficult for many an adolescent, he and his family moved back to Dorpat where his father took up a position at the university again. It was hard for the young Harnack to leave Erlangen (AZH 19). His father had also remarried by this time. It was, however, a return to the aristocratic existence of the leading Prussian citizenry of the region. To his life's end, that part of the Baltic was "home" to Harnack; the outcome of World War I and the effect it had on the region troubled him deeply (AZH 20). As early as 1868 he resented the "Russification" of so many aspects of life there, especially the pres-sure that was put on everything German (AZH 21).

He concluded his secondary education at Dorpat a brilliant student; his interest in theology well established. Shortly before the final exam-inations he wrote to his closest friend of Erlangen days, Stintzing:

"You will have heard that I am going to study theology. I do not know whether you are one of those who look down on everything called religion and theology with disdain or indifference. And yet, no matter how one looks at Christianity and possibly regards it as a mistake, is it not of real value to pursue the history of this mistake and to discover which world-shaking events and transformations this mistake has caused? . . . The longer I live . . . the more I discover daily that all problems and conflicts finally go back to the religious dimension . . . and why the Christian point of view can never be quite discarded. That is why I am an enthusiastic theologian; I hope to find in this scholarly discipline (*Wissenschaft*) the *way* towards solving the major problems of our life. . . . I do not desire to be given the fulness of ready-made statements of faith, rather, I want to produce every statement in that web by myself and then make it my own" (AZH 23). As shall be seen later, in this are the roots of Harnack's theological liberalism: the need to understand, to know religion historically and to relate it to all other historical phenomena, to push beyond the merely dogmatic or creedal to the living core or essence of religious truths and then to defend the self-won insights with frankness, integrity and reason.

At eighteen, he entered the University of Dorpat and the male student fraternity Livonia; unlike many other fraternity students in Prussia he refused to fight duels. His father influenced him profoundly with his rigorous application of scholarly method and strong attachment to Luther's work and personality. Another of his teachers, Moritz von Engelhardt, introduced him to the necessity and rigors of textual criticism and the study of original sources. Those influences were to shape Harnack's entire academic life. In 1872 he left Dorpat to study at the University of Leipzig where, in the course of a year, he wrote his doctoral dissertation and, within another year, his habilitation-dissertation. He flourished in that ancient centre of learning and commerce, now a key city in the new, first German *Reich*. Lutheran orthodoxy shaped the theological faculty, but the precision of textual and historical criticism governed the scholarly work of its professors. Harnack's first dissertation was entitled "Source Criticism and the History of Gnosticism" (AZH 43); it reaped great praise from his former teacher, Engelhardt, for whom Harnack's methodological precision was confirmation that, in spite of Lutheran orthodoxy, it was possible to pursue scholarly excellence (AZH 44). His praise confirmed the young Harnack in his own insistence on the primacy of method in theological study, a view he reaffirmed fifty years later in his correspondence with Karl Barth. The *Habilitationsschrift* was written in the remarkably short period of five months; according to university regulations, it had to be written in Latin. Its title was "*De Appelis Gnosi monarchica*". Once that thesis had been accepted he had to pass an oral examination for which he had to propose theses for public debate. Among them are two which augured things to come in his theological position as a mature scholar: "It is not possible to write a *life* of Jesus" and "There is no other method for the exegesis of Holy Scripture than the grammatical-historical one" (AZH 46).

In the Autumn of 1875 Harnack began his long career as a university teacher; at the same time, he started a "church-history society" which met regularly at his apartment. His first course of lectures was on gnosticism, a subject he was never to lose interest in; one hundred and twenty students enrolled in it (AZH 47). He was much liked by his students; and when he received a call to the university of Giessen in 1878 they mounted a counter-action, which included sending a delegation to the minister of education of Saxony, to have Harnack remain at Leipzig.

While at Leipzig he took up with remarkable energy the task of providing critical editions of texts, or of revising existing ones, which did not meet scholarly standards. This called for precise chronological tables and geographical details. He rejoiced in maps and tables as essential aids in the study of history. One of his major works, *The Mission and Expansion of Christianity in the First Three Centuries*, contains maps which he drew himself (AZH 56). The second interest which was also to mark his work till the end, namely the study of church-history as an integral part of the entire intellectual history of humankind, resulted from his work at Leipzig. Harnack maintained that these two histories have to be studied by means of the same methods even though God's revelation is contained in the history of the church. "How is such a dual aspect to be sustained?" is the methodological question the young professor asked. And how are creeds and dogmas to be studied as being both of individual faith and public history?

When he left Leipzig he had published ninety works and before he accepted the call to a full professorship at Giessen he had turned down already two other similar invitations (AZH 62). Another significant event of his days at Leipzig needs mention: in 1877 Harnack met Albrecht Ritschl, who was teaching in Göttingen. It was this theologian in whom Harnack saw genuine potential for Christianity as an ecclesial institution in the modern intellectual climate. "The future of Protestantism as a religion and a spiritual power lies in the direction which Ritschl has indicated" (AZH 64). To his life's end Harnack pointed to him as an example and point of orientation which would rescue theology from romantic diversions and irrationalism.

From 1879 to 1886 Harnack taught at the University of Giessen in the state of Hesse. Just before he arrived, there were only fifteen students in the theology faculty. Such numbers were new to him as was the fact that as the head of the department (as we would say today) he had both to deal with administrators and act as one himself. The number of students grew exponentially in his days at Giessen, as did his organizational and administrative skills. One day he went to see a sick student in his residence and found him with other students playing dominoes. The other students did not know Harnack. When they asked what he was he replied: a theologian. You must be in your upper years of study, they said, to which he answered: yes, the full professor years (AZH 82).

In December 1879 Harnack and Amalie Thiersch were married. She was a Roman Catholic and they had met in Leipzig. On their honeymoon Harnack was taken very ill and they had to rush home from their trip.

"It was decided to return to the home in Giessen immediately. Inexplicable pains in the back and head, sleeplessness, fever and nausea produced a picture of illness which the doctors, including his father-in-law, who had rushed to their side, could not diagnose. Some spoke of neuralgia, others urged electric treatment and Thiersch recommended champagne to raise the spirit, which caused quite a stir in little Giessen. Harnack had to cancel his lectures; only weeks later could he resume them, and then only when resting at home on a sofa. His young spouse took the opportunity . . . to listen in. But the pains and the other symptoms of illness did not leave; a stay at the spa in Wiesbaden did not help either. Then, one warm summer day in May brought a surprising and happy change. Harnack was resting on the sofa, his shirt-sleeves rolled up, when his spouse discovered in his elbow, almost wholly covered by skin, one half of a thick, rusting darning-needle; she was able to remove it after a small incision. The other half, that with the eye, was located further up in the arm and removed surgically. That needle, which had entered the body with some piece of clothing, had wandered through the body and caused pain and other disturbances in nerves and muscles. Gone were the shadows which had covered the first months of marriage" (AZH 86).

Four children, three daughters and then a son, were born in Giessen between 1881 and 1886. All the while Harnack worked hard as the new editor of the prestigious *Theologische Literaturzeitung* and began his monumental *History of Dogma*. For nearly thirty years he edited the journal; in Giessen alone he wrote two hundred reviews for it, including works in French, English and Russian. This work attracted the attention of scholars outside Germany and, in turn, brought students to

Giessen from England, the United States and Switzerland (AZH 83). But Harnack also imposed his theological orientation on the *Literaturzeitung*, reaping both support and opposition. At the personal level he tried to hold together what, at the level of scholarship, had to be separated: namely personal relations of friendship and the rigorous pursuit of truth in the academic manner. When the first volume of *History of Dogma* appeared it became apparent that many would not remain friends. In the church he was seen by many to be heretical, while in the academy others lamented his unmoving orthodoxy; public debates turned *ad hominem* in their attacks.

In the course of thirteen months he wrote the first volume of the *History*, while working on it he smoked so heavily that he became totally exhausted and had to stay in a sanatorium to recover (AZH 98). The book appeared in December 1885; it was intended to create "reflective restlessness" in the readers with, as Harnack saw it, the current, dangerously confused situation of Christian faith. In a letter to his friend Loofs he wrote:

"I believe that we cannot move onward without an element of iconoclasm. Since we may not act iconoclastically in a direct fashion, just because neither the pulpit nor the church's instruction are the place for such action, our books have to present that dimension. We have to have it there if we want to free Protestantism from its false entanglements and prepare for the crisis which has to come if our Christian and educated people are to have confidence again, not in this or that isolated item, but in the whole of evangelical Christianity. I do not want to spare any student of theology this incisive crisis. All three possible consequences of that crisis, namely dropping theology altogether, hardening one's need for authority or seeking understanding, are more desirable than this mushy stew of emotion and thought which students store up at university through sheer indifference only to sprinkle it with what is called 'experience on the job' which turns out to be no more than simple routine. Given the way things stand today, the best teacher, in my view, is the one who knows how to combine a living witness to the gospel with a *fortiter scandalizare* (an energetic scandalizing) and to whom the one is as much an inner need as the other" (AZH 103).

The response was not long in coming; the chief critique was that Harnack made use of the New Testament and Christianity as *sources*, rather than as *norms*, for the formation of personal faith (AZH 104). But it was his father's critique which troubled him the most.

"Our difference is not a theological, but a profound, directly Christian difference. I would deny Christ were I to gloss over it. For whoever regards the fact of the resurrection as you do — to mention only the all-important and main issue — is, in my view, no longer a Christian theologian" (AZH 105).

The fame of the book — and it was, after all, only the first of several volumes — prompted Harvard University to offer Harnack a position; he declined in the hope that the discussions concerning a post in Prussia would lead to a fruitful conclusion. As it turned out he left Giessen in 1886 and went to Marburg. The Harnacks stayed there for two years. But Marburg was not Prussia, it was still Hesse. Nevertheless, Harnack found there an open and regular dialogue with clergy who found his intellectual integrity, however much it differed from their faith position, his concern for practical issues and his growing appreciation of "social questions" truly encouraging. Marburg brought Harnack into a close personal and working relationship with Wilhelm Herrmann, the systematic theologian with whom he cooperated in several joint publications and other academic projects.

In 1887 the second volume of *History of Dogma* appeared; like volume one, it was over five hundred pages in length, covering the development of the Church's teaching from the beginning of the fourth century to the time of Augustine. It was the labor for this work which gave rise to Harnack's predilection for Augustine; in him, as in Goethe, he found a rich source of wisdom, understanding and faith. He had need for such inspiration for the University of Berlin and the Prussian Ministry of Education had made the move to call him, only to face the most rigorous opposition from Prussian church-officials. The press entered the controversy and the spectacle became unworthy of both academia and Church. The issues for the Church were these: (1) Harnack's questioning of the authorship of the gospel of John, Ephesians and I Peter, denying their apostolicity, (2) Harnack's views regarding miracles, especially those of the Virgin Birth, the Resurrection and the Ascension and (3) his denial that Jesus instituted baptism in the name of the Triune God (AZH 119). The Ministry of Education used the controversy adroitly to isolate the officials of the Church. In the midst of the debates Emperor Frederick died, leaving the matter to his successor to decide. This catapulted the new ruler into a hot political issue: for if he decided against Harnack it would have signalled a victory of the Church over the state, of clericalism over science. At least that is how it looked in the ongoing press-debates. Finally, on September 17th 1888, the Emperor signed the call to Harnack to join the faculty of the University of Berlin, adding the comment that, in his university, he did not want to have any bigots (AZH 127).

Harnack now entered the university he was to serve till the end of his life. He took up his position of church-historian, convinced that the chief area of this discipline werè the first six centuries of the Church, being the most important period for theologians.

"The fact that we are not advancing in theology as we ought is to a large extent the result of the habit of many church-historians to cultivate one-sidedly the history of the Reformation or of the Middle Ages and to manifest only a sub-standard sense in relation to ancient church-history. . . . Since *all* our *decisive* problems in the history of the Church relate to the sphere of *ancient* history, we must demand that every church-historian be at home in that period. . . . In theological education everything depends on students knowing how Catholicism *came into being*, how it is related to early Christianity, how dogma, cult and constitution *arose* and how they are to be judged. Future clergy may safely forget the details of [recent] church-history but not how to answer those questions. . . . [Otherwise] the whole study of church-history is useless and those clergy, once in a parish, will be subject to the church-press and to the power-claims of a false tradition. . . . Neither *exegesis* nor *dogmatics* will lead us to a healthy progress and to increasingly purer comprehension of what is original and of value, but a better known *history*. Not exegesis and dogmatics, but the conclusions of church-historical research, once they become the common good, will break the bonds of burdensome and conscience-breaking tradition. Cardinal Manning once uttered the frivolous phrase: overcome history with dogma; we declare the opposite: illumine dogma with history; as Protestants we are confident that in doing so we do not tear down but build up" (AZH 129-31).

For many these were "fighting words" but Harnack never modified their meaning and the action they implied.

The expectations of the monarch, the government and the university were the right kind of challenge to a mind like Harnack's, to his energies and devotion to scholarship. He blossomed in the "Protestant freedom of spirit," as his biographer put it (AZH 134), the freedom which is both the source and the goal of liberalism.

On October 23rd 1888 Harnack delivered his inaugural lecture; the early morning lectures of his first semester at Berlin drew between four and five hundred students! Then, four years later, in 1892, he became involved in the feud over the Apostles' Creed. He had been publicly sympathetic to the wish for a new creed-like expression of Christian faith so that the dimension of personal credibility could take over from that of mere credulity in worship. But he kept out of the public discussion until a delegation of students came to him for advice in relation to their plans. The response he gave them, published shortly thereafter in the liberal journal *Christliche Welt*, landed like a fox in a henhouse. He prefaced a separate study on the Creed with the nine points he had given the students; what a stir they caused can be gauged from the fact that the little study enjoyed the small total of twenty-seven editions! (AZH 151). According to Harnack's biographer, who was his own daughter and who is entitled to see things with a particular predisposition, there was "a horde of small, yelping dogs, those pious twisters of truth and that unholy simplemindedness" which went on the attack against Harnack as a "forger in the pits of heathenism." The Catholic press spoke of his "anti-Christian teaching" (AZH 151).

But the positive responses were just as forceful and clear; all of which put stress on the government. What helped was that two years earlier Harnack had been elected to the prestigious Academy of Sciences, for that meant that his *academic* reputation was beyond question. The issue, therefore, became one of the freedom of theology as an academic discipline from what Harnack and others quickly called the tutelage of the Church. The minister of education at the time, Bosse, made a distinction in his handling of the dispute over the appointment: he spoke of *Wahrheit* (truth) and of *Wahrhaftigkeit* (truthfulness), suggesting to Harnack that in the pursuit of *Wahrheit* there is a duty to *Wahrhaftigkeit* (AZH 155), which was his way of saying that, given love for truth and the openness to follow wherever it leads, there is still the imperative of the virtue of perspicacity in things political. The minister's perspicacity led to the establishment of a professorship in theology for a person of the "other" camp; though filling this post turned into another headache. The eminent Adolf Schlatter finally agreed to accept the call to what the press quickly came to call the "punitive professorship" (AZH 156). Schlatter held the post for five years and was succeeded in 1898 by Reinhold Seeberg who, in time, wrote his own widely used history of dogma.

Harvard University renewed its offer to Harnack but met with a second refusal even though Charles W. Eliot, who had written on behalf of the university, said in the letter that:

"the President and Fellows would not propose to a professor in the

University of Berlin that he take a professorship in Harvard University did they not suppose that in this particular case an absolute freedom from all restrictions — governmental, academic or social — a freedom of thought and speech would be a weighty consideration" (AZH 157).

The observers on the far away shores of Massachussetts had accurately assessed what the protagonists in academia and Church were fighting over in Berlin: the freedom of theology. What they might not have been so clear about was from or for what theology wanted to be free. As Harnack saw it in 1896, when he gave an address on the current situation of Protestantism, the matter was this: (1) we must not give up the task of expressing the ancient, evangelical faith in a new, simple and clear way, using the language of today; (2) we must become more flexible and diverse in expressing our religious life and more refined in our social conscience and (3) despite resistance, we must build up the Church and exercise patience (AZH 160).

There is much which could be examined in detail from Harnack's well-over forty year-long life and work in Berlin. One could refer to his growing involvement in social action, his aversion to what he called "Manchesterdom" or the *laisser faire, laisser aller* of public policy (AZH 162) and his similarly strong opposition to the platforms of the Social Democrats. He believed that Christian faith called its adherents to sacrificing as individuals so that they might act charitably as the servants of all. The journal *Christliche Welt*, which had been founded in 1886 by several of Harnack's students, upheld this ideal of individual service as expressing the road towards a world which could call itself Christian. Harnack combined this virtue with his firm conviction that the gospel of Jesus had proclaimed how infinitely valuable each human soul was in the community of equals under the fatherhood of God. In 1903 Harnack accepted the presidency of the Evangelical-Social Congress which he had helped found thirteen years earlier, precisely to further this ideal and its demands. It was also his way of opposing the politics of the Social Democrats, an aim he shared with his monarch. For Harnack, in contrast to the Religious Socialists of the Ragaz-Kutter line, the Church's call was to be nothing but the guardian of the gospel, she is not expected to do things other than proclaim a strong, comforting faith which overcomes the cares of this world. But just as it is certain that Christian faith is about eternity and not about time here and now, so it is certain that the Church must serve the people here and now; this meant that she has to help establish conditions under which the gospel can be

18

truly grasped. One of Harnack's last publications bears the title (in translation): *Help the Children of Berlin Who Need Recreation*, showing his commitment to such service (AZH 171).

One could also speak of Harnack's illustrious teaching career in Berlin, of his research and administration. Within a year of his arrival, he completed and published the third and final volume of *History of Dogma* (1889). He continued the immensely demanding task of editing the Church Fathers and spent the year at the turn of the century lecturing on the nature of Christianity. It was as if he wanted to assist the new century in keeping what had been good in the 19th century, while forging ahead in shaping its own, authentic affirmations. He himself put it like this: these lectures are to serve "understanding and peace" and not cause strife (AZH 181). Unlike Schleiermacher who, a century earlier, had addressed the despisers of religion while enlightening them on the character of Christianity, Harnack addressed the many who had become alien to the Church and who did not know of their own religious gifts. When the lectures were eventually published — a student had diligently, and without Harnack's knowledge, made a stenographic record of them which he then gave Harnack, who was immensely pleased — Harnack chose for the collection's motto Matthew 15:27, which he had imprinted in Greek: ah, yes, Lord, but even little dogs eat the crumbs that fall from their masters' table (AZH 182). The book, again, caused a storm, no one kept quiet. A woman reported in public that her initially positive impression of the book had been shattered when, on vacation at a North Sea resort, she observed how Harnack had turned into a pagan sybarite, for he had dined on lobster and champagne (AZH 185). (As it turned out the champagne was her imagination's invention!) But there were also many who found renewed access to Jesus, access which was personal rather than mediated by dogma, creed and institution. It was a way to Jesus said to be granting and demanding freedom.

Berlin stimulated Harnack. His election to the Academy of Sciences of Prussia, which admitted him under the category of historian because the by-laws allowed no membership to theologians, permitted him to engage in projects which depended on team-work. In 1891 a major project was launched to prepare a scholarly edition of the Greek Church Fathers; the first volume appeared two years later surveying what materials had to be edited. It took over a thousand pages to describe the survey alone! A series of fifty volumes were planned, to be published over a period of twenty years; Harnack was to be the principal editor. Many scholars who, in the *Streit der Fakultäten* — as Kant referred to the squabble among faculties in the academy — about which was truly the most scientific, would side with the natural sciences, came to see in their colleague Harnack that theology could actually be a truly *scholarly* discipline, a *Wissenschaft.* As a kind of relaxing "diversion," Harnack took on the writing and publication of the history of the Prussian Academy; the project began in 1896 and he presented the finished four volume work to the Academy on the occasion of its bicentenary, in 1900. It had given him a wide range of contacts with people of diverse disciplines and approaches from which his own perspective could only benefit. People associated such a perspective, as they now perceived it in Harnack, with the idea of the "renaissance man," the person of remarkable breadth of knowledge held together in an integrated unity. During the bicentenary, which was conducted at the Emperor's command with full pomp and circumstance, Harnack gave an address which he concluded with these words:

"Science is not the only task of humankind, nor is it its highest; yet those to whom this task has been entrusted are to pursue it with all their heart and strength. However different the epochs of science are in their unfolding, the task remains basically the same at all times: to keep the sense for truth pure and alive and to recreate this world, given to us as a cosmos of powers, into a cosmos of ideas. May it be given to our Academy in its third century to cooperate in this work of humankind; may the powers of darkness be absent from it; may the light which was in the beginning illumine its way and may the word which was in the beginning radiate in its spirit" (AZH 207).

A classic expression of the lofty liberalism of the Western world's Enlightenment mind!

The dawn of the new century raised, as it always seems to have done, a concern with what lay ahead. Harnack himself seems not to have had a sense of what might face the world to which he had become so committed, namely the world of the academy, of scholarship, of the Imperial Court, of Germany and, finally of the Church. He continued with his astonishingly busy work and its related schedule.

He used to begin his day well before 7 am, sometimes even conducting seminars at that hour; after his marriage in 1879 it became a rule that, after the evening meal, no work was to be done; "in my home there is to be no more working after 8 pm" he declared, and the focus of attention was to be the family (AZH 209). He received an average of seventy-five pieces of correspondence a week which required responses, all of which he wrote by hand, usually within forty-eight hours! One asks what organization and support had to be in place to make that possible. And he regularly read Goethe whose maxims and reflections he valued immensely for their "wisdom of life" (AZH 213).

The proclaimer of the "essence of Christianity" to the men and women of 19th and 20th century modernity became the rector of the University of Berlin as he was giving shape to that theology in 1900. It is as if he never believed himself to have already enough to do. He had given himself to a perception of Christianity which grew out of historical knowledge rather than out of the insights which are gained from focusing on the individual soul's religious experience. Theology had to be based, in his view, on the public, institutional and historically discernible segment or deposit in which the individual religion of each person may well live in fullness and integrity. By temperament and conviction Harnack was a person of "culture" who would depart, with some abhorrence, from the mysterious and dark in the human psyche to the pure air of ideas, "from cult to dogma, from miracle to organization, from mysticism to speculation," as one of his colleagues once put it (AZH 229).

At this time Harnack became troubled by the fact that his relationship to the Church was so heavily overcast. He had always wanted to serve the Church but it did not even call upon him to sit on commissions to examine his own students for their fitness to serve the Church or their theological readiness. The Church, and for that matter some of his own colleagues, regarded him as someone who held an unbelieving theology. He tried to have himself nominated for positions in the synod of Brandenburg but found no one prepared to do so. Eventually he said "goodbye inwardly to the Church as it appeared to him in its visible manifestation" (AZH 230-1). Instead, he embraced a life of extensive administrative responsibilities in the government of Kaiser Wilhelm II. The chief focus of these activities was the freedom of scholarship. A firm step towards that goal was his appointment as Director-General of the Royal Library in Berlin in March 1905. The dean at the university reduced his teaching-load to seven hours a week. A new professor was appointed to pick up the slack: Harnack's personal friend and former student, Karl Holl (AZH 250). Nine years later, in the year World War I broke out, Harnack was able to preside at the opening of the huge new library building on the famous Unter den Linden, Berlin's elegant main avenue; his work had enlarged the staff from one hundred and fifty to over three hundred and the budget had increased annually by exponential growth figures. The Emperor rewarded his chief librarian that day be granting him a knighthood; from the 22nd March 1914 onward Harnack and his descendants were to call themselves von Harnack. The motto of the new family coat-of-arms, chosen by von Harnack himself, was the ancient Christian invocation of the Spirit: *Veni Creator Spiritus* (AZH 260).

The personal relationship between the Emperor and Harnack had flourished well since the bicentenary celebrations of the Academy of Sciences in 1900. Harnack's biographer-daughter recounts numerous meetings between the two; at times they met together with only one other person present. She refers in particular to meetings of the two with Houston Stewart Chamberlain, the author of the widely acclaimed study on the foundations of the 19th century which had had a strong impact on German intellectual circles.[2] For reasons personal and political, the religious dimension was kept out of their discussions; what drew the Emperor to Harnack was the latter's scholarly breadth and administrative acumen. Wilhelm II believed himself clearly to be ruling by God's grace, *dei gratia,* just as he believed with similar firmness in the global responsibilities said to be resting on the shoulders of his Germany (AZH 262). His own personal tradition introduced a strong military outlook into that mix. Harnack became enmeshed in that configuration, reacting to some of it with openness, rejecting other aspects.

His scholarly activity as theologian/historian continued unabated. Between 1900 and 1914 he published 455 books, studies, reviews and lectures; his friends urged him to slow down and conserve his energy. But he was driven by the feeling that both the freedom and dignity of *Wissenschaft,* of scholarship, needed his rigorously methodic and circumspect example. The major works of those years were *The Mission and Expansion of Christianity in the First Three Centuries,* the seven (!) volumes of studies on the New Testament, a new, and the final, edition of his *History of Dogma,* four volumes of his speeches and essays, *The Constitution and Law of the Church in the First Two Centuries,* and, of course, the numerous new volumes of the critical edition of the Greek Church Fathers, appearing under his general editorship. In 1903 he accepted the presidency of the *Evangelisch-Sozialer Kongress,* a position he kept for eight years. When he was elected at the annual meeting at Darmstadt he declared: "Our social legislation is on the advance, but how creeping an advance it is. We are doing good, but slow, work in our fatherland. In every sphere our bureaucratic apparatus, in other respects our greatest strength, manifests itself as a source of delay. . . . In such circumstances no organization which pursues progress may withdraw from responsibility" (AZH 288). Harnack steered a middle course between those who owned the means of production, especially the large industrial concerns of Germany, on the one hand, and the Social Democrats, on the other. He said that private property was not only a right but, in fact, the basic condition of Western culture. At the same time he saw *his* basic difference with the Social Democrats to be their anti-religious outlook. "Social-Democracy does not want to know anything about the foundation on which we build, namely the moral spirit of the gospel, and it does not wish to accept the state as it has emerged historically, having become for us the land of our fathers. There can be no compromise" (AZH 290). Where the Social Democrats wanted radical changes, Harnack would invoke the idea of progress and call on them to cooperate within the realistic conditions of society and culture. His own call for reforms, for example, on the inheritance tax, housing or strike legislation, met with little, if any, support from the political left whereas the Emperor was not alienated by it, due probably to Harnack's stature in Prussian society.

The scholarly world outside Germany paid increasing attention to this man. At the time of his death Harnack was not only a member of the Prussian Academy of Sciences but also of the academies of Amsterdam, Gotenburg, Naples, Oslo, Rome, Stockholm and Uppsala, as well as a corresponding or honorary member of those of London, Paris, Vienna and Dublin. The War brought suspension of membership in some cases; in most this was resumed soon afterwards. His lectures were well received wherever he went, be it St. Louis in 1904, Harvard or Yale, Rome or London. *The Manchester Guardian* called him "our Harnack" after a very successful lecture in England on February 6th 1911 (AZH 296). He had lectured on peace; since 1908 Harnack had been involved in efforts to reduce and avoid what he and others feared to be belligerence between Germany and France. On the occasion of a visit by British clergy to the University of Berlin on June 5th 1909, he said at the conclusion of a speech that: "on the soil of science and Christianity the cry 'war' is as madness, a cry out of an abyss from which we have long ago emerged" (AZH 301). Yet he was troubled that His Majesty's Government did not declare publicly that its relations with Germany were friendly, no matter how critical they might otherwise be. Harnack wanted to unite scholars and scientists around what he held to be their common goal and vision in the two countries; he emphasized what German science had achieved and had still to complete and called on the

English to strive now for such a goal as well for, surely, this would create a deeper understanding and prevent war. He was to be most deeply disappointed when "the guns of August" began to roar in 1914.

Harnack's position in German scholarship was not lost on the Emperor; as he saw it, Harnack embodied the best of what he took to be a true Prussian: diligence, loyalty, patriotism, objectivity and German cosmopolitanism. When the University of Berlin celebrated its 100th anniversary in October 1911, the Emperor announced, on the occasion of dedicating a new assembly-hall, that a new academy was to be established, and that it was to bear his name: the *Kaiser Wilhelm Gesellschaft zur Förderung der Wissenschaften*. Its aim was to advance the sciences. Many quickly recognized that Germany was finally to have what the Rockefellers, Carnegies, Rothschilds and Nobels had given their countries; much was made of the fact that this society was a gift from the Emperor and would, therefore, leave science free from any attachment to private capitalism. Once again, Germany had done the right thing only better (AZH 329). Harnack was chosen to be the first president, with one of the Krupp family as his vice-president. Preparation for and then the actual conduct of the War saw an accelerated expansion of the work of the numerous institutes founded by the society. The theologian Harnack presided over a society the focus of which was chiefly technological and scientific, in the sense of the physical sciences. It was clear that his personality was able to create cooperation among diverse specialists, and interest among those of wealth for an institution which served the interests of the public and of industry and of university. It was truly a tribute of high recognition when the society named its new head-office complex in Berlin, completed and dedicated in 1929, the *Adolf von Harnack Haus*. (Even though the society now bears another name, the *Max Planck Gesellschaft*, the building, albeit in the service of the United States Military, still bears its original name.)

The War came. On the evening of August 4th Harnack accepted the Kaiser's wish that he compose the Emperor's appeal to the German nation. When he sat down to write the text, the "hostile" nations were France and Russia, but before he had finished, word came to him that Great Britain had joined them. Harnack was stunned by the news; when eleven British theologians wrote him on August 27th 1914 an open letter containing an attack on German scholarship, he responded in indignation. The wound of that attack never healed completely. In 1909 he had written a memorandum in which he argued that Germany's greatness rested on two pillars: its defensive forces and its scholarship. He

24

said that it was the duty of Prussia, in accordance with its glorious tradition, to assure that both were maintained in strong form (AZH 348). Harnack was a signatory to several public declarations in which this thought found expression; one was published in German newspapers on September 4th 1914 under the title "*An die evangelischen Christen im Auslande*" (to Protestant Christians outside Germany), another on October 4th 1914 under the title "*An die Kulturwelt*" (to the world of culture). In the former one reads among other statements the following:

"Our people could not engage in this struggle with so clear a conscience were it not for the fact that leading men of church, scholarship and commerce tried on numerous occasions to make this fratricide impossible. . . . The responsibility for it, we declare with calm certitude before our brothers everywhere, does not rest on our people. . . . We are deeply convinced that we have to lay the blame on those who for a long time have woven the net of conspiracy against Germany and who have now thrown it on us in order to suffocate us."[3]

In the latter one reads *inter alia*:

"It is not true that the fight against our so-called militarism is not a fight against our culture, as our enemies hypocritically allege. Without German militarism German culture would long ago have vanished from the earth. [Our militarism] grew out of [our culture] for its protection. . . . Germany's army and Germany's people are one. This consciousness today makes seventy million Germans without distinction of education, class and party one brotherhood. . . . We call out to you: believe us, believe that we shall fight this fight to the end as a people of culture to whom the legacy of a Goethe, a Beethoven, a Kant is as holy as its hearth and soil."[4]

Throughout the War Harnack stayed in close touch with the several institutes of the Kaiser-Wilhelm Society and knew, among other things, of the research on and testing of the deadly combat gases which Dr. Fritz Haber was developing in Göttingen for use by the German army (AZH 348). He attacked the view that the War was showing how bankrupt religion actually was, claiming instead that the experience of the outbreak of war had unearthed deep and often hidden sources of religious life.

"In place of individual life, no longer the highest of goods, there is something ideal such as one's country's life or a great good to be won for all of humankind. . . . This highspirited disposition, ready to embrace life and death equally, is very closely akin to religion. It is, in actual fact, people who had hitherto nothing in common with religion, knowing it only through its official forms, people who had neglected their inner life, who now feel themselves borne up high on the wings of religion and, as if by magic, sense themselves freed from the weight which clung to their feet, gaining a new relation to their brothers and an awareness of the transcendent meaning of their lives" (AZH 350).

To the end of the War and, it seems safe to say, to the end of his life, Harnack believed that the War had been waged to assure a peace which would be more noble than the peace which had led to the War in the first place. He rejected what he called a "flat" pacifism, namely the rejection of all war on principle, and favoured the pacifism which, although repulsed by the horrors of war, will still enter into it for the sake of a "higher" peace which is the peace God's kingdom promises (AZH 351). To him the War had been a call into the reflection on his nation's weaknesses which needed to be replaced by moral strengths; at the same time it was necessary to know what to preserve and even strengthen of the religious, moral and national energies which had been released by the War. He joined in organized efforts to protect the life at home of children and of young people, to eradicate diseases such as tuberculosis and venereal disease; he cooperated in efforts to improve housing, support couples who were willing to marry at a younger age, and to make continuing education more widely available. He raised his voice against industrialists who made huge profits from the War and in a number of other ways urged specific reforms of public life (AZH 353ff). With colleagues in the academy and in administration he discussed what *kind* of peace had to be assured; as they saw it, it had to be free from any seeds of future wars. And having become the vice-chair of the German National Committee, a grouping of politicians seeking to prepare for a realistically attainable peace, Harnack insisted that no politically independent people should be made part of the German Empire, even though that meant that his beloved Baltic could never become German (AZH 361).

The defeat and revolution of late 1918 came as no surprise to him although he was not prepared for their day to day actuality. He had grown quite concerned over the way the Emperor and his ministers had conducted the War, seemingly, in his view, with disregard for the values of German scholarship, values he believed firmly to represent the values of the whole civilized world's academic and cultural community. In early 1919 he wrote to Holl

"we have sinned not only in relation to Mammonism: we have not discerned the signs of the times and our overestimation of our power and might was worse than a false calculation or deception. I sense almost no readiness for repentance and changes of will embracing the whole people. This realization is the most burdensome of our pain. Of this I am certain: if *we* are not to bear the entire cost of the world-revolution, then we must begin to think differently and change our moral feelings in relation to the social dimensions of life and to the inner and outer life" (AZH 374).

He welcomed the move towards a democratic order but saw that it alone could not be made to carry the whole burden of the renewal of Germany.

"We have to resist Mammonism, godlessness and the loss of ideals . . . for otherwise we will not be spared Bolshevism. New liberal forms alone achieve nothing; they will only have to give way to more 'liberal' ones if they are not permeated by a public spirit, seriousness and the courage for sacrifice" (AZH 375).

In a sermon he preached on February 2nd 1919 at the university, he laid out seven basic principles for a new Germany that would live out the kind of peace he had longed for.

1 Without a national consciousness there can be no peoplehood; without humaneness no real greatness.
2 Without authority there can be no organization.
3 Without personality there can be no life that is worth living.
4 Without determination to overcome class-divisions there can be no internal peace.
5 Without capital there can be no culture.
6 Without power there can be no state.
7 Without selflessness and the fear of God there can be no future (AZH 375).

He sided with the new constitution, not so much because he agreed with it but because he wanted to help rebuild the nation along the lines of these principles. Several government figures recognized this in the course of the next years, calling on Harnack for advice or to invite his participation, especially in relation to matters of the academy. As he once put it, he did participate in the new order in order not only to make the best of the given situation but to make it even better. He joined no political party, even though several of them asked him to do so. He was even invited to accept the ambassadorship to the United States of America in the autumn of 1921 but, believing himself to be hard to replace in the circles of German scholarship at so crucial a time, he refused the offer (AZH 394). In fact, the time became for him one of renewed scholarly concentration. He was still president of the Kaiser-

Wilhelm Society and, until 1921, director-general of the Royal Library. He kept on sending his annual reports of the former to his sovereign-in-exile who always responded in acknowledgment and appreciation. And Harnack successfully resisted moves to have the Society's name changed (AZH 384).

During the War Harnack had found little time for major scholarly work and even though he did publish a significant number of limited studies on matters church-historical, there were none to which he had devoted the energies comparable to, for example, *The Mission and Expansion of Christianity*. In early 1920 he found an old, yet new love and by the end of June of that year he completed the manuscript for his *Marcion, das Evangelium vom fremden Gott* (Marcion, the gospel of the alien God). Fifty years earlier, as a nineteen year old student, he had won a gold medal at the University of Dorpat, with a study on Marcion and the responses of Tertullian to his teachings. Ever since then, Harnack had wanted to expand on that study and gathered material for it in order to write a major monograph on this "heretic." It was his intention to reconstruct as completely as possible Marcion's two-part canon, his gospel and his *apostolikon*, as well as the biblical-theological arguments which prefaced the collection of "contradictions" between the two testaments, the famous/infamous *Antitheses*. The part of the book Harnack was to publish in 1920 remains to this day his outstanding contribution to the study of Marcion; the more provocative part, namely Harnack's interpretations, has, on the whole, not survived critical challenge. According to Harnack, Marcion was the real creator of the Catholic church; "by his organizational and theological ideas and by his activity Marcion gave the decisive impetus to the creation of the early Catholic church and provided it with a model; what is more, he deserves the credit for first grasping and carrying out the idea of a canonical collection of Christian writings, the New Testament."[5] Furthermore, Harnack argued, that once one has rid Marcion of certain period-bound notions and perceptions, such as those of ancient cosmology and unhistorical interpretations of Scripture, one will come to see in him a religious personality which, in certain respects, is the final link in the chain from the prophets to Jesus and Paul (AZH 398). For Marcion's gospel speaks of a god — the alien god — who has nothing to do with the miserable and soiled creation and its course of events but who nonetheless comes in a redeemer who is perfect love and nothing but love. Gone is the justice of punishment, gone also rigorous legalism. The redeemer exposes the god of this creation and the pursuit of that god's justice to be the reason why creation is in misery. Harnack claims that *this* gospel appeals to the deep longings of the post-War generation. Closely linked to that aspect of Marcion's gospel is his rejection of the Old Testament, his separation of the "righteous" god of Judaism from the god of the New Testament. Harnack stood with Marcion here and formulated the noteworthy, if not notorious, thesis that "in the second century, the rejection of the Old Testament would have been a mistake and the great Church rightly refused to make that mistake; the retention of it in the sixteenth century was due to a fatal legacy from which the Reformation was not yet able to withdraw; but for Protestantism since the nineteenth century to continue to treasure it as a canonical document is the result of a religious and ecclesiastical paralysis."[6] Here, too, Harnack believed that he was meeting the perception of a widespread religious and ecclesiastical paralysis on the part of many people, a paralysis which needed to be lifted; he was sure that if the Church would only be courageous enough to liberate itself from dogmatic faith and relegate the whole Old Testament to the level to which Luther had relegated the *Apocrypha,* namely as materials "good and useful to peruse" and stop treating it as sacred scripture, this sense of paralysis would be lifted and a genuinely new beginning would set in (AZH 399-400).

The reactions ranged from very positive to very negative; Harnack felt buoyed up by them and found new energies in himself for more, similar work. He turned to Augustine once again, believing that he had words of encouragement and solace to speak to the post-War world. He put together a collection of that church-father's maxims and reflections, edited, translated and published them.

"Those who read Augustine today ask themselves inevitably what progress we have made since in relation to the virtues which radiate from this work: the sense of reality, the deep longing for truth, the love of neighbor, the energy in the formation of common life, the tenderness of conscience, warmth of heart, nobility of language and of the forms of spiritual intercourse. We have made progress in none of these; we have gained a more useful knowledge of nature and have become more adept in technology! And yet, a monumental progress is to be noted, the brutality of the World-War and of our World-Peace notwithstanding: a half-measure of all these virtues has, in one way or another, become a commonplace of humankind; we call it 'civilization'. Compared to it, the time of Augustine must seem to be one of barbarism, slavery and tyranny. Those who have attained to more than that half-measure and still long for more, rightly despise and hate the level of civilization currently reached; such hate is the necessary precondition for moving beyond such a level. A different stage can be reached only if a new Augustinianism dominates to the same extent as does today's civilization, an Augustinianism in which the fear of God, as the source of all higher goods, permeates human knowledge and intention, sustains true freedom and creates a covenant of justice and peace. Such a covenant will be Christian-Augustinian or it will not be at all; it will stand erect and free without the antiquated scaffolding in the removal of which the centuries have exhausted themselves" (AZH 402-3).

This is probably the finest expression by Harnack himself of what theological liberalism would say about itself.

At the age of seventy, in 1921, Harnack retired from the directorship of the Royal Library and from his university teaching position, though he had to succeed himself in the latter for two more years as the appointment of Lietzmann was not ratified until then. But he also accepted many invitations to lecture; in many of the addresses he gave at that time he expressed his growing concern with the emergence of theological patterns and methods which, at least in his eyes, went contrary to his own vision. The biographer puts Harnack's perception succinctly:

"He feared that the generation of younger theologians was moving in a dangerous direction. He was concerned over the decline in the respect for historical research. What he found was rather a romantic leaning towards the primitive, a tendency to draw all knowledge from the depths of one's soul. All this merely supplanted a methodical analysis of the sources. But this tendency seemed to be controllable, partially due to Harnack's own work. . . . On the whole a shift in emphasis was noticeable in the world of theological endeavour, yet one was able at least to understand one another's language, one could assume that all strove for the same end" (AZH 412-3).

It was as if two worlds, separate and unrelated, encountered each other when Harnack and one of his former students, Karl Barth, met again in 1920 at a conference at which both were to present lectures. Afterwards a deeply shaken Harnack confessed to a friend that:

"the effect of Barth's lecture was just staggering. Not one word, not one sentence could I have said or thought. I saw the sincerity of Barth's speech, but its theology frightened me. . . . The severity of the charges made in that address is still very vivid in my mind. Instead of losing any of its force, it appears to me more and more hazardous, yes, in a way even scandalous. This impression is in no way softened by the consideration that this sort of religion is incapable of being translated into real life, so that it must soar above life like a meteor rushing towards its disintegration" (AZH 415).

After a little more than two years he entered the fray with his "Fifteen Questions to the Despisers of Scientific Theology". And when that dialogue came to an unresolved and unresolveable conclusion, Harnack used one of the guest-lecture series to make his point again. In 1926, during the lectures on "The Formation of Christian Theology and the Church's Dogma," he indicated that to him the new theological developments were wholly incomprehensible at best — "I have no antenna for such speculation" he said at the time (AZH 416) — or, at worst, narrow in scope and sectarian:

"It is encouraging to see the seriousness of intention in our contemporary theology and its desire to address itself to the main issues of theology. But how weak it is as a science . . . how expressionistic its logic and how shortsighted its view of history. . . . What seems to be lost completely is the link between theology and the *universitas litterarum* and culture. There are rather new links between this evangelical theology and Catholicism and Romanticism. But let us hope that we have here no more than the cocoon-stage of something that some day will turn out to be a genuinely evangelical butterfly" (AZH 417-8).

It is a painful irony that, at the time when Harnack found himself quite unable to redirect the scholarship of the discipline to which he had given, for more than half a century, the lion's-share of his energies and spirit, he should also receive from President Hindenburg a citation of great honor which lauded Harnack as the bearer of the cultural heritage of Germany: *Dem Träger deutscher Bildung* (AZH 409). The ecumenical movement claimed his attention, although his declining physical strength kept him from accepting the invitations to participate in the conferences at Stockholm (1925), Lausanne (1927) and Prague (1928). His strong wish was that the churches establish clarity on the question of the person of Jesus and of his place in the creeds. He saw this to be the issue on which the unity of the churches would be determined. The two-nature doctrine of Christ was *the* speculation which Harnack sought to have removed in favor of a broad consensus in which the individual Christian conscience could then decide freely how to view Christ's being. But as long as that *skandalon* remained, the way into the Church would remain barred to many people who, unable to bind themselves to such a doctrine, had to remain free from such dogmatism and free for a new form of confessing their faith in Christ (AZH 422-3).

Harnack gave the last years of his life to the *Kaiser-Wilhelm Gesellschaft* and to a final formulation of how he saw the attainment of certain knowledge. One of the last sentences he wrote was *"Wissenschaft ist die Erkenntnis des Wirklichen zu zweckvollem Handeln"* (science or scholarship is the cognition or knowledge of reality in the service of purposeful activity) (AZH 427). This was expressed too in the short essay on the stages of such knowledge which he meant to be his legacy to those younger scholars who had, in his view, not yet given in to "romanticism," that desire to discover truth in the impressionisms of subjectivity. Over against such subjectivity stood the truth and reality which the historian, in an "objectivity" marked by intense and unrestrained listening to what is "out there," seeks to discern with clearly laid out methods. And as a theologian the scholar serves the search for truth historically whereas as an historian the scholar interprets the truth thus found theologically.

It was given to Adolf and Amalie von Harnack to celebrate their golden wedding anniversary on December 27th 1929 in the newly dedicated Harnack-Haus. Harnack gave a meditation on Genesis 1:18 and began it by citing the opening line of a poem by Eichendorff which — what curious coincidence! — also stands at the beginning of Richard Strauss' final composition, written in 1949 and also in sight of his life's end: *Wir sind durch Not und Freude gegangen Hand in Hand,* (we have gone through pain and joy hand in hand). Harnack had one more birthday, on May 7th 1930 he turned seventy-nine years of age. That evening the family gathered for prayer and meditation; Harnack led in it and reflected on the words of Isaiah 40:27-29: "God, give strength to the tired and to the powerless new energy." These words gave great solace to all present until they discovered, after his death, that on that same day he had written in the margin of his Bible, next to that text: "my sadness is so great that I do not know where to turn" (AZH 440).

He became quite ill after his birthday but was still determined to be present at the 18th General Meeting of the Kaiser-Wilhelm Society in Heidelberg later that month. He was able to travel, accompanied by his spouse, but had to be hospitalized soon after their arrival. For two weeks, in full possession of his mind and in the company of his family, he read, answered correspondence, arranged for the celebration of one of the maids' ten years of service in the Harnack home in Berlin (AZH 441) and then on June 10th 1930, at 6 o'clock in the evening, his life ebbed away.

A huge company of people mourned his death; his ashes were laid to rest in Berlin, under a simple stone on which the simple words of the family crest are written: *Veni Creator Spiritus.*

II

Harnack's thought is, by general agreement, "liberal," but what does it mean to call it "liberal theology at its height"? Does the term "liberal" have so unequivocal a meaning that that assertion is clear in its meaning?

As used here, "liberal" derives its meaning partly from Harnack's *own* work, partly from specific aspects it shares with the work of other theologians labelled "liberal" and partly from the insights of critics who wanted to do what "liberals" had done but do it better or more appropriately.

Harnack's work manifests a powerful conviction in relation to the imperative of freedom: the freedom of thought, of pursuing truth on every path, the freedom from interference by those who have been given authority in human institutions, from human declarations and rules so that conscience may develop as fully as possible. But that freedom is also inseparable from responsibility, the responsibility towards the object and subject of human action and speech, towards the rigors of human discourse and enquiry. Harnack's "liberalism," as it is seen by the author, was his thinking and speaking in responsibility and openness, coupled with a broad personal modesty. That modesty can be seen in his awareness that there were limits to what he saw and said. But they were not limits set, speaking now in theological terms, by dogmatics, as an academic discipline, or by dogmas, affirmations defined by duly authorized people, to be affirmed and held to be true for the sake of salvation; such limits were seen to be antithetical to other, highly characteristic features of the "liberal" position. Among those were the confidence in the human, finite, spirit, the reverence for the dignity, competence and authority of the power of human thought and the ability to be able to transcend one's subjectivity in the endeavor to attain to genuine objectivity. In Harnack's "liberal theology" one perceives an incorruptible reasonableness *and* an unshakeable religious faith; there is his sense of giving his all for the freedom of theology in the very centre of his awareness that he was dependent on the "absolute" spirit which to pray for was the task of believing Christian theologians. His faith was a faith that *knows* because it was held by, but not the consequence of, courageous and free thought.

No claim is being made that such features are to be found only in the theology of this "liberal," Adolf von Harnack; what is being claimed is that his theology manifests these, essentially laudable, characteristics. There are others which belong to a more general description of "liberal theology" as such.

Liberal theology is

" a theology in the succession of Descartes, primarily and definitely interested in human, and particularly the Christian, religion within the framework of our modern outlook on the world, considering God [and God's] work and . . . word from this point of view, and adopting the critical attitude towards the message of the Bible and ecclesiastical tradition — to this extent, an anthropocentric theology. . . . The task of free theological study (it could never be too reverently and strenuously undertaken) was just to study Christian doctrine, as it developed in accordance with its inner necessity, and illuminate it by considering the question of its real meaning . . . [giving] it a critical yet positive examination and exposition; in other words, to raise it from the level of intuition to that of pure concept."[7]

"Liberal theology," as a scholarly discipline, and "liberal" faith, as a faith that knows, are "modern" since they embrace the Cartesian assertion that to be human at all is to be about the enterprise of cognitive appropriation of reality. The dignity of human beings resides exactly in their ability, God-given, no doubt, to *comprehend*, to get reality into the grasp of the mind (or the will or the hand). Such grasp is not arbitrary but methodic, according to Descartes and, consequently, the faith that knows not only knows God and creation but also knows *how* it knows. Hence the necessity of affirming confidence in the human mind and its workings, the preoccupation with method (or "methodology") and its objectivity, the reverence for the competence and authority, in one word the "dignity," of the power of thought. The anthropocentricity mentioned above refers to the long-held Cartesian declaration that the only way for humans not to doubt anything we claim to know is not to rely on our *experience*, but on the mind's self-certainty. In somewhat technical terminology, what Descartes, and much of modern scholarship, suggested was that the noetic *ratio* of the mind's comprehension is univocally expressive of the ontic *ratio* of what is being comprehended; the basic assumption was that there exists a perfect correlation or symmetrical relationship between faith and revelation, between faith and that which it claims to be its subject-matter.[8] Descartes' method, in the final analysis, reduces the distance between the knower and the known to such an extent that the known can no longer appear to be a limit on the knower. The limit-free knower is, therefore, radically free from, but also radically free for, reality. This is the anthropocentrism referred to which readily turns into *methodological* egocentricity since the *subjectivity* of another being cannot set limits to the grasp of the knowing subject's comprehension. For example, God is no limiting "subject" to such cognition since in the formal relations established by our pure, ontological concepts and constructs no limiting negation can occur by that which those concepts and constructs noetically name; only our meanings and our naming can change. Such is the freedom of modern, Cartesian comprehension.

When critics of "liberal theology" indicate what they would do better or more appropriately they speak also of what they would abandon in it; their critique also helps specify what "liberal" in relation to theology means in this book.

"Liberal theology" is a theology that insists on freedom as the one, unrelinquishable condition in its pursuit of truth. It is clearly a condition no one, indeed, ought to neglect. It is a question of considerable weight for theology, however, how the condition of that freedom is established, how that freedom is perceived and for which interests it is being defended. It seems true, indeed, that the truth sets us free but it makes a significant difference if the liberation wrought by the truth is held to be a liberation into the neutrality of the all-seeing arbiter or into the commitment of a disciple. Liberal theology is perceived to have decided that it is the former: freedom allows fundamentally for the mediating weighing of, and opting between, various possibilities while urging the contemplation of some higher unity, of the existence of which there can be no doubt. The freedom held here is one in which one would not freely choose to renounce one's freedom; one would not decide to become "bound". Rather, this freedom holds fast to its higher vantage-point where comparing, assessing, discussing and judging remain forever open possibilities. If and when a stand is taken in this theology, it is not because one "can do no other; God help me. Amen," but because one believes that, even though other stands could quite well have been taken, this is the one which appeared most in accord with reason but may well be altered should it appear later that a yet more reasonable stand should be taken. It is reassuring to know that tomorrow is a new day and changes in one's position are possible. Again, it is important to state that all human position-taking, with one exception, is *human* self-commitment, commitment chosen as a *human* option for which one holds full, individual responsibility. One binds oneself, so to speak, freely in the knowledge that one can always unbind oneself equally freely. Such binding is the very triumph, the very affirmation of freedom.

The exception is the commitment to Christian faith, according to one of the sharpest critics of "liberal theology," Karl Barth. Such a commitment or decision is final for in it the possibility of doing otherwise in the future has been given up. This is because the commitment is to God as the absolute, limiting reality for us humans. In the language of liturgy, the decision for God is a decision for one who is "Lord." The freedom not to be committed at a future time has been given up precisely because God is God. Of course, humans can do all sorts of things other than have faith in this God; one may well choose or create deities which are free from everything limiting on humans. But humans can not have faith in this God and, in this faith, continue in the wish not to have faith at another time.[9] The decision for God, if it is the God who is *God,* is unconditional. To speak of God as the absolute, limiting reality suggests that, for example, human speech and knowledge of God arise precisely where it has pleased God to become revealed to human beings or that God is to be sought not in the sphere of the possibilities we determine as being open to comprehension, namely reason, experience and intuitive understanding *as human faculties;* instead God is to be found in God's self-manifestation.

"For this is liberalism in the Church: faith is chosen, for good reasons, with seriousness and conviction, but chosen as one of our human options. One gives witness to that faith, but one is not ready to overlook all the many other options next to faith which could have been taken up in that same freedom. At bottom, one has time for them still or again. Certainly, one wants to serve God and only God, but one wants to do that from that elevated position from the vantage-point of which serving Mammon is a serious option. The triumph belongs, precisely because one wants to serve God, to one's freedom, the freedom in which one stands at the center. That center it is which is being affirmed. There is time for comparisons and for assessments, in short: for oneself. In this situation where one has, basically, time for oneself and one's options, Christian faith is to be understood, confessed, explained and proclaimed. But that means that it is understood, confessed, explained and proclaimed in relation to the

36

understanding of the human self for which one happens to have time just now, that is, the one which is of one's time, which is "modern." At one time people said Christian faith had to be understood in relation to morality, at another in relation to reason, at yet another in relation to humanity, to culture. . . . As a child of this or that time, as a participant in its history, its spirit, particular opinions and convictions, one affirmed and grasped now this, now that anthropology as being the only correct one and faith, well, faith must be in relation, no matter what, to the human being thus understood. Otherwise faith would be — *horribile dictu* — suspended in mid-air. That faith must have such a relation, that is to say, that it must at all events be moral, reasonable, humane . . . has quietly become peculiarly self-evident and important. . . . One needs to ask: what is more certain and important: the *relation* of faith to morality, reason, humanity, culture . . . in short, the *relation* to humans, no matter what anthropology they have made their own at the time, or faith itself?"[10]

That question highlights the anthropocentricity spoken of earlier. For the question, with slight changes in terminology, shows that the issue for liberal theology is, in fact, the noetic *ratio* (method), rather than the ontic *ratio* (the limiting substance of faith) and that, secondly, that limiting substance is quietly taken for granted. This does not have to mean — and it certainly does not mean that in Harnack's theology — that faith is at a disadvantage in relation to epistemology. What it does mean is that the theologian has claimed the freedom to arbitrate between the two *ratios*. But does not such a stance change the nature of faith? Is not faith itself a matter now of mediating, weighing, assessing and judging, just like any of our human options?

Here is a freedom which sees itself free only in relation to what it can accomplish autonomously. And if in that freedom theologians fail to be in the "correct" relationship to morality, reason, ideology, etc., their work is seen to be suspect: speculative, sectarian, orthodox, neo-orthodox, or the like. It may, of course, well be so, but the basis for that judgment is narrowed to the claims of modernity, however conceived.

When Harnack confronted theologies which began, like his, with the conviction that the truth does, indeed, make us free but then said that that meant it is God's *revelation* which is the work and gift of freedom, he countered with having no antenna for such language. To claim that it is the freedom of God, precisely as the freedom which sets absolute limits, which establishes and guarantees human freedom towards God and neighbor, freedom in scholarship and politics, was to Harnack sheer speculation. He rejected the dialectics which held that the decision for faith or discipleship was a decision in which our freedom became bound to and by the limits the other, be it God or neighbor, places on one's subjecthood but that such bondage was, in fact, true freedom. "I do not become a slave but free when I hear the revelation of this free God," the God who is free to become bound to the creatures to whom this God turns in covenantal grace.[11] It is possible, however, that Harnack understood only too well what was at stake, namely that the freedom always to be able to remain the judge in a superior vantage-position was utterly rejected and that that meant nothing less than a wholly other theology, a wholly other noetic *and* ontic *ratio.* It seems unlikely that he would have conceded that his own aims were dealt with better or more appropriately; he usually believed that people were reverting to a pre-Enlightenment position rather than moving forward with liberal theology beyond liberal theology.

The height of liberal theology, which Harnack is claimed here to represent, is reflected in all the positive and critical aspects just presented. Readers will discover his incorruptible reasonableness in the rigors of his methodic approach, his unflagging confidence in the competence and authority of thought and its power. Harnack's unshakeable religious faith is similarly apparent. But the focus of his work is, clearly, not the Christian faith *qua* faith but as an expression of what is taken to be a basic human characteristic: religion. As a theologian he focused on the real *meaning* of Christian faith-expressions and, as an historian, on how that meaning arose, developed and changed; as a theologian/historian he asked how adequate the various historical and current expressions were in relation to the real meaning of the Christian religion. This combination, in which the theologian Harnack was, above all, an historian and, as an historian, above all a convinced theologian[12] expresses a situation in the scholarly world of the late 19th and 20th centuries, namely the indissoluble tie between Christianity and culture, religion and the formation of the human character (what the Germans call *Bildung*). In that situation one sees the predominance of the *relation* of faith to the modern human being over faith in addition to the general consciousness of method as that which, finally, assures the legitimacy of science and scholarship and their claim to authoritativeness. Another way of putting this is to say that the general conviction concerning the freedom to be able, always and ultimately, to judge was that meticulous adherence to the standards of reason and of method would assure that freedom.

There is a remarkable passage in Harnack's lecture of 1920 "What Has History to Offer as Certain Knowledge Concerning the Meaning of World Events?" which is included in this selection of his texts. In that passage he says the following: "*homo sum, nil historicum a me alienum puto* [I am human and consider nothing of history alien to me]. . . . Everything which has happened and is still happening in history, *that you are yourself* and everything depends on your appropriating it consciously. That is why whatever happens in history . . . can become your inner possession and meld perfectly with our higher life. We are allowed . . . to illumine history by means of our experience . . ., assured that from [it] we will surely understand history. . . . We must expand, with Faust, the ego that is ours into the whole world's ego. This occurs . . . as we, in noble hunger, take into ourselves the whole of world-happening and all of history's great and good personalities, transforming all into the fibres of our being."[13]

That is both genuine and ecstatic liberalism, for in that fashion we also appropriate, that is to say master, Jesus, that good personality, his religion and revelation. Jesus is in himself no limiting entity; what draws our attention is what he said, what kind of human being he was. Whatever reverence we give him is due entirely to the fact that he and his message perfectly meld with our higher life.

A similarly pure expression of liberalism, in the form of faith that *knows*, is to be found in the two following items from Harnack's *What Is Christianity?* One observes, nowadays perhaps with a sense of astonishment, how sure he was about the faith of others, how calmly convinced he was that he understood it well.

"Measured by the experience of the senses and by exact knowledge, not only are the different religions a paradox, but so are all religious phenomena. They introduce an element, and pronounce it to be the most important of all, which is not cognisable by the senses and flies in the face of things as they are actually constituted. But all religions other than Christianity are in some way or other so bound up with the things of the world that they involve an element of earthly advantage, or, as the case may be, are akin in their substance to the intellectual and spiritual condition of a definite epoch."[14]

This judgment of negativity in relation to non-Christian religions is made even more sharply in the next item. Responding to the challenge that Jesus had introduced nothing really new in relation to the preaching of his ancestors in the faith, Harnack said that:

"it is quite true that what Jesus proclaimed . . . was also to be found in the prophets, and even in the Jewish tradition of [his] time. The Pharisees themselves were in possession of it; but unfortunately they were in possession of much else besides. With them it was weighted, darkened, distorted, rendered ineffective and deprived of its force, by a thousand things which they also held to be religious and every whit as important as mercy and judgment. They reduced everything to one dead level, wove everything into one fabric; the good and holy was only one woof in a broad earthly warp. . . . Take the people of Israel and search the whole history of their religion; take history generally, and where will you find a message about God and the good that was ever so pure and so full of strength . . . as we hear and read of in the gospels? Pharisaical teachers had proclaimed that everything was contained in the injunction to love God and one's neighbor. They spoke excellently; the words might have come out of Jesus' mouth. But what was the result of their language? . . . All that they did was weak and, because weak, harmful."[15]

It is only consistent that faith which *knows*, once it has established what religion or faith mean in terms of pure concepts, will make decisions about a different religion or faith, firmly convinced *that* such decisions can be made in the manner of an evaluative judgment. It is the stance of liberalism at its height. It is true that liberalism also asserted that every person has the freedom to seek salvation in the manner most reasonable to her/him and that that freedom needed to be defended. Still, liberal theology would not relinquish the certainty that the genuinely original and truly valuable of religion is to be found in Christianity. It would not defend that view in terms of dogmatics — Harnack is reported to have said to someone who helped set up his personal library that dogmatics goes into the section of *belles lettres*[16] — it demonstrated this view in what it believed to be a manner free of all metaphysics, namely historically. But when the attack on that view came under the heading of "historicism," Harnack charged the critics with being unscientific. For him the system of dogmatics had to give way to the system of Christian history.[17]

Finally, it should be pointed out that historians of Christian theology refer to "liberal theology at its height" in the term "neo-Protestantism"; it refers to the already cited belief that Christian faith must not be in opposition to, but in community with, the general consciousness expressed in culture, science and *Bildung*, such as the *universitas litterarum*. The triumph of Harnack's amazingly diversified life and work was to overcome the divergence between modern society and Christian religion and establish a relation between them on the basis of scholarly, dependable knowledge. And that relation clearly included, as an essential and decisive aspect of the culture of modern society, the social work each particular community required.

This liberal theology was not a theology of the Church but one of culture. For that reason, it is also known as "*Kulturprotestantismus*," cultural Protestantism. The name was not the choice of liberal theology; it wanted to become the theology of the Church, a Church, however, which had also chosen to be a Church in relation to modernity. The primary addressee was the cultured individual of modern times who sought, in freedom from any strictures which associating with the institutional Church was believed to bring, to be religious and cultured, a person of reason *and* faith. And it found a strong, positive echo among that public for it held out the chance to provide successfully two much treasured values: the freedom of theology and the freedom of the individual to be, and remain, the final and authoritative arbiter.

A Postscript

The reader will become aware of Harnack's irritating habit of quoting a variety of poets, writers and journalists without citing the source. The editor decided that the absence of such references, which to search out would have been a huge task, does not reduce the clarity of the image of Harnack's life and work.

SELECTED TEXTS

1

HISTORY AS A SCIENCE IN THE SERVICE OF THEOLOGY: METHOD AND CERTAINTY

The strength of every scholarly discipline resides, in no small way, in the precision of its methods and in the care with which they are applied. Harnack shared this conviction with the academicians of his age but he also sensed that the humanities were expected to be even more meticulous about "recognized methodologies" than, let us say, the natural sciences. His discipline was theology, the method he chose as a theologian was that of "the modern science of history" (see p. 66). One may say, therefore, that as a theologian he was an historian and as an historian he was a theologian. His intention in that scholarly pursuit was to "change people mired in their elemental drives and in sadness into pure and courageous ones," to demonstrate that "the most important part of our destiny lies in our hands." (see pp. 62-63).

The following selections speak of Harnack's quest for a rigorously "scientific" theology, one which can rightly claim its place in the academy. The first text, written within a year of Harnack's death, is the most precise, but also the barest, of his utterances on his method. It is a kind of testament to a generation of students who struggled to maintain the integrity of his particular historical-theological, theological-historical approach in face of the growing critique of "historicism," as that approach came to be called. Harnack was aware of the critique when he delivered the lecture which represents the earliest selection in this section. In it, as in his lengthy lecture at the Aarau Student-Conference in 1920, he sought to demonstrate that with a rigorously controlled historical method, applied to the claims of the religious consciousness of Christians, those claims can be proven to be certain and true. He sensed no polemics against his position in 1899/1900 when he delivered his lectures on the nature of Christianity at the University of Berlin. He was then the undisputed master of scholarly theology; in 1923, when he and his erstwhile student Karl Barth engaged in public debate, he manifested a mounting bewilderment at the apparent rejection of the seemingly firm conclusions of his work, especially that "in the study of . . . the Christian religion" history "has the first word," (see p. 166) which was, after all, to what he had dedicated his life's work.

STAGES OF SCIENTIFIC KNOWLEDGE

Life was nearly over for Harnack even though he may have wished to be in his prime again, were that possible, in order to set out a definitive methodology for the pursuit of truth in the historical sciences. He did not wish to develop a metaphysics of history, rather, he sought a way on which it would be possible to know with certainty, by means of precise steps of analysis and interpretation, what life's architectonics, ideas and purposes are. This little document sums up how Harnack saw his own approach towards that goal; it was written in 1929 and published, posthumously, in 1930 in the anthology Aus der Werkstatt des Vollendeten; *the translation, prepared by the editor, was made from the text in* Ausgewählte Reden und Aufsätze, *pp. 177-80.*

Science is knowledge of reality for purposeful action. Science has its stages. The first and lowest stage consists of determining, analyzing and ordering. Important natural scientists have tried to limit "pure" science to this stage alone, but in this they will not succeed. The structure of our understanding, as well as of reality opening up to us and of the relationship among phenomena, require that we enter upon a second stage.

The second stage is determined by the knowledge of the original interrelationship among things. Here one deals with numbers, weights, and measures relating to the knowledge of the forces in the world insofar as they can be represented as operative quantitatively and mechanistically. Our reason is a born mathematical physicist; it abstracts, reckons and measures like such a one. A number of greater and lesser persons of education have maintained that all science is comprised in this knowledge of the mechanics of the world, but that science also gives rise to and embraces a perfect and completely satisfying world-view. Thus, they spoke of the "world-view of the natural scientist," suggesting at the same time that this would be the only possible and tenable view. Their comments notwithstanding, this kind of knowledge has its limits. For even inanimate nature surrounding us opens up for us a view of natural history which we are unable to contest by means of the mechanics which correspond to this abstractive method; we are led by that view towards a sublime metaphysics. There are other reasons to question their conviction. In the world around us we do not observe mere quantities or forces operating mechanistically, not even a motley abundance of puzzling differentiations among those forces. What surrounds us is "life." We know and experience ourselves as a part of this "life" and observe it as an abundance of centers which, however conditioned, are nonetheless independent. It is characteristic of these living beings that they appear in forms made up of harmonious parts, that the whole is always greater than the parts, that each is its own world, and yet that all touch one another harmoniously. Indeed, each of these living beings presents itself as complete, final and, therefore, as a self-contained value; and yet, everything alongside is mutually conditioned, thereby forming a link towards the next higher being. If one understands as pure science the specific method of thought characteristic of the second, mechanistic stage, one must admit that, in its final form, life cannot be understood at all "scientifically."

Nevertheless, life is not shut off to thought. Investigating life is the third stage of knowledge. In this matter Goethe was a master. At present it is Uexküll [a professor of biology, who opposed mechanistic views of nature] who must be named particularly for his endeavors to investigate the life-movement of every living form. He determined the "world" of each one of them to be the environment and perceptual reality unique to each and, in addition, recognized how the wider world acts on each species and how each makes its way in that wider world; each form and each individual within that form has its own "perceptual reality" which is "the world" for it. From this perspective life is seen as an unending variety of living groups each of which is a world unto itself. We are confronted by not simply *one* world but by an abundance of them. To know them one must determine, analyze and order, as in the first stage, but now with a greater engagement; here new questions are raised concerning usefulness and adaptability, concerning the idea as well as direction and purpose. I would not wish to be misunderstood here: science, as I have briefly described it under the second stage, can only be pursued as it is at present; it rightly resists all interference and, as mechanics, must be kept completely "pure." We should not deny it our sympathy and admiration and fervently desire its every advance. Only the illusion should cease that it encompasses everything worth knowing and is capable of offering a complete picture of the world. For alongside it there is a knowledge of concrete reality and of life, half known and half unknown by everyone and practiced by each living form, since without such knowledge it is not possible to live. It is the task of the third stage of scientific knowledge to pursue this knowledge of life as intentionally as that of mechanics, to seek it in both the all-encompassing and the individual and then, by means of this knowledge, not only render the totality of phenomena into the well-analyzed environment of humankind but also grasp that environment's architectonics, course, ideas and purposes.

The fourth stage of knowledge, closely related to the third, is directed towards the knowledge of humankind. Here, the conscious spirit meets us with its ideas, norms and values. At this stage the science of history comes into its own, of history which is more than the development of technology, of the forms of human alliance and of their speech. History begins only where the binding idea of norms and values comes to light. Not only natural laws are operative in history; in it lives the spirit which gives birth to the idea, to values and norms, that is to say, to laws of freedom.

This last and highest stage of scientific knowledge flows into philosophy which is itself, however, no "science." Philosophy is an aristocratic activity and cultivates a synthesis which is not everyone's concern. One must not forget that humanity has not found its upward way by the light of the torches of individual insights gained through quantitative examination but under the guidance of men who had a vision of a central sun and had the courage to advance from physics to metaphysics, from history to metahistory, from ethics to metaethics. The pursuit of philosophy is not everyone's concern, and one must respect the standpoint of those who do not make it a part of their own labor. However, even when one is unable to participate in the work of philosophy, its incomparable value still forces itself upon us from history, and one honors an undertaking which is beyond one's powers.

*

WHAT HAS HISTORY TO OFFER AS CERTAIN KNOWLEDGE CONCERNING THE MEANING OF WORLD EVENTS?

On April 17th 1920 Adolf von Harnack, within one year of retiring from his academic duties, and Karl Barth, within one year of beginning his, met at Aarau, Switzerland; both had been invited to give lectures at the famed Studentenkonferenz. *Barth, Harnack's one-time student, spoke on "Biblical Questions, Insights and Vistas"; earlier in the day his former teacher had spoken on the subject of the selection to follow. While he believed that he was addressing the post World War I generation which longed for firm answers along lines of renewed certainty, Barth went about radically questioning the entire enterprise of building on the kind of foundations his teacher had just developed. For Harnack the experience was a turning point, and he now sought for the remaining years of his life to formulate his "science of understanding." The text, given here in the editor's translation, was first published in 1923 in the anthology* Erforschtes und Erlebtes, *pp. 171-95.*

Why are people preoccupied with history? What legitimates the pursuit of that subject? Do we pursue it for entertainment? Is it a "diversion?" The 18th century believed that it was just that. But if that is so, then it is better to busy oneself with novels, romances and dramas; they are generally more entertaining than history. Shakespeare's royal dramas, for example, are more interesting than the story of English royal history. Again: do we engage in history simply in order to satisfy our elementary thirst for knowledge? It may well be that, under certain circumstances, an individual will devote an entire life to the satisfaction of this thirst; on the other hand, every thinking person should direct that thirst for knowledge also towards the area of history. However, if knowledge of history is, and ought to be, a task which is given to all humankind as an essential part of knowledge, then it must have the dimensionality of the present and be related to our actions, for we are not in this world to entertain ourselves or become lost in thought *but, rather, to further reality and serve our neighbor.* No one, including the historian, may withdraw from this task. "History" must go and welcome this task; otherwise we ought to leave it behind ourselves and turn to other preoccupations. We study history not merely to learn or merely to know what happened, but to free ourselves from the *past* wherever it has become a burden, to be enabled to do what is right in the *present* and to prepare the *future* suitably and with prudence. Only when we are enabled to do so by means of "history" is its right proven to take its place alongside the other great tasks which are given to humankind.

What has history to offer as certain knowledge concerning the meaning of world events? Your question, it seems to me, harbors an unexpressed doubt or anxiety. It is for that reason that I have divided it into two questions: (1) *Does history really offer certain knowledge?* and (2) *Which knowledge does history offer about the meaning of world events and what value does that knowledge have?*

I

Does history really offer certain knowledge? Scepticism is expressed on several fronts. The logician comes forward, asserting that one could never make the crucial experiment in history and that it is impossible to exclude any one factor in order to determine exactly what history and its course would be like without that factor. The examining magistrate comes forward, instructing us that it is just not possible to prove simple facts of a case even the next day despite numerous witnesses because the cause and the order of events, motives and fault are so rapidly covered in thick fog and statements come to stand against statements. Finally, the diplomat joins the others, informing us with that ever so telling smile that all of so-called "modern history" (and much more so that of Antiquity and the Middle Ages) is a convenient fable, a legend which every political party shapes to its own purposes; the most important acts are lacking or closed to the historian and, even if they were all on hand and accessible, only half of what really took place would show up in the files, mixed in with much falsehood, both hidden and open. Those who write, for example, a history of Luther or of the Reformation today write *their* history of Luther or the Reformation. Everywhere, this pattern is repeated.

Taken together, these objections are unanswerable, indeed, one may even reinforce them: it is indisputable, as the old Latin adage puts it: *historia quo accuratius eo falsius narratur*: history becomes the more inaccurate the more accurately one recites it with all circumstances and motives included. Goethe's ringing lament is all too justified: do you believe that from mouth to ear yields much honest profit? (*Glaubst du denn von Mund zu Ohr sei redlicher Gewinn?*) And yet, we may give reply to the logician, the magistrate and the diplomat: the history of which you speak is not at all the history with which we are concerned. We are no seekers of motives, no interpreters of what is at the inner core; we are not the note-takers at the world's judgment. We do not want to hear *histories* but know *history*. Histories are a heap of glimmering and gleaming stones of different densities; history, on the other hand, is *one* great majestic crystal. It is necessary to distinguish sharply between history and biography. The aim of historical research is to exclude the subjective element entirely and to construct an edifice of the greatest objectivity, whereas biography has to re-experience its protagonists in order to raise them anew to life. This task claims all spiritual and physical energies and is an "artful" one for only thus can the re-creation succeed. The subjective character is not only not excluded here but is, in fact, clearly needed, for a biography can never be other than a double, always the autobiography of the biographer. Therefore, only when a number of biographies are taken together is objectivity approached.

We return to history. Is there in it something firm and secure? Our answer is an unqualified "yes." There is an abundance of significant data the truth of which simply cannot be questioned. *In the first place,* there are the major events which, as such and in their succession, are not subject to doubt. From the Persian Wars to the Great War we just experienced those events are firmly established in their overall scope and order, no matter whether one thinks of the Roman Empire, the Barbarian Invasion, Charlemagne's Empire, the Reformation, the Thirty Years War, or dozens of similar historical events of the world. Why these facts are well established need not concern us now, even though there is here and there some uncertainty still about the exact year and day. You all know that they are well established and that one need not waste a single word in refutation if someone were to declare that there never was a Barbarian Invasion or that the Reformation occurred in the 17th century or that Napoleon and his Empire never existed.

In the second place, there are the monuments from all epochs of the last 2500 years and beyond. By monuments I mean all that which is still extant from bygone ages, be it buildings, statues, inscriptions, coins, documents, handwriting, etc. Their quantity is immeasurable; all thought of forgery is excluded in relation to the majority of them. One can as little forge the Egyptian Pyramids as the ruins of the great edifices of Assyria and Babylon or the frieze of the Parthenon or Dante's *Divine Comedy.* This or that statue, this or that coin or inscription may be a forgery but Greek sculpture cannot be the work of a mediaeval forgery-ring and the many hundreds of thousands of Babylonian, Persian and Roman inscriptions must belong to the epochs to which they claim to belong. But what an abundance of rich knowledge flows from these monuments! What does an Egyptian pyramid, a Greek temple with its works of art, a Gothic cathedral, what do the coins and documents of all ages not teach the thoughtful observer! From them all, one cultural epoch after another arises, firmly profiled in their thinking, their strength and orientation. The life of religion, of politics, scholarship and home, in their great and small actions, is reawakened and the past, as if it were imperishable, stands next to the present.

In the third place, there are the institutions which the numerous ages before us have created for themselves, all the way to the ancient Babylonian Law Code. By institutions I mean everything deposited in the form of legislation, lawbooks, ordinances, contracts, agendas, liturgies, school regulations, economic arrangements, and the like. In them I see the true products of historical development to which the study of history has to direct itself in the first instance if not even exclusively. More of this later. It is enough to indicate here that, even though forgeries have been discovered in this category and a few uncertainties still remain, the genuineness of these institutions is now so well established, due in part to the possession of the monuments referred to earlier, that any defence of authenticity is superfluous.

Some object that that may indeed be so but, still, little is gained from this since valid knowledge is obtained only where *laws* are established. Can history establish such laws?

The first thing to be said in reply is that simply noting facts in their interrelation and succession alone is highly instructive even without any prescribed reason for doing so. From the perception of reality and its rich life there flows a fullness of impression which broadens and deepens soul and spirit. We educate our children with the help of picture-books and the picture-book of history gives adults a continuing education through such perception for the remainder of their lives. Nothing can replace such education. Moreover, the character and significance of "law" is often overrated. Even in the natural sciences "law" is not nearly as "objective" an entity as many present-day natural scientists still imagine. Under critical scrutiny many "laws" turn out to be only preliminary conclusions, more or less fruitful hypotheses, provisional, and not absolute laws. The recently promulgated theory of relativity itself limits laws like Newton's: they are valid only in a particular area. This theory also finds support from Spengler's arguments which have brought to light the restrictive arbitrariness of different cultural epochs in relation to their perception of space, size, number and time. Not a few "proven" causal relationships have now also revealed themselves to be tautologies or differences in observation or variations in linguistic expression. Even if some of these "low grade" laws give us better understanding than a statement as profound as: there is a draft because the wind is blowing, they still cannot serve as a true enrichment of knowledge.

In the rigorous sense of the word history cannot establish laws, even if it can show, as we shall see later, that under certain conditions there must of necessity be decline while under other circumstances there will be an upswing. Such insight can, however, always be traced back to the tautology that force will always present itself only as force and weakness as weakness. The reason why "history" cannot establish laws is because its objects are only seldom enumerated, measured and weighed and because the factors on which it rests are in part too complicated, in part beyond calculation.

There is, first of all, the *elementary* factor: all those things which surround and are connected with us in various but inescapable ways: the soil, the climate, the basic physical and spiritual qualities, ability and character, hunger and love, the place where we eat and the amount there is to eat. So powerful is this factor, of which "economics" is comprised, that an entire school of historians maintains that the whole course of history, including the history of ideas, is to be understood solely from it and believes itself able to reconstruct history as a struggle for economic existence.

Then, there is the factor which I would like to call the *cultural* factor. The present is to be found in each moment of history and everyone of those moments is determined by the capital of traditions, institutions, authorities, knowledge, attitudes and customs accumulated to that time. No matter what an individual's relation to those aspects, there is no escape from their grasp. They work with the gentle force of a second nature; they determine simply everything. As the example of many historians shows, it is easy to be tempted to present all of history, excluding its elementary foundation, as the history of culture in development, as political history in the broadest sense of that word.

Next to these two there is a third factor: the *individual.* Not only the powerful one, who makes history, not only the genius, but each and every individual. It has been rightly said that "*individuum est ineffabile.*" That is: the individual embodies an element which is inexhaustible and which defies explanation. This insight holds true not only for the human individual, it holds for everything individual per se, only the more so for the human one. Given the particular nature of our spirit we are compelled to press towards the "One" through the formulation of ever more comprehensive concepts. That nature offers us both deepening enlightenment and difficult illusions. Still, it is not hard for us to classify all phenomena in an ascending order and, with increasing abstraction, allow their attributes and characteristics to merge perfectly with the "All-One" which we name by various names according to circumstances and taste. In this way we may truly ascend indeed, whereas for the descent we lack a compass. How one is to take even the first step from the "All-One," whether we name it matter, power, energy or give it an ideal name, and offer an initial explication in order to succeed in the long descent to actual phenomena evades our knowledge so perfectly that even surmise ceases. That there are organisms, plants, roses: even this we can know only as fact and assert nothing about their why and wherefore. However, that *this* rose stands before us with its particular complex of characteristics and that it, if tested, has absolutely *no exact equal*, is utterly ineffable. Similarly, precisely why *this* individual appears at *this* moment, is inexpressible and unexplainable. That is no less true of the unimportant individual than of the important one, but only with the latter does that fact strike us. When does genius appear? When the mighty man? It is said that he, too, is merely an exponent of his time and circumstance and that he would come when he must. However much the "great man" is a child of his time, he is also greater than it and, therefore, a phenomenon beyond calculation. The assertion that he will come when he must is idle talk. How often has "time been fulfilled" and the waiting was in vain! How often and eagerly was he expected and yet he did not come! But what mighty workings are there in history as a consequence of his appearance that were all incalculable in advance! How impossible it is, therefore, to establish laws for the course of history.

But there is more. First, there is that which we call by the puzzling words "fate" and "chance" and which pertains not only to the individual but, also, to thousands of facts, frustrating all calculations. Almost all *events* which bring latent forces to reality produce unforeseen combinations and open powerful new orders of causation and are for us "by chance." The wind, or a child at play, or evil intention can cause an overhanging rock to fall and that fall may be of no consequence or "by chance" create the worst misfortune. And so it is in both the little and the big things in life. Even when all the origins of an event are clear and intelligible to us, why and how it began, why certain lines crossed today and not yesterday, remains hidden from us as a rule. Second, even in those processes which seem governed rigorously by law, like those which depend on the elementary factor named above, an incalculable element appears. For natural constrictions do not apply to humans as they do to wood and stone, but as to a living and, therefore, responding being; these responses differ from one being to another. An earthquake, a famine, a war, and the like, has indeed the same effect on all in certain basic ways. However, entirely different consequences follow for diverse individuals; some allow themselves to become discouraged and despairing, others create a chorus of virtue from adversity. Some become selfish and cowardly, others courageous and ready to sacrifice.

It was so in the days of Fichte and Schleiermacher, so it was in the World War we have experienced, so it is always. A Greek philosopher once noted that humans are not stirred up by things but by their conception of things. That means nothing other than that each important event produces two types of reaction, an elementary one and one which arises in the soul and spirit; often enough, the latter is the more important and is the one beyond calculation.

Even though it is impossible, according to what has been set out here, to establish laws of history, we none the less possess an excellent, albeit not infallible, means by which to organize the abundance of its phenomena, to make them transparent and *to understand* them, namely *analogy*. Analogy is a special means of induction. In the writing of history it has always been practiced and valued highly. It is Spengler's merit to have brought its significance clearly to the fore in his profound and thought-provoking work *The Decline of the West*. In the study of history he was the first to sing the praise of analogy. He, too, was the first to show what a striking analogy exists between all the mental and spiritual phenomena of a given epoch and, then, how the drama of ascent, flowering, decline and fall unfolds in every great epoch. In that work he has taught us that, all the way from the understanding of space, time and number via mathematics, music, the creative arts, scholarship and the shaping of ordinary life up to the reflection on the Whole in philosophy and religion, *one* and the same forming, law-giving and symbolizing spirit or style is at work in every epoch. He has called attention to the fact that the stages on the course of historical processes are surprisingly alike, even to the fine detail, in all of the important periods so that one must speak of the "contemporaneousness" of segments of distant ages. The indicators of time do, indeed, revolve around the same dial in every age.

In fact, it is no different for adults as it is for children: practically everything the latter learn before they start school they learn by observation and analogy; it is no different for scholars. To be sure, conclusions drawn from analogy are initially only surmises; how seriously one can err is shown daily by children's hasty conclusions. But learning consists for the most part of the corrections made in one's conclusions via analogy. However, in the process surmises become ever more probable and finally advance to presumptive evidence. And such evidence it is on which eventually the entire certainty of the conduct of our lives and of what is maintained in the science of history comes to rest; it is what is erroneously called laws of history.

But can historians prophesy on the basis of their historical knowledge? Can they be prophets of the future? No one has contested this more clearly and rigorously than Jakob Burckhardt; he has denied every possibility of foretelling the future just because there are no laws of history. Spengler, on the other side, opened his work with the declaration that historians, through blindness or lack of understanding, have hitherto missed their calling. For him the highest, indeed the essential task of the knowledge of history, was to prophesy the future; according to him, that task was not merely somewhat feasible but, in actual fact, entirely possible. He came to this astonishing conclusion precisely through the demonstration of the importance of analogy. Faced with those two opposing assertions, I must make a decision, something which, as a rule, causes me some unease. As I see it, *the truth lies in the middle*; still, Burckhardt is closer to the truth. Spengler comes to his astonishing conclusion through a colossal overestimation of analogy in that he is quite serious in maintaining that if only one delineates a cultural sphere correctly error is ruled out and that whatever in history does not fit into the analogical scheme is negligible. I will deal with that again in the next part, here it is enough to say that historians may not affix their torch and plumb-line to the bow of their ship but only to its helm, for the torch illumines only the way already traveled and the plumb-line fathoms only the depths and shallows already traversed. But as sailors, as a rule, do not err in their conclusions about the nature of what still lies before them when they compare their most recent findings with earlier ones — it is, of course, possible to confuse a sandbar with the shore — so historians will not frequently be mistaken when they relate their conclusions about the past to what lies ahead; just as sailors become more certain in their surmises as they grow in experience, so historians will also become more certain in their calculations regarding the future as they grow in their experience of life and history.

To sum up: the question: *does history really offer certain knowledge?* is answered by saying that history, moving back into shrouded antiquity, offers each succeeding age an abundance of certain and significant facts from all dimensions of life. It can make them evident and transparent not only in particular instances but, by means of analogy, order them into unified groups and bring understanding of their sequence through surmise and presumptive evidence. On the basis of such surmises history can look into the future, given the proviso that, as in forecasting the weather, error is possible. But here as there, prediction should not be shunned simply because of the possibility and frequent actuality of error.

II

Which knowledge does history offer about the meaning of world events and what value does that knowledge have? — We come now to the main question. I build here on what I have already said about *institutions*. We study history ultimately in order to know institutions. Whether we are dealing with war, diplomacy, politics or art and science, Church and school, etc., historical research must be directed steadily towards learning to know what results development has led to. We meet those results in the form of contracts, constitutions, law codes, school curricula and organization, Church organization, liturgies, catechisms, etc.

In this study we discern further that *nothing at all*, not even great men and the genius, *makes a lasting impression on the human community that has not taken form in institutions.* If we are unable to trace a significant and successful historical development into the institutions it has brought forth, then either the development is still incomplete or our knowledge of it is. However impressive the effectiveness of the individual, however immeasurable the influence of person on person, the totality which social groups as such represent is influenced permanently only by an institution which, whether written or unwritten, gives clear expression of itself in the form it imposes, the goals it inspires and the authority it exercises.

It is in the nature of these institutions that they be taken together and studied in terms of the sequence of those which are similar, on the one hand, and in terms of the apposition of those which are simultaneous, on the other. This provides both longitudinal and cross sections for the study of history. Simple coordination such as this reveals quickly the life and movement evident in those sections. The longitudinal sections show us the *direction* of the movement as well as how *strength* and *weakness* alternated in it; the cross sections show us the *character* and the *style* of any given moment together with its greater or lesser *unity*.

No other historian in recent decades has practised the art of "sectioning" with the virtuosity of a Spengler nor has anyone given such profound interpretation to those sections as he did; at the same time no one has been as mistaken as he about them. He excelled, to be sure, in making cross sections and in depicting the character and style of individual epochs, even though he forced some of his subject-material and often his cross-cuts look more like a zig-zag than a straight line. His longitudinal cuts, on the other hand, are to a large extent arbitrary, even beyond comprehension. For example, he claims that with the coming of

Christianity a new major epoch took rise: however, from the 7th century onward Islam carried the epoch and not Christianity. Then, around the year 1000 an entirely new period began in his view for Western Europe, the period in the decline and fall of which we now stand; for it ancient Christianity is no more than an encumbrance to be borne, a sheath under whose cover the ancient form was utterly transformed. But Spengler does not see that, at least for the first half of this period, the Church-father Augustine was the great teacher and that, on the other hand, new forces made themselves felt in the middle of this period. On the contrary, he sees in Islam the actual continuation of Christianity which is not even accurate for the Orient, even though Islam is the bearer of culture in that region. Still, that culture is not an independent one but is that of Persia-Greece. One can calmly await the counter-evidence to Spengler since he did not even attempt to prove his claims.

But let us return to our subject. The longitudinal and cross sections provide the first step in the search for meaning in history. The longitudinal sections, we said, teach us to recognize *direction* and *force*. Something extraordinary is achieved, however, with that for it is the decisive question to determine in which direction something moved and what force is employed. In history one should not ask too quickly about "right or wrong," "true or false," but enquire primarily about direction. For example, Platonic philosophy or Catholic theology may be false in many or all points but, compared to what went before, they have permanent value in their *direction*. If the gaze is fixed firmly on historical development, no matter whether it is political, scholarly, artistic, religious, or the like, then the dead succession of events comes not only alive but also open to interpretation and understanding, especially if one takes into account at the same time with what force a phenomenon resisted and overcame its opposition and where and why direction was changed. It may just be that the times changed; in fact, time is in and of itself the strongest factor operative in the change of direction, since every particularity exists only in its relationship to others while relationships are subject to the constant change of time. Just as the relationship of children to their parents changes all the time and, finally, the aging child becomes very much like the graying parent, so it is with the relationship of institutions in their apposition one to the other. May I use a mathematical comparison: let us designate the original relationship of two magnitudes $a:b$ and call the time factor n; the new quotient becomes $a+n:b+n$. One sees at once that even if the first fraction is very small, the second one can approximate the first only if it is big enough. But this is what, time and again, one observes in history: institutions dislocate themselves in the relationship of direction simply because they are not all of the same age; from such dislocations come conflicts without any outside agency. In addition to those dislocations we also see in many places changes in direction which are caused by persons who act with a powerful *force*. Frequently, the new direction which they established had been clearly indicated in the past but lacked the power to come into operation. History shows clearly in its longitudinal sections how much comes into existence through the presence of such force; it is equal in importance with direction, for direction remains unactualized unless it is assisted by force. The epoch maker is always a powerful person, indeed, often it is only such a person who makes an epoch.

Cross sections, on the other hand, recall the individuality of an epoch by calling attention to its character and style; they allow the apparently divided, disparate and accidental to appear as the representation of a greater unity. Greek state-constitution, Greek mathematics, Greek sculpture and Greek religion and philosophy belong together as do Gothic cathedrals, mediaeval scholarship and mediaeval government. From the neglected riches of the many and of the individual there develops the sense required to conceive of the epoch's extensive wealth of character and style of thought. Those riches can be clearly comprehended and described. What insight! However, at the same time, the feeling of missing such unity is kindled where such unity is not yet, or no longer, present as is the recognition that attention is to be paid to disintegration of and decline in character and style.

Thus, already in its first step the scholarly study of history, in its critical contemplation of things, offers great things for the interpretation of world events. Through longitudinal and cross sections it teaches the recognition of direction and change in direction, life and stagnation, the differentiation of power and weakness and the valuing of character and style of epochs.

Let us take the next step. *All institutions originate in ideas.* This statement is true also in relation to purely economic institutions. It is quite unthinkable that one could ever discover, between heaven and earth, an institution that had not been previously there in the idea. To be sure, all history is the history of institutions but behind this history there live ideas and the history of ideas. Therefore, just as surely as everything which is only ideology and not yet institution is not yet history, so also all of the history of institutions is unprobed as long as the motivating ideas are unknown. The ideas are, however, the *spirit*.

We must now speak of the spirit. All history is *history of the spirit* (*Geistesgeschichte*) and has an inner happening for its foundation; *the spirit, however is one*. Whether we possess much or little of it, it is always one and the same spirit working in us and in everything brought forth by history. With that we are led back to ourselves out of the enormous life of history or, rather, a deep unity between all events and the nature of our own higher existence is discovered. The old phrase "*homo sum, nil humanum a me alienum puto*" [I am human and consider nothing human alien to me] can also be expressed as "*homo sum, nil historicum a me alienum puto*" [I am human and consider nothing historical alien to me]. But that still says too little. Everything which has happened and is still happening in history: *that you are yourself* and everything depends on your appropriating it consciously. That is why whatever happens in history is not only much more understandable for us than nature and its processes but also can become our own inner possession and meld perfectly with our higher life. We are allowed for that very reason to illumine history by means of our own experience and life circumstances, assured that from them we will surely understand history in growing measure for it is spirit which unveils spirit. This is the interpretation of history on the second step.

Permit me a brief digression. In the light of what has just been said how utterly scanty looks the currently oft repeated assertion that nothing is to be learned from history, that it is, rather, necessary to turn back to our own personal experience or, as the even more careless would have it, we are in the world to "live it up." No!, the opposite is true: we must expand, with Faust, the ego that is ours into the whole world's ego. This occurs — I know I speak boldly — as we, in noble hunger, take into ourselves the whole of world-happening and all of history's great and good personalities, transforming all into the fibres of our being. "Those who fail to give themselves account of the past three millennia remain in the dark, ignorant, living merely from day to day." Not only those who speculate are "like the animal in a dry pasture, led around in a circle by a wicked spirit while all around is a rich, green meadow," but also those who seek to restrict all to their own experience. In the merry-go-round around one's own ego one may well be dazzled by the voyage but it is like the child's trip on the wooden horse at a country-fair; one stays put in the same place and sees nothing new. To broaden oneself inwardly through history does not only belong to education, *it is education*. Such education connects itself harmoniously to the inner life of the spirit. We shall remain wretched and in bondage if we limit ourselves to ourselves; we shall become rich and free if we enter every door of history and make ourselves at home in its spacious rooms.

The knowledge that history, as history of institutions, is history of ideas further clarifies for us a problem that is frequently misinterpreted. With apparent justification "institutions" and "life" are often placed in sharp opposition one to another, whereupon it is said that precisely for their opposition one must free oneself from history because it cripples the independence and freshness of life through its institutions. They are the real enemy of ideas and of life and one will master institutions only if one ignores or resists them. It is true that ideas and institutions stand in a continuing struggle, but they are not in it because they are opposites of some kind such as that ideas are something alive while institutions are something dead. No!, an idea cannot enter completely into an institution and every institution seeks somehow to assert itself even when it has lost every right still to exist. Therefore, a struggle must continually prevail between ideas and some institutions for which reason there is justification for turning away from history *if* it is a turning away from the outmoded. But even that does not change the fact that institutions originate in ideas and are of the spirit. One cannot even resist the outmoded by ignoring it or turning one's back on history. The outmoded is opposed only by obliterating it on the basis of a correctly understood history.

Over the two steps on the interpretation of history depicted thus far there arises a third one on which alone the understanding of world events comes to completion. At the present time this step is still much debated. It has to do with whether one can infer from history itself a *measure of value* for what it produces or whether one must, *as an historian,* avoid all valuation, that is to say, whether one ought to determine simply what *is* in relation to history but not what *ought to be.* One major school maintains this and speaks of valuation as of an ungainly preoccupation since the science of history itself is in a position only to establish the factual.

One might object in the first instance that, as long as there have been recorders of history — and it is still so today — no great work of history has yet appeared in which the author has refrained from all valuation. This argument is not entirely persuasive because the historian's weakness could be to blame for that fact. But it is in the substance of history itself, that is to say, it is the longitudinal and cross sections of history which deliver a measure of value if the primary condition is granted that *life is something of utter value.* Whoever takes the position that since everything comes into existence it is, therefore, also worthy of perishing, is beyond the scope of discussion. But that attitude, as is well known, was proposed by the devil. Whoever, on the other hand, rejects it has in the preservation of life and its advance a standard by which to measure and evaluate the processes of history. Obviously, this preservation and advance are not about the physical life of the individual person but about the higher spiritual life of the whole since, in the end, even the physical life of the individual person is dependent on that higher spiritual life because humans are "political beings."

If one applies this measure it becomes clear that the *orientation towards the conservation and preservation of life* is correct and that its opposite is false, further, that *force (Kraft)* is of value and that *weakness* corrupts and, finally, that *unity* in character and style is a value and carelessness an evil. Here we have the measure for an evaluative assessment of world events without having to borrow from religion. Because everything crumbles under certain circumstances and we, ourselves, also fall to pieces bit by bit while, under other circumstances, life is preserved, it follows that the one is bad and the other good. As to what those circumstances are history makes unmistakably clear: to preserve life alone is the direction and force in which humans and humankind is set free "from the dominion of that which binds all" or, as the Bible puts it, "from slavery to the passing nature," that is to say, from servitude to the merely natural and to one's own empirical ego. Destructive to life, not only to the life of the whole but also to that of the individual, is the direction which raises to pre-eminence the physical well-being of the individual and, with that, the struggle of all against all. No word confirms the course of world-history more assuredly than that of Jesus: that they who seek to save their lives only will surely lose it. The course of world events shows that behind the direction which strives energetically to rise up over the merely natural and egoism there lurk chaos and death.

One aspect of this powerful direction is that it seeks to expand everywhere towards unity. It cannot remain focused on one narrow line but must, permeating all things and advancing on all sides, become character and style and function as an organism. That organism is *culture*; it cannot exist as such if it is not active in subjugating all merely natural phenomena without rest and embracing everything. Should culture lose its restless striving, its never restful ascent and its push towards unity, it begins at once to harden into mere civilization; immediately the decay of its dying members sets in until barbarism arises which is the more shocking the more plentiful are the masks and the grimaces into which the higher values of a better day have been changed.

Every direction rising above the merely natural, every force, every struggle for unity and style carries its own reward in itself: the preservation of life. And every descending direction, every weakness, every loss of character and of style carries its own punishment in itself: the decay and decomposition of life. *Augustine* was the first to learn this from world-history and he preached it with the tongues of humans and of angels, he, the first true and mighty interpreter of world events. He was also the one who, bright of eye and courageous, placed the idea of *life* into the center of Christian scholarship. He said that all being and all life is good unless it is phantom-being and life. He calls it God's work. We are indebted to him for even more: with great clarity he saw that all human striving and acting depends exclusively and solely on *love*, either on the love of self and of the merely natural or on another, a higher love. "*Faciunt malos vel bonos mores mali vel boni amores*" [is it good and bad loves which shape good and bad mores]. He never doubted that this other, higher love was the love of God planted by the creator deep in the human heart: "You have made us for yourself." Historical knowledge cannot attain to this if it limits itself solely to its own area although, in the end, it does come close to this knowledge for, according to this argument, it recognizes the paradoxical fact that all worthwhile events in history are determined by the powerful striving towards a higher ascent over the merely natural up to, even, the joyful renunciation of one's empirical life, determined also by the high appreciation of a mysterious "whole" and "one" which is grasped with a passionate desire. There is no doubt: humankind works in history "as if God existed," as if, originating from a higher source, it had to recapture that origin through purposeful activity in which all of its members are brought into unity. Religion is that which names this striving the love of God and neighbor. Measured empirically, this striving is completely irrational, an enthusiastic striving towards something which one neither sees nor hears and which is experienced as a powerful and blessed feeling for life.

Another observation has to be added to this perception of the great motor of history's higher life. We stated at the outset that "biography" was a special task to be distinguished from "history." The most important achievement of biography is that it engenders in us awe of great and good people. In teaching us acquaintance with people who have reached greater heights than we, whose knowledge is more profound, whose intentions purer and whose striving more persistent than ours, biography binds us to them with a mysterious bond, raises us towards them and fills us with noble sentiments of awe for them. But as enthusiastic striving towards the "whole-one" is irrational, beyond reason, so, too, is this awe. Such striving and awe are alike as well in the power they both possess to fill us completely, to purify and energize us. "The best in history," Goethe said "is the enthusiasm it calls forth." That is true if enthusiasm is the passionate striving towards the whole and the awe in face of the personal manifestation of the great and good. If one takes a close look at history it is apparent that humankind, as a growing unity, has received imperishable gifts only from a few hands. And yet, each of us has met someone higher, purer, more forceful by whose help we have been enabled to stand up.

We have attempted to determine how history may help interpret world events. A few questions remain which are closely connected with what has been presented here.

Is there any progress in history? Many a serious observer denies it. Spengler believes himself to have given proof against the notion of progress; cultures, he says, are like great balls or bubbles which arise slowly, reach maximum elevation and then slowly shrivel up and pass away. Each is an entity in itself, without any connection to its preceding and succeeding culture; none achieves a greater content of truth than another since "truth" is in actuality a matter of dreams, unattainable; no culture possesses a truth greater than that of another culture since humanity remains always the same without any higher and lower. Even if one disregards the contradictions into which Spengler was drawn and leaves aside the basic philosophical question involved, there are two things which may be said against him right away. First, it is factually incorrect to think of cultures as of pearls strung one next to the other without any mutual connection; cultures, rather, flow one into the other and work with the huge capital received from the culture replaced. They transform this capital in a most wonderful way and without it they would not even exist. Second, one kind of progress can be demonstrated without reserve throughout the course of history in terms of the science of knowing and prevailing over nature. Spengler, it is true, denies this too, but he basically walks around the problem instead of dealing with it head-on. But if progress is not to be denied in *one* dimension of culture, as it is beyond doubt that, from the days of the Egyptians and Babylonians onward, the great edifice of science, which has achieved more and more unity in all the changes of cultures, has progressively developed, then the wretched notion is eliminated that in history one worthless cycle of thinking and striving replaces another and all hope is reduced to the comfortless outlook that the bursting bubble of today will not be the last one.

Is there continual progress in history? Certainly not. Rather, we can observe disastrous regress even if, at times, it turns out to have been only an apparent one or is subsequently seen to have been the onset of further progress.

Can progress cease altogether and humanity sink again to the natural stage by way of barbarism? History is unable to answer this question.

Is world history the world judgment? This question is to be denied in relation to small and particular events but not in relation to the overall process, in accordance to what has been presented here, for false directions, weakness and desultoriness surely lead to decay and downfall; whereas upward striving, force and unity lead to the securing of life. However, in respect to the interpretation and evaluation of events, historians must practice restraint not only because "God does not call in the accounts every day" but also because they themselves, as a rule, are so much part of the events that it is not possible to be impartial and because often enough they are unable to know clearly whether a force, in the process of waning, has not already become a hindrance and whether the new that is striving to emerge is not a dangerous revolt but is, instead, to be greeted as liberation and salvation. Mature understanding of life can accomplish as much here as it can in relation to prophecy even though it, too, is not immune to error.

And finally: *does not preoccupation with history lead to quietism and does it not paralyse determined work and life?* Today many follow Nietzsche and give an affirmative answer and turn away from history. But whoever does not want to hear the majestic organ music of world events, as it has sounded through three millennia, must remain satisfied with the bellstroke of the moment, but that is a bad exchange. History paralyses only when one does not allow its deepest content to touch one's being. As we have seen, that content is to be found in the upward-striving direction, in the development of force, in the striving towards unity and in the great and good personalities. All of these, however, have the inner strength to draw us into themselves and to fill us with life. Truly, "to understand everything is to forgive everything" is not the last word of history; that word is the life-giving impulse to take one's place among the heroes and, following them, work with them. "In vain I resist this striving which resides day and night in my breast." How could history be a paralysing entity? No! history seeks to change people mired in their elemental drives and in sadness into pure and courageous ones, more:

in view of the great and good personalities who have acted with force in history, we come to learn that we, too, do not stand helplessly before an immoveable fate but that, instead, the most important part of our destiny lies in our own hands. Therefore, grasp *amor fati* to yourselves, that is to say, lay hold of destiny with a high spirit and shape it accordingly.

*

CHRISTIANITY AND HISTORY

Harnack delivered this lecture before a large audience in Berlin in October 1895; the repercussions of his position in the debate over the place of the Apostles' Creed in public worship were still much in the air. Critics had charged him with dissolving Christian truths in the acids of his historical-critical scholarship and were curious now to see how he might argue the triumph of the historian's work over the affirmations of faith. Those, on the other hand, who had sided with him in calling for a modern creed were wondering whether he would buy back some of his critical views of orthodoxy, given those repercussions. His object in this lecture was to show in what sense the Christian religion can be said to be dependent on historical facts and when the veracity of those events is either proved or disproved.

The translation is that of T. B. Saunders from the German text of 1896; it appeared in English under the title used here also in 1896.

The name of Jesus Christ of Nazareth . . . neither is there salvation in any other: for there is no other name under heaven given among men, whereby we may be saved.

Such is the creed of the Christian Church. With this creed she began; in the faith of it her martyrs have died; and today, as eighteen hundred years ago, it is from this creed that she derives her strength. The whole meaning and purport of religion — life in God, the forgiveness of sins, consolation in suffering — she couples with Christ's person; and in so doing she associates everything that gives life its significance and its permanent value, nay the Eternal itself, with an historical fact; maintaining the indissoluble unity of both.

But is such a connexion defensible? Will it bear intelligent examination? When all history seems to be a ceaseless process of growth and decay, is it possible to pick out a single phenomenon and saddle it with the whole weight of eternity? especially when it is a phenomenon of the past.

If Christ's person were still among us, the matter would perhaps be different. But although we are separated from it by many centuries and an intricate and confusing tradition, we are told, nevertheless, that we must cling to it as though it were endowed with an eternal presence, and acknowledge it as the rock of our life. Is that possible? Is it right? This is a question which has occupied thoughtful Christians in all ages, and it involves the most careful inquiry into the essential nature and the just claims of Christianity; in a word, into the relation between Christianity and history. All that I can attempt in these brief pages is to indicate the nature of the question, and to offer some considerations by which its meaning and importance may be estimated.

I may begin by mentioning the encouraging fact that the great assault made by the eighteenth century on the connexion between religion and history has been repelled. This assault found its pregnant expression in the principle laid down by Lessing: *Historical truth, which is accidental in its character, can never become the proof of the truths of Reason, which are necessary.*

The principle may, indeed, be right; everything depends upon the way in which it is construed. But in the way in which it was understood by Lessing's own generation, influenced as that generation was by Rousseau, it is wrong. It is the outcome of the whole of the superficial philosophy of the eighteenth century. According to that philosophy, everything that has happened in the way of history is of trivial moment; it is an accident; nay, it even cramps and fetters the mind; and there is no salvation anywhere but in the two forces which that generation described as *Nature* and *Reason.* They were regarded as forces that were invariable and constituted once for all; and no true blessing was to be obtained outside of them. It was believed that every man from the creation downwards possessed in his reason a fixed capital, which was capable of supplying him with everything that might be needful for a virtuous and happy life. It was believed, further, that man was fitted into the framework of nature, and was in harmony with it; and that he had only to unfold his powers in accordance with nature, in order to become a glorious specimen of his kind.

In this view of the world, history was no longer a necessity; for a man could receive absolutely nothing from it which he did not already possess. To the consistent adherents of this view, its logical outcome was that history seemed a strange and wrong-headed venture; and the cry was all for renouncing its tyranny, and for returning to the freedom of nature. It is true that Lessing himself made great efforts to do justice to history; but his efforts were uncertain, and they were but little understood. His generation had no concern for anything but the truths of reason, alleged to be eternal, and the "natural religion" which it had rediscovered; and in possession of these blessings, it looked down on "the accidents of history" with contempt, and cut the bond between them and religion. All historical religions, so the eighteenth century taught, are at the best only the one true, natural religion in disguise — the religion which always was and always will be — and of this religion Reason, fixed and unalterable, is the only content. By the side of it, even Christianity and its founder can make no special or particular claim; for everything that is particular is accidental, superfluous, and intellectually mischievous.

Now today this view of the world is not, it is true, extinct; but it has been refuted. In no respect has the spirit of the nineteenth century so strongly opposed the spirit of the eighteenth as in this.

It is a change which we owe to Herder and the leaders of the romantic movement; we owe it to Hegel and his great pupil Ranke; we owe it, not least of all, to the powerful reaction of the Christian faith. The illusion of a ready-made reason, existing from the beginning, has been dispelled; the idol of a "divine nature" has been unmasked; the vast problem involved in the facile notion of a "natural religion" has been revealed. In the place of shallow talk about divine nature and profane history, about the "eternal truths of reason" and casual records, we have arrived at the knowledge of *history*, of the history from which we have received what we possess, and to which we owe what we are. In this process two conceptions, above all, came to the front with increasing clearness: *development* and *personality*. They involve an opposition; but it is an opposition which determines the work of the historian in dealing with his facts.

When the meaning of history came to be accurately understood, religion was restored to its place; for religion is no ready-made structure, but a growth; and it is a growth that falls within the history of humanity. Its developments are no mere outward semblance: they are a reality. Its prophets and founders have been prophets and founders indeed; for they have raised humanity to a higher level. Reverence for the spirit that prevails in history, and gratitude to all those from whom we have received any benefit — and without it we should have been the poorer in our inner and outer life — must, therefore, govern our views of that science.

Here we have a critical spirit very different from that which pervaded the so-called age of Enlightenment. The assault which the eighteenth century directed against the connexion between history and religion has, in fact, proved a failure. But other assaults have been taking shape in our own time. There is a whole array of them.

The first proposition that meets us is this: It is just because the Christian religion is a part of history, and consequently of that *development* of which all history consists, that it is no more than a link in that development; and therefore its founder cannot be allowed any peculiar or unique position.

We succeeded, let us say, in defeating this attack. A fresh opponent then starts up with the objection that even though the founder of the Christian religion may have been an incomparable man, he lived many centuries ago; and it is therefore impossible to go to him with our troubles and sorrows, and to lay hold of him as the rock of our life: it is not the *person* which we have any longer to consider, but the *doctrine*, the *principle*.

If, in the end, this opponent be also routed, there is still one more. We are told that we may speak of Jesus Christ as we will, and he may have been all that we say, but that we cannot be certain of it; for where our idea of him has not been destroyed by historical criticism, it has been rendered doubtful; and, even though it were more trustworthy than it is, still the facts of history can never be known with a certainty that would entitle us to make them the foundation of our religious belief.

These are the three barriers that have been opposed to the creed of the Church on the score of history; and it is on these three questions that the whole of the controversy turns. Every form of doubt, whether secret or open, deals in the main with these questions; and in some shape or other they are doubts which have been entertained and pondered by us all.

I PERSONALITY AND DEVELOPMENT

Now, as regards the first assault: it is the most comprehensive, but also the weakest, of the three.

It is perfectly true that the strength of our modern conception of history lies in the effort which we everywhere make to trace the *development* of things, and to show how one thing has grown out of another. That this is the true task of the historian is a proposition which can no longer be disputed. There can be no manner of doubt that it is only by this method that a true understanding of history can be attained; and even those who condemn the modern science of history cannot escape the influence of its method. They do the same work as is done by those whom they condemn, but they do not succeed in doing it so well; nay, they do it badly and imperfectly.

However, a man must be infatuated to maintain that, because all history is a history of development, it can and must be described as a process of material or mechanical change. Up till now the attempts that have been, and are still being, made in this direction carry their own refutation with them. At the very most, it is only in the sphere of political economy that we can trace a certain stringent order of phenomena, where the struggle for material existence is supreme; but even there this stringent order is always being disturbed by elements of a non-material character, which exert a powerful influence.

In the history of intellectual and moral ideas, the rough-and-ready way of explaining cause by environment alone breaks down altogether. I admit that even here much may be accounted for in this way, much more than earlier generations suspected: the necessity that drives and compels has often been the mother of progress; and even today we can see causes at work, and watch the process of growth. But without the strength and the activity of an individual, of a *personality*, nothing great, nothing that will bring us farther on our way, can be accomplished. Whence comes the strength of the strong, and the deed of the doer? Whence comes it that the knowledge that might advance us, the thought that might save us, is transmitted from one generation to another as barren and worthless and dead as a stone, until some one seizes it and strikes it into fire? Whence comes that higher order of marriage, where a thought so unites with a soul that each is merged in the other, and belongs to the other, and masters the will? Whence comes the courage that conquers the resistance of a dull and unfeeling world? Whence comes the living power that begets a living conviction?

It is a very limited psychology which fails to see that these are the real levers of history. All that its adherents ask is whether the man has said anything new; and if so, whether it cannot be deduced from something that went before; and they profess themselves content if they ascertain that it was only "relatively" new, and that nothing very wonderful has happened after all. No! not only in the beginning was the Word, the Word that was at once Deed and Life; but the living, resolute, indomitable Word, namely, the *person*, has always been a power in history, along with and above the power of circumstance. Here, too, it is true, there are intervening links and developments. No torch lights itself; one prophet rouses another; but this mysterious development we can never fathom — we can only feel it.

What is true of history in general, and of all the lines on which intellectual and spiritual life is enacted, is true in the highest sense of religion, which is the profoundest subject of which history treats. *Man shall not live by bread alone, but by every word that proceedeth out of the mouth of God.* Never have the two great central elements of all life and action been more clearly and simply expressed; and our historians still have a lesson to learn from these words, if they are not to lose their way.

Of religion it is true that it, too, has been developed, and that it is in a state of constant development. From its history it may be shown that it has had to yield to the stress of trouble and danger: the trouble that teaches men to pray, the danger that deadens them and makes them grasp at a straw. But the same history tells us also, that no aspiration and no progress have ever existed without the miraculous exertion of an individual will, of a *person*. It was not what the person said that was new and strange — he came when the time was fulfilled and spoke what the time required — but how he said it; how it became in him the strength and power of a new life; how he transmitted it to his disciples. That was his secret, and that was what was new to him. Mankind looks up with reverence to all the great minds that have been given to it — the thinkers, the artists, the heroes — but it is only the prophets and the founders of religion that it worships; for it feels that here a power has been at work which frees it from the world, and lifts it above the things of every day.

But if we thus put all prophets and founders of religion into one class, it may be said that we, in our turn, are doing away with the significance of the founder of the Christian religion. That is certainly not the case; for there is no concrete or specific conception embracing the differences to be found among those whom we rightly call prophets and founders of religion. Every one of them is a power for himself, and must be judged by himself. There have been founders of religion both sacred and profane; there have been sublime prophets and strange prophets. An inexhaustible wealth of gift and power has been diffused among them; but the measure of it, their bearing, the goal of their efforts, every circumstance of their lives, differs with each of them. If this difference were disregarded, nothing would be clear. It would be a piece of presumptuous folly to attempt to lay down, at the outset, the measure of the Spirit — that is, of the Spirit of God — which has borne sway in these individuals.

But it is only of One that we know that he united the deepest humility and a purity of will with the claim that he was more than all the prophets who were before him: the Son of God. Of him alone we know that those who ate and drank with him, glorified him not only as their Teacher, Prophet, and King, but also as the Prince of Life, as the Redeemer and

Judge of the world, as the living power of their existence — *it is not I that live, but Christ in me* — and that presently a band of the Jew and Gentile, the wise and the foolish, acknowledged that they had received, from the abundance of this one man, grace for grace. This fact, which lies open to the light of day, is unique in history; and it requires that the actual personality behind it should be honored as unique.

II PERSONALITY AND PRINCIPLE

This disposes of the first objection: that no special or unique position can be attributed to the person of Jesus Christ, because of the presumption that all history takes the form of development.

But now we have to deal with a serious attack. Even though the founder of the Christian religion may have been an incomparable man, he lived, we are told, many centuries ago; and therefore it is impossible to take him up into our religious life, and adopt him as its foundation: it is no longer the person that we have to consider, but the doctrine, or, as it is sometimes called, the *principle.* Nay, the objection is still more severely stated thus: Religion is wholly a matter of relation to God — God and the soul, the soul and God — everything that intrudes upon this mutual relation destroys its exclusive character, and impairs its fervor and its freedom.

I might try to meet this attack by referring to the ecclesiastical doctrine of redemption and reconciliation through Jesus Christ; but I am afraid that if I did so I should hardly make myself clear; for in the form in which the Church has stated that doctrine, it belongs to the things which in these days are least understood, and therefore most open to doubt. Such is the fact; how far it is warranted is a matter of opinion. I shall therefore attempt to proceed by a different path.

Well then! it is quite true: religion is a relation of the soul to God, and nothing more. That a man should find God and possess him as *his* God — should live in the fear of him, trust him, and lead a holy and blessed life in the strength of this feeling — that is the substance and the aim of religion. We can carry our conception of religion no further, nor can we allow any alien element to subsist alongside of it. Religion is ordering our ways and committing our troubles to the love and care of him who rules.

The stronger and purer our feeling of devotion, the more surely is it comprehended in this utterance. It is a truth which has been attested by Christ's disciples in all ages; it was attested by Christ himself in teaching us the Lord's Prayer; and therefore we cannot condemn the theologians who tell us that it is the sum and substance of religion.

But what holds good of all moral ideas, holds good in the highest sense of religion: it is one thing to be sensible of their truth, it is another to be possessed of their power. We may recognize and acknowledge the claims of the Christian religion, the peace and beauty of the religious life, and yet be quite incapable of raising ourselves to its level. It may hover before our eyes and shine with the radiance of a star; and yet not burn like a fire in our hearts. We may have the keenest sense of the bonds that we would escape, and yet be totally unable to set ourselves free. Not only may we be so — we are so. There is no one who has had this feeling, or who has it again and again, and is delivered from it, but knows that he has been delivered because God has spoken to him. The man who fails to hear the voice of God for himself is without religion. *Speak, Lord, for thy servant heareth*, is the only form in which a religious life is possible.

As the conduct of human life is manifold and various, so, too, is the voice of God. But we know that there are few among us who hear and understand the voice of God, in the secret sphere of their inner personal life, without human help and intervention. The truth is, rather, that one Christian educates another; heart kindles heart; and the strength to will what we approve comes from the mysterious Power by which one life awakens another. At the end of the series of messengers and agents of God stands Jesus Christ. They point back to him, and it is from him that has sprung the river of life which they bear in themselves as their own. Various indeed is the measure of their conscious relation to him — who could deny it! — but they all live on him and through him.

Here we have a fact which gives an incomparable significance to this personality, as a force still working in history. But the objection with which we have to deal is not yet exhausted. Jesus Christ, it is said, remains, after all, a power of the past; although it is a power which continues in effect. But when the Christian faith sends us back to him, that is not the view which it takes. We must endeavor to get a closer grasp of what this faith means, in order to understand how far its view is right, supposing that the faith is right at all.

The Christian faith is not, as is so often maintained, a gentle exaltation of our earthly life, or a comfort and relief in its troubles and trials. No! it is decision for God and against the world. It is an eternal life that is involved: the recognition that in and above Nature and her changes there is a realm of sanctity and love, a city not built with hands, whose citizens we are to be; and with this message there comes to us the demand that we should cleanse our hearts and deny ourselves.

We are here confronted with an alternative which determines our inner life. It is, indeed, a contest; but is victory possible? is there then, in truth, a higher Reality, compared with which the world is as nothing? or do our feelings and presentiments delude us? May it not be that we are altogether confined within the sphere of mechanical nature, the sphere of our earthly existence, and that we are waging a miserable war with our own shadows, with phantoms and specters? That is the question of questions, the doubt of doubts.

Well! as long as the Christian faith has existed, these doubts and questions have been resolved by looking to Jesus Christ: resolved, not in the form of philosophical demonstration, but by looking with a confident trust to the image of his life. When God and everything that is sacred threatens to disappear in darkness, or our doom is pronounced; when the mighty forces of inexorable nature seem to overwhelm us, and the bounds of good and evil to dissolve; when, weak and weary, we despair of finding God at all in this dismal world — it is then that the personality of Christ may save us. Here we have a life that was lived wholly in the fear of God — resolute, unselfish, pure; here there glows and flashes a grandeur, a love, which draws us to itself. Although it was all a continual struggle with the world; though bit by bit one earthly possession after another fell away, and at last the life itself came to an ignominious end; yet no soul can avoid the thought that whoso dies thus, dies well: he dies not, but lives. For it was in this life and death that there first dawned upon mankind the assurance of an eternal life, and a divine love which overcomes all evil, nay, sin itself. It is in the presence of a glory which is beyond the reach of death, that we have come to perceive the vanity of the world and of all earthly possessions.

Eighteen hundred years separate us from this history; but if we seriously ask ourselves what it is that has given us the courage to believe that in the history of the world God prevails, not only by moral and intellectual forces, but by his presence in the midst of it; if we ask what it is that leads us to believe in an eternal life — our answer is, that we make bold to believe it in reliance upon Christ. *Jesus lives, and with him I live also.* He is the firstborn among many brothers; he is our surety for the reality of a future world.

So it is, then, that God speaks to us through him. It was testified of Christ that he was the *Way*, the *Truth*, and the *Life*; as such he is still revealed to our inmost feelings, and therein consists his presence to us.

71

As surely as everything depends on the soul finding God and becoming one with him, so surely is he the true Savior, Guide, and Lord who leads the soul to God. When the Christian Church proclaims of him that he lives, it is a truth which is still attested today; and the Church is also right in reminding us of his sufferings and his death. But we will not speak of these things now; nor will we speak of them at all after the fashion in which they are so often treated. That the sufferings of the just form the saving element in history, is a truth which we feel in the measure in which our senses are alive to the gravity of the moral issue, and open to the influence of personal sacrifice. But "we draw a veil over the sufferings of Christ, for the very reason that we hold them in such reverence. In our judgment it is an unwarrantable and audacious thing to treat these deep mysteries, in which the divine depths of suffering lie hidden, as an object of barter — to keep an account in them, or to toy and trifle with them; nor to rest until the most worthy of all actions is made to look common and insipid" (Goethe).

We ought not to forget that faith in Christ is never more than a mere cry of *Lord, Lord,* if it does not pass into the strength of allegiance in the good cause. Not those did he himself call his brothers and his sisters, who desired to see him, or to raise aloft his name in the world; but those who do the will of his Father in heaven. It is by this utterance that we have always to judge the Christian's faith.

III PERSONALITY AND HISTORY

That in spite of the eighteen hundred years which separate us from him, Jesus Christ can have, nay has, a place in the religious life of the Christian; that his personality, and not his doctrine alone, is still today *set for the rising again of many* — I have tried to show. But a third and final attack confronts us. You may, we are told, talk of Jesus Christ as you will, and he may have been all that you say, but you cannot be certain of it; for where our idea of him has not been destroyed by historical criticism, it has been rendered doubtful; and even though it were more trustworthy than it is, still the facts of history can never be known with a certainty that would entitle us to make them the foundation of our religious belief.

This objection is the most serious of the three; and if it were in all respects justifiable, it would go ill with us.

"Where our idea of him has not been destroyed by historical criticism, it has been rendered doubtful." At the first blush it looks as if this were indeed the case. I pass over such results of criticism as flourish today, and tomorrow are cast into the oven; I speak only of those which are brought before us again and again with increasing force. If we direct our attention first of all to the external historical facts, we find that the tradition as to the incidents attending the birth and the early life of Jesus Christ has been shattered; and so too has been the credibility of many of the stories which were told of him. We find, too, that criticism cannot allay the ancient doubts raised by the reports of what took place on the first Easter morning. As regards the picture of his life, as regards his discourses and the doctrine he taught, the historical way of looking at them seems to transform them altogether.

The man who reads his Bible in a homely way is wont to treat all the characteristic features which he encounters in that book as above and beyond time. He sees and feels such things only as he takes to form the true kernel of the narrative: things which concern himself; and it was by these that the Christian doctrine was formerly established by the Church. But the historical way of looking at them may not, and will not, overlook the concrete elements in and by which the life and the doctrine were actually fashioned in their day. It seeks for points of connexion with the Old Testament and its developments, with the religious life of the synagogue, with contemporary hopes for the future, with the whole intellectual and spiritual condition of the world of Greece and Rome; and it finds that the evidence of such connexion is unmistakable. The consequence is, that the sayings and discourses of the Lord, and the image of his life itself, not only take their color — and it is a very definite color — from the history of the time, but they are also seen to possess certain definite limitations. They belong to their time and their environment; and they could not exist in any other. But they lose no particle of their power and validity, unless it can be shown that the main lineaments of the personality of Christ, and the sense and true point of his sayings, have been altered. I cannot discover that historical criticism has effected any such change.

The same is true of the testimony which he gave of himself. I admit that if historical research had proved that he was an apocalyptic enthusiast or a visionary, whose image and utterances were invested with a purity of aim and a sublimity of thought only by the refining influence of later times, it would be another matter. But who has proved that, and who could prove it? For besides the four written gospels we possess a fifth, unwritten; and in many respects its voice is clearer and more effective than those of the other four — I mean the united testimony of the first Christian community. It enables us to gather what was the prevailing impression made by this personality, and in what sense his disciples understood his words and the testimony which he gave of himself. It is true that his clothes — the outward form of his doctrine — were part of the heritage; but the great and simple truths which he came to preach, the personal sacrifices which he made, and his victory in death, were what formed the new life of his community; and when the apostle Paul with divine power described this life as a life in the Spirit (Romans 8), and again as a life in love (1 Corinthians 13), he was only giving back the light which had dawned upon him in and through Jesus Christ his Lord. This is a simple matter of fact, which no historical criticism can in any way alter. All that it can do is to place it in a clearer light, and so increase our reverence for the divinity which was revealed in radiance in a Son of Abraham, amid the wreck and refuse of a narrow world. Let the plain Bible-reader continue to read his gospels as he has hitherto read them; for in the end the critic cannot read them otherwise. What the one regards as their true gist and meaning, the other must also acknowledge to be so.

But the facts, the facts! I do not know how there can be a greater fact than the one which I have just been describing. By the side of it, what can any historical detail signify?

We are told, however, that an historical detail has a very obvious significance; that it is only the external fact, nay, the miraculous fact, which can afford us the final and only certainty that there exists a reality corresponding to our belief; that the objects of our belief are not mere phantoms of thought, but that God himself governs the course of history, and is leading it to its goal.

I am well aware of the gravity of this assertion, and I am far from disputing anyone's right to make it if he chooses. If God would but rend the heavens and come down, that we might behold him! — it is a cry that is often heard. But I know, too, that it is not born out of the depth and strength of the faith which the apostle Paul describes, and that it readily falls under the utterance of the Lord: *Except ye see signs and wonders, ye will not believe.* Great is the power of external authority in matters of religion; great is the power of signs and wonders; but only where their substance lies can faith and devotion find their ultimate assurance. Their substance is God the Lord; it is reliance on Jesus Christ, whose word and spirit are even today a witness to the heart of the power of God.

Woe to us if it were otherwise; if our faith rested on a number of details, to be demonstrated and established by the historian. It would be mere sophistry for any historian to claim that he had achieved such a task; for it is assuredly true that no detail of the past can attain such a degree of evidential certainty that it could form the foundation for bricks and mortar, let alone a whole eternity. Testimonies, documents, assertions — when all is said, to what do they amount?

There is, I admit, a difference between fact and fact. The actual external details are always a matter of controversy; and in this sense Lessing was perfectly right when he warned us against coupling matters of the highest moment with "accidental truths of history," and hanging the whole weight of eternity on a spider's thread. But the spiritual purport of a whole life, of a personality, is also an historical fact: we are certain of it by the effect which it produces; and it is here that we find the link that binds us to Jesus Christ. It is a feeling which is one with devotion itself; and this is what the same Lessing meant when he spoke the word of deliverance: "Even though we may be unable to remove all the objections that may be made against the *Bible*, nevertheless, in the heart of all Christians who have attained to an inner sense of its essential truths, *Religion* remains steadfast and intact."

But are we to say that such external details as have been handed down are of no significance whatever? Who would be so shortsighted, or so frivolous, as to maintain such a proposition? Because we cannot build upon them, they are far from having no significance. First of all, we have to examine whether they are not actually true after all. Much that was formerly rejected has been re-established on a close investigation, and in the light of comprehensive experience. Who in these days, for example, could make such short work of the miraculous cures in the gospels as was the custom of scholars formerly?

Then, too, it may be said of all that is told of Jesus Christ, that it is written as a *lesson* for us. That is a consideration which in our controversies is often unduly overlooked; but it is in keeping with the objects of the oldest writers, and the practice of the oldest teachers. In matters of religious tradition it is the peculiarity of much that passes for historical, that the spiritual meaning to be found in it is its most important feature. Where something is maintained as an historical fact, it is more often than not a defense of the article of faith bound up with it. It is through the formula, *Conceived of the Holy Ghost*, that the dogma of the Divine Sonship of Jesus Christ is proclaimed; in and with the message of the Ascension we are taught that he lives and rules with the Father.

This leads us to another aspect of the religious significance of external details, which is closely related to that which I have been mentioning. They have been to faith what the prop is to the vine, or a sheltering screen to the tender plant. They have given it support and guidance, or they have protected its growth from the influence of wind and weather; and the service which they have rendered in the past, they still render today to many. The difficulty is that one man's faith requires a strong stake to prop it, or some kind of protective shelter; whilst another finds the prop break in his hands, and his faith bloom only in the free light of the sun.

Finally, much in the New Testament that is recorded as history, much that affects us most deeply, is not only told us as a lesson, but, in the form in which it is given, it possesses a deep *symbolical* significance. I know none of the leading events of the narrative of which that cannot be said. The same spirit which revealed to our eyes the power and the glory of a divine life, so far as mankind is able to grasp it, has also veiled the truth for us with a delicate web of significant legend, a poetry that moves the heart, and has thus brought it home in picture and parable.

That the stories which are told of Christ possess this manifold significance, will be obvious to everyone who considers the history of Christianity with an open mind and a humble heart. It is an interpretation of the facts which is not without its dangers; for on the one hand it may readily lead a man to foist his own mind upon history, to confuse the plant with the prop, and so to conjure up grave difficulties; and on the other, it may deaden the force of historical facts as real facts, and the personality of Christ as a real personality. However, the difficulties which have arisen here are not of our making, and we cannot resolve them in any arbitrary fashion of our own. Rather let us trust to that divine guidance which knows what is good for us; let us proclaim truly, and with a pure mind, the knowledge which we have received; and then let us endeavor to understand the profound saying, that natural strength and the crutch that supports it come from the same source (Goethe).

It may, perhaps, have been expected that I should speak of other matters: of the changes which Christianity has experienced in the course of its history, or of the blessings which it has spread abroad in the world. But a knowledge of the fundamental question, namely, how far religion and history are connected, and how they are united in the evangelical faith, is more important than anything else. This evangelical faith need fear no test that can be applied to it. It can bear a strict and methodical scrutiny of the facts which form its historical foundation; nay, for its own sake it must demand such a scrutiny; for while it has no concern with Pilate's speculative question — what is truth? — yet the knowledge of the truth is assigned as its mission, and there, too, its promise will be fulfilled. (*CH: 17-68*)

*

WHAT IS CHRISTIANITY?

(First Selection)

Harnack is best known today in the theological world for this course of lectures. It is the most translated and reprinted of his books as it sums up many of his views about the Christian religion. Nowhere else are they found again as succinctly and eloquently as in this work.

All but the third section of this reader draw on What Is Christianity? *In the following selection Harnack's historical-theological method is set out; it was done with the audience in mind: between 500 and 600 students from all faculties of the university, augmented by admirers and "spies" from the city, were present for each of the 16 lectures.*

The book was first published in German in 1900 and in the same year in English, in the translation by T. B. Saunders. This selection is from pages 1-18.

LECTURE I

The great English philosopher, John Stuart Mill, has somewhere observed that mankind cannot be too often reminded that there was once a man of the name of Socrates. That is true; but still more important is it to remind mankind again and again that a man of the name of Jesus Christ once stood in their midst. The fact, of course, has been brought home to us from our youth up; but unhappily it cannot be said that public instruction in our time is calculated to keep the image of Jesus Christ before us in any impressive way, and make it an inalienable possession after our schooldays are over and for our whole life. And although no one who has once absorbed a ray of Christ's light can ever again become as though he had never heard of him; although at the bottom of every soul that has been once touched an impression remains, a confused recollection of this kind, which is often only a "superstition," is not enough to give strength and life. But where the demand for further and more trustworthy knowledge about him arises, and a man wants positive information as to who Jesus Christ was, and as to the real purport of his message, he no sooner asks for it than he finds himself, if he consults the literature of the day, surrounded by a clatter of contradictory voices. He hears some people maintaining that primitive Christianity was closely akin to Buddhism, and he is accordingly told that it is in fleeing the world and in pessimism that the sublime character of this religion and its profound meaning are revealed. Others, on the contrary, assure him that Christianity is an optimistic religion, and that it must be thought of simply and solely as a higher phase of Judaism; and these people also suppose that in saying this they have said something very profound. Others, again, maintain the opposite; they assert that the gospel did away with Judaism, but itself orginated under Greek influences of mysterious operation; and that it is to be understood as a blossom on the tree of Hellenism. Religious philosophers come forward and declare that the metaphysical system which, as they say, was developed out of the gospel is its real kernel and the revelation of its secret; but others reply that the gospel has nothing to do with philosophy, that it was meant for feeling and suffering humanity, and that philosophy has only been forced upon it. Finally, the latest critics that have come into the field assure us that the whole history of religion, morality, and philosophy, is nothing but wrapping and ornament; that what at all times underlies them, as the only real motive power, is the history of economics; that, accordingly, Christianity, too, was in its origin nothing more than a social movement and Christ a social deliverer, the deliverer of the oppressed lower classes.

There is something touching in the anxiety which everyone shows to rediscover himself, together with his point of view and his own circle of interest, in this Jesus Christ, or at least to get a share in him. It is the perennial repetition of the spectacle which was seen in the "Gnostic" movement even as early as the second century, and which takes the form of a struggle, on the part of every conceivable tendency of thought, for the possession of Jesus Christ. Why, quite recently, not only, I think, Tolstoi's ideas, but even Nietzsche's, have been exhibited in their special affinity with the gospel; and there is perhaps more to be said even upon this subject that is worth attention than upon the connexion between a good deal of "theological" and "philosophical" speculation and Christ's teaching.

But nevertheless, when taken together, the impression which these contradictory opinions convey is disheartening: the confusion seems hopeless. How can we take it amiss of anyone, if, after trying to find out how the question stands, he gives it up? Perhaps he goes further, and declares that after all the question does not matter. How are we concerned with events that happened, or with a person who lived, nineteen hundred years ago? We must look for our ideals and our strength to the present; to evolve them laboriously out of old manuscripts is a fantastic proceeding that can lead nowhere. The man who so speaks is not wrong; but neither is he right. What we are and what we possess, in any high sense, we possess from the past and by the past — only so much of it, of course, as has had results and makes its influence felt up to the present day. To acquire a sound knowledge of the past is the business and the duty not only of the historian but also of every one who wishes to make the wealth and the strength so gained his own. But that the gospel is a part of this past which nothing else can replace has been affirmed again and again by the greatest minds. "Let intellectual and spiritual culture progress, and the human mind expand, as much as it will; beyond the grandeur and the moral elevation of Christianity, as it sparkles and shines in the gospels, the human mind will not advance." In these words Goethe, after making many experiments and laboring indefatigably at himself, summed up the result to which his moral and historical insight had led him. Even though we were to feel no desire on our own part, it would still be worth while, because of this man's testimony, to devote our serious attention to what he came to regard as so precious; and if, contrary to his declaration, louder and more confident voices are heard today, proclaiming that the Christian religion has outlived itself, let us accept that as an invitation to make a closer acquaintance with this religion whose certificate of death people suppose that they can already exhibit. . . .

What is Christianity? It is solely in its historical sense that we shall try to answer this question here; that is to say, we shall employ the methods of historical science, and the experience of life gained by studying the actual course of history. This excludes the view of the question taken by the apologist and the religious philosopher. On this point permit me to say a few words.

Apologetics holds a necessary place in religious knowledge, and to demonstrate the validity of the Christian religion and exhibit its importance for the moral and intellectual life is a great and a worthy undertaking. But this undertaking must be kept quite separate from the purely historical question as to the nature of that religion, or else historical research will be brought into complete discredit. Moreover, in the kind of apologetics that is now required no really high standard has yet been attained. Apart from a few steps that have been taken in the direction of improvement, apologetics as a subject of study is in a deplorable state: it is not clear as to the positions to be defended, and it is uncertain as to the means to be employed. It is also not infrequently pursued in an undignified and obtrusive fashion. Apologists imagine that they are doing a great work by crying up religion as though it were a job-lot at a sale, or a universal remedy for all social ills. They are perpetually snatching, too, at all sorts of baubles, so as to deck out religion in fine clothes. In their endeavor to present it as a glorious necessity, they deprive it of its earnest character, and at the best only prove that it is something which may be safely accepted because it can do no harm. Finally, they cannot refrain from slipping in some Church programme of yesterday and "demonstrating" its claims as well. The structure of their ideas is so loose that an idea or two more makes no difference. The mischief that has been thereby done already and is still being done is indescribable. No! the Christian religion is something simple and sub-lime; it means one thing and one thing only: Eternal life in the midst of time, by the strength and under the eyes of God. It is no ethical or social *arcanum* for the preservation or improvement of things generally. To make what it has done for civilization and human progress the main question, and to determine its value by the answer, is to do it violence at the start. Goethe once said, "Mankind is always advancing, and man always remains the same." It is to *man* that religion pertains, to man, as one who in the midst of all change and progress himself never changes. Christian apologetics must recognize, then, that it is with religion in its simple nature and its simple strength that it has to do. Religion, truly, does not exist for itself alone, but lives in an inner fellowship with all the activities of the mind and with moral and economical conditions as well. But it is emphatically not a mere function or an exponent of them; it is a mighty power that sets to work of itself, hindering or furthering, de-stroying or making fruitful. The main thing is to learn what religion is and in what its essential character consists; no matter what position the individual who examines it may take up in regard to it, or whether in his own life he values it or not.

But the point of view of the philosophical theorist, in the strict sense of the word, will also find no place in these lectures. Had they been delivered sixty years ago, it would have been our endeavor to try to arrive by speculative reasoning at some general conception of religion, and then to define the Christian religion accordingly. But we have rightly become sceptical about the value of this procedure. *Latet dolus in generalibus.* We know today that life cannot be spanned by general con-ceptions, and that there is no general conception of religion to which actual religions are related simply and solely as species to genus. Nay, the question may even be asked whether there is any such generic conception as "religion" at all. Is the common element in it anything more than a vague disposition? Is it only an empty place in our innermost being that the word denotes, which every one fills up in a different fashion and many do not perceive at all? I am not of this opinion; I am convinced, rather, that at bottom we have to do here with something which is common to us all, and which in the course of history has struggled up out of torpor and discord into unity and light. I am convinced that Augustine is right when he says, "Thou, Lord, hast made us for thyself, and our heart is restless until it finds rest in thee." But to prove that this is so; to exhibit the nature and the claims of religion by psychological analysis, including the psychology of peoples, is not the task that we shall undertake in what follows. We shall keep to the purely historical theme: What is the Christian religion?

Where are we to look for our materials? The answer seems to be simple and at the same time exhaustive: Jesus Christ and his gospel. But however little doubt there may be that this must form not only our point of departure but also the matter with which our investigations will mainly deal, it is equally certain that we must not be content to exhibit the mere image of Jesus Christ and the main features of his gospel. We must not be content to stop there, because every great and powerful personality reveals a part of what it is only when seen in those whom it influences. Nay, it may be said that the more powerful the personality which a man possesses, and the more he takes hold of the inner life of others, the less can the sum-total of what he is be known only by what he himself says and does. We must look at the reflection and the effects which he produced in those whose leader and master he became. That is why a complete answer to the question, What is Christianity?, is impossible so long as we are restricted to Jesus Christ's teaching alone. We must include the first generation of his disciples as well — those who ate and drank with him — and we must listen to what they tell us of the effect which he had upon their lives.

But even this does not exhaust our materials. If Christianity is an example of a great power valid not for one particular epoch alone; if in and through it, not once only, but again and again, great forces have been disengaged, we must include all the later products of its spirit. It is not a question of a "doctrine" being handed down by uniform repetition or arbitrarily distorted; it is a question of a *life*, again and again kindled afresh, and now burning with a flame of its own. We may also add that

Christ himself and the apostles were convinced that the religion which they were planting would in the ages to come have a greater destiny and a deeper meaning than it possessed at the time of its institution; they trusted to its spirit leading from one point of light to another and developing higher forces. Just as we cannot obtain a complete knowledge of a tree without regarding not only its root and its stem but also its bark, its branches, and the way in which it blooms, so we cannot form any right estimate of the Christian religion unless we take our stand upon a comprehensive induction that shall cover all the facts of its history. It is true that Christianity has had its classical epoch; nay more, it had a founder who himself was what he taught — to steep ourselves in him is still the chief matter; but to restrict ourselves to him means to take a point of view too low for his significance. Individual religious life was what he wanted to kindle and what he did kindle; it is, as we shall see, his peculiar greatness to have led men to God, so that they may thenceforth live their own life with him. How, then, can we be silent about the history of the gospel if we wish to know what he was?

It may be objected that put in this way the problem is too difficult, and that its solution threatens to be accompanied by many errors and defects. That is not to be denied; but to state a problem in easier terms, that is to say in this case inaccurately, because of the difficulties surrounding it, would be a very perverse expedient. Moreover, even though the difficulties increase, the work is, on the other hand, facilitated by the problem being stated in a larger manner; for it helps us to grasp what is essential in the phenomena, and to distinguish kernel and husk.

Jesus Christ and his disciples were situated in their day just as we are situated in ours; that is to say, their feelings, their thoughts, their judgments and their efforts were bounded by the horizon and the framework in which their own nation was set and by its condition at the time. Had it been otherwise, they would not have been men of flesh and blood, but spectral beings. For seventeen hundred years, indeed, people thought, and many among us still think, that the "humanity" of Jesus Christ, which is a part of their creed, is sufficiently provided for by the assumption that he had a human body and a human soul. As if it were possible to have that without having any definite character as an individual! To be a man means, in the first place, to possess a certain mental and spiritual disposition, determined in such and such a way, and thereby limited and circumscribed; and, in the second place, it means to be situated, with this disposition, in an historical environment which in its turn is also limited and circumscribed. Outside this there are no such things as "men." It at once follows, however, that a man can think, speak, and do absolutely nothing at all in which his peculiar disposition and his own age are not coefficients. A single word may seem to be really classical and valid for all time, and yet the very language in which it is spoken gives it very palpable limitations. Much less is a spiritual personality, as a whole, susceptible of being represented in a way that will banish the feeling of its limitations, and with those limitations, the sense of something strange or conventional; and this feeling must necessarily be enhanced the farther in point of time the spectator is removed.

From these circumstances it follows that the historian, whose business and highest duty it is to determine what is of permanent value, is of necessity required not to cleave to words but to find out what is essential. The "whole" Christ, the "whole" gospel, if we mean by this motto the external image taken in all its details and set up for imitation, is just as bad and deceptive a shibboleth as the "whole" Luther, and the like. It is bad because it enslaves us, and it is deceptive because the people who proclaim it do not think of taking it seriously, and could not do so if they tried. They cannot do so because they cannot cease to feel, understand and judge as children of their age.

There are only two possibilities here: either the gospel is in all respects identical with its earliest form, in which case it came with its time and has departed with it; or else it contains something which, under differing historical forms, is of permanent validity. The latter is the true view. The history of the Church shows us in its very commencement that "primitive Christianity" had to disappear in order that "Christianity" might remain; and in the same way in later ages one metamorphosis followed upon another. From the beginning it was a question of getting rid of formulas, correcting expectations, altering ways of feeling, and this is a process to which there is no end. But by the very fact that our survey embraces the whole course as well as the inception we enhance our standard of what is essential and of real value.

We enhance our standard, but we need not wait to take it from the history of those later ages. The thing itself reveals it. We shall see that the gospel in the gospel is something so simple, something that speaks to us with so much power, that it cannot easily be mistaken. No far-reaching directions as to method, no general introductions, are necessary to enable us to find the way to it. No one who possesses a fresh eye for what is alive, and a true feeling for what is really great, can fail to see it and distinguish it from its contemporary integument. And even though there may be many individual aspects of it where the task of distinguishing what is permanent from what is fleeting, what is rudimentary from what is merely historical, is not quite easy, we must not be like the child who, wanting to get at the kernel of a bulb, went on picking off the leaves until there was nothing left, and then could not help seeing that it was just the leaves that made the bulb. Endeavors of this kind are not unknown in the history of the Christian religion, but they fade before those other endeavors which seek to convince us that there is no such thing as either kernel or husk, growth or decay, but that everything is of equal value and alike permanent. *(C: 1-15)*

*

The oftener I re-read and consider the gospels, the more do I find that the contemporary discords, in the midst of which the gospel stood, and out of which it arose, sink into the background. I entertain no doubt that the founder had his eye upon *man* in whatever external situation he might be found — upon *man* who, fundamentally, always remains the same, whether he be moving upwards or downwards, whether he be in riches or poverty, whether he be of strong mind or of weak. It is the consciousness of all these oppositions being ultimately beneath it, and of its own place above them, that gives the gospel its sovereignty; for in every man it looks to the point that is unaffected by all these differences. The thesis of the decadent age and the religion of the wretched may serve to lead us into the outer court; it may even correctly point to that which originally gave the gospel its form; but if it is offered us as a key for the understanding of this religion in itself, we must reject it. . . .

In history absolute judgments are impossible. This is a truth which in these days — I say advisedly, in these days — is clear and incontestable. History can only show how things have been; and even where we can throw light upon the past, and understand and criticize it, we must not presume to think that by any process of abstraction absolute judgments as to the value to be assigned to past events can be obtained from the results of a purely historical survey. Such judgments are the creation only of feeling and of will; they are a subjective act. The false notion that the understanding can produce them is a heritage of that protracted epoch in which knowing and knowledge were expected to accomplish everything; in which it was believed that they could be stretched so as to be capable of covering and satisfying all the needs of the mind and the heart. That they cannot do. This is a truth which, in many an hour of ardent work, falls heavily upon our soul, and yet — what a hopeless thing it would be for mankind if the higher peace to which it aspires, and the clearness, the certainty and the strength for which it strives, were dependent on the measure of its learning and its knowledge. *(C: 17-18)*

*

REVELATION AND THEOLOGY: THE BARTH-HARNACK CORRESPONDENCE

A little more than two years after the student-conference at Aarau, on January 11th 1923, Harnack published his "Fifteen Questions"; he did not have Barth specifically in mind when he wrote them, although he was one of those from whom Harnack wanted an account. Barth wrote his replies in one sitting, so to speak, and published them in the same journal, Christliche Welt, *on February 8th. They provided the concreteness to which Harnack addressed his "Open Letter," published on March 8th. Barth's lengthy "Answer" appeared on April 26th and the quite "unconcluding" "Postscript" of Harnack, breaking off the correspondence, though not the relationship between them, appeared on May 24th. The editors and readers of the journal had had a real feast in theological controversy, even though little had been resolved.*

The translation was prepared by the editor from the German text which was published in Karl Barth, Theologische Fragen und Antworten, *1957, pp. 7-31.*

See also the editor's study of that correspondence: Revelation and Theology. An Analysis of the Barth-Harnack Correspondence of 1923, *pp. 29-53.*

HARNACK

Fifteen questions to the despisers of scientific theology

(1) Is the religion of the Bible, or are its revelations, so completely a unity that in relation to faith, worship and life one may simply speak of "the Bible"? If this is not so, may one leave the determination of the content of the gospel solely to the individual's heuristic knowledge (*Erfahrung*), to his subjective experience (*Erlebnis*), or does one not rather need here historical knowledge and critical reflection?

(2) Is the religion of the Bible, or are its revelations, so completely a unity and so clear that historical knowledge and critical reflection are not needed for a correct understanding of their meaning? Or are they

the converse, namely so incomprehensible and indescribable that one must simply wait until they radiate out in man's heart because no faculty of man's soul or mind can grasp them? Are not both these assumptions false? Do we not need, for an understanding of the Bible, next to an inner openness, historical knowledge and critical reflection?

(3) Is the experience of God (*Gotteserlebnis*) different from the awakening of faith or identical with it? If it is different, what distinguishes it from uncontrollable fanaticism? If it is identical, how can it come about otherwise than through the preaching of the gospel? And how can there be such preaching without historical knowledge and critical reflection?

(4) If the experience of God (*Gotteserleben*) is contrary to or disparate from all other experience (*Erleben*), how is the necessity of a radical withdrawal from the world to be avoided or how is one to escape the sophism that one has to remain in the world since even the withdrawal from it is based on a decision of the will and thus something worldly?

(5) If God and the world (life in God and life in the world) are complete opposites, what is one to make of the close union, indeed the equivalence of the love of God and the love of one's fellow, which comprise the core of the gospel? How is this equivalence possible without the highest valuation of morality?

(6) If God and the world (life in God and life in the world) are complete opposites, how does education in godliness, that is in goodness, become possible? But how is education possible without historical knowledge and the highest valuation of morality?

(7) If God is simply unlike anything said about him on the basis of the development of culture, on the basis of the knowledge gathered by culture, and on the basis of ethics, how can this culture and in the long run one's own existence be protected against atheism?

(8) If Goethe's pantheism, Kant's conception of God or related points of view are merely opposites of real statements about God, how can it be avoided that these statements are given over to barbarism?

(9) But if the converse is true, namely that here as in all physical and spiritual developments opposites are at one and the same time steps and steps are opposites, how can this basic knowledge be grasped and furthered without historical knowledge and critical reflection?

(10) If the knowledge that God is love is the highest and final knowledge of him and if love, joy and peace are his sphere, how may one remain forever between door and hinge, how may one give autonomous standing to what are transition points in Christian experience (*Erfahrung*) and thus perpetuate their dread?

(11) "Whatever is true, honorable, just, gracious, if there is any excellence, anything worthy of praise, think on these things" — if this liberating admonition still stands, how can one erect barriers between the experience of God (*Gotteserlebnis*) and the good, the true and the beautiful, instead of relating them with the experience of God by means of historical knowledge and critical reflection?

(12) If all sin is nothing other than the lack of reverence and love, how can this lack be checked other than by the preaching of God's holy majesty and love? How dare one introduce all kinds of paradoxes and whims here?

(13) If it is certain that whatever is subconscious, sensory, numinous, spell-binding (*Fascinos*), etc., remains sub-human as long as reason has not taken hold of, comprehended, purified and protected it in its unique essence, how can one rebuke this reason, yes even wish to eradicate it? And what has one to offer once this Herostratean deed is done?[1]* Is not even gnostic occultism rising up now out of the rubble?

(14) If the person of Jesus Christ stands at the center of the gospel, how else can the basis for reliable and communal knowledge of this person be gained but through critical-historical study so that an imagined Christ is not put in place of the real one? What else besides scientific theology is able to undertake this study?

(15) Granted that there are inertness, short-sightedness and numerous ills, yet is there any other theology than that which has strong ties, and is in blood-relationship, with science in general? Should there be one, what persuasiveness and value belong to it?

Berlin-Grünewald   Adolf von Harnack

BARTH

Fifteen answers to Professor Adolf von Harnack

In reference to the title (of your questions): someone objecting to that form of Protestant theology which has become determinative since Pietism and the Enlightenment, especially during the last fifty years of German history, is not necessarily a "despiser of scientific theology." The point of the objection is that *this* particular theology might have moved further away from its theme than is good. (The Reformation was the last instance where it was stated clearly.)

*For numbered footnotes see pp. 323ff.

(1) *The one revelation of God* might be considered the theme of theology and this beyond the "religion" and the "revelations" of the Bible. "Historical knowledge" could tell us that the communication of the "content of the gospel" can be accomplished, according to the assertion of the gospel, only through an act of this "content" itself. But "critical reflection" could lead to the conclusion that this assertion is founded in the essence of the matter (the relation of God and man) and is therefore to be seriously respected. The "scientific character" of theology would then be its adherence to the recollection that its object *was once subject* and must become that again and again, which has nothing to do whatever with one's "heuristic knowledge" (*Erfahrung*) and "experience" (*Erlebnis*) in themselves.

(2) "Inner openness, heuristic knowledge, experience, heart" and the like on the one hand and "historical knowledge and critical reflection" on the other are possibilities which can be equally helpful, irrelevant or obstructive to the "understanding" (*Verstehen*) of the Bible. It is understood through neither this nor that "function of the soul or mind" but by virtue of *that* Spirit which is identical with the content of the Bible and that by *faith*.

(3) The so-called "experience of God" (*Gotteserlebnis*) is therefore as different as heaven and earth from the faith awakened by God and is *practically* indistinguishable from "uncontrolled fanaticism." But why *could* it not be a more distinct or more confused symptom of and a testimony to the awakening of faith? Faith does come about *practically* through preaching, but preaching comes about through "the Word of the Christ" (no matter in what state the preacher's historical knowledge and critical reflection are). The task of theology is at one with the task of preaching. It consists in the reception and transmission of the Word of the Christ. Why should "historical knowledge and critical reflection" not be of preparatory service in this?

(4) The faith awakened by God will never be able to avoid completely the necessity of a more or less radical protest against this world as surely as it is a hope for the promised but invisible gift. A theology, should it lose the understanding of the basic distance which faith posits between itself and this *world*, would in the same measure have to lose sight of the knowledge of God the *Creator*. For the "utter contrast" of God and the world, the *cross*, is the only way in which we as *human beings* can consider the original and final *unity* of Creator and creature. Sophistry is not the realization that even our protest against the world cannot justify us before God. It is rather the common attempt to bypass the cross by

means of a shallow doctrine of creation.

(5) The coordination of the love of God and the love of man which the gospel makes is precisely the most forceful reference to the fact that the relation between our "life in the world" and our "life in God" is one of "utter contrast" which is overcome only through the miracle of the eternal God himself. Or is there a stranger, more incomprehensible factor in this world, one more in need of God's revelation, than one's "fellowman"? "Highest valuation of morality" — gladly, but do we *love* our neighbor? Are we capable of it? And if we do *not* love *him*, what about our love of *God*? What shows more plainly than this "core" (not of the gospel, but of the law) that God does not give life unless he takes it first?

(6) "No one can come to me unless the Father who sent me draws him and I will raise him up at the last day."

(7) Statements about God derived from "the development of culture, from the knowledge gathered by culture and from ethics" may as expressions of special "experiences of God" (*Gotteserlebnisse*) (e.g. the experiences of the War) have their significance and value in comparison with the experiences of primitive peoples who do not yet know such great treasures. (Consider, for example, the significance and value of the statements of the War-theologians of all countries.) *These* statements can definitely not be considered as the "preaching of the gospel" (3). Whether they *protect* culture and the individual "against atheism" or whether they *sow* atheism, since they come out of polytheism, would remain an *open* question in each individual case.

(8) "Real statements about God" are made in any way only where one is aware of being confronted by *revelation* and therefore of being placed under judgment instead of believing oneself to be on a pinnacle of culture and religion. Under this judgment stand together with all other statements about this subject also those of Goethe and Kant. Schleiermacher's alarm about "barbarism" is to be rejected as non-essential and irrelevant because the gospel has as much and as little to do with "barbarism" as with culture.

(9) It may be that *in the sphere* of human statements about God "opposites are at one and the same time steps and steps are opposites, as in all physical and spiritual development," yet it is still true that between *God's* truth (which may be expressed in human terms also) and *our* truth there is only contrast, only an *either-or*. (It is more urgent, for *theology* in any case, to "grasp" and to "develop" *this* knowledge!) Humility, yearning and supplication, will always be the first and also the last thing *for us*. The way from the old to the new world is *not* a stairway, *not* a develop-

ment in any sense whatsoever; it is a being born anew.

(10) If the knowledge that "God is love" is the *highest* and *final knowledge about God,* how can one consistently pretend to be in possession of it? Is not the "transition point" just as long in duration as time? Is not *our* faith also always unfaith? Or should we believe in our *faith?* Does not faith live by being faith in God's *promise?* Are we saved in a way other than in *hope?*

(11) "The peace of God which is higher than our understanding," Phil. 4:7. The "barrier" of this "higher" is a basic and insurmountable one. If he does "keep our hearts and minds in Christ Jesus" and thus makes *possible* the admonition of Phil. 4:8 ("Whatever is true . . ."), then *as such* he is *higher* than our understanding. There is a relation between him and what *we* call good, true and beautiful, but this relation is precisely the "barrier," the divine *crisis,* on the basis of which alone one may first speak seriously about the good, the true and the beautiful.

(12) If sin should perhaps be more than a "lack of reverence and love," namely man's *fall* from *God* and his being lost in a godlikeness the end of which is *death,* then the preaching of God's holy majesty and love is a task which does not seem to spare our human thinking and speaking from wandering on *curious* ways. A *spectator*-theology may then speak of "all kinds of paradoxes and whims." He who is in a position to solve this — but *this* same — task more easily must show how it is done. Historical knowledge tells us that Paul and Luther were *not* in that position.

(13) *Which* theological tradition is it that, having begun with the apotheosis of "feeling," has apparently landed happily in the swamp of the psychology of the unconscious? *Who* thought that a special "religious" source of knowledge could be opened up apart from critical reason? And *ad vocem* "gnostic occultism": which theology is at every moment notoriously close to the danger of losing its ablest devotees to Dr. Steiner?

(14) The reliability and communality of the knowledge of the person of Jesus Christ as the center of the *gospel* can be none other than that of the God-awakened *faith.* Critical-historical study signifies the deserved and necessary end of *those* "foundations" of the knowledge which are no foundations at all since they have not been laid by God himself. Whoever does not yet know (and this applies to all of us) that we *no* longer know Christ according to the flesh, should let the critical study of the Bible tell him so. The more radically he is frightened the better it is for him and for the matter involved. This might turn out to be the service which "historical knowledge" can render to the actual task of theology.

(15) If theology were to regain the courage to face up to concrete objectivity (*Sachlichkeit*), the courage to bear witness to the *Word* of revelation, of judgment and of *God's* love, the outcome might well be that "science in general" would have to seek "strong ties and a blood-relationship" with theology instead of the other way around; for it would be better perhaps also for jurists, physicians and philosophers if they knew what theologians ought to know. Or should the present fortuitous *opinio communis* of others really be the instance through which we have to let our work be judged as to its "persuasiveness and value"?

Göttingen   Karl Barth

HARNACK

Open letter to Professor Karl Barth

I thank you for replying to my "fifteen questions." They were addressed to you *also*, yes, especially to you.

Your answers have made a few things clearer to me, but for that very reason the opposition between us has become all the clearer. I shall try to show this in what follows. Other things have remained totally obscure for me or perhaps they have become so, especially your answer to my first question. Despite much hard effort, it is wholly incomprehensible to me. Since very much depends on this basic question, one of the main issues, namely your concept of revelation, stays under the cover of a heavy fog.

Concerning the title of my questions and question 15: you see in contemporary scientific theology an unstable and transitory product which has been in the making since Pietism and the Enlightenment and that it has the value of an *opinio communis* only. I see in it the only possible way of grasping the object epistemologically. This way is old and new at the same time, new because it has attained to greater clarity and maturity only since the eighteenth century and old because it began when man started thinking. You say that "the task of theology is at one with the task of preaching"; I reply that the task of theology is at one with the task of science in general. The task of preaching is the pure presentation of the Christian's task as a witness to Christ. You transform the theological professorship into the pulpit-ministry (and desire to hand over to secular disciplines what is known as "theology"). On the basis of the whole course of Church-history I predict that this undertaking will not lead to edification but to dissolution. Or is what you have to say meant to act only as a "ferment"? No one could make this his intention and surely it is not part of your plan. Nevertheless, I acknowledge the ferment: the courage to be objective, the courage to be a witness.

Concerning questions 2 and 3: I cannot see what in your opinion is to remain when one is obliged to do away with "inner openness, heuristic knowledge, experience, heart, historical knowledge and critical reflection" in connexion with the understanding of the religion of the Bible. It is true, you say the "religion of the Bible is understood by virtue of that Spirit which is identical with the content of the Bible and that by faith," but since you add "the so-called experience of God is thus as different as heaven and earth from the awakening of faith by God and is practically indistinguishable from uncontrolled fanaticism," your "thus" is as incomprehensible to me as the justification of your illustration or your determination of the relation between the experience of God and faith. I am unable to speak about things incomprehensible. To my joy you subscribe to the thesis "faith comes from the preaching of the Word of the Christ," but just as your "the Christ" in place of "Jesus Christ" looks unfortunate to me in view of Church-historical considerations, my suspicions are heightened because of the context in which you use the Pauline "we know Christ no longer according to the flesh." So, we do not know the historical Jesus Christ of the gospels any more? How am I to understand that? By the theory of the exclusive inner word? Or by which of the many other subjectivistic theories?

Concerning question 4: it grieves me that you gave it a very devious answer only; "the faith awakened by God will never be able to avoid completely (!) the necessity of a more or less (!) radical protest against this world as surely as it is a hope for the promised but invisible gift." Are you by any chance not quite sure about this point? It would have been better then to postpone the answer. But since it looks half-baked it lacks either understanding or the courage to witness.

Concerning question 5: you answer my question about the love of God and the love of one's neighbor in terms of a problematical conceptuality of "the neighbor" and "love of the neighbor" which is especially characteristic of your theology, yes, but not of the gospel which knows no problems here at all. In your presentation I see a very great separation from the simple gospel.

Concerning question 6 (about the possibility of education in godliness): you simply answer with John 6:44. If that is all you have to say here, then you condemn all Christian pedagogy and sever, like

Marcion, every link between faith and the human. In my view you have the example of Jesus against you.

Concerning questions 7 and 9: you assert that in each individual case it is an open question whether the cognition of God, evolved in the history of man, excepting revelation, protects against or sows atheism. This is only half an answer to my question as to whether God is *not at all* whatever is said about him on the basis of the development of culture, on the basis of the knowledge gathered by culture and on the basis of ethics. Or may I assume that you reject such an assertion with me? Hardly! For your sentence "the gospel has as much and as little to do with barbarism as with culture" can be understood only as a radical denial of every valuable understanding of God within the history of man's thought and ethics. Your point of view becomes completely plain when you say that "between God's truth and our truth there is only contrast, only an either-or. The way from the old to the new world is not a stairway, not a development in any sense whatsoever, but rather a being born anew." Does this not exclude the belief that one's being a Christian happened precisely in that way, while at the same time one admits that God let it happen on a stairway on which eternal values had already been given? Remember Augustine's account of his becoming a Christian!

Concerning questions 10 and 11: your answers to them are in my view those which move away the furthest from the Christianity of the gospel on account of the problematics into which you draw the Christian faith. You said that the transition point from godlessness to God lasts for every Christian as long as time; *our* faith, you said, is also always unfaith; we are saved only in hope; there is a relation between what we call good, true and beautiful and the peace of God only insofar as a barrier is also a relation, etc. By answering my questions like this, in terms of what Christianity still lacks and of what we all know, you shatter what we already possess, for you make the Christian's confidence . . . in which he is allowed to live, an illusion, and his joy, which is to fill his life, you turn into frivolity. You will dispute this, but what you put in their place is the description of a state of mind which in the best of cases only a handful may know as the peace of God, a state of mind which is in no way a necessary precondition for all Christian humility.

From this vantage point your answer to question 12 becomes understandable. The simple gospel out of which Jesus told his understandable and comforting parables for the salvation of souls does not suit you; Christian preaching rather can "not spare man's thinking and speaking from wandering on curious paths." How many will ever be able to understand you, seeing that you are wholly submerged in highly sub-lime psychology and metaphysics? Then you turn surprisingly to Paul and Luther. But even here I have no doubt that today too every Christian will find it easier to live according to their teaching and example than to yours. But are Paul and Luther examples to be emulated? Can we slip on their armour? Must we smaller ones torment ourselves in order to experience what they did? It is — and now let me be prob-lematical for once — our strength and at the time our destiny to have experienced Paul and Luther. Against this destiny will work only the comforting word which precisely they call out to us: I believe in the forgiveness of sins.

You did not answer question 13 but merely left it with the remark that prevalent theology or one of its developments has led into the swamp of the psychology of the unconscious and into occultism. Since that ques-tion was not directed to you but to another address, I can remain silent here although I must say that occultism is by divine decree the punish-ment for every form of contempt of reason and science and that every period of time has only one science.

For question 14 I also miss a succinct answer. Does the awakening of faith, insofar as it includes the knowledge of the person of Jesus Christ as the center of the gospel, take place without regard for his historical person? If this is to be answered negatively, can faith dispense with his-torical knowledge of that person? If this is to be answered affirmatively, can the critical-historical study of this person with regard to faith be something irrelevant or is it not rather absolutely necessary? What you say here in relation to biblical science may be formulated like this: the most radical biblical science is always right and thank heaven for that, because now we may be rid of it. This point of view, known to the point of nausea from recent, second-rate Church-history, opens the gate to every suitable fantasy and to every theological dictatorship which dis-solves the historical ingredient of our religion and seeks to torment the conscience of others with one's own heuristic knowledge.

I do sincerely regret that the answers to my questions only point out the magnitude of the gap that divides us. But then neither my nor your theology matters. What does matter is that the gospel is correctly taught. Should however your way of doing this come to prevail it will not be taught any more; it will rather be given over into the hands of devo-tional preachers who freely create their own understanding of the Bible and who set up their own dominion.

Yours respectfully
von Harnack

BARTH

An answer to Professor Adolf von Harnack's open letter

Esteemed Dr von Harnack

It is not necessary to state explicitly that your extensive discussion of my answers to your questions is an honor for which I am grateful to you. Nevertheless I enter with hesitation upon the task of giving more information to you about my theological thoughts. The editor thought it something which in view of your letter was the natural thing to do. But you yourself have stated that my answers have shown you only the gap that divides us. Is it not pointless and annoying to pose further riddles to you now and more than likely to most of the readers of *Christliche Welt*? My position is unpleasant in yet another way: the first time you posed real questions to which I, as one of those to whom they were addressed, had to answer as well or as badly as I could. In your letter, however, you confront me as someone — and I have absolutely no intention of challenging your right in this, you, who are one of my revered teachers of former times — who has accomplished his tasks, has obtained knowledge and who, because of the experience and the reflections of a rich life, has no time and no ear not only for answers different from those he would himself give but also for questions other than his own. Is there any further answer to be given to questions? Is the discussion not over? But since you wanted to tell me that it was not my answers you had in mind when you raised your original questions — something I never doubted — I think that I owe it to you and to our listeners to confess that I do consider my answers open to debate, but that still for the time being and until I am shown a better way I reserve all else to myself. Nonetheless, your objections cannot deter me from continuing to ask along the line of those answers. Allow me, therefore, to touch again on every point and to draw some of them together. For a real understanding of my continued opposition I would refer to my publications as well as to those of my friends Gogarten and Thurneysen, something you would do also were you in a similar situation. (For the other group of those to whom you addressed yourself I assume no responsibility.) More to the general public as to you I would like to say that in the end no effective repudiation of our views will be possible without a serious study of our point of view.

You see in what you call "scientific theology" "the only possible way of grasping the object epistemologically" and you call it "new because it has attained to greater clarity and maturity only since the eighteenth century, old since it began when man started to think." I hope that I am not reading anything into your position when I assume, based on that explicit reference to the eighteenth century, that the Reformers Luther and Calvin (together with that unfortunate tribe of "revival preachers") would fail to qualify as "scientific theologians," whereas Zwingli and Melanchthon might not. I would also assume that for you the idea of considering the Apostle Paul (in addition to whatever else he was) as one of those theologians is quite out of the question. Be that as it may, I believe I know "thinking men" in earlier and later centuries who as theologians pursued wholly different ways from those which since the eighteenth century have been regarded as normal, men whose scientific quality (should "scientific quality" mean objectivity) it would in my opinion be hazardous to doubt. The appeal to Paul's or Luther's theology is for you nothing but a presumptuous attempt at imitation. On this side of the "gap" the process looks relatively simple. We have been irresistibly impressed by the material superiority of those and other older theologians, however little they may fit into the present scheme of the guild. We, therefore, cannot feel ourselves relieved, by the protest of the spirit of modern times (which perhaps has to learn to understand itself first!) nor by the faith in the forgiveness of sins (!) which you invoked, of our duty to consider the fundamental point of departure of those theologians more seriously in regard to its total justification than was done especially in recent theology in spite of all the research into Paul and the enthusiasm for Luther. There can be no question of any repristination here whatsoever. It is my private view that the exercise of repristinating a classical theological train of thought, which in the days of medieval and Protestant scholasticism was known as "theology," is probably more instructive than the chaotic business of today's faculties for which the idea of a determinative *object* has become strange and monstrous in face of the determinate character of the *method*. But I also think I know that this *same* kind of thing can and should not return and that we must think *in* our time *for* our time. Actually the point is not to keep the historical-critical method of biblical and historical research developed in the last centuries away from the work of theology, but rather to fit that method, and its refinement of the way questions are asked, into that work in a meaningful way. I think I said this in my answers 2, 3, and 14 and may thus be permitted to express astonishment that you still accuse me of regarding critical biblical science as something "devious," of wishing to be "rid of it," and must therefore be threatened with the punishment of occultism which is decreed by "divine order" for despisers of reason and science. What I must defend myself against is not historical criticism but rather the foregone conclusiveness with which — and this is characteristic also of your present statements — the task of theology is *emptied*, that is to say, the way in which a so-called "simple gospel," discovered by historical criticism *beyond* the "Scriptures" and *apart from* the "Spirit," is given the place which the Reformers accorded to the "Word" (the correlation of "Scripture" and "Spirit"). Such a gospel can be called "God's Word" only metaphorically because it is at best a human impression of it. The sentence so repugnant to you and others, to the effect that the task of theology is at one with the task of preaching is for me an *inevitable* statement of the *program* (in the carrying out of which, of course, many things must still be considered). In this I assume it is conceded that the preacher must by right proclaim "the Word" and not perhaps his own heuristic knowledge, experiences, maxims and reflections. You have said that the truth of preaching and of faith come about "through the Word of the Christ." (The definite article before "Christ" is of no consequence to me at all.) If the transmission of this "Word" is the preacher's task then it is also that of the theologian (who finds himself at least in virtual personal union with the former). The tactical and practical differences in accomplishing this are obvious as is the understanding that some of the things which belong to the lectern are to be left out in the pulpit and vice versa. The *theme*, however, which the theologian must pursue in history and which he must strive to express in a manner appropriate to his situation, cannot be a *second* truth *next to* that which he is obliged to present as a preacher. *That* was self-evident in the beginnings of Protestant theology (I think especially of Zürich and Geneva). I cannot see how the subsequent abstract separation of "scholarly" and "edifying" thought and speech can be derived from the essence of the matter. However, if it be right to assume the unity of the theologian's and the preacher's task, what is completely ruled out as a theme for one as well as for the other, along with everything that is merely human impression and not God's Word, is a "simple gospel" which as alleged "revelation" remains in the Bible, after the sufficient ground of cognition for all revelation, given in the correlation of "Scripture" and "Spirit," has been radically eliminated.

But at this point arises your categorical declaration that my "*concept of revelation*" is "*totally*" (the italics are yours!) "incomprehensible" to you. You had asked in question 1 how one might come to find out what the content of the gospel is without historical knowledge and critical reflection. I answered in the first instance that the gospel itself tells us that this understanding occurs exclusively through an action (through deed and word) of this very "content" (of God or Christ or the Spirit). Surely you will not demand individual citations for this thesis. In the second instance I said concerning critical reflection that it cannot be good to reverse the order and turn "Thus says the Lord" into "Thus hears man." If there is a way to *this* "content," then the content itself must be the way; the speaking voice must be the listening ear. All other ways do not lead to this goal, all other ears do not hear this voice. The fact that God is himself the goal as well as the way is something — and I gladly concede this — which to *me* as to *you* is *totally* incomprehensible, not only "fog," but, to speak with Luther, darkness. If you were to tell me that one cannot believe in a way from God *to us*, to which there does not correspond apparently any way from us *to God* (for it is always most exclusively God's way *to us*), I could only reply that deep down in my heart I think exactly the same. But then, is it not already included, quite apart from what the Bible says about it on every page, in the concept of revelation (and really not only in *my* concept!) that one cannot "believe" it? Would it not be better to renounce this high-sounding word if revelation were only the designation of a very sublime or a very deep but still a possible human discovery? Or should we theologians, if we do not wish to do this, not get up enough courage to let our theology begin with the perhaps essentially sceptical but nevertheless clear reminder of the "totally incomprehensible," inaudible and unbelievable, the *really* scandalous testimony that God himself has said and done something, something *new* in fact, outside of the correlation of all human words and things, but which *as* this new thing he has injected *into* that correlation, a word and a thing next to others but *this* word and *this* thing? I am not talking now of the possibility of accepting this testimony. I only ask whether we should not for once *reckon* more soberly with the fact that what is called Christianity made its first and for us recognizable beginning with this testimony? This testimony, which historical criticism cannot analyze enough, and which will not cease being *this* testimony when thus analyzed, I call in its totality "the Scriptures." The delineation of "the Scriptures" over against other scriptures appears to me a secondary question. Should an extra-canonical writing contain in a notable fashion this very testimony, there can be no *a priori* impossibility of letting this testimony speak through it also, no, quite to the contrary. From this observation, however, to the canonization of *Faust*, for example, there is a long way which a discerning Church just will *not* travel.

The Scriptures then witness to revelation. One does not have to believe it, nor *can* one do it. But one should not deny that it witnesses to revelation, *genuine* revelation that is, and not to a more or less concealed religious possibility of man but rather to the possibility of God, namely that *he* has acted under the form of a human possibility — and this as *reality.* According to this testimony, the Word became flesh, God himself became a human-historical *reality* and that this took place in the *person of Jesus Christ.* But from this it by no means follows for me that this event can also be an object of human-historical *cognition*; this is excluded because and insofar as *this* reality is involved. The existence of a Jesus of Nazareth, for example, which can of course be discovered historically is not *this* reality. A historically discernible "simple gospel," discernible because it is humanly plausible, a "simple gospel" which causes no scandal, a "simple gospel," that is, in your sense, a word or a deed of this Jesus which would be nothing other really than the realization of a human possibility — would not be *this* reality. I doubt whether it is possible at any cogent point to separate one word or one deed of Jesus from the background of this reality, even considered only historically, that is, from the Scripture which witnesses to revelation and so to the scandal it causes and then proceed to interpret it as the "simple gospel" in your sense. Why, for example, I regard this as impossible in reference to the command to love God and one's neighbor, I mentioned in my fifth answer, for which you have chastised but not refuted me. I can now only in passing enter protest against your description of the parables of Jesus (*die Gleichnisse Jesu*) as "understandable and comforting" parables (*Parabeln*)[2] and I hope to have in both cases at least some historians on my side. But even of you could succeed in claiming some point or other in the tradition for your position, it would merely mean that this point is *not*, or *is* only in context with other points, the object of the testimony or the kerygma which is surely in your judgment also the sole issue for the New Testament writings. The object of the testimony has been made known by the apostles and evangelists to such an extent as *revelation*, as the action of God himself, it has been thrust back so deeply into an impenetrable hiddenness and *protected* so strongly from every desire for *direct* perception, that not only all statements which obviously refer to this "center of the gospel," found for example in that rather threatening bundle in the second article of the Creed, but in fact the "Sermon on the Mount" as well, the parabolic and polemical speeches of Jesus and the account of his passion, all leave the circumspect reader with the conclusion that there can be no question of speaking here of a direct historical *comprehensibility* of this "historical" *reality* (revelation). All that is com-

99

prehensible is always that other which makes up the historical context of the alleged revelation.

Beyond this "other" that barrier goes up and the scandal, the fable or the miracle threatens. The historical reality of Christ (as revelation, as "center of the gospel") is not the "historical Jesus" whom an all too eager historical research had wanted to lay hold of in disregard of the very warnings made in the sources themselves (coming upon a banality which has been and shall be proclaimed in vain as a pearl of great price). Nor is it, as you said, an imagined Christ but rather the *risen one,* or let us say with more restraint in view of our little faith: the Christ who is *witnessed to* as the risen one. That is the "evangelical, the historic Jesus Christ" and otherwise, that is, apart from the testimony to him, apart from the revelation which must here be believed, "we know him no longer." In this sense I think I can legitimately appeal to 2 Corinthians 5:16. At this decisive point, that is, in answering the question: what makes Jesus the Christ? in terms of the reference to the *resurrection,* one is indeed left from man's point of view with what you called "totally" incomprehensible. And I gladly confess that I would a hundred times rather take the side of the No, the refusal to believe which you proclaim on the basis of this fact, than the talents of a "positive" theology which ends up making what is incomprehensible altogether self-evident and transparent once again, for that is an emptying and a denying of revelation which with its apparent witness to the revelation is worse than the angriest refusal to believe which at least has the advantage of being suited to the subject matter. My declaration of sympathy for the "most radical" biblical science was meant in this sense. The theology of the Reformers did not need this negative discipline because it still had the courage not to avoid the scandal of revelation. It thus never raised the question of a historically discernible core of the gospel. *We* need it, however, because we have fallen into this impossible question through flight from the scandal. I see the theological function of historical criticism especially in the task of making clear to us *a posteriori* that there is *no road* this way, and that in the Bible we have to do with testimonies and *only* with *testimonies.* I notice that this is the function it has in fact fulfilled among us since David Friedrich Strauss, and done so excellently in its own way, even if it is not widely understood and above all unaware of what it was doing.

The *acceptance* of this unbelievable testimony of the Scriptures I call *faith.* Again I do not claim that this is a discovery of *my* theology. I do ask, however, what else faith could be — disregarding sentimentalities — but the obedience I give to a human word which testifies to the Word of God as a word addressed to me, as if it were itself God's Word? Let no one have any delusions here about the fact that this is an unprecedented event, that here one must speak of the *Holy Spirit* if all the objections Herrmann rammed into our heads against a "mere credence" in historical facts *apart* from this basis of cognition are not to hold good. Therefore I distinguish faith as *God's working* on us (for only he can say to us, in such a way that we will hear it, what *we* can *not* hear, 1 Corinthians 2:9) from all known and unknown human organs and functions, even our so-called "experiences of God." Is that such an unheard-of novelty? Must I, as one of the Reformed tradition, ask whether Luther's explication of the third article in the *Small Catechism* is valid or not? Do you really not see that through the rash abandonment of *this* concept of faith in favor of the lentil-pottage of a less paradoxical one, the doors have been opened to the anthroposophic *tohuwabohu* of faith and occult "capabilities" of man, confronted with which official theology is simply at a loss?

It has to be thus: whatever may be said against the possibility of revelation can with equal strength be said also against the possibility of faith. That leaves us with this as the *second* excluded possibility: God who according to the witness of the Scriptures has spoken "the Word of Christ" speaks that Word also to *me through* the witness of the Scriptures empowered through the *testimonium Spiritus Sancti internum,* so that I *hear* it and by hearing it *believe.* Is this the "theory of the exclusive inner word" or one of the many "other subjectivistic theories"? In your third question you yourself spoke of the *awakening* of faith. I agree, but hold that what we are concerned with here, as also in the "understandable and comforting parable" of the prodigal son, Luke 15:32, is the awakening of someone dead, that is, with *God's miracle* just as in revelation. Indeed, I have no confidence in any objectivity other than the one described in this way or in terms of the correlate concepts of "Scripture" and "Spirit," least of all in the pontifications of a science which would first have to demonstrate its absolute superiority over the subjectivist activity of the "preachers of awakening" by means of results.

But then, honored Sir, you have conjured up against me the shadow of Marcion with the assertion that I "sever the link between faith and the human." May I ask how you derive that from my answers 2 and 3? Have I really made *tabula rasa* with those human organs, functions and experiences? It is not my intention to do this. I really think that man goes on living whether he believes it or not, that he goes on as man, in time, in the world of things, dependent from his point of view exclusively on his own human possibilities. I think I also know that man's faith can at every moment be completely described as "inner openness," "heuristic knowledge," "experience," "religion," "historical knowledge," "critical reflection," etc., just as the testimony of revelation also *can*, yes, *must* be described as a piece of unpleasantly dark human intellectual and cultural history (unless God himself intervenes!). But I would do no "severing" at all here or there (that would only be a completely senseless undertaking!); I would rather say that the human is the relative, the testimony, the parable and thus not the absolute *itself* on some pinnacles or heights of development as one would certainly conclude from your statements. The human rather is the *reference* (understood or not understood) to the absolute. In view of this the historically and psychologically discernible, that which we know in ourselves and others as "faith" would be a witness to and a symptom of that action and miracle of God on us, of that faith, in other words, which, created through the "Word" and "steeped in the Word" is, as Luther said, our righteousness before God himself. The religions of the Bible, with which you began your first question, would in the same way be witness to and symptom of the historical reality of God's incarnation. But the ground for knowing both justifying faith and revelation would be God's action on us through his Word. Does my point of view really not become clear to you?

However, and here I think I come to the nerve of all your objections, I am indeed *content* with the testimonial character of all that which occurs here and there in time and as a result of man. I explicitly *deny* the possibility of positing anything relative as absolute, somehow and somewhere, be it in history or in ourselves, or in Kierkegaardian terms, of going from testimony to "direct statement." If I do not wholly misunderstand the Bible and the Reformation, the latter is and must remain, in the most exclusive sense, God's concern. The fact that eternity becomes time, that the absolute becomes relative, that God becomes man (and *thus* — and only thus — in each case the reverse also!), in other words, the fact that the matter involved coincides with the sign pointing to it and *thus* the coincidence of the sign with the matter to which it points, as Luther, with final insight, remarked in his teaching on the Lord's Supper, while touching on the natural-titanic presumptuousness of the *homo religiosus*, is true only as the "Word and work of God," as the act of the Trinity itself. This act can only be *witnessed to* and *believed* because it is revealed. It is never a historical-psychological reality which becomes directly cognizable for example in our religious experience, in the *dénouements* of our consciences, in the relations between man and man, even in the purest of them, in the thoughts of Goethe and Kant about God or in whatever towers of human god-likeness you may mention. When this reality becomes cognizable here or there, then the miracle has occurred which we cannot *deny*, with which, however, we cannot *reckon* as with any other possibility or even with a general truth. We must worship it when it is *present* (present as the miracle of God!). My rejoinder to your reproof of "severing" (which I cannot acknowledge as justified), is that you empty faith by asserting a continuity between the "human" and faith just as you empty revelation by saying that there is a continuity between history and revelation. I do not sever; I do repudiate every continuity between hither and yonder. I speak of a dialectical *relation* which points to an *identity* which cannot be established nor, therefore, presumed by us. *Parabolic* value only is, therefore, to be given to the images of those stairways which "Christian" *biography* of all ages is in the habit of unfolding before us (an undertaking which despite or rather in view of Augustine is just as promising as it is ambiguous). *Parabolic* value only is to be given to the efforts also and successes of "Christian" *pedagogy*, which truly and for good reason has never been able to be rid of heathenism. We honor and do not dishonor this pedagogy when we put it under the hope and judgment of John 6:44. *Parabolic* value is, however, also to be given to all "Christian" protest against the world which as a human undertaking (why do you insist on concluding that I am irresponsible here? I shall repeat my "devious" answer in its full form) is really a more or less "radical" protest only, a "half-baked," a small protest, a demonstration, a gesture which can never, never wish to anticipate and realize the end of this world and the coming of the kingdom. Parable, parable only can be all "becoming" in view of the birth from death to life through which alone (but only on the way which God takes and is), we come from the truth of man to the truth of God.

Still in connexion with the charge of Marcionism, you demand from me a full answer to the question "whether God is simply unlike anything said about him on the basis of the development of culture, on the basis of the knowledge gathered by culture and on the basis of ethics." Very well, then, but may I ask you really to listen to my whole answer. *NO*, God is "absolutely not at all that," as surely as the Creator is not the creature or even the creation of the creature. But precisely in this *NO*, which can be uttered in its full severity only in the faith in revelation, the creature recognizes itself as the work and the possession of the Creator. Precisely in this *NO* God is known as *God*, as the source and the goal of the *thoughts* of God which man, in the darkness of his culture and his decadence, is in the habit of forming. For this *NO*, posited with finality by revelation, is not without the "deep, secret *YES* under and above the *NO*" which we should "grasp and hold to with a firm faith in God's Word" and "confess that God is right in his judgment against us, for then we have won." This is how it is with that *NO*: "nothing but *YES* in it, but always deep and secretly and always seeming to be nothing but *NO*." What lover of contradictoriness might have said that? Kierkegaard or Dostoyevsky? No, Martin Luther! (*E.A.* 11, 120). Is Luther to be suspected then of Marcionism too? According to Zwingli, yes, but I think that you and I understand him better than that. So, why should you not understand *me* a little better at the same time? Does the human really become insignificant when, in the faith in revelation, its *crisis* occurs which makes forever impossible every identification between here and the beyond, excepting always the one which it does not become us to express (about the end of all things foreseen in 1 Corinthians 15:28)? Does it really not become full of significance and promise, really serious and possible precisely through being moved out of the twilight of supposed fulfilment into the light of real *hope*? Is it really *not* enough for *us* to have and to behold in the transitory the parable of the intransitory, to live in it and to work for it, to be glad as men that we have at least the *parable* and to suffer as men under the fact that it is *only* the parable, *without*, however, anticipating the "swallowing up of death in victory" in a spurious consciousness of eternity exactly *because* the great temporal *significat* applies to the greater eternal *est* and nothing else? Have I really made "*tabula rasa*"?

Yes, you say so, honored Sir, and you must know *why*, although you cannot deduce it from my statements. I am afraid that you *must* really misunderstand me *precisely at this point*, even if we could agree about revelation and faith. Why is it that right here, where of all things the existential question of our relation to God and the world, where the confirmation in hope of faith in revelation is involved, you unambiguously exchange the role of the defender of *science* for that of the defender of the so-called "Christian" possession? Why the lament about the "sublimity" of my metaphysics and psychology, as if all of a sudden *popular intelligibility* were for you the standard of right theology? What is the meaning of measuring the distances which, more here and less there, separate me from the "Christianity of the gospels," as if the topic of our discussion were all of a sudden the *Christian nature* of my theology? What is the meaning of the charge of "commending" a "state of mind," unpalatable to you, when the point of your scientific misgivings was that neither revelation nor faith was made understandable by me in the familiar, "simple" fashion as a state of mind, when, in other words, *the state of mind* was introduced by you into our discussion? Why all those strong words about "illusion," "frivolity," "lover of contradictoriness," etc., when you have certainly not demonstrated, from my perhaps unsatisfactory, but nevertheless circumspect answers, the right to such tumultuous conclusions and accusations? How am I to explain the transition from instruction to admonition and how am I to answer it? You can surely guess that I too have angry thoughts about the connexion between the *scientific* character of your theology, which causes you to repudiate what I (and not only I) call revelation and faith, and your own *Christian position*, which comes out into the open in the idea that Paul's "saved in hope" must be suspected as "problematical." I too would be in the position of registering strongest scruples and of uttering very sharp words where the misunderstanding between us seems so hopeless. Yet what else would I do then but seal this hopelessness on my part too, something that must not be done? It is better in every respect to break off here.

Yet let me repeat: I do not intend to entrench myself in those positions in which you, honored Sir, and our voluntary-involuntary audience in this conversation have seen me, simply because I know how frighteningly relative *everything* is that one can *say* about the great subject which occupies you and me. I know that it will be necessary to speak of it in a way quite different from that of my present understanding. I would like to be able to listen attentively in the future to whatever *you* also will have to say. But at this time I cannot concede that you have driven me off the field with your questions and answers, although I will gladly endure it when it really happens.

Respectfully Yours
Karl Barth

HARNACK

A postscript to my open letter to Professor Karl Barth

Professor Barth has given a very detailed answer to my open letter. I thank him for his full presentation. To my disappointment I cannot continue the discussion now and in this journal, since the number and weight of the problems are too great to be dealt with briefly and in this place. But there are two things which I would not like to leave unsaid.

(1) Paul and Luther are for me not primarily subjects but objects of scientific theology as is Professor Barth and all those who express their

Christianity as prophets or witnesses like preachers, whether they do it in biblical commentaries or in dogmatic writings etc. Scientific theology and witnessing are often enough mixed together in life, but neither can remain healthy when the demand to keep them separate is invalidated. Both are objective, not only the witnessing, as one may conclude from Professor Barth's statements, but the kind of objectivity is a very different one in each case. A scientific-theological presentation *can* also inspire and edify, thanks to its object, but the scientific theologian whose *aim* it is to inspire and to edify brings a foreign flame to his altar. For as there is only *one* scientific method there is also only *one* scientific task: the pure cognition of its object. Whatever other fruit falls to science as a reward is an unexpected gift.

(2) Revelation is not a scientific concept; science can neither draw together under one generic concept nor explain in terms of "revelation" the God-consciousness of the paradoxical preaching of founders of religion and prophets (and religious experiences in general). There is no future, however, in the attempt to grasp a "Word" of this kind as something so purely "objective" that human speaking, hearing, grasping, and understanding can be eliminated from its operation. I have the impression that Professor Barth tries something like that and calls in a dialectic in this attempt which leads to an invisible ridge between absolute religious scepticism and naive biblicism — the most tormenting interpretation of Christian experience and Christian faith! But since for centuries it has again and again been presented, the only thing to change is its background, it may be justified individually and must, therefore, be treated with respect. But can it create a community and are the blows justified with which it beats down everything that presents itself as Christian experience? Will there be any room left on that glacial bridge for the children and friends of him who, interpreting the Christian faith in this and never any other way, has been able to find a foothold on it? Would it not be better for him to admit that he is playing *his* instrument only and that God has still other instruments, instead of erecting a rigid either-or?

In Barth's answers there becomes apparent in several places a certain sensitiveness which is intensified even to the assertion that my replies sounded like "admonition." I cannot be judge in my own case; hence I am glad to say that no other desire moved me in my letter than to reach clarity *vis-à-vis* a theologian friend.

Berlin   Adolf von Harnack

2

THE GOSPEL, EARLY CHRISTIANITY AND THE HISTORY OF DOGMA AND CHURCH

This section occupies itself with the description of Harnack's thesis that the good news, taught by Jesus of Nazareth, being a living entity, entered a both glorious and horrid history from a Palestinian rootage to the rank of a world-religion. The latter has peculiar and identifiable characteristics which are themselves to be welcomed and rejected in the name of the gospel. The historian Harnack is highly interested in observing what happened to a significant phenomenon of human culture; the believer Harnack wishes to discern how a simple, yet deeply powerful religious truth fares in the course of the changes which mark all history; the Protestant, to be specific, the Lutheran, Harnack seeks to understand how his own ecclesial identification arose in the history he observes and how it is to be justified with historical argumentation. Finally, the German, Harnack, living at a juncture of his nation's self-awareness pregnant with aspirations reaching beyond its own community, needs to place all of these factors into a simple, coherent, convincing and intellectually-morally compelling whole. Theological and cultural liberalism at its finest and, also, its most obvious!

The selections comprising this section range over a period of time even longer than that covered in the previous section. The main burden is carried by the pivotal work of Harnack as a theologian: the lectures What is Christianity? *They were delivered during the winter semester of 1899-1900, at the University of Berlin, before an audience of over 600, once a week for one hour. In their author's lifetime, the book had a publication record of 11 editions in Germany alone, with 71000 copies printed, and translation into 14 languages. These figures tell the significance of the lectures for their time and the importance of them in Harnack's work.*

The three pieces written after those lectures develop, in their way, points Harnack had already made in 1899/1900, but they now also respond to the wide-ranging critique which Das Wesen des Christentums *had elicited. The critique was both scholarly and ad hominem, which testifies to the division in the churches over the place of the freedom of theology. The latest of the selections in the section, that of 1926, manifests the critique associated with "dialectical theology."[3] Even as responses to critics, these selections show Harnack's most mature thinking on matters which had occupied him for over half a century.*

OUTLINES OF THE HISTORY OF DOGMA

When it became clear that students needed quicker access to the overall sweep of his multi-volumed study of dogma and its theological orientation, Harnack prepared the "Outlines." The first edition of it appeared in 1889 and a second, revised one, two years later. It was quickly translated into English, French and Russian. The introduction, which comprises this selection, traces the theological line by which Harnack himself interpreted the birth and subsequent growth of Christian dogma; it is the key, so to speak, to the system of history he was establishing. In this selection, as in the next one from What Is Christianity?, *the thesis maintained is that Christian dogma was the result of the intrusion of Hellenism into the gospel of Jesus and its triumph over it, turning Jesus' work into the gospel about Jesus.*

The translation was prepared by E. K. Mitchell; the text is from the book Outlines of the History of Dogma, *p. 1-36.*

PROLEGOMENA TO THE DISCIPLINE

I.   Idea and Aim of the History of Dogma

1. Religion is a practical affair with mankind, since it has to do with our highest happiness and with those *faculties* which pertain to a holy life. But in every religion these faculties are closely connected with some definite *faith* or with some definite *cult*, which are referred back to divine *revelation.* Christianity is that religion in which the impulse and power to a blessed and holy life is bound up with faith in God as the Father of Jesus Christ. So far as this God is believed to be the omnipotent Lord of heaven and earth, the Christian religion includes a particular *knowledge* of God, of the world and of the purpose of created things; so far, however, as this religion teaches that God can be truly known only in Jesus Christ, it is inseparable from historical knowledge.

2. The inclination to formulate the content of religion in *Articles of Faith* is as natural to Christianity as the effort to *verify* these articles with reference to science and to history. On the other hand the universal and supernatural character of the Christian religion imposes upon its adherents the duty of finding a statement of it which will not be impaired by our wavering knowledge of nature and history; and, indeed, which will be able to maintain itself before every possible theory of nature or of history. The problem which thus arises permits, indeed, of no absolute solution, since all knowledge is relative; and yet religion

essays to bring her absolute truth into the sphere of relative knowledge and to reduce it to statement there. But history teaches, and every thinking Christian testifies, that the problem does not come to its solution; even on that account the *progressive efforts* which have been made to solve it are of value.

3. The most thorough-going attempt at solution hitherto is that which the Catholic Church made, and which the churches of the Reformation (with more or less restrictions) have continued to make, viz.: Accepting a collection of Christian and pre-Christian writings and oral traditions as of divine origin, to deduce from them a system of doctrine, arranged in scientific form for apologetic purposes, which should have as its content the knowledge of God and of the world and of the means of salvation; then to proclaim this complex system (*of dogma*) as the *compendium* of Christianity, to demand of every mature member of the Church a faithful acceptance of it, and at the same time to maintain that the same is a necessary preparation for the blessedness promised by the religion. With this augmentation the Christian brotherhood, whose character as "Catholic Church" is essentially indicated under this conception of Christianity, took a definite and, as was supposed, incontestable attitude toward the science of nature and of history, expressed its religious faith in God and Christ, and yet gave (inasmuch as it required of all its members an acceptance of these articles of faith) to the thinking part of the community a system which is capable of a wider and indeed boundless development. *Thus arose dogmatic Christianity.*

4. The aim of the *history of dogma* is, (1) To explain the *origin* of this dogmatic Christianity, and, (2) To describe its *development.*

5. The *history of the rise* of dogmatic Christianity would seem to close when a well-formulated system of belief had been established by scientific means, and had been made the "*articulus constitutivus ecclesiæ*," and as such had been imposed upon the entire Church. This took place in the transition from the 3rd to the 4th century when the Logos-Christology was established. The *development* of dogma is *in abstracto* without limit, but *in concreto* it has come to an end. For, (a) the *Greek* Church maintains that its system of dogma has been complete since the end of the "Image Controversy"; (b) the *Roman Catholic* Church leaves the possibility of the formulating of new dogmas open, but in the Tridentine Council and still more in the Vatican has it in fact on political grounds rounded out its dogma as a legal system which above all demands obedience and only secondarily conscious faith; the Roman Catholic Church has consequently abandoned the original motive of dogmatic Christianity and

has placed a wholly new motive in its stead, retaining the mere semblance of the old; (c) The *Evangelical* churches have, on the one hand, accepted a greater part of the formulated doctrines of dogmatic Christianity and seek to ground them, like the Catholic Church, in the Holy Scriptures. But, on the other hand, they took a different view of the authority of the Holy Scriptures, they put aside tradition as a source in matters of belief, they questioned the significance of the empirical Church as regards the dogma, and above all they tried to put forward a formulation of the Christian religion, which goes directly back to the "*true understanding of the Word of God.*" Thus in principle the ancient dogmatic conception of Christianity was set aside, while however in certain matters no fixed attitude was taken toward the same and reactions began at once and still continue. Therefore is it announced that the history of Protestant doctrine will be excluded from the history of dogma, and within the former will be indicated only the position of the Reformers and of the churches of the Reformation, out of which the later complicated development grew. Hence the history of dogma can be treated as relatively a completed discipline.

6. The claim of the Church that the dogmas are simply the exposition of the Christian revelation, because deduced from the Holy Scriptures, is not confirmed by historical investigation. On the contrary, it becomes clear that dogmatic Christianity (the dogmas) in its conception and in its construction was *the work of the Hellenic spirit upon the gospel soil.* The intellectual medium by which in early times men sought to make the gospel comprehensible and to establish it securely, became inseparably blended with the content of the same. Thus arose the dogma, in whose formation, to be sure, other factors (the words of sacred scripture, requirements of the cult, and of the organization, political and social environment, the impulse to push things to their logical consequences, blind custom, etc.) played a part, yet so that the desire and effort to formulate the main principles of the Christian redemption, and to explain and develop them, secured the upper hand, at least in the earlier times.

7. Just as the formulating of the dogma proved to be an illusion, so far as the same was to be the *pure* exposition of the gospel, so also does historical investigation destroy the other illusion of the Church, viz.: that the dogma, always having been the same therein, have simply been explained, and that ecclesiastical theology has never had any other aim than to explain the unchanging dogma and to refute the heretical teaching pressing in from without. The formulating of the dogma indicates rather that theology constructed the dogma, but that the Church must

ever conceal the labor of the theologians, which thus places them in an unfortunate plight. In each favorable case the result of their labor has been declared to be a *reproduction* and they themselves have been robbed of their best service; as a rule in the progress of history they fell under the condemnation of the dogmatic scheme; whose foundation they themselves had laid, and so entire generations of theologians, as well as the chief leaders thereof, have, in the further development of dogma, been afterwards marked and declared to be heretics or held in suspicion. Dogma has ever in the progress of history devoured its own progenitors.

8. Although dogmatic Christianity has never, in the process of its development, lost its original style and character as a work of the spirit of perishing antiquity upon gospel soil (*style of the Greek apologists and of Origen*), yet it experienced first through Augustine and later through Luther a deeper and more thorough transformation. Both of these men, the latter more than the former, championed a new and more *evangelical* conception of Christianity, guided chiefly by Paulinism; Augustine however hardly attempted a revision of the traditional dogma, rather did he co-ordinate the old and the new; Luther, indeed, attempted it, but did not carry it through. The Christian quality of the dogma gained through the influence of each, and the old traditional system of dogma was relaxed somewhat — this was so much the case in Protestantism that one does well, as remarked above, no longer to consider the symbolical teaching of the Protestant churches as wholly a recasting of the old dogma.

9. An understanding of the dogmatico-historic process cannot be secured by isolating the special doctrines and considering them separately (Special History of Dogma) after that the epochs have been previously characterized (General History of Dogma). It is much better to consider the "general" and the "special" in each period and to treat the periods separately, and as much as possible to prove the special doctrines to be the outcome of the fundamental ideas and motives. It is not possible, however, to make more than four principal divisions, viz.: I. The Origin of Dogma. II. a. The Development of Dogma in accordance with the principles of its original conception (Oriental Development from Arianism to the Image-Controversy). II.b. The Occidental Development of Dogma under the influence of Augustine's Christianity and the Roman papal politics. II.c. The Three-fold Issuing of Dogma (in the Churches of the Reformation — in Tridentine Catholicism — and in the criticism of the rationalistic age, *i.e.*, of Socinianism).

10. The history of dogma, in that it sets forth the process of the origin and development of the dogma, offers the very best means and methods of freeing the Church from dogmatic Christianity, and of hastening the inevitable process of emancipation, which began with Augustine. But the history of dogma testifies also to the *unity* and continuity of the Christian faith in the progress of its history, in so far as it proves that certain fundamental ideas of the gospel have never been lost and have defied all attacks.   (*OHD*: 1-8)

*

PRESUPPOSITIONS OF THE HISTORY OF DOGMA

III. Introductory

1. The gospel appeared in the "fulness of time." And the *gospel* is *Jesus Christ.* In these sentences the announcement is made that the gospel is the climax of a universal development and yet that it has its power in a personal Life. Jesus Christ "destroyed not," but "fulfilled." He witnessed a new life before God and in God, but within the confines of Judaism, and upon the soil of the Old Testament whose hidden treasures he uncovered. It can be shown, that everything that is "lofty and spiritual" in the psalms and prophets, and everything that had been gained through the development of Grecian ethics, is reaffirmed in the plain and simple gospel; but it obtained its power there, because it became life and deed in a *Person*, whose greatness consists also in this, that he did not remould his earthly environment, nor encounter any subsequent rebuff, — in other words, that he did not become entangled in his times.

2. Two generations later there existed, to be sure, no united and homogeneous *Church*, but there were scattered throughout the wide Roman empire confederated congregations of Christian believers (churches) who, for the most part, were Gentile-born and condemned the Jewish nation and religion as apostate; they appropriated the Old Testament as theirs by right and considered themselves a "new nation," and yet as the "ancient creation of God," while in all departments of life and thought certain sacred *forms* were gradually being put forward. The existence of these confederated Gentile Christian communities is the preliminary condition to the rise of dogmatic Christianity.

The organization of these churches began, indeed, in the apostolic times and their peculiar constitution is negatively indicated by the free-

112

ing of the gospel from the Jewish church. While in Islam the Arabic nation remained for centuries the main trunk of the new religion, it is an astonishing fact in the history of the gospel, that it soon left its native soil and went forth into the wide world and realized its universal character, not through the transformation of the Jewish religion, but by developing into a world-religion *upon Græco-Roman soil. The gospel became a world-religion in that, having a message for all mankind, it preached it to Greek and barbarian, and accordingly attached itself to the spiritual and political life of the world-wide Roman empire.*

3. Since the gospel in its original form was Jewish and was preached only to the Jews, there lay in this transition, which was brought about, in part gradually and without disturbance, and in part through a severe crisis, consequences of the most stringent kind. From the standpoint of the history of the Church and of dogma, the brief history of the gospel within the bounds of Palestinian Judaism is accordingly a paleontological epoch. And yet this remains the *classical epoch*, not only on account of the Founder and of the original testimony, but quite as much because a *Jewish* Christian (Paul) recognized the gospel as the power of God, which was able to save both Jew and Greek, and because he designedly severed the gospel from the Jewish national religion and proclaimed the Christ as the *end* of the Law. Then other Jewish Christians, personal disciples of Jesus, indeed, followed him in all this (see also the 4th Gospel and the Epistle to the Hebrews).

Yet there is in reality no chasm between the older brief epoch and the succeeding period, so far as the gospel is in itself universalistic, and this character very soon became manifest. But the means by which Paul and his sympathizers set forth the universal character of the gospel (proving that the Old Testament religion had been fulfilled and done away with) was little understood, and, *vice versa*, the manner and means by which the Gentile Christians came to an acceptance of the gospel, can only in part be attributed to the preaching of Paul. So far as we now possess in the New Testament *substantial* writings in which the gospel is so thoroughly thought out that it is prized as the *supplanter* of the Old Testament religion, and writings which at the same time are not deeply touched with the Greek spirit, does this literature differ radically from all that follows.

4. The growing Gentile Church, notwithstanding Paul's significant relation toward it, did not comprehend, nor really experience the crisis, out of which the Pauline conception of the gospel arose. In the Jewish propaganda, within which the Old Testament had long since become

liberalized and spiritualized, the Gentile Church, entering and gradually subjecting the same to itself, seldom felt the problem of the reconciliation of the Old Testament with the gospel, since by means of the allegorical method the propaganda had freed themselves from the letter of the law, but had not entirely overcome its spirit; indeed they had simply cast off their national character. Moved by the hostile power of the Jews and later also of the Gentiles and by the consciousness of inherent strength to organize a "people" for itself, the Church as a matter of course took on the form of the thought and life of the world in which it lived, casting aside everything polytheistic, immoral and vulgar. Thus arose the new organizations, which with all their newness bore testimony to their kinship with the original Palestinian churches, in so far as, (1) the Old Testament was likewise recognized as a primitive revelation, and in so far as, (2) the strong spiritual monotheism, (3) the outlines of the proclamation concerning Jesus Christ, (4) the consciousness of a direct and living fellowship with God through the gift of the Spirit, (5) the expectation of the approaching end of the world, and the earnest conviction of the personal responsibility and accountability of each individual soul were all likewise maintained. To these is to be added finally, that the earliest Jewish-Christian proclamation, yes, the gospel itself, bears the stamp of the spiritual epochs, out of which it arose, — of the Hellenic age, in which the nations exchanged their wares and religions were transformed, and the idea of the worth and accountability of every soul became widespread; so that the Hellenism which soon pressed so mightily into the Church was not absolutely strange and new.

5. The history of dogma has to do with the Gentile Church only — the history of theology begins, it is true, with Paul — but in order to understand historically the basis of the formation of doctrine in the Gentile Church, it must take into consideration, as already stated, the following as antecedent conditions: (1) *The gospel of Jesus Christ,* (2) *The general and simultaneous proclamation of Jesus Christ in the first generation of believers,* (3) *The current understanding and exposition of the Old Testament and the Jewish anticipations of the future and their speculations,* (4) *The religious conceptions and the religious philosophy of the Hellenistic Jews,* (5) *The religious attitude of the Greeks and Romans during the first two centuries, and the current Græco-Roman philosophy of religion.*

IV. *The Gospel of Jesus Christ According to His Own Testimony*

The gospel is the good news of the *reign* of the Almighty and Holy God, the Father and Judge of the world and of each individual soul. In this reign, which makes men citizens of the heavenly kingdom and gives them to realize their citizenship in the approaching aeon, the *life* of every man who gives himself to God is secure, even if he should immediately lose the world and his earthly life; while those who seek to win the world and to keep their life fall into the hands of the Judge, who condemns them to hell. This reign of God, in that it rises above all ceremonies and statutes, places men under a *law*, which is old and yet new, viz.: Whole-hearted *love* to God and to one's neighbor. In this love, wherever it controls the thoughts in their deepest springs, that *better justice* is exemplified which corresponds to the *perfection* of God. The way to secure this righteousness is by a *change of heart, i.e.* by self-denial and humility before God and a heart-felt trust in him. In such humility and trust in God the soul realizes its own unworthiness. The gospel, however, calls even sinners, who are so disposed, unto the kingdom of God, in that it assures them satisfaction with his justice, *i.e.*, guarantees them *the forgiveness of the sins* which have hitherto separated them from God. In the three-fold form, however, in which the gospel is set forth, (God's sovereignty, higher justice [law of love] and forgiveness of sin) it is inseparably connected with Jesus Christ. For in the proclamation of the gospel, Jesus Christ everywhere called men unto himself. In him is the gospel *word* and *deed*; it is his meat and drink and, therefore, is it become his personal life, and into *this life* he would draw all men. He is *the Son*, who knows the Father. Men should see in him how kind the Lord is; in him they may experience the power and sovereignty of God over the world and be comforted in this trust; him, the meek and gentle-hearted One, should they follow; and inasmuch as he, the holy and pure One, calls sinners unto himself, they should be fully assured that God through him forgives sin.

This close connexion of his *gospel* with his *person,* Jesus by no means made prominent in *words*, but left his disciples to experience it. He called himself the Son of Man and led them on to the confession that he was their Master and Messiah. Thereby he gave to his lasting significance for them and for his people a comprehensible expression, and at the close of his life, in an hour of great solemnity, he said to them that his death also like his life was an imperishable service which he rendered to the "many" for the forgiveness of sins. By this he raised himself above the plane of all others, although they may already be his brethren; he claimed for himself a unique significance as the *Redeemer* and as the *Judge*; for he interpreted his death, like all his suffering, as a triumph, as the transition to *his glory*, and he proved his power by actually awakening in his disciples the conviction that he still lives and is Lord over the dead and the living. The religion of the gospel rests upon this faith in Jesus Christ, *i.e.* looking upon him, that historical Person, the believer is convinced that *God* rules heaven and earth, and that God, the Judge, is also Father and Redeemer. The religion of the gospel is the religion which frees men from all legality, which, however, at the same time lays upon them the highest moral obligations — the simplest and the severest — and lays bare the contradiction in which every man finds himself as regards them. But it brings *redemption* out of such necessities, in that it leads men to the gracious God, leaves them in his hands, and draws their life into union with the inexhaustible and blessed life of Jesus Christ, who has overcome the world and called sinners to himself.

V.   The General Proclamation concerning Jesus Christ in the First Generation of His Adherents

1. Men had learned to know Jesus Christ and had found him to be the Messiah. In the first two generations following him everything was said about him which men were in any way able to say. Inasmuch as they knew him to be the risen one, they exalted him as the Lord of the world and of history, sitting at the right hand of God, as the way, the truth and the life, as the prince of life and the loving power of a new existence, as the conqueror of death and the king of a coming new kingdom. Although strong individual feeling, special experience, scriptural learning and a fantastic tendency gave from the beginning a form to the confession of him, yet common characteristics of the proclamation can be definitely pointed out.

2. The content of the disciples' belief and the general proclamation of it on the ground of the certainty of the resurrection of Jesus, can be set forth as follows: Jesus is the Messiah promised by the prophets — he will come again and establish a visible kingdom — they who believe in him and surrender themselves entirely to this belief, may feel assured of the grace of God and of a share in his future glory. A new community of Christian believers thus organized itself within the Jewish nation. And this new community believed itself to be *the true Israel* of the messianic times and lived, accordingly, in all their thoughts and feelings in the

future. Thus could all the Jewish apocalyptic expectations retain their power for the time of the second coming of Christ. For the fulfillment of these hopes the new community possessed a guarantee in the sacrificial death of Christ, as also in the manifold manifestations of the Spirit, which were visible upon the members upon their entrance into the brotherhood (from the beginning this introduction seems to have been accompanied by baptism) and in their gathering together. The possession of the Spirit was an assurance to each individual that he was not only a "disciple" but also a "called saint," and, as such, a priest and king of God. Faith in the God of Israel became faith in God the *Father*; added to this was faith in Jesus, the Christ and Son of God, and the witness of the gift of the Holy Spirit, *i.e.* of the Spirit of God and Christ. In the strength of this faith men lived in the fear of the judge and in trust in God, who had already begun the redemption of his own people. The proclamation concerning Jesus, the Christ, rested first of all entirely upon the Old Testament, yet it had its starting-point in the exaltation of Jesus through his resurrection from the dead. To prove that the entire Old Testament pointed toward him, and that his person, his work, his fate were the actual and verbal fulfillment of the Old Testament prophecies, was the chief interest of believers, in so far as they did not give themselves entirely to expectations of the future. This reference did not serve at once to make clear the meaning and worth of the messianic work — this it did not seem to need — but rather to establish the Messiah-ship of Jesus. However, the Old Testament, as it was then understood, gave occasion, through the fixing of the person and dignity of Christ, for widening the scope of the thought of Israel's perfected theocracy. And, in addition, faith in the exaltation of Jesus to the right hand of God caused men to think of the beginning of his existence in harmony therewith. Then the fact of the successful Gentile conversion threw a new light upon the scope of his work, *i.e.* upon its significance for all mankind. And finally the personal claims of Jesus led men to reflect on his peculiar relation to God, the Father. On these four points speculation began already in the apostolic age and it went on to formulate new statements concerning the person and dignity of Christ. In proclaiming Jesus to be the Christ men ceased thereby to proclaim the gospel, because the keeping of all which Jesus had commanded was to be included as a matter of course and so did not especially engage the thoughts. That this must be for the future a questionable digression is plain enough; for since everything depends upon the appropriation of the person of Jesus, it is not possible for a personal life to be appropriated through *opinions* about the person, but only through the record of the *concrete personality*.

3. Upon the basis of the plain words of Jesus and in the consciousness of the possession of the Spirit men were already assured of a *present possession* of the forgiveness of sin, of righteousness before God, of the full knowledge of the divine will and of the call into the future kingdom. In the acquiring of these blessings, surely not a few realized the consequences of the first coming of the Messiah, *i.e.* his work, and they referred especially the forgiveness of sin to the death of Christ, and eternal life to his resurrection. But no theories touching the relation of the blessings of the gospel to the history of Christ were propounded; Paul was the first to develop a theology upon the basis of the death and resurrection of Christ and to bring it into relations with the Old Testament religion.

4. This theology was constructed in opposition to the legalistic righteousness of the pharisees, *i.e.*, to the official religion of the Old Testament. While its form was thereby somewhat conditioned, its power rested in the certainty of the new life of the Spirit, which the risen one offered, who through his death overcame the world of the flesh and of sin. With the thought that righteousness comes through faith in God who raised Jesus from the dead and fulfilled the Law by the legal way of the crucifixion of the Christ upon the cross, Paul wrenched the gospel from its native soil and gave it at the same time through his Christological speculation and his carrying out of the contrast of flesh and spirit, a characteristic stamp which was comprehensible to the Greeks, although they were ill prepared to accept his special manner of reconciling it with the Law. Through Paul, who was the first theologian, the question of the Law (in theory and practice) and the principles of missionary activity accordingly became the absorbing themes in the Christian communities. While he proclaimed freedom from the Law and baptized the heathen, forbidding them to become Jews, others now for the first time consciously made the righteousness of Christian believers dependent upon the punctilious observance of the Law and rejected Paul as an apostle and as a Christian. Yet the chief disciples of Jesus were convinced, perhaps not a little influenced by the success of Paul and conceded to the heathen the right to become Christians without first becoming Jews. This well attested fact is the strongest evidence that Christ had awakened among his personal disciples a faith in himself, which was dearer to them than all the traditions of the fathers. Yet there were among those who accepted the Pauline mission various

opinions as to the attitude which one should take toward heathen Christians in ordinary life and intercourse. These opinions held out for a long time.

As surely as Paul had fought his fight for the *whole* of Christendom, so sure also is it that the transformation of the original form of Christianity into its universal form took place *outside* of his activity (proof: the Church at Rome). The Judaism of the diaspora was long since surrounded by a retinue of half-bred Grecian brethren, for whom the particular and national forms of the Old Testament religion were hardly existent (see VII). And, farther, this Judaism itself had begun to transform for the Jews the old religion into a universal and spiritual religion without casting aside its forms, which were rather considered significant symbols (mysteries). The gospel, being received into these circles, completed simply and almost suddenly the process of spiritualizing the old religion, and it stripped off the old forms as shells, replacing them at once in part by new forms (*e.g.*, circumcision is circumcision of the heart, likewise also baptism; the sabbath is the glorious kingdom of Christ, etc.). The outward withdrawal from the synagogue is also here a clear proof of the power and self-consciousness of the new religion. The same developed itself rapidly in consequence of the hatred of the Jews, who adhered to the old faith. Paul exerted an influence, and the destruction of Jerusalem cleared up entirely the obscurities which still remained.

VI.   The Current Exposition of the Old Testament and the Jewish Future Hope, in their Bearing on the Earliest Formulation of the Christian Message

1. Although the method of the pedant, the casuistic handling of the Law and the extortion of the deepest meaning of the prophecies, had been in principle done away with by Jesus Christ, the old school-exegesis still remained active in the Christian churches, and especially the unhistorical local-method in the exposition of the Old Testament, as well as the allegoristic and the Haggada; for a sacred text — and as such the Old Testament was considered — ever invites men in the exposition of it to disregard its historical conditions and interpret it according to the needs of the time. Especially wherever the proofs of the fulfillment prophecy, *i.e.*, of the Messiah-ship of Jesus was concerned, the received point of view exercised its influence, as well upon the exposition of the Old Testament as upon the conception of the person, fate and deeds of Jesus. It gave, under the strong impression of the history

of Jesus, to many Old Testament passages a foreign sense and enriched, on the other hand, the life of Jesus with new facts, throwing the emphasis upon details which were often unreal and seldom of prime importance.

2. The Jewish apocalyptic literature, as it flourished after the time of Antiochus Epiphanes, was not forbidden within the circles of the first believers of the gospel, but rather was it retained and read as an explanation of the prophecies of Jesus and, as it were, cultivated. Although the content of the same appeared modified and the uncertainty regarding the person of the Messiah who was to appear in judgment was done away with, the earthly sensuous hopes were by no means wholly repressed. Confused pictures filled the fancy, threatened to obscure the plain and earnest description of the judgment which every individual soul is sure of, and drove many friends of the gospel into a restless turmoil and into a detestation of the state. Consequently the reproduction of the eschatological discourses of Jesus became indefinite; even things wholly foreign were mingled therewith, and the true aim of the Christian life and hope began to waver.

3. Through the apocalyptic literature, the artificial exegesis and the Haggada, a mass of mythological and poetical ideas crowded into the Christian communities and were legitimized. The most important for the succeeding times were the speculations in regard to the Messiah, which were drawn in part from the Old Testament and the apocalypses and in part were constructed in accordance with methods whose right no one questioned and whose adoption seemed to give security to the faith. Long since in the Jewish religion men had given to everything that is and that happens an existence within the knowledge of God, but they had in reality confined this representation to that only which is really important. The advancing religious thought had above all included individuals also, that is, the most prominent, within this speculation which should glorify God, and so a pre-existence was ascribed also to the Messiah, but of such a nature that by virtue of it *he abides with God during his earthly manifestation.* In opposition to this, the Hellenic ideas of pre-existence rooted themselves in the distinguishing of God and matter; spirit and flesh. According to the same the Spirit is pre-existent and visible nature is only a shell which it assumes. Here was the soil for ideas about the incarnation, the assumption of a second nature, etc. In the time of Christ these Hellenic ideas influenced the Jewish and thus both were so spread abroad that even the most prominent Christian teachers adopted them. The religious convictions (see V. 2), that (1) the estab-

lishment of the kingdom of God upon the earth and the sending of Jesus as the perfect mediator was from eternity the highest purpose in God's plan of salvation, that, (2) the glorified Christ has entered into his own proper position of God-like dominion, that, (3) in Jesus God has revealed himself, and that he therefore excels all Old Testament mediators, yes, the angel-powers themselves — these convictions were so *fixed* (not without the influence of Hellenic thought) that Jesus pre-existed, *i.e.* that in him a heavenly being of like rank with God, older than the world, yes even its creating principle, has appeared and assumed our flesh. The religious root of this speculation lay in sentences such as I. Pet. 1, 20; its forms of statement were varied even according to the intelligence of the teacher and his familiarity with the apocalyptic theology or with the Hellenic philosophy of religion, in which intermediate beings (above all the Logos) played a great rôle. Only the Fourth Evangelist — he hardly belongs to the 1st century — saw with perfect clearness that the pre-earthly Christ must be established as God being in the beginning with God, in order not to endanger the content and significance of the revelation of God in Christ. In addition there prevailed in wide circles such conceptions also as recognized in a spiritual communication at his baptism the equipment of the man Jesus (see the genealogies, the beginning of the Gospel of Mark) for his office, or found upon the basis of Isaiah 7 in his miraculous birth (from a virgin) the germ of his unique being. (The rise and spread of this representation is wholly indistinct to us; Paul seems not to have known it; in the beginning of the 2nd century it is almost universal.) On the other hand, it is of great significance that every teacher who recognized the *new* in Christianity as *religion* ascribed pre-existence to Christ.

Supplement — A reference to the witness of prophecy, to the current exposition of the Old Testament, to apocalyptic writings and valid methods of speculation was not sufficient to clear up every new point which cropped out in the statement of the Christian message. The earliest brotherhoods were enthusiastic, had prophets in the midst of them, etc. Under such conditions facts were produced outright continually in the history (*e.g.*, as particularly weighty, the ascension of Christ and his descent into hell). It is farther not possible to point out the motive to such productions, which first only by the creation of the New Testament canon reached a by no means complete end, *i.e.*, now became enriched by comprehensible mythologumena.

VII.   The Religious Conceptions and the Religious Philosophy of the Hellenistic Jews in their Bearing on the Transformation of the Gospel Message

1. From the remnants of Jewish-Alexandrian literature (reference is also made to the Sibylline oracles as well as to Josephus) and from the great propaganda of Judaism in the Græco-Roman world, it may be inferred that there was a Judaism in the diaspora to whose consciousness the cultus and the ceremonial law disappeared entirely behind the monotheistic worship of God without images, behind the moral instruction and the faith in a future reward beyond. Circumcision itself was no longer absolutely required of those converted to Judaism; one was also satisfied with the cleansing bath. The Jewish *religion* seemed here transformed into a common human *morality* and into a monotheistic *cosmology*. Accordingly the thought of the theocracy as well as the messianic hope grew dim. The latter did not entirely fail, however, but the prophecies were valued chiefly for the proof of the antiquity of the Jewish monotheism, and the thought of the future spent itself in the expectation of the destruction of the Roman empire, of the burning of the world and — what is weightiest — the *general judgment.* That which is specifically Jewish preserved itself under a high regard for the Old Testament, which was considered as the fountain of all wisdom (also for the Greek philosophy and the elements of truth in the non-Jewish religions). Many intelligent men also observed punctiliously the Law for the sake of its symbolical significance. Such Jews, together with their converts from the Greeks, formed a new Judaism upon the foundation of the old. And these prepared the soil for the christianizing of the Greeks, as well as for the establishment within the empire of a great Gentile Church free from the Law; under the influence of Greek culture it developed into a kind of universal society with a monotheistic background. As religion it laid aside the national forms, put itself forward as the most perfect form of that "natural" religion, which the Stoa had discovered. But in that way it became more *moralistic* and lost a part of the *religious* energy, which the prophets and psalmists possessed. The inner union of Judaism and the Hellenistic philosophy of religion indicates a great advance in the history of religion and culture, but the same did not lead to strong religious *creations.* Its productions passed over into "Christianity."

2. The Jewish-Alexandrian philosophy of religion had its most noted defender in Philo — the perfect Greek and the sincere Jew, who turned the religious philosophy of his time in the direction of Neo-Platonism and prepared the way for a Christian theology, which was able to rival

the philosophy. Philo was a Platonist and a Stoic, but at the same time a revelation-philosopher; he placed the final end in that which is above reason and therefore the highest power in the divine communication. On the other hand, he saw in the human *spirit* something divine and bridged over the contrast between *God* and creature-*spirit*, between nature and history, by means of the personal-impersonal *Logos*, out of which he explained religion and the world whose material, it is true, remained to him wholly perishable and evil. His ethical tendencies had, therefore, in principle a strong ascetic character, however much he might guard the earthly virtues as relative. Virtue is freedom from the sensuous and it is made perfect through the touch of divinity. This touch surpasses all knowledge; the latter, however, is to be highly prized as the *way*. Meditation upon the world is by Philo dependent upon the need of happiness and freedom, which is higher than all reason. One may say that Philo is therefore the first who, as a philosopher, gave to this need a clear expression, because he was not only a Greek, but also a Jew imbued with the Old Testament within whose view, it is true, the synthesis of the Messiah and of the Logos did not lie.

3. The practical fundamental conceptions of the Alexandrian philosophy of religion must, in different degrees, have found an entrance very early into the Jewish-Christian circles of the diaspora, and through the same also into the Gentile-Christian; or rather the soil was already prepared wherever these thoughts became widespread. After the beginning of the 2nd century the philosophy of Philo also became influential through Christian teachers, especially his *logos-doctrine*, as the expression of the unity of religion, nature and history; and *above all his fundamental hermeneutic principles*. The systems of Valentine and Origen presuppose the system of Philo. His fine dualism and allegorical art ("the Biblical alchemy") became acceptable also to the learned men of the Church; to find the *spiritual* meaning of the sacred text, in part alongside the letter and in part outside, was the watchword of scientific Christian theology, which in general was possible only upon such a basis, since it strove, without recognizing a *relative* standard, to unify the monstrous and discordant material of the Old Testament and the Gospel, and to reconcile both with the religion and scientific culture of the Greeks. Here Philo was a master, for he first in the largest sense poured the new wine into the old wine-skins — a procedure in its ultimate intention justified, since history is a unit; but in its pedantic and scholastic execution the same was a source of illusions, of unreality and finally of stultification.

*VIII.   The Religious Disposition of the Greeks and Romans in the First
Two Centuries and the Contemporary Græco-Roman Philosophy of Religion*

1. In the age of Cicero and Augustus the people's religion and the religious sense in general was almost entirely wanting in cultured circles, but after the end of the 1st century of our era a revival of the religious sense is noticeable in the Græco-Roman world, which affected all grades of society and seemed after the middle of the 2nd century to grow stronger from decennium to decennium. Parallel with it went the not fruitless attempt to restore the old national cults, religious usages, oracles, etc. Meanwhile the new religious needs of the time did not reach a vigorous or untroubled expression through this effort, which was made in part from above and in part by artificial means. The same sought, far more in accordance with the wholly changed conditions of the times, to find new forms of gratification (intermingling and intercourse of nations — downfall of the old republican constitutions, institutions and classes — monarchy and absolutism — social crises and pauperism — influence of philosophy, religion, morality and law — cosmopolitanism and human rights — influx of oriental cults — knowledge of the world and satiety). Under the influence of philosophy a disposition toward *monotheism* was developed out of the downfall of the political cults and the syncretism. Religion and *individual morality* became more closely united: *Spiritualization of the cults, ennobling of man, idea of ethical personality, of conscience and of purity. Repentance and pardon* became of importance, also inner union with the divinity, longing for *revelation (asceticism and mysterious rites as a means of appropriating the divine)*, yearning after a painless, eternal life beyond the grave (apotheosis); the earthly life as a phantom life (self-control and resurrection). Just as in the 2nd century the *moral* swing was the stronger, so in the 3rd century the religious increased more and more — thirst for *life*. Polytheism was not thereby overcome, but only shoved aside upon a lower plane, where it was as active as ever. The *numen supremum*, highest mystery, revealed its fulness in a thousand forms (demi-gods), going upward (apotheosis, emperor cult, "*dominus ac deus noster*", "our lord and God") and downward (manifestations in nature and in history). The soul itself is a super-earthly being; the ideal of the perfect man and of the leader (redeemer) was developed and sought after. The new remained in part concealed by the old cultus forms, which the state and piety protected or restored; there was a feeling-around after forms of expression, and yet the wise, the skeptic, the pious and the patriot capitulated to the cultish traditions.

2. The formation of social organizations, on the one hand, and the founding of the monarchical world-wide Roman empire, on the other, had the greatest significance as regards the development of something new. Everywhere there sprang up that cosmopolitan feeling, which points beyond itself, there toward the practice of charity, here toward the uniting of mankind under *one* head and the wiping out of national lines. The Church appropriated, *piece for piece*, the great apparatus of the earthly Roman empire; in its constitution, perhaps, it also saw the portrayal of the divine economy.

3. Perhaps the most decisive factor in the change of the religious-ethical attitude was the philosophy, which in almost all its schools had more and more brought ethics forward and deepened the same. Upon the soil of Stoicism, Posidonius, Seneca, Epictetus and Marcus Aurelius, and upon the soil of Platonism, men like Plutarch had achieved an ethical-outlook, which in its principles (knowledge, resignation, trust in God) was obscure, yet in some particulars scarcely admits of improvement. Common to them all is the great value put upon the *soul.* A religious bent, the desire for divine assistance, for redemption and for a life beyond, comes out distinctly in some of them; most clearly in the Neo-Platonists and those who anticipated them in the 2nd century (preparation by Philo). Characteristics of this mode of thought are the dualistic contrasting of the divine and the earthly, the abstract idea of God, the assertion of the unknowableness of God, skepticism in regard to sense-experience and distrust of the powers of reason; at the same time great readiness to investigate and to utilize the results of the previous scientific labors; and farther, the demand for freedom from the sensuous through asceticism, the want of an authority, belief in a higher revelation and the fusing of religion, science and mythology. Already men began to legitimize the religious *fantasie* within the realm of philosophy, by reaching back and seizing the myths as the vehicle of the deepest wisdom (romanticism). The theosophical philosophy which had thus equipped itself was from the standpoint of natural science and clear thinking in many ways a retrogression (yet not in all particulars, *e.g.* the Neo-Platonic psychology is far better than the Stoic); but it was an expression for the deeper religious needs and the better self-knowledge. The inner life with its desires was now altogether the starting-point for all thought concerning the world. Thoughts of the divine, gracious providence, of the kinship of all men, of the common fraternal love, of the ready and willing forgiveness of wrong, of the indulgent patience, of the insight into their own weaknesses were no

less the product of the practical philosophy of the Greeks for wide circles, than the conviction of the inherent sinfulness, of the need of redemption and of the value of a human soul which finds its rest only in God. But men possessed no sure *revelation*, no comprehensive and satisfactory *religious communion*, no vigorous and religious *genius* and no conception of *history*, which could take the place of the no longer valuable political history; men possessed no *certitude* and they did not get beyond the wavering between the fear of God and the deification of nature. *Yet with this philosophy, the highest the age had to offer, the gospel allied itself, and the stages of the ecclesiastical history of dogma during the first five centuries correspond to the stages of the Hellenistic philosophy of religion within the same period.* (*OHD*. 10-36)

*

WHAT IS CHRISTIANITY?

(Second Selection)

This selection from Harnack's "best-seller" describes "the gospel of Jesus," the message of Jesus' preaching. Harnack distinguished between the gospel of and the gospel about Jesus. This selection, being about the former, deals with what Harnack calls the original and essential aspect of the Christian religion. Materials from the second to the fifth lectures make up this selection and are taken from pp. 19-77.

Our first section deals with the main features of the message delivered by Jesus Christ. They include the form in which he delivered what he had to say. We shall see how essential a part of his character is here exhibited, for "he spoke as one having authority and not as the scribes."

Our authorities for the message which Jesus Christ delivered are — apart from certain important statements made by Paul — the first three gospels. Everything that we know, independently of these gospels, about Jesus' history and his teaching, may be easily put on a small sheet of paper, so little does it come to. In particular, the fourth gospel, which does not emanate or profess to emanate from the apostle John, cannot be taken as an historical authority in the ordinary meaning of the word. The author of it acted with sovereign freedom, transposed events and put them in a strange light, drew up the discourses himself, and illustrated great thoughts by imaginary situations. Although, therefore, his work is not altogether devoid of a real, if scarcely recognizable, traditional element, it can hardly make any claim to be considered an authority for Jesus' history; only little of what he says can be accepted, and that little with caution. On the other hand, it is an authority of the first rank for answering the question: What vivid views of Jesus' person, what kind of light and warmth, did the gospel disengage?

These gospels are not, it is true, historical works any more than the fourth; they were not written with the simple object of giving the facts as they were; they are books composed for the work of evangelization. Their purpose is to awaken a belief in Jesus Christ's person and mission; and the purpose is served by the description of his deeds and discourses, as well as by the references to the Old Testament. Nevertheless they are not altogether useless as sources of history, more especially as the object with which they were written is not supplied from without, but coincides in part with what Jesus intended. The gospels are not "party tracts"; neither are they writings which as yet bear the radical impress of the Greek spirit. In their essential substance they belong to the first, the Jewish, epoch of Christianity, that brief epoch which may be denoted as the palæontological. That we possess any reports dating from that time, even though, as is obvious in the first and third gospel, the setting and the composition are by another hand, is one of those historical arrangements for which we cannot be too thankful. Criticism today universally recognizes the unique character of the gospels. What especially marks them off from all subsequent literature is the way in which they state their facts. This species of literary art, which took shape partly by analogy with the didactic narratives of the Jews, and partly from catechetical necessities — this simple and impressive form of exposition was, even a few decades later, no longer capable of exact reproduction. From the time that the gospel was transferred to the broad ground of the Græco-Roman world it appropriated the literary forms of the Greeks, and the style of the evangelists was then felt to be something strange but sublime. When all is said, the Greek language lies upon these writings only like a diaphanous veil, and it requires hardly any effort to retranslate their contents into Hebrew or Aramaic. That the tradition here presented to us is, in the main, at first hand is obvious.

How fixed this tradition was in regard to its form is proved by the third gospel. It was composed by a Greek, probably in the time of Domitian; and in the second part of his work, the Acts of the Apostles — besides the preface to the first — he shows us that he was familiar with the literary language of his nation and that he was an excellent master of style. But in the gospel narrative he did not dare to abandon the traditional type: he tells his story in the same style as Mark and Matthew, with the same connexion of sentences, the same color, nay, with many of precisely the same details; it is only the ruder words and expressions, which would offend literary taste, that are sparingly corrected. There is another respect, too, in which his gospel strikes us as remarkable: he assures us at the beginning of it that he has "had perfect understanding of all things from the very first," and has examined many accounts. But if we test him by his authorities, we find that he has kept in the main to Mark's gospel, and to a source which we also find appearing again in Matthew. These accounts both seemed to him, as a respectable chronicler, to be preferable to the crowd of others. That offers a good guarantee for them. No historian has found that it is possible or necessary to substitute any other tradition for the one which we have here.   (C: 19-22)

*

But the miraculous element, all these reports of miracles! Many have allowed themselves to be frightened by them into roundly denying the credibility of the gospels. But, on the other hand, historical science in this last generation has taken a great step in advance by learning to pass a more intelligent and benevolent judgment on those narratives, and accordingly even reports of the marvellous can now be counted amongst the materials of history and turned to good account. I owe it to you and to the subject briefly to specify the position which historical science today takes up in regard to these reports.

In the first place, we know that the gospels come from a time in which the marvellous may be said to have been something of almost daily occurrence. People felt and saw that they were surrounded by wonders, and not by any means only in the religious sphere. Certain spiritualists among us excepted, we are now accustomed to associate the question of miracles exclusively with the question of religion. In those days it was otherwise. The fountains of the marvellous were many. Some sort of divinity was, of course, supposed to be at work in every case; it was a god who accomplished the miracle; but it was not to every god that people stood in a religious relation. Further, in those days, the strict conception which we now attach to the word "miracle" was as yet unknown; it came in only with a knowledge of the laws of nature and their general validity. Before that, no sound insight existed into what was possible and what was impossible, what was rule and what was exception. But where this distinction is not clear, or where, as the case may be, the question has not yet been raised at all in any rigorous form, there are no such things as miracles in the strict sense of the word. No one can feel anything to be an interruption of the order of nature who does not yet know what the order of nature is. Miracles, then, could not possess the significance for that age which, if they existed, they would possess for ours. For that age all wonders were only extraordinary events, and, even if they formed a world by themselves, it was certain that there were countless points in which that other world mysteriously encroached upon our own. Nor was it only God's messengers, but magicians and charlatans as well, who were thought to be possessed of some of these miraculous powers. The significance attaching to "miracles" was, therefore, in those days a subject of never-ending controversy; at one moment a high value was set upon them and they were considered to belong to the very essence of religion; at another, they were spoken of with contempt.

In the second place, we now know that it is not after they have been long dead, nor even after the lapse of many years, that miracles have been reported of eminent persons, but at once, often the very next day. The habit of condemning a narrative, or of ascribing it to a later age, only because it includes stories of miracles, is a piece of prejudice.

In the third place, we are firmly convinced that what happens in space and time is subject to the general laws of motion, and that in this sense, as an interruption of the order of nature, there can be no such things as "miracles." But we also recognize that the religious man — if religion really permeates him and is something more than a belief in the religion of others — is certain that he is not shut up within a blind and brutal course of nature, but that this course of nature serves higher ends, or, as it may be, that some inner and divine power can help us so to encounter it as that "everything must necessarily be for the best." This experience, which I might express in one word as the ability to escape from the power and the service of transitory things, is always felt afresh to be a miracle each time that it occurs; it is inseparable from every higher religion, and were it to be surrendered, religion would be at an end. But it is an experience which is equally true of the life of the individual and of the great course of human history. How clearly and logically, then, must a religious man think, if, in spite of this experience, he holds firmly to the inviolable character of what happens in space and time. Who can wonder that even great minds fail to keep the two spheres quite separate? And as we all live, first and foremost, in the domain not of ideas but of perceptions, and in a language of metaphor, how can we avoid conceiving that which is divine and makes us free as a mighty power working upon the order of nature, and breaking through or arresting it? This notion, though it belong only to the realm of fantasy and metaphor, will, it seems, last as long as religion itself.

In the fourth place, and lastly, although the order of nature be inviolable, we are not yet by any means acquainted with all the forces working in it and acting reciprocally with other forces. Our acquaintance even with the forces inherent in matter, and with the field of their action, is incomplete; while of psychic forces we know very much less. We see that a strong will and a firm faith exert an influence upon the life of the body, and produce phenomena which strike us as marvellous. Who is there up to now that has set any sure bounds to the province of the possible and the actual? No one. Who can say how far the influence of soul upon soul and of soul upon body reaches? No one. Who can still maintain that any extraordinary phenomenon that may appear in this domain is entirely based on error and delusion? Miracles, it is true, do not happen; but of the marvellous and the inexplicable there is plenty. In our present state of knowledge we have become more careful, more hesitating in our judgment, in regard to the stories of the miraculous which we have received from antiquity. That the earth in its course stood still; that a she-ass spoke; that a storm was quieted by a word, we do not believe, and we shall never again believe; but that the lame walked, the blind saw, and the deaf heard, will not be so summarily dismissed as an illusion.

From these suggestions you can arrive for yourselves at the right position to take up in regard to the miraculous stories related in the gospels, and at their net results. In particular cases, that is to say, in the application of general principles to concrete statements, some uncertainty will always remain. So far as I can judge, the stories may be grouped as follows — (1) Stories which had their origin in an exaggerated view of natural events of an impressive character; (2) stories which had their origin in sayings or parables, or in the projection of inner experiences on to the external world; (3) stories such as arose in the interests of the fulfillment of Old Testament sayings; (4) stories of surprising cures effected by Jesus' spiritual force; (5) stories of which we cannot fathom the secret. It is very remarkable, however, that Jesus himself did not assign that critical importance to his miraculous deeds which even the evangelist Mark and the others all attributed to them. Did he not exclaim, in tones of complaint and accusation, "Unless ye see signs and wonders, ye will not believe"? He who uttered these words cannot have held that belief in the wonders which he wrought was the right or the only avenue to the recognition of his person and his mission; nay, in all essential points he must have thought of them quite otherwise than his evangelists. And the remarkable fact that these very evangelists, without appreciating its range, hand down the statement that Jesus "did not many mighty works there because of their unbelief," shows us, from another and a different side, with what caution we must receive these miraculous stories, and into what category we must put them.

It follows from all this that we must not try to evade the gospel by entrenching ourselves behind the miraculous stories related by the evangelists. In spite of those stories, nay, in part even in them, we are presented with a reality which has claims upon our participation. Study it, and do not let yourselves be deterred because this or that miraculous story strikes you as strange or leaves you cold. If there is anything here that you find unintelligible, put it quietly aside. Perhaps you will have to leave it there for ever; perhaps the meaning will dawn upon you later and the story assume a significance of which you never dreamt. Once more, let me say: do not be deterred. The question of miracles is of relative indifference in comparison with everything else which is to be found in the gospels. It is not miracles that matter; the question on which everything turns is whether we are helplessly yoked to an inexorable necessity, or whether a God exists who rules and governs, and whose power to compel nature we can move by prayer and make a part of our experience. (C. 24-30)

*

Jesus lived in religion, and it was breath to him in the fear of God; his whole life, all his thoughts and feelings, were absorbed in the relation to God, and yet he did not talk like an enthusiast and a fanatic, who sees only one red-hot spot, and so is blind to the world and all that it contains. He spoke his message and looked at the world with a fresh and clear eye for the life, great and small, that surrounded him. He proclaimed that to gain the whole world was nothing if the soul were injured, and yet he remained kind and sympathetic to every living thing. That is the most astonishing and the greatest fact about him! His discourses, generally in the form of parables and sayings, exhibit every degree of human speech and the whole range of the emotions. The sternest tones of passionate accusation and indignant reproof, nay, even irony, he does not despise; but they must have formed the exception

131

with him. He is possessed of a quiet, uniform, collected demeanor, with everything directed to one goal. He never uses any ecstatic language, and the tone of stirring prophecy is rare. Entrusted with the greatest of all missions, his eye and ear are open to every impression of the life around him — a proof of intense calm and absolute certainty. . . .

His eye rests kindly upon the flowers and the children, on the lily of the field — "Solomon in all his glory is not clothed like one of them" — on the birds in the air and the sparrows on the house-top. The sphere in which he lived, above the earth and its concerns, did not destroy his interest in it; no! he brought everything in it into relation with the God whom he knew, and he saw it as protected in him: "Your Father in heaven feeds them." The parable is his most familiar form of speech. Insensibly, however, parable and sympathy pass into each other. Yet he who had not where to lay his head does not speak like one who has broken with everything, or like an heroic penitent, or like an ecstatic prophet, but like a man who has rest and peace for his soul, and is able to give life and strength to others. He strikes the mightiest notes; he offers men an inexorable alternative; he leaves them no escape; and yet the strongest emotion seems to come naturally to him, and he expresses it as something natural; he clothes it in the language in which a mother speaks to her child. (C: 34-37)

*

When he came forward, another was already at work among the Jewish people: John the Baptist. Within a few months a great movement had arisen on the banks of the Jordan. It differed altogether from those messianic movements which for several generations had by fits and starts kept the nation alive. The Baptist, it is true, also proclaimed that the kingdom of God was at hand; and that meant nothing less than that the day of the Lord, the judgment, the end, was then coming. But the day of judgment which John the Baptist announced was not the day when God was going to take vengeance upon the heathen and raise up his own people; it was the day of judgment for this very people that he prophesied. . . .

Questions force themselves upon us at this point which have often been answered and still are again and again put. It is clear that John the Baptist proclaimed the sovereignty of God and his holy moral law. It is also clear that he proclaimed to his fellow-countrymen that it was by the moral law that they were to measure, and that on this alone everything was to turn. He told them that what they were to care about most was to be in a right state within and to do good deeds. It is clear, lastly, that there is nothing over-refined or artificial in his notion of what was good; he means ordinary morality. It is here that the questions arise.

Firstly: if it was only so simple a matter as the eternal claims of what is right and holy, why all this apparatus about the coming of the day of judgment, about the axe being laid to the root of the trees, about the unquenchable fire, and so on?

Secondly: is not this baptism in the wilderness and this proclamation that the day of judgment was at hand simply the reflection or the product of the political and social state of the nation at the time?

Thirdly: what is there that is really new in this proclamation and had not been already expressed in Judaism?

These three questions are very intimately connected with one another.

Firstly, then, as to the whole dramatic eschatological apparatus about the coming of the kingdom of God, the end being at hand, and so on. Well, every time that a man earnestly, and out of the depths of his own personal experience, points others to God and to what is good and holy, whether it be deliverance or judgment that he preaches, it has always, so far as history tells us, taken the form of announcing that the end is at hand. How is that to be explained? The answer is not difficult. Not only is religion a life in and with God; but, just because it is that, it is also the revelation of the meaning and responsibility of life. Every one who has awakened to a sense of religion perceives that, without it, the search for such meaning is in vain, and that the individual, as well as the multitude, wanders aimlessly and falls: "they go astray; every one turns to his own way." But the prophet who has become conscious of God is filled with terror and agony as he recognizes that all mankind is sunk in error and indifference. . . .

The prophet's gaze penetrates the course of history; he sees the irrevocable end; and he is filled with boundless astonishment that the godlessness and blindness, the frivolity and indolence, have not long since brought everything to utter ruin and destruction. That there is still a brief moment left in which conversion is possible seems to him the greatest marvel of all, and to be ascribed only to God's forbearance. But certain it is that the end cannot be very far off. This is the way in which with every great cry for repentance the idea of the approaching end always arises. The individual forms in which it shapes itself depend upon contemporary circumstances and are of subordinate importance. It is only the religion which has been built up into an intellectual system that does not make this emphasizing of the end all-important; without such emphasis no actual religion is conceivable, whether it springs up anew like a sudden flame or glows in the soul like a secret fire.

I pass now to the second question: whether the social and political conditions of the time were not causes of the religious movement. You are aware that at the time of which we speak the peaceful days of the Jewish theocracy were long past. For two centuries blow had followed upon blow. . . . So far as human foresight went, it looked as if no improvement in its position could ever again be effected; the lie seemed to be given to all the glorious old prophecies; the end appeared to have come. How easy it was at such an epoch to despair of all earthly things, and in this despair to renounce in utter distress what had once passed as the inseparable accompaniment of the theocracy. How easy it was now to declare the earthly crown, political possessions, prestige and wealth, strenuous effort and struggle, to be one and all worthless, and in place of them to look to heaven for a completely new kingdom, a kingdom for the poor, the oppressed, the weak, and to hope that their virtues of gentleness and patience would receive a crown. And if for hundreds of years the national God of Israel had been undergoing a transformation; if he had broken in pieces the weapons of the mighty, and derided the showy worship of his priests; if he had demanded righteous judgment and mercy — what a temptation there was to proclaim him as the God who wills to see his people in misery that he may then bring them deliverance! We can, in fact, with a few touches construct the religion and its hopes which seemed of necessity to result from the circumstances of the time — a miserabilism which clings to the expectation of a miraculous interference on God's part, and in the meantime, as it were, wallows in wretchedness.

But although the terrible circumstances of the time certainly disengaged and developed many ideas of this kind, and easily account for the wild enterprises of the false Messiahs and the political efforts of fanatical pharisees, they are very far from being sufficient to explain John the Baptist's message. They do, indeed, explain how it was that deliverance from earthly things was an idea which seized hold of wide circles, and that people were looking to God. Trouble makes men pray. But trouble in itself does not give any moral force, and moral force was the chief element in John the Baptist's message. In appealing to it, in proclaiming that everything must be based on morality and personal responsibility, he took a higher point of view than the feeble piety of the "poor," and

134

drew not from time but from eternity. . . .

John the Baptist's message, and — let me say it at once — the message which Jesus himself delivered appealed to those who expected nothing of the world or of politics. . . . Whence came the power, the inflexible power, which compelled others? This leads us to the last of the questions which we have raised.

Thirdly, what was there that was new in the whole movement? Was it anything new to set up the sovereignty of God, the sovereignty of the good and the holy, in opposition to all the other elements which had forced their way into religion? Did John the Baptist, did Christ himself, bring in anything that had not been proclaimed long before? Gentlemen, the question as to what is new in religion is not a question which is raised by those who live in it. What is there that can have been "new," seeing that mankind existed so long before Jesus Christ and had seen so much in the way of intelligence and knowledge? Monotheism had long been introduced, and the few possible types of monotheistic religious fervor had long made their appearance here and there, and had taken possession of whole schools, nay, of a whole nation. Can the religious individualism of that psalmist ever be surpassed in depth and vigor who confessed: "Lord, when I have thee, I ask not after heaven and earth"? Can we go beyond what Micah said: "He hath showed thee, O man, what is good; and what doth the Lord require of thee but to do justly and to love mercy, and to walk humbly with thy God"? Centuries have passed since these words were spoken. "What do you want with your Christ," we are asked, principally by Jewish scholars; "he introduced nothing new." I answer with Wellhausen: It is quite true that what Jesus proclaimed, what John the Baptist expressed before him in his exhortations to repentance, was also to be found in the prophets, and even in the Jewish tradition of their time. The pharisees themselves were in possession of it; but unfortunately they were in possession of much else besides. With them it was weighted, darkened, distorted, rendered ineffective and deprived of its force, by a thousand things which they also held to be religious and every whit as important as mercy and judgment. They reduced everything to one dead level, wove everything into one fabric; the good and holy was only one woof in a broad earthly warp. You ask again, then: "What was there that was new"? The question is out of place in monotheistic religion. Ask rather: "Had what was here proclaimed any strength and any vigor"? I answer: Take the people of Israel and search the whole history of their religion; take history generally, and where will you find any message about God and the good that was ever

135

so pure and so full of strength — for purity and strength go together — as we hear and read of in the gospels? As regards purity, the spring of holiness had, indeed, long been opened; but it was choked with sand and dirt, and its water was polluted. For rabbis and theologians to come afterwards and distill this water, even if they were successful, makes no difference. But now the spring burst forth afresh, and broke a new way for itself through the rubbish — through the rubbish which priests and theologians had heaped up so as to smother the true element in religion; for how often does it happen in history that theology is only the instrument by which religion is discarded! The other element was that of strength. Pharisaical teachers had proclaimed that everything was contained in the injunction to love God and one's neighbor. They spoke excellently; the words might have come out of Jesus' mouth But what was the result of their language? That the nation, that in particular their own pupils, condemned the man who took the words seriously. All that they did was weak and, because weak, harmful. Words effect nothing; it is the power of the personality that stands behind them. But he "taught as one having authority and not as the scribes." Such was the impression of him which his disciples received. His words became to them "the words of life," seeds which sprang up and bore fruit. That was what was new. . . .

When he appeared, he, too, it is true, like John proclaimed: "Repent, for the kingdom of God is at hand"; but his message became one of joy as he delivered it. The traditions about him contain nothing more certain than that his message was an "evangel," and that it was felt to bring blessing and joy. With good reason, therefore, the evangelist Luke began his narrative of Jesus' public appearance with the words of the prophet Isaiah: "*The Spirit of the Lord is upon me, because he hath anointed me to preach the gospel to the poor; he hath sent me to heal the broken-hearted, to preach deliverance to the captives and recovering of sight to the blind, to set at liberty them that are bruised, to preach the acceptable year of the Lord.*" Or in Jesus' own words: "*Come unto me all ye that labor and are heavy laden and I will give you rest. Take my yoke upon you, and learn of me; for I am meek and lowly of heart; and ye shall find rest unto your souls. For my yoke is easy and my burden is light.*" These words dominated Jesus' whole work and message; they contain the theme of all that he taught and did. They make it at once obvious that in this teaching of his he left John the Baptist's message far behind. The latter, although already in silent conflict with the priests and the scribes, did not become a definite signal for contradiction. "The falling and the rising again," a new humanity opposed to the old, the God-man — Jesus

Christ — was the first to create. He came into immediate opposition with the official leaders of the people, and in them with ordinary human nature in general. They thought of God as of a despot guarding the ceremonial observances in his household; he breathed in the presence of God. They saw him only in his law, which they had converted into a labyrinth of dark defiles, blind alleys and secret passages; he saw and felt him everywhere. They were in possession of a thousand of his commandments, and thought, therefore, that they knew him; he had one only, and knew him by it. They had made this religion into an earthly trade, and there was nothing more detestable; he proclaimed the living God and the soul's nobility.

If, however, we take a general view of Jesus' teaching, we shall see that it may be grouped under three heads. They are each of such a nature as to contain the whole, and hence it can be exhibited in its entirety under any one of them.

Firstly, the kingdom of God and its coming.

Secondly, God the Father and the infinite value of the human soul.

Thirdly, the higher righteousness and the commandment of love.

That Jesus' message is so great and so powerful lies in the fact that it is so simple and on the other hand so rich; so simple as to be exhausted in each of the leading thoughts which he uttered; so rich that every one of these thoughts seems to be inexhaustible and the full meaning of the sayings and parables beyond our reach. But more than that — he himself stands behind everything that he said. His words speak to us across the centuries with the freshness of the present. It is here that that profound saying is truly verified: "Speak, that I may see thee." (C: 39-51)

*

I. THE KINGDOM OF GOD AND ITS COMING

. . . Jesus, like all those of his own nation who were really in earnest, was profoundly conscious of the great antithesis between the kingdom of God and that kingdom of the world in which he saw the reign of evil and the evil one. This was no mere image or empty idea; it was a truth which he saw and felt most vividly. He was certain, then, that the kingdom of the world must perish and be destroyed. But nothing short of a battle can effect it. With dramatic intensity battle and victory stand like a picture before his soul, drawn in those large firm lines in which the prophets had seen them. At the close of the drama he sees himself seated at the right hand of his Father, and his twelve disciples on thrones judging the twelve tribes of Israel; so objective was this picture to him, so completely in harmony with the ideas of his time. Now we may take the view — and not a few of us take it — that in these dramatic pictures, with their hard colors and contrasts, we have the actual purport of Jesus' message and the fundamental form which it took; and that all his other statements of it must be simply regarded as secondary. We may say that they are all variations of it more or less edifying, variations which were added, perhaps, only by later reporters; but that the only positive factor is the dramatic hope for the future. In this view I cannot concur. It is considered a perverse procedure in similar cases to judge eminent, epoch-making personalities first and foremost by what they share with their contemporaries, and on the other hand to put what is great and characteristic in them into the background. The tendency as far as possible to reduce everything to one level, and to efface what is special and individual, may spring in some minds from a praiseworthy sense of truth, but it has proved misleading. More frequently, however, we get the endeavor, conscious or unconscious, to refuse greatness any recognition at all, and to throw down anything that is exalted. There can be no doubt about the fact that the idea of the two kingdoms, of God and of the devil, and their conflicts, and of that last conflict at some future time when the devil, long since cast out of heaven, will be also defeated on earth, was an idea which Jesus simply shared with his contemporaries. He did not start it, but he grew up in it and he retained it. The other view, however, that the kingdom of God "cometh not with observation," that it is already here, was his own.

For us, gentlemen, today, it is difficult to reconcile, nay, it is scarcely possible to bridge over, such an opposition as is involved, on the one side in a dramatic picture of God's kingdom existing in the future, and on the other in the announcement that "it is in the midst of you," a still and mighty power in the hearts of men. But to understand why it was that with other historical traditions and other forms of culture no opposition was felt to exist between these views, nay, that both were able to exist side by side, we must reflect, we must steep ourselves in the history of the past. . . .

Truly the historian's task of distinguishing between what is traditional and what is peculiar, between kernel and husk, in Jesus' message of the kingdom of God is a difficult and responsible one. How far may we go? We do not want to rob this message of its innate character and color, we do not want to change it into a pale scheme of ethics. On the other hand, we do not want to lose sight of its peculiar character and strength, as we should do were we to side with those who resolve it into the general ideas prevailing at the time. The very way in which Jesus distinguished between the traditional elements — he left out none in which there was a spark of moral force, and he accepted none which encouraged the selfish expectations of his nation — this very discrimination teaches us that it was from a deeper knowledge that he spoke and taught. But we possess testimonies of a much more striking kind. If anyone wants to know what the kingdom of God and the coming of it meant in Jesus' message, he must read and study his parables. He will then see what it is that is meant. The kingdom of God comes by coming to the individual, by entering into his soul and laying hold of it. True, the kingdom of God is the rule of God; but it is the rule of the holy God in the hearts of individuals; *it is God himself in his power.* From this point of view everything that is dramatic in the external and historical sense has vanished; and gone, too, are all the external hopes for the future. Take whatever parable you will, the parable of the sower, of the pearl of great price, of the treasure buried in the field — the word of God, God himself, is the kingdom. It is not a question of angels and devils, thrones and principalities, but of God and the soul, the soul and its God. (C: 53-56)

*

When John the Baptist in prison was disturbed by doubts as to whether Jesus was "he who was to come," he sent two of his own disciples to him to ask him himself. There is nothing more touching than this question of the Baptist's, nothing more edifying than the Lord's answer. But we will not dwell upon the scene. What was the answer? "Go and shew John again those things which you do hear and see: the blind receive their sight, and the lame walk, the lepers are cleansed, and the deaf hear, the dead are raised up, and the poor have the gospel preached to them." That is what the "coming of the kingdom" means, or, rather, it is there already in this saving activity. By vanquishing and banishing misery, need and disease, by the actual influence which Jesus was exerting, John was to see that a new day had dawned. The healing of the possessed was only a part of this saving activity; the activity itself, however, was what Jesus denoted as the meaning and the seal of his mission. It was, then, to the wretched, to the sick, and to the poor, that he addressed himself; but not as a moralist and without any trace of weak-minded sentimentality. He makes no division of evils into departments and groups; he spends no time in asking whether the sick one "deserves" to be healed; he is far, too, from having any sympathy for pain and death. He nowhere says that disease is salutary and that evil is a blessing. No! disease he calls disease, and health he calls health. To him all evil, all misery, is something terrible; it is part of the great realm of Satan. But he feels the power of the Savior within him. He knows that progress is possible only by overcoming weakness and healing disease.

But he goes further. It is by his healing, above all by his forgiving sin, that the kingdom of God comes. This is the first complete transition to the conception of the kingdom of God as the power that works inwardly. As he calls the sick and the poor to him, so he calls sinners also, and it is this call which is all-important. "The Son of Man is come to seek and to save that which was lost." Here for the first time everything that is external and merely future is abandoned: it is the individual, not the nation or the state, which is redeemed; it is new men who are to arise, and the kingdom of God is to be at once their strength and the goal at which they aim. They search for the treasure hidden in the field and find it; they sell all that they have and buy the pearl of great price; they are converted and become as children; but thereby they are redeemed and made God's children and God's champions. . . .

At a later period the view of the kingdom, according to which it was already come and still comes in Jesus' saving activity, was not kept up by his disciples: nay, they continued to speak of it as of something that was solely in the future. But the thing itself retained its force; it was only given another title. It underwent the same experience as the conception of the "Messiah." As we shall see hereafter, there was scarcely anyone in the Church of the Gentiles who sought to explain Jesus' significance by regarding him as the "Messiah." But the thing itself did not perish.

The essential elements in the message of the kingdom were preserved. The kingdom has a triple meaning. Firstly, it is something supernatural, a gift from above, not a product of ordinary life. Secondly, it is a purely religious blessing, the inner link with the living God; thirdly, it is the most important experience that a man can have, that on which everything else depends; it permeates and dominates his whole existence, because sin is forgiven and misery banished.

This kingdom, which comes to the humble and makes them new men and joyful, is the key that first unlocks the meaning and the aim of life. This was what Jesus himself found, and what his disciples found. It is a supernatural element alone that ever enables us to get at the meaning of life; for natural existence ends in death. But a life that is bound up with death can have no meaning; it is only sophisms that can blind us to this fact. But here the kingdom of God, the Eternal, entered into time. "Eternal light came in and made the world look new." This is Jesus' message of the kingdom. Everything else that he proclaimed can be brought into connexion with this; his whole "doctrine" can be conceived as a message of the kingdom.

II. GOD THE FATHER AND THE INFINITE VALUE OF THE HUMAN SOUL

To our modern way of thinking and feeling, Christ's message appears in the clearest and most direct light when grasped in connexion with the idea of God the Father and the infinite value of the human soul. Here the elements which I would describe as the restful and restgiving in Jesus' message, and which are comprehended in the idea of our being children of God, find expression. I call them *restful* in contrast with the impulsive and stirring elements; although it is just they that are informed with a special strength. But the fact that the whole of Jesus' message may be reduced to these two heads — God as the Father, and the human soul so ennobled that it can and does unite with him — shows us that the gospel is in nowise a positive religion like the rest; that it contains no statutory or particularistic elements; *that it is, therefore, religion itself.* It is superior to all antithesis and tension between this world and a world to come, between reason and ecstacy, between work and isolation from the world, between Judaism and Hellenism. It can dominate them all, and there is no factor of earthly life to which it is confined or necessarily tied down. Let us, however, get a clearer idea of what being children of God, in Jesus' sense, means, by briefly considering the Lord's Prayer. . . .

It was communicated by Jesus to his disciples at a particularly solemn moment. They had asked him to teach them how to pray, as John the Baptist had taught his disciples. Thereupon he uttered the Lord's Prayer. It is by their prayers that the character of the higher religions is determined. But this prayer was spoken — as every one must feel who has ever given it a thought in his soul — by one who has overcome all inner unrest, or overcomes it the moment that he goes before God. The very apostrophe of the prayer, "Our Father," exhibits the steady faith of the man who knows that he is safe in God, and it tells us that he is certain of being heard. Not to hurl violent desires at heaven or to obtain this or that earthly blessing does he pray, but to preserve the power which he already possesses and strengthen the union with God in which he lives. No one, then, can utter this prayer unless his heart is in profound peace and his mind wholly concentrated on the inner relation of the soul with God. All other prayers are of a lower order, for they contain particularistic elements, or are so framed that in some way or other they stir the imagination in regard to the things of sense as well; whilst this prayer leads us away from everything to the height where the soul is alone with its God. And yet the earthly element is not absent. The whole of the second half of the prayer deals with earthly relations, but they are placed in the light of the eternal. In vain will you look for any request for particular gifts of grace, or special blessings, even of a spiritual kind. "All else shall be added unto you." The name of God, his will, and his kingdom — these elements of rest and permanence are poured out over the earthly relations as well. Everything that is small and selfish melts away, and only four things are left with regard to which it is worth while to pray — the daily bread, the daily trespass, the daily temptations, and the evil in life. There is nothing in the gospels that tells us more certainly what the gospel is, and what sort of disposition and temper it produces, than the Lord's Prayer. With this prayer we ought also to confront all those who disparage the gospel by representing it as an ascetic or ecstatic or sociological pronouncement. It shows the gospel to be the fatherhood of God applied to the whole of life; to be an inner union with God's will and God's kingdom, and a joyous certainty of the possession of eternal blessings and protection from evil.   (C: 59-65)

*

This highest estimate of a man's value is based on a transvaluation of all values. To the man who boasts of his possessions he says: "Thou fool." He confronts everyone with the thought: "Whosoever will lose his life shall save it." He can even say: "He that hateth his life in this world shall keep it unto life eternal." This is the transvaluation of values of which many before him had a dim idea; of which they perceived the truth as through a veil; the redeeming power of which — that blessed mystery — they felt in advance. He was the first to give it calm, simple, and fearless expression, as though it were a truth which grew on every tree. It was just this that stamped his peculiar genius, that he gave perfectly simple expression to profound and all-important truths, as though they could not be otherwise; as though he were uttering something that was self-evident; as though he were only reminding men of what they all know already, because it lives in the innermost part of their souls.

In the combination of these ideas — God the Father, providence, the position of men as God's children, the infinite value of the human soul — the whole gospel is expressed. But we must recognize what a paradox it all is; nay, that the paradox of religion here for the first time finds its full expression. . . . Religion gives us only a single experience, but one which presents the world in a new light: the eternal appears; time becomes means to an end; man is seen to be on the side of the eternal. This was certainly Jesus' meaning, and to take anything from it is to destroy it. In applying the idea of providence to the whole of humanity and the world without any exception; in showing that humanity is rooted in the eternal; in proclaiming the fact that we are God's children as at once a gift and a task, he took a firm grip of all fumbling and stammering attempts at religion and brought them to their issue. Once more let it be said: we may assume what position we will in regard to him and his message, certain it is that thence onward the value of our race is enhanced; human lives, nay, we ourselves, have become dearer to one another. A man may know it or not, but a real reverence for humanity follows from the practical recognition of God as the Father of us all.

III. THE HIGHER RIGHTEOUSNESS AND THE COMMANDMENT OF LOVE

This is the third head, and the whole of the gospel is embraced under it. To represent the gospel as an ethical message is no depreciation of its value. The ethical system which Jesus found prevailing in his nation was both ample and profound. To judge the moral ideas of the pharisees solely by their childish and casuistical aspects is not fair. By being bound up with religious worship and petrified in ritual observance, the morality of holiness had, indeed, been transformed into something that was the clean opposite of it. But all was not yet hard and dead; there was some life still left in the deeper parts of the system. To those who questioned him Jesus could still answer: "You have the law, keep it; you know best yourselves what you have to do; the sum of the law is, as you yourselves say, to love God and your neighbor." Nevertheless, there is a sphere of ethical thought which is peculiarly expressive of Jesus' gospel. Let us make this clear by citing four points.

Firstly: Jesus severed the connexion existing in his day between ethics and the external forms of religious worship and technical observance. He would have absolutely nothing to do with the purposeful and self-seeking pursuit of "good works" in combination with the ritual of worship. He exhibited an indignant contempt for those who allow their neighbors, nay, even their parents, to starve, and on the other hand send gifts to the temple. He will have no compromise in the matter. Love and mercy are ends in themselves; they lose all value and are put to shame by having to be anything else than the service of one's neighbor.

Secondly: in all questions of morality he goes straight to the root, that is, to the disposition and the intention. It is only thus that what he calls the "higher righteousness" can be understood. The "higher righteousness" is the righteousness that will stand when the depths of the heart are probed. Here, again, we have something that is seemingly very simple and self-evident. Yet the truth, as he uttered it, took the severe form: "It was said of old ... but I say unto you." After all, then, the truth was something new; he was aware that it had never yet been expressed in such a consistent form and with such claims to supremacy. A large portion of the so-called Sermon on the Mount is occupied with what he says when he goes in detail through the several departments of human relationships and human failings so as to bring the disposition and intention to light in each case, to judge a man's works by them, and on them to hang heaven and hell.

Thirdly: what he freed from its connexion with self-seeking and ritual elements, and recognized as the moral principle, he reduces to *one* root and to *one* motive — love. He knows of no other, and love itself, whether it takes the form of love of one's neighbor or of one's enemy, or the love of the Samaritan, is of one kind only. It must completely fill the soul; it is what remains when the soul dies to itself. In this sense love is the new life already begun. But it is always the love which *serves*, and only in this function does it exist and live.

Fourthly: we saw that Jesus freed the moral element from all alien connexions, even from its alliance with the public religion. Therefore to say that the gospel is a matter of ordinary morality is not to misunderstand him. And yet there is one all-important point where he combines religion and morality. It is a point which must be felt; it is not easy to define. In view of the Beatitudes it may, perhaps, best be described as *humility*. Jesus made love and humility one. Humility is not a virtue by itself; but it is pure receptivity, the expression of inner need, the prayer for God's grace and forgiveness, in a word, the opening up of the heart to God. In Jesus' view, this humility, which is the love of God of which we are capable — take, for instance, the parable of the pharisee and the publican — is an abiding disposition towards the good, and that out of which everything that is good springs and grows. "Forgive us our trespasses even as we forgive them that trespass against us" is the prayer at once of humility and of love. This, then, is the source and origin of the love of one's neighbor; the poor in spirit and those who hunger and thirst after righteousness are also the peacemakers and the merciful. It was in this sense that Jesus combined religion and morality, and in this sense religion may be called the soul of morality, and morality the body of religion. We can thus understand how it was that Jesus could place the love of God and the love of one's neighbor side by side; the love of one's neighbor is the only practical proof on earth of that love of God which is strong in humility. (*C:* 68-73)

*

The history of religion marked an enormous advance, religion itself was established afresh, when through poets and thinkers in Greece on the one hand, and through the prophets in Palestine on the other, the idea of righteousness and a righteous God became a living force and transformed tradition. The gods were raised to a higher level and civilized; the warlike and capricious Jehovah became a holy being in whose court of judgment a man might trust, albeit in fear and trembling. The two great provinces of religion and morality, hitherto separated, were now brought into close relation; for "the Godhead is holy and just." It is *our* history that was then developed; for without that all-important transformation there would be no such thing as "mankind," no such thing as a "history of the world" in the higher sense. The most immediate result of this development may be summed up in the maxim: "What ye would not that men should do unto you, do ye also not unto them." Insufficient and prosaic as the rule may seem, yet, if extended so as to cover all human relationships and really observed, it contains a civilizing force of enormous strength.

But it does not contain the ultimate step. Not until justice was compelled to give way to mercy, and the idea of brotherhood and self-sacrifice in the service of one's neighbor became paramount — another reestablishment of religion — was the last advance accomplished that it was possible and necessary to make. Its maxim, "What ye would that men should do unto you, do ye also unto them," also seems prosaic; and yet rightly understood it leads to the summit and comprises a new method of apprehension, and a new way of judging one's own life. The thought that "he who loses his life shall save it," runs side by side with this maxim and effects a transvaluation of values, in the certainty that a man's true life is not tied to this span of time and is not rooted in material existence.

I hope that I have thus shown, although briefly, that in the sphere of thought which is indicated by "the higher righteousness" and "the new commandment of love" Jesus' teaching is also contained in its entirety. As a matter of fact, the three spheres which we have distinguished — the kingdom of God, God as the Father and the infinite value of the human soul, and the higher righteousness showing itself in love — coalesce; for ultimately the kingdom is nothing but the treasure which the soul possesses in the eternal and merciful God. It needs only a few touches to develop this thought into everything that, taking Jesus' sayings as its groundwork, Christendom has known and strives to maintain as hope, faith, and love. (C: 76-77)

*

THE TWO–FOLD GOSPEL IN THE NEW TESTAMENT

At the 5th International Congress of Free Christianity and Religious Progress, held in Berlin in 1910, Harnack put together, in succinct form, his views of the "two" gospels, or better: the dual aspect of the gospel as found in the New Testament. One aspect is associated with Jesus and his message, the gospel which provides sublime insight so that we might act purposefully; the other is associated with Paul and the subsequent teachers of the early Church, the gospel which seeks to discern who Jesus was and how he became the savior. In its simplicity, Jesus' message raises us to the higher life of religion; the gospel about him draws us into Hellenistic metaphysics.

The translation was provided by the staff of the Congress itself and appeared, intially, in the Congress-proceedings. Subsequently, the address was printed as a separate pamphlet; in England the pamphlet appeared in 1911 which text is the one used here.

Perhaps there is no other word amongst the great central conceptions of Christianity which has gone through so manifold and rich a history in Christendom as the word "gospel" (evangel, evangelical). This history, already begun in apostolic ages, has not even today reached its end, for the word gospel (evangel, evangelical) is ever being laid claim to in new senses. Some of these have only the geographical or limited meaning of a state Church. Therefore I am by no means sure that all the meanings in which the word is today used in the different Churches are known to me. If we look at German Christendom we see that the Protestants call themselves evangelical in contradistinction to the Roman Catholics,

146

and that by the word "gospel" they understand first and foremost the message of the free grace of God in Christ in contradistinction to the Law, as well as the hierarchy and the priesthood. We however see also that amongst them small circles, desirous of uniting their members more closely, and feeling a lack of real earnestness in the great Churches, claim for themselves the term evangelical in quite a special sense, perhaps under the title of "evangelical community" or something similar. We further recognize that the words "evangelical" and "Protestant" produce a certain amount of friction, as the more liberal evangelicals prefer to call themselves "Protestants," the Conservative Protestants preferring to be known as "evangelicals." We notice also that the term "evangelical" is used in such a manner as to indicate that one is neither strictly Lutheran nor strictly a Calvinist, but adheres to the great and fundamental ideas of the Reformation.

But in addition to this it must not be forgotten that in German Protestantism the "gospel" means Jesus' preaching of the kingdom of God.

Just at this point a contradiction arises in the common use of the term, for whilst on the one hand the definition of "gospel" in the sense of the message of the free grace of God in Christ is so conceived that the teaching of Jesus Christ, the Son of God, alone is the gospel, in other quarters the gospel is looked upon as the gospel of Jesus in contradistinction to this apostolic announcement. The same word is also used for the teachings of St. Paul, and for the message of Jesus in sharp contrast to the Pauline teachings. In the latter sense the thought of the kingdom of God as the specific content of the gospel is urged, or also the Sermon on the Mount, the Beatitudes, or simply the "ethics" of Jesus. With this one approaches the Roman Catholic way of speaking, which, especially since the time of St. Francis — the matter and the term are however much more ancient — designates certain sayings of Jesus "evangelical counsels" and attempts in its rules for the monks the reproduction of the highest commands of Jesus for the attainment of Christian perfection. According to this in certain commands of the Sermon on the Mount and in Matthew 10 the culmination of the gospel is to be sought, and "evangelical" in its fullest sense is he only who literally fulfills these commands, and at the same time withdraws himself from the life of the world. With this is connected the thought of wholly following in the steps of, and imitating the apostles, but above all Christ himself, and the gospel appears as the direction to order one's life as far as possible according to the pattern of the humble life and bitter sufferings of Jesus. Something of this has been transmitted to Protestant Christians also by means of devotional literature; the evangelical communities especially, to whom we have already alluded, have been more or less strongly influenced by the conception ever since the 17th century.

At this point then (*les extrêmes se touchent*) Liberal Protestantism comes into touch with Pietism, insofar as they both, even if in very different ways, look on the gospel as a rule for the direction of life.

So extraordinarily manifold, then, and in some instances contradictory, are the current meanings attached to the words "gospel" and "evangelical" in a single ecclesiastical domain. In opposition to this it is doubly important to go back to the oldest times and to determine definitely what the word gospel means in the Old Testament.

Have the many different meanings, which the word receives today, their roots already in the New Testament? As a matter of fact it is so. No one can deny that already there the word gospel is used in very different senses. . . .

This much however is certain, that one must speak of a two-fold gospel in the New Testament. There "gospel" is a message of joy preached to the poor, the meek, the peacemakers, and them that have a clean heart: it is a message that the kingdom of God is nigh, and that this kingdom will take away the sorrows of the poor in spirit, will fill them with righteousness, and will bring them all the blessings which attend the accepted children of God. And there is also in the New Testament the teaching that the Son of God came down from heaven, was made man, and through his death and resurrection, has redeemed believers from their sins, from death and Satan, and so has made real the everlasting salvation of God. Here also the gospel is the message of the kingdom of God, but it appears fully accomplished in the preaching of Jesus Christ, since it is only through belief in him as the crucified and risen savior that man can win the kingdom of heaven. The question as to how the second gospel arose, and how it is related to the first is well known to be one of the most disputed problems of Church-historical investigation. It has constantly been maintained that the second gospel in contradistinction to the first is something quite new, that so far as it contains what we call historical Christianity, it depicts a new religion in which Jesus Christ himself has very little or no part, and that the apostle Paul was the author of this religion. Some, and indeed the majority, of those who hold this opinion, hold this second gospel to be new only as distinct from the first, but in itself to be much the older.

Their opinion is that it existed already before the time of Christ, and that it had already perhaps existed in and with the, at that time, current dogma of the Jewish Messiah — it may be in some syncretistic Jewish group — or it may go back to the widely spread heathen representation of a God dying and rising again.

In order to find out which of these fundamental suppositions is the right one it must first be clearly laid down that the idea of the importance of the apostle Paul in laying the foundation of the "second" gospel must be much, or I would rather say, very considerably modified.

The declaration that "Christ died for our sins, according to the Scriptures," St. Paul indicates to be a traditional, therefore a generally accepted article of faith of the first rank; and he says the same concerning the resurrection of Christ.

According to this it is certain that the first apostles also, as well as the congregation at Jerusalem, shared this conviction and doctrine. This is also proved by the first chapter of the Acts of the Apostles — the credibility of which is undisputable in this respect.

Therefore the problem must be moved chronologically from St. Paul to the period of the first disciples of Christ, who had already preached the dying of Christ for sin and his resurrection. If they preached it, however, they recognized it at once as the main factor, therefore as the gospel within the gospel, and this, indeed, is clearly shown in the oldest written gospel that we have, namely in that according to St. Mark. The whole work of St. Mark is so disposed and composed that death and resurrection appear to be the aims of the whole presentation.

Even if St. Mark was admittedly influenced by the preaching of Paul, yet the gospel specially written for the Jews — that according to St. Matthew — had the same form. It could not then have been new to the Christians of Palestine.

If, therefore, the earliest conception of the gospel stands nearer to that of St. Paul than many critics admit, St. Paul, on the other hand, stands also nearer to this conception than many of his judges imagine. The gospel of Christ is with St. Paul not the gospel concerning Christ but the gospel which Christ preached.

St. Paul has indeed expressed himself in some places in his Epistles, that Christ is the content of the gospel; full of meaning and important however as this is, it is nevertheless to be regarded as an abridged mode of speaking.

The gospel according to St. Paul is the announcement, predicted by the prophets, of the salvation of God brought about by the death and resurrection of Christ.

In addition to this one must further notice, what an important part the idea the "kingdom of God" also plays with him in order not to become a more rigorous Paulite in the representation of the theology of St. Paul, than the apostle was himself. The idea of the founding of the kingdom and its fulfillment through the Son is for St. Paul also the first and most comprehensive one.

If therefore the most ancient teaching of the kingdom of heaven, and St. Paul's preaching of the crucified and risen savior — i.e. the "first" and the "second" gospel — draw historically nearer together than would at first sight appear, still the question arises as to where the sources of the "second gospel" are to be sought.

One may at once premise, that however one may seek the answer to this question, the task will be no light one. A belief that has penetrated so quickly and so victoriously, and has taken the place of the teaching of Jesus himself, must possess many and strong roots; it must in fact have proceeded from interlacing roots of especial strength.

If my standpoint be correct there are four conceptions which have worked together here. They lie (1) in the teaching of Christ himself, (2) in the messianic views of the then existing Judaism, (3) in the theology of St. Paul, and (4) in certain religious conceptions regarding widely circulated myths of the heathen world. All these could not but co-operate, and have co-operated in producing the Church's belief in redemption as connected with the person of Jesus Christ, and causing it to appear as the groundwork of Christian teaching.

I. The message of Jesus comes into consideration here, in as much as he preached not only the necessity and the reality of the remission of sins, but also undoubtedly associated his person and work with it. He not only claimed the power to forgive sins, but at the celebration of the Last Supper he also associated his death with the setting free of souls.

But even if one were to deny this, this much is at any rate certain, that the attachment of his person, i.e. the body of disciples, was willed by him.

He, however, who followed him, could not but discover and know him to be in some sense "the way" to the Father, and to all the blessings of heaven. ("Come unto me.")

II. That the Messiah would suffer and die was certainly not the general expectation of Judaism in the time of Christ. This expectation, however, was not entirely lacking, for after John the Baptist had been beheaded, many in spite of this held him to be the Messiah, and believed that he had risen from the dead. His death, therefore, had no validity against his Messiahship. One sees from this that in the case referred to the question of a suffering Messiah occupied their minds, and was not disposed of by a simple negative.

But the Old Testament prophecies also must have prepared the way for a suffering Messiah, especially Isaiah 53. If its acceptation was striven against in wide circles, an evasion of it, because of the ruling exegesis, was not easily possible.

As soon as the personal Messiah was brought into the foreground — and just at the time of Christ the messianic expectations seemed to have grown stronger — it could not be otherwise than that at least individual teachers would see themselves forced to the acceptation that in passages like Isaiah 53 the discourse is of the Messiah.

If, however, the personal Messiah was referred to in Isaiah 53, then not only were his suffering and death to be expected, but also the meaning of salvation through his death appeared to be taught in plain words.

III. The reasoning of St. Paul was throughout antithetical, and his spirit never rested till he had led everything up to great and moving contrasts and brought it to a paradoxical form. If he had on the one hand learnt from the Old Testament: "Cursed be he that hangs on the cross," and on the other had gained the belief that "Christ died for us sinners according to the Scriptures," then the bald "according to the Scriptures" could not suffice him; much more was it necessary to clearly show the "wherefore" of this. It must be proved that Jesus, through the very fact that he was accursed, had brought salvation to man.

This could, however, only be proved when the death on the cross appeared as the most necessary, and therefore the main factor of the life of Christ.

It was the most necessary factor, because nothing is more necessary than to satisfy the justice of God and his holy laws, which demand the death of the sinner. This satisfaction was consummated in the obedient death of Christ, and the demands of the law are now satisfied; they have moreover also become void, because Christ suffered death not as an individual man, but as the second Adam and Son of God. But this logical and juridical consideration of the matter was not sufficient for the apostle, since the other great event, the resurrection, did not get its just recognition, nor did it suffice for his reasoning when directed towards the actual condition of man. Man is, as experience shows, ruled by the lusts of the flesh, which lead to death. He can then only be helped, when this sinful desire has been taken away, and the Spirit of God, the Spirit of Life, has been instilled in him in its stead.

Christ through his death has overcome and put an end to the sins of the flesh, and as he manifested himself through his resurrection as Spirit, he now begins an inworking upon man which overcomes the carnal flesh and sets in its place the Holy Spirit as its guiding principle. Thus the heavenly Christ, who died and rose again, is not only the great exemplar of the overcoming of the flesh by the Spirit, but also the moving power in the new creation of mankind, which, through him, becomes "a new creature."

IV. It is utterly improbable that St. Paul arrived at the central conception of a Son of God, who died and rose again, through the myths of Western Asia; the premises of his reasoning and the historical premises which lay in the death on the cross and the belief in the resurrection of Jesus must of themselves have led him up to it. But it is quite possible that the idea underlying those myths had won some influence over him, without his being aware of it, not only upon the cosmological development of the idea, but also upon the determination and power with which the apostle advanced it. Wherever St. Paul came, from Syria to Corinth, the myth of a God dying and rising from the dead must have confronted him in various forms.

This myth, which originally was symbolical of the most general and most important natural occurrences, had had a history extending over a long period, in which it had become the expression of hopes of immortality and moral purification without losing completely its original meaning.

But however this may be if the apostle Paul was at all — and if so how much — indebted to this myth, of one thing at any rate there can be no doubt, and that is that the preaching of a crucified and risen God must have touched in a wonderful and liberating manner the hearts of thousands, who had hitherto received this belief from uncertain and obscure sources, and who now obtained it from a history, which had as it were, taken place only yesterday, and the witnesses of which they now saw before them.

The message of the death and resurrection of the God Jesus Christ, who had become man, became the gospel of the Church at large, and has taken its place side by side with Christ's teaching of the kingdom of heaven, its benefits and its ethical demands.

Apparently — and especially so when one takes the doctrine of the Churches into consideration — the "second gospel" almost supplanted the "first." But this is not even true as regards doctrine. Not only does the "first gospel" live in the hearts of those who take the Christian religion in earnest, but it is also not lacking in the dogmas of the Churches;

it is, indeed, a decisive point of departure among them.

The currents of both gospels flow through the whole of Church history and doctrinal development; one may distinguish the one from the other though they are not separated, and the strength of the life of Christendom seems to depend on the fact that neither one of these two currents is victorious over the other, and that they indeed have one source.

How then does the present age stand with regard to both these gospels? A superficial review would incline one to the conclusion that it goes forth to welcome the one, that is free from miracles and mythologies, but refuses to accept the other all the more decisively because it contains the representation of a God become man, and his death and resurrection. But this conclusion is not the final one. The paramount issue today is not the miraculous or non-miraculous, but the question whether the soul of man has an eternal value which distinguishes it from all else; whether moral goodness is a conventional product, or a life-principle of the spirit; and whether there be a living and saving God or not.

He who denies these questions — and they are denied in large circles at the present time, as well as in the name of science — must reject Jesus' gospel of the kingdom of heaven, and all the ideas, thoughts and pre-scriptions of the Sermon on the Mount. He must put in their place an entirely new ethic — if indeed an ethic can be spoken of at all.

That is what is actually taking place, and so the first "gospel," the gospel of Jesus, is today engaged in a bitter struggle for its ultimate premises, and with them everything else is attacked. On the other hand one can say that the times are today more favorable to the "second gospel" than they were in some former periods. Not only does "modern positive" theology defend it in its transmitted form, but also the latest phase in the development of philosophy meets it halfway. Philosophers of the School of Hegel and Hartmann assure us that the profoundest philosophical and religious knowledge is contained in the "second gospel." The agreement of these philosophers with Christian theology can matter little or nothing to the latter if they thereby eliminate the per-sonality of Christ, and frame an ideal poem out of his appearance, his suffering and death. The support, which they offer to Christian belief, is therefore of slight value.

The "second gospel" is untenable in the form of a "twofold-nature" doctrine since it is contrary to historical, and in fact every possible form of knowledge.

Every assertion about Jesus Christ which has not as its framework that he was man, is not to be accepted, since it is at variance with the historical portraiture of the life of Christ. But the "second gospel" is in no way refuted through this admission. Even if it is certain that no God appeared, and that no God died and rose again, it is equally certain that we know absolutely nothing of God through our senses and knowledge of nature, and that therefore the personal higher life and ethics are the only realm in which we can come into touch with God.

God is holiness and God is love. If this be so, God is then only manifest in the personal life, that is, in men. He works by means of men, saves through men, and completes his work through men. And for men in this sense there is no conception of a species since they here come only into consideration as individuals and separately. To what degree however God has endowed the individual and made him his instrument for others we can learn solely from the facts themselves, i.e., from history; no philosophy is able to enlighten us or determine hard and fast lines.

The "second gospel" teaches that God has made Jesus of Nazareth Lord and Christ for mankind, that his work was God's work, and history has set its seal upon it. This seal is not the seal of the Church — for the great spread and dominion of Christianity can of itself prove nothing — but it consists in the fact that for almost 1900 years and to the present day faith in Jesus Christ has produced children of God who know that they are redeemed; who lift themselves above the world without despising it, who are filled with burning love and energy towards their brethren, and who joyfully go their way because they have found God, and hence even in the midst of time live for eternity.

This "double gospel," as it is set forth in the New Testament, is just as necessary at the present day, as it has been necessary in all periods of the past.

The "first gospel" contains the **Truth**, the "second" contains the **Way**, and both together bring **Life**.

It is by no means necessary that every one be fully conscious that Jesus Christ is the way by which he has come to the truth. Christ is thereby also Christ that one brother becomes a Christ to another.

It is always personal life in God, which communicates itself to others, and whereby alone new life can be produced, for not only in the case of the prophets does it hold good that one must anoint the other.

Behind them all stands Jesus Christ. To him belongs whoever has found God, and whoever has found him, the more he advances the more will he go forward in the certainty that Jesus is the Christ. (*TG:* 3-11)

WHAT IS CHRISTIANITY?

(Third Selection)

This selection presents Harnack's analysis of the development of the notion of the person of Christ, of Christology, and of the origins of the Creeds as affirmations, within the context of Christian worship, required for solemn recital by those who sought admission into the Church. Harnack's concern here is to show how that development represents the initial departure from Jesus' preaching.

THE GOSPEL AND THE SON OF GOD, OR THE CHRISTOLOGICAL QUESTION

... The forces of the gospel appeal to the deepest foundations of human existence and to them only; it is there alone that their leverage is applied. If a man is unable, then, to go down to the root of humanity, and has no feeling for it and no knowledge of it, he will fail to understand the gospel, and will then try to profane it or else complain that it is of no use.

We now, however, approach quite a different problem: What position did Jesus himself take up towards the gospel while he was proclaiming it, and how did he wish himself to be accepted? We are not yet dealing with the way in which his disciples accepted him, or the place which they gave him in their hearts, and the opinion which they formed of him; we are now speaking only of his own testimony of himself. But the question is one which lands us in the great sphere of controverted questions which cover the history of the Church from the first century up to our own time. In the course of this controversy men put an end to brotherly fellowship for the sake of a *nuance*; and thousands were cast out, condemned, loaded with chains and done to death. It is a gruesome story. On the question of "Christology" men beat their religious doctrines into terrible weapons, and spread fear and intimidation everywhere. This attitude still continues: Christology is treated as though the gospel had no other problem to offer, and the accompanying fanaticism is still rampant in our own day. Who can wonder at the difficulty of the problem, weighed down as it is with such a burden of history and made the sport of parties? Yet anyone who will look at our gospels with unprejudiced eyes will not find that the question of Jesus' own testimony is insoluble. ...

Before we examine Jesus' own testimony about himself, two leading points must be established. In the first place, he desired no other belief in his person and no other attachment to it than is contained in the keeping of his commandments. Even in the fourth gospel, in which Jesus' person often seems to be raised above the contents of the gospel, the idea is still clearly formulated: "If ye love me, keep my commandments." He must himself have found, during his labors, that some people honored, nay, even trusted him, without troubling themselves about the contents of his message. It was to them that he addressed the reprimand: "Not everyone that saith unto me Lord, Lord, shall enter into the kingdom of heaven; but he that doeth the will of my Father." To lay down any "doctrine" about his person and his dignity independently of the gospel was, then, quite outside his sphere of ideas. In the second place, he described the Lord of heaven and earth as his God and his Father; as the greater, and as him who is alone good. He is certain that everything which he has and everything which he is to accomplish comes from this Father. He prays to him; he subjects himself to his will; he struggles hard to find out what it is and to fulfil it. Aim, strength, understanding, the issue, and the hard *must*, all come from the Father. This is what the gospels say, and it cannot be turned and twisted. This feeling, praying, working, struggling and suffering individual is a man who in the face of his God also associates himself with other men.

These two facts mark out, as it were, the boundaries of the ground covered by Jesus' testimony of himself. They do not, it is true, give us any positive information as to what he said; but we shall understand what he really meant by his testimony if we look closely at the two descriptions which he gave of himself: the *Son of God* and the *Messiah* (the Son of David, the Son of Man).

The description of himself as the Son of God, messianic though it may have been in its original conception, lies very much nearer to our modern way of thinking than the other, for Jesus himself gave a meaning to this conception which almost takes it out of the class of messianic ideas, or at all events does not make its inclusion in that class necessary to a proper understanding of it. On the other hand, if we do not desire to be put off with a lifeless word, the description of himself as the Messiah is at first blush one that is quite foreign to our ideas. Without some explanation we cannot understand, nay, unless we are Jews, we cannot understand at all, what this post of honor means and what rank and character it possesses. It is only when we have ascertained its meaning by historical research that we can ask whether the word has a significance which in any way survives the destruction of the husk in which it took shape in Jewish political life.

Let us first of all consider the designation, "Son of God." Jesus in one of his discourses made it specially clear why and in what sense he gave himself this name. The saying is to be found in Matthew, and not, as might perhaps have been expected, in John: "No man knoweth the Son but the Father; neither knoweth any man the Father, save the Son, and he to whomsoever the Son will reveal him." It is "knowledge of God" that makes the sphere of the divine Sonship. It is in this knowledge that he came to know the sacred being who rules heaven and earth as Father, as *his* Father. The consciousness which he possessed of being *the Son of God* is, therefore, nothing but the practical consequence of knowing God as the Father and as his Father. Rightly understood, the name of Son means nothing but the knowledge of God. Here, however, two observations are to be made: Jesus is convinced that he knows God in a way in which no one ever knew him before, and he knows that it is his vocation to communicate this knowledge of God to others by word and by deed — and with it the knowledge that men are God's children. In this consciousness he knows himself to be the Son called and instituted of God, to be *the* Son of God, and hence he can say: *My* God and *my* Father, and into this invocation he puts something which belongs to no one but himself. How he came to this consciousness of the unique character of his relation to God as a Son; how he came to the consciousness of his power, and to the consciousness of the obligation and the mission which this power carries with it, is his secret, and no psychology will ever fathom it.... He is certain that he knows the Father, that he is to bring this knowledge to all men, and that thereby he is doing the work of God. Among all the works of God this is the greatest; it is the aim and end of all creation. The work is given to him to do, and in God's strength he will accomplish it. It was out of this feeling of power and in the prospect of victory that he uttered the words: "The Father hath committed all things unto me." Again and again in the history of mankind men of God have come forward in the sure consciousness of possessing a divine message, and of being compelled, whether they will or not, to deliver it. But the message has always happened to be imperfect; in this spot or that, defective; bound up with political or particularistic elements; designed to meet the circumstances of the moment; and very often the prophet did not stand the test of being himself an example of his message. But in this case the message brought was of the profoundest and most comprehensive character; it went to the very root of mankind and, although set in the framework of the Jewish nation, it addressed itself to the whole of humanity — the message from God the

157

Father. Defective it is not, and its real kernel may be readily freed from the inevitable husk of contemporary form. Antiquated it is not, and in life and strength it still triumphs today over all the past. He who delivered it has as yet yielded his place to no man, and to human life he still today gives a meaning and an aim — he *the Son of God.*

This already brings us to the other designation which Jesus gave of himself: *the Messiah....*

The idea of a Messiah and the messianic notions generally, as they existed in Jesus' day, had been developed on two combined lines, on the line of the kings and on that of the prophets. Alien influences had also been at work, and the whole idea was transfigured by the ancient expectation that God himself in visible form would take up the government of his people. The leading features of the messianic idea were taken from the Israelitish kingdom in the ideal splendor in which it was invested after the kingdom itself had disappeared. Memories of Moses and of the great prophets also played a part in it. (*C:* 124-131)

*

Although the messianic doctrines prevalent in the Jewish nation in Jesus' day were not a positive "dogma," and had no connexion with the legal precepts which were so rigidly cultivated, they formed an essential element of the hopes, religious and political, which the nation entertained for the future. They were of no very definite character, except in certain fundamental features; beyond these the greatest differences prevailed. The old prophets had looked forth to a glorious future in which God would himself come down, destroy the enemies of Israel, and work justice, peace, and joy. At the same time, however, they had also promised that a wise and mighty king of the house of David would appear and bring this glorious state of things to pass. They had ended by indicating the people of Israel itself as the Son of God, chosen from amongst the nations of the world. These three views exercised a determining influence in the subsequent elaboration of the messianic ideas. The hope of a glorious future for the people of Israel remained the frame into which all expectations were fitted, but in the two centuries before Christ the following factors were added: (i) The extension of their historical horizon strengthened the interest of the Jews in the nations of the world, introduced the notion of "mankind" as a whole and brought it within the sphere of the expected end, including, therefore, the operations of the Messiah. The day of judgment is regarded as extending to the whole world, and the Messiah not only as judging the world but as ruling it as well. (ii) In early times, although the moral purification of the people had been thought of in connexion with the glorious future, the destruction of Israel's enemies seemed to be the main consideration; but now the feeling of moral responsibility and the knowledge of God as the holy one became more active; the view prevails that the messianic age demands a holy people, and that the judgment to come must of necessity also be a judgment upon a part of Israel itself. (iii) As individualism became a stronger force, so the relation of God to the individual was prominently emphasized. The individual Israelite comes to feel that he is in the midst of his people, and he begins to look upon it as a sum of individuals; the individual belief in providence appears side by side with the political belief, and combines with the feeling of personal worth and responsibility; and in connexion with the expectation of the end, we get the first dawn of the hope of an eternal life and the fear of eternal punishment. The products of this inner development are an interest in personal salvation, and a belief in the resurrection, and the roused conscience is no longer able to hope for a glorious future for all in view of the open profanity of the people and the power of sin; only a remnant will be saved. (iv) The expectations for the future become more and more transcendent; they are increasingly shifted to the realm of the supernatural and the supramundane; something quite new comes down from heaven to earth, and the new course on which the world enters severs it from the old; nay, this earth, transfigured as it will be, is no longer the final goal; the idea of an absolute bliss arises, whose abode can only be heaven itself. (v) The personality of the long-expected Messiah is sharply distinguished, as well from the idea of an earthly king, as from the idea of the people as a whole, and from the idea of God. Although he appears as a man amongst men, the Messiah retains scarcely any messianic traits. He is represented as with God from the first beginnings of time; he comes down from heaven, and accomplishes his work by superhuman means; the moral traits in the picture formed of him come into prominence; he is the perfectly just man who fulfils all the commandments. Nay, the idea that others benefit by his merits forces its way in. The notion, however, of a suffering Messiah, which might seem to be suggested by Isaiah 53, is not reached. (C: 132-34)

*

The idea which was formed of the Messiah must have been as contradictory as the hopes to which it was meant to respond. Not only were people's formal notions about him continually changing — questions were being raised, for instance, as to the sort of bodily nature which he would have; above all, his inmost character and the work to which he was to be called appeared in diverse lights. But wherever the moral and really religious elements had begun to get the upper hand, people were forced to abandon the image of the political and warlike ruler, and let that of *the prophet*, which had always to some extent helped to form the general notions about the Messiah, take its place. That he would bring God near; that somehow or other he would do justice; that he would deliver from the burden of torment within — this was what was hoped of him. . . .

We shall never fathom the inward development by which Jesus passed from the assurance that he was the Son of God to the other assurance that he was the promised Messiah. But when we see that the idea which others as well had formed of the Messiah at that time had, by a slow process of change, developed entirely new features, and had passed from a political and religious idea into a spiritual and religious one — when we see this, the problem no longer wears a character of complete isolation. That John the Baptist and the twelve disciples acknowledged Jesus to be the Messiah; that the positive estimate which they formed of his person did not lead them to reject the shape in which he appeared, but, on the contrary, was fixed in this very shape, is a proof of the flexible character of the messianic idea at the time, and also explains how it was that Jesus could himself adopt it. "Strength is made perfect in weakness." That there is a divine strength and glory which stands in no need of earthly power and earthly splendor, nay, excludes them; that there is a majesty of holiness and love which saves and blesses those upon whom it lays hold, was what he knew who in spite of his lowliness called himself the Messiah, and the same must have been felt by those who recognized him as the king of Israel anointed of God.

How Jesus arrived at the consciousness of being the Messiah we cannot explain, but still there are some points connected with the question which can be established. An inner event which Jesus experienced at his baptism was in the view of the oldest tradition the foundation of his messianic consciousness. It is not an experience which is subject to any criticism; still less are we in a position to contradict it. On the contrary, there is a strong probability that when he made his public appearance he had already settled accounts with himself. . . .

By this, however, I do not mean that, so far as he himself was concerned, he had nothing more to learn in the course of it. Not only had he to learn to suffer, and to look forward to the cross with confidence in God, but the consciousness of his Sonship was now for the first time to be brought to the test. The knowledge of the "work" which the Father had intrusted to him could not be developed except by labor and by victory over all opposition. What a moment it must have been for him when he recognized that he was the one of whom the prophets had spoken; when he saw the whole history of his nation from Abraham and Moses downwards in the light of his own mission; when he could no longer avoid the conviction that he was the promised Messiah! No longer avoid it; for how can we refuse to believe that at first he must have felt this knowledge to be a terrible burden? Yet in saying this we have gone too far; and there is nothing more that we can say. But in this connexion we can understand that the evangelist John was right in making Jesus testify over and over again: "I have not spoken of myself; but the Father which sent me; he gave me a commandment, what I should say, and what I should speak." And again: "For I am not alone, but I and the Father that sent me."

But however we may conceive the "Messiah," it was an assumption that was simply necessary if the man who felt the inward call was to gain an absolute recognition within the lines of Jewish religious history — the profoundest and maturest history that any nation ever possessed, nay, as the future was to show, the true religious history for all mankind. The idea of the Messiah became the means — in the first instance for the devout of his own nation — of effectively setting the man who knew that he was the Son of God, and was doing the work of God, on the throne of history. But when it had accomplished this, its mission was exhausted. Jesus was the "Messiah," and was not the Messiah; and he was not the Messiah, because he left the idea far behind him; because he put a meaning into it which was too much for it to bear. Although the idea may strike us as strange we can still feel some of its meaning; an idea which captivated a whole nation for centuries, and in which it deposited all its ideals, cannot be quite unintelligible. In the prospect of a messianic period we see once more the old hope of a golden age; the hope which, when moralized, must necessarily be the goal of every vigorous movement in human life and forms an inalienable element in the religious view of history; in the expectation of a personal Messiah we see an expression of the fact that it is *persons* who form the saving element in history, and that if a union of mankind is ever to come about by their deepest forces and highest aims being brought into accord, this same mankind must agree to acknowledge *one* lord and master. But beyond this there is no other meaning and no other value to be attached to the messianic idea; Jesus himself deprived it of them.

With the recognition of Jesus as the Messiah the closest possible connexion was established, for every devout Jew, between Jesus' message and his person; for it is in the Messiah's activity that God himself comes to his people, and the Messiah who does God's work and sits at the right hand of God in the clouds of heaven has a right to be worshipped. But what attitude did Jesus himself take up towards his gospel? Does he assume a position in it? To this question there are two answers; one negative and one positive.

In those leading features of it which we described in the earlier lectures the whole of the gospel is contained, and we must keep it free from the intrusion of an alien element: God and the soul, the soul and its God. There was no doubt in Jesus' mind that God could be found, and had been found, in the law and the prophets. "He hath showed thee, O Man, what is good; and what doth the Lord require of thee, but to do justly, and to love mercy, and to walk humbly with thy God." He takes the publican in the temple, the widow and her mite, the lost son, as his examples; none of them know anything about "Christology," and yet by his humility the publican was justified. These are facts which cannot be turned and twisted without doing violence to the grandeur and simplicity of Jesus' message in one of its most important aspects. To contend that Jesus meant his whole message to be taken provisionally, and everything in it to receive a different interpretation after his death and resurrection, nay, parts of it to be put aside as of no account, is a desperate supposition. No! his message is simpler than the Churches would like to think it; simpler, but for that very reason sterner and endowed with a greater claim to universality. A man cannot evade it by the subterfuge of saying that as he can make nothing of this "Christology" the message is not for him. Jesus directed men's attention to great questions; he promised them God's grace and mercy; he required them to decide whether they would have God or Mammon, an eternal or an earthly life, the soul or the body, humility or self-righteousness, love or selfishness, the truth or a lie. The sphere which these questions occupy is all-embracing; the individual is called upon to listen to the glad message of mercy and the Fatherhood of God, and to make up his mind whether he will be on God's side and the eternal's, or on the side of the world and of time. *The gospel, as Jesus proclaimed it, has to do with the Father only and not with the Son.* This is no paradox, nor, on the other hand, is it "rationalism," but the simple expression of the actual fact as the evangelists give it.

But no one had ever yet known the Father in the way in which Jesus knew him, and to this knowledge of him he draws other men's attention, and thereby does "the many" an incomparable service. He leads them to God, not only by what he says, but still more by what he is and does, and ultimately by what he suffers. It was in this sense that he spoke the words, "Come unto me all ye that labor and are heavy laden, and I will give you rest;" as also, "The Son of Man came not to be ministered unto, but to minister and to give his life a ransom for many." He knows that through him a new epoch is beginning, in which, by their knowledge of God, the "least" shall be greater than the greatest of the ages before; he knows that in him thousands — the very individuals who are weary and heavy laden — will find the Father and gain life; he knows that he is the sower who is scattering good seed; his is the field, his the seed, his the fruit. These things involve no dogmatic doctrines; still less any transformation of the gospel itself, or any oppressive demands upon our faith. They are the expression of an actual fact which he perceives to be already happening, and which, with prophetic assurance, he beholds in advance. When, under the terrible burden of his calling and in the midst of the struggle, he comes to see that it is through him that the blind see, the lame walk, the deaf hear, the poor have the gospel preached to them, he begins to comprehend the glory which the Father has given him. And he sees that what he now suffers in his person will, through his life crowned in death, remain a fact efficacious and of critical importance for all time: *He is the way to the Father, and as he is the appointed of the Father, so he is the judge as well.*

Was he mistaken? Neither his immediate posterity, nor the course of subsequent history, has decided against him. It is not as a mere factor that he is connected with the gospel: *he was its personal realization and its strength, and this he is felt to be still.* Fire is kindled only by fire; personal life only by personal forces. Let us rid ourselves of all dogmatic sophistry, and leave others to pass verdicts of exclusion. The gospel nowhere says that God's mercy is limited to Jesus' mission. But history shows us that he is the one who brings the weary and heavy laden to God; and, again, that he it was who raised mankind to the new level; and his teaching is still the touchstone, in that it brings men to bliss and brings them to judgment. . . .

THE GOSPEL AND DOCTRINE, OR THE QUESTION OF CREED

We need not dwell long on this question, as on the essential points — everything that it is necessary to say has already been said in the course of our previous observations.

The gospel is no theoretical system of doctrine or philosophy of the universe; it is doctrine only insofar as it proclaims the reality of God the Father. It is a glad message assuring us of life eternal, and telling us what the things and the forces with which we have to do are worth. By treating of life eternal it teaches us how to lead our lives aright. It tells us of the value of the human soul, of humility, of mercy, of purity, of the cross, and the worthlessness of worldly goods and anxiety for the things of which earthly life consists. And it gives the assurance that in spite of every struggle, peace, certainty, and something within that can never be destroyed, will be the crown of a life rightly led. What else can "the confession of a creed" mean under these conditions but to do the will of God, in the certainty that he is the Father and the one who will recompense? Jesus never spoke of any other kind of "creed." Even when he says: "Whosoever shall confess me before men, him will I confess also before my Father which is in Heaven," he is thinking of people doing as he did; he means the confession which shows itself in feeling and action. How great a departure from what he thought and enjoined is involved in putting a "Christological" creed in the forefront of the gospel, and in teaching that before a man can approach it he must learn to think rightly about Christ. That is putting the cart before the horse. A man can think and teach rightly about Christ only if, and insofar as, he has already begun to live according to Christ's gospel. There is no forecourt to his message through which a man must pass; no yoke which he must first of all take upon himself. The thoughts and assurances which the gospel provides are the first thing and the last thing, and every soul is directly arraigned before them.

Still less, however, does the gospel presuppose any definite knowledge of nature, or stand in any connexion with such knowledge; not even in a negative sense can this contention be maintained. It is religion and the moral element that are concerned. The gospel puts the living God before us. Here, too, the confession of him in belief in him and in the fulfillment of his will is the sole thing to be confessed; this is what Jesus Christ meant. So far as the knowledge is concerned — and it is vast — which may be based upon this belief, it always varies with the measure of a man's inner development and subjective intelligence. But to possess the Lord of heaven and earth as a Father is an experience to which nothing else approaches; and it is an experience which the poorest soul can have, and to the reality of which he can bear testimony.

An experience — it is only the religion which a man has himself experienced that is to be confessed; every other creed or confession is in Jesus' view hypocritical and fatal. If there is no broad "theory of religion" to be found in the gospel, still less is there any direction that a man is to begin by accepting and confessing any ready-made theory. Faith and creed are to proceed and grow up out of the all-important act of turning from the world and to God, and creed is to be nothing but faith reduced to practice. (*C.* 136-148)

*

The gospel is based upon the antithesis between Spirit and flesh, God and the world, good and evil. Now, in spite of ardent efforts, thinkers have not yet succeeded in elaborating on a monistic basis any theory of ethics that is satisfactory and answers to the deepest needs of man. Nor will they succeed. In the end, then, it is essentially a matter of indifference what name we give to the opposition with which every man of ethical feeling is concerned: God and the world, the here and the beyond, the visible and the invisible, matter and spirit, the life of impulse and the life of freedom, physics and ethics. That there is a unity underlying this opposition is a conviction which can be gained by experience; the one realm can be subordinated to the other; but it is only by a struggle that this unity can be attained, and when it is attained it takes the form of a problem that is infinite and only approximately soluble. It cannot be attained by any refinement of a mechanical process. *Von der Gewalt die alle Wesen bindet, befreit der Mensch sich, der sich überwindet.* It is by self-conquest that a man is freed from the tyranny of matter. This saying of Goethe's excellently expresses the truth that is here in question. It is a truth which holds good for all time, and it forms the essential element in the dramatic pictures of contemporary life in which the gospel exhibits the antithesis that is to be overcome. I do not know how our increased knowledge of nature is to hinder us from bearing witness to the truth of the creed that "The world passeth away, and the lust thereof, but he that doeth the will of God abideth for ever." We have to do with a dualism which arose we know not how; but as moral beings we are convinced that, as it has been given us in order that we may overcome it in ourselves and bring it to a unity, so also it goes back to an original unity, and will at last find its reconciliation in the great far-off event, the realized dominion of the Good.

Dreams, it may be said; for what we see before our eyes is something very different. No! not dreams — after all it is here that our true life has its root — but patchwork certainly, for we are unable to bring our knowledge in space and time, together with the contents of our inner life, into the unity of a philosophic theory of the world. It is only in the peace of God which passeth all understanding that this unity dawns upon us.

(C. 150-151)

*

THE FORMATION OF CHRISTIAN THEOLOGY AND OF THE CHURCH'S DOGMA

Harnack delivered a series of lectures at the University of Bonn in 1926 under this title. Both the question of theological method and how theology and dogma arose are much on his mind. He is also on the defensive before the attacks on the part of newer theological insights associated with an orientation someone had called "dialectical theology." He makes a distinction between theologies that edify an individual believer's soul and theologies that create communities; the former are charismatic, the latter objective as they rely on current philosophies which seek to establish valid, theoretical principles of knowledge. In Harnack's view, the former should remain strictly the prerogative of preaching, of the pulpit, whereas the latter should keep to the arena of the lecterns of academia. The translation was prepared by the editor; the material was chosen from the book Die Entstehung der christlichen Theologie und des kirchlichen Dogmas, *published in 1927, pp. 1-2 and 87-90.*

(From the Preface)
In choosing this topic I was governed by the desire to acquaint students of theology with a major problem of Church-history, one in which, as everywhere else in history, the issue is to discern what is real and true. I wish to do so at a time which, preoccupied with life and death questions, is in danger of underestimating the critical question of truth and, as a consequence, of doing away with rigorously methodical study, indeed, of repudiating that question and study as "historicism." History nowhere has the final word, to be sure, but in the scholarly study of religions and of the Christian religion in particular it does have the first word everywhere.

166

The topic ... was chosen for another reason as well: I have read on no less than four occasions recently in the work of quite different theologians that a new foundation and method for discerning the Christian religion in history and doctrine was now available. Each of the theologians provides a different foundation and method. Still, it is being claimed that a new beginning will be made on the basis of this new situation; everything needs to be reworked from the ground up. All this will require much time but the promise is there of something truly satisfactory to emerge and to take the place of antiquated theologies. One is glad about such announcements if their authors and prophets do, indeed, behold something new rather than, under the spell of the new, try more or less consciously to reconstitute an old orthodoxy. There is a duty, however, to demonstrate that the old scholarly theology has not died out, that it, too, likes to learn something new and that the methodic and educational tradition, to which this theology is committed, has its advantages. ...

The high degree of independence which marks the Christian religion and its oldest developments are attested by the fact that they can be lifted out of the general history of an age and portrayed in a particular fashion without seriously affecting their essence and manifestation....

(From the Conclusions)
From its inception, that is to say beginning with St. Paul, Christian theology was charismatic. Other charismatic theologies followed St. Paul's immediately and there have been others since.[4] But from the earliest times of the Church the theology which based itself on objective revelation and on contemporary idealistic philosophy, in which reason was apparent, has been victorious because it promised a generally valid exposition of the Christian religion. If it is granted that the particular idealistic philosophy is reason (*die Vernunft*) itself and if objective revelation has, in fact, been correctly determined, then this theology has a right to exist. If these two points are not granted then this theology breaks down and must be replaced, but not only by such however valuable complementary efforts as those of Irenaeus and Origen. This does not answer the question whether Christian theology must shun all ties with idealistic philosophy, but then the oldest development of Christian theology denies this anyway. Theologies which have not entered into a relationship with such a philosophy have never become a theology of the *Church*. Brittle charismatic theologies were never more than ferments of some effectiveness. A theology from within is never scho-

larly theology . . . it is, rather, something else, something higher; it is confession. Only theology from without can create community. We lament that the insufficiency of such a theology is so plainly evident, but no one can change that. Should any attempt it, however, they will fail and create confusion for theology. Let them stick, instead, to their task: preaching.

The Church's dogma and its separate dogmas arose in the confluence of apologetic theology and its anti-gnostic affirmations of faith. It follows that no external authority may be conferred upon them, for the *external* authority claimed for those affirmations, be it the authority of the "apostolic" rule of faith or that of Holy Scripture, is most fragile. As a collection, like that of the Old Testment which the synagogue established, the New Testament is lacking in external authority: the churches established it in a lengthy process and, fortunately, hardly ever tried to relate this collection as such back to the apostles or place it on a legendary foundation such as the legend of the Septuagint. Whatever the New Testament is lacking in external authority is more than made up by the inner substance of eternity in its individual writings. The more or less fanciful attempts, both strained and playful in their manner, to construct an "organic sum of Scripture" and to demand for it the *formal* authority which cannot be established for the collection *qua* collection, have to be met by the seriousness and dignity of faith and of scholarly work (*Wissenschaft*). At the same time reference has to be made to the fortunate consequence of the creation of the New Testament, namely that it diminished the place of the Old Testament in the Church.[5] One can see this happening already in Irenaeus; even if that fateful method of interpretation, namely allegory, always blurred the opposition and distinction between the testaments, the Church, nevertheless, kept that opposition and distinction alive and related them to the clear opposition and distinction which St. Paul recognized between the two covenants. To base a Christian insight of faith, a dogma, exclusively on the Old Testament, as did the ancient apologists, even if this is done in an individual case only, would be a most precarious, yes, inadmissible undertaking in the Church.

There exists no external formal authority either for individual dogmas or the Church's dogma; they are not the sure word of God nor can they become it. What is to be regarded as God's word, which demands and creates faith and its obedience, demonstrates itself to our conscience by its very content. That word is in no way sealed exclusively in Holy Scripture or creed; no, the Christian community, the Church, plants and increases it by means of the living, spoken word. That word is utterly indispensable, for it is not only the prophet who calls forth the prophet, it is also the Christian who calls forth the Christian.

*

WHAT IS CHRISTIANITY?

(Fourth Selection)

This selection, from pages 152-189, deals with Christianity in the Apostolic times, especially with the work of Paul. It continues the treatment of how the Christian religion developed into a creedal or dogmatic religion and why. The comment attributed to Harnack, that Paul was the only one who understood Jesus and he misunderstood him, finds expression in this selection.

THE CHRISTIAN RELIGION IN THE APOSTOLIC AGE

The inner circle of the disciples, the band of twelve whom Jesus had gathered around him, formed itself into a community. He himself founded no community in the sense of an organized union for divine worship — he was only the teacher and the disciples were the pupils; but the fact that the band of pupils at once underwent this transformation became the ground upon which all subsequent developments rested. What were the characteristic features of this society? Unless I am mistaken there were three factors at work in it: (i) The recognition of Jesus as the living *Lord*; (ii) the fact that in every individual member of the new community — including the very slaves — religion was *an actual experience*, and involved the consciousness of a living union with God; (iii) the leading of *a holy life* in purity and brotherly fellowship, and the expectation of the *Christ's return in the near future*.

Jesus Christ the Lord: in thus confessing their belief in him his disciples took the first step in continuing their recognition of him as the authoritative teacher, of his word as their permanent standard of life, of their desire to keep "everything that he commanded them." But this does not express the full meaning attaching to the words "the Lord": nay, it is far from touching their peculiar significance. The primitive community called Jesus its Lord because he had sacrificed his life for it, and because its members were convinced that he had been raised from the dead and was then sitting on the right hand of God. There is no historical fact more certain than that the apostle Paul was not, as we might perhaps expect, the first to emphasize so prominently the significance of Christ's death and resurrection, but that in recognizing their meaning he stood exactly on the same ground as the primitive community. "I delivered unto you first of all," he wrote to the Corinthians, "that which I also received, how that Christ died for our sins according to the Scriptures, and that he was buried, and that he rose again the third day." Paul did, it is true, make Christ's death and resurrection the subject of a particular speculative idea, and, so to speak, reduced the whole of the gospel to these events; but they were already accepted as fundamental facts by the circle of Jesus' personal disciples and by the primitive community. In these two facts it may be said that the permanent recognition of Jesus Christ, and the reverence and adoration which he received, obtained their first hold. They formed the ground on which the whole Christological theory rested. But within two generations from his death Jesus Christ was already put upon the highest plane upon which men can put him. As men were conscious of him as the living Lord, he was glorified as the one who had been raised to the right hand of God and had vanquished death, as the prince of life, as the strength of a new existence, as the way, the truth, and the life. The messianic ideas permitted of his being placed upon God's throne, without endangering monotheism. But, above all, he was felt to be the active principle of individual life: "It is not I that live, but Christ that liveth in me"; he is "my" life, and to press onwards to him through death is great gain. . . . It was just the death "for our sins," and the resurrection, which confirmed the impression given by his person, and provided faith with a sure hold: he died as a sacrifice for us and he now lives.

There are many today who have come to regard both these positions as very strange; and their attitude towards them is one of indifference — towards the death, on the ground that no such significance can be attributed to a single event of this kind; towards the resurrection, because what is here affirmed to have happened is incredible.

It is not our business to defend either the view which was taken of the death, or the idea that he had risen again; but it is certainly the historian's duty to make himself so fully acquainted with both positions as to be sensible of the significance which they possessed and still possess. That these positions were of capital importance for the primitive community has never been doubted; even Strauss did not dispute it; and the great critic, Ferdinand Christian Baur, acknowledged that it was on the belief in them that the earliest Christian communion was built up. It must be possible, then, for us in our turn to get a feeling and an understanding for what they were; nay, perhaps we may do more; if we probe the history of religion to the bottom, we shall find the truth and justice of ideas which on the surface seem so paradoxical and incredible lying at the very roots of the faith.

Let us first consider the idea that Jesus' death on the cross was one of expiation. Now, if we were to consider the conception attaching to the words "expiatory death" in the alien realm of formal speculation, we should, it is true, soon find ourselves in a blind alley, and every chance of our understanding the idea would vanish. We should be absolutely at the end of our tether if we were to indulge in speculations as to the necessity which can have compelled God to require such a sacrificial death. Let us, in the first place, bear in mind a fact in the history of religion which is quite universal. Those who looked upon this death as a sacrifice soon ceased to offer God any blood-sacrifice at all. The value attaching to such sacrifices had, it is true, been in doubt for generations, and had been steadily diminishing; but it was only now that the sacrifices disappeared altogether. They did not disappear immediately or at one stroke — this is a point with which we need not concern ourselves here — but their disappearance took place within a very brief period and was not delayed until after the destruction of the temple. Further, wherever the Christian message subsequently penetrated, the sacrificial altars were deserted and dealers in sacrificial beasts found no more purchasers. If there is one thing that is certain in the history of religion, it is that the death of Christ put an end to all blood-sacrifices. But that they are based on a deep religious idea is proved by the extent to which they existed among so many nations, and they are not to be judged from the point of view of cold and blind rationalism, but from that of vivid emotion. If it is obvious that they respond to a religious need; if, further, it is certain that the instinct which led to them found its satisfaction and therefore its goal in Christ's death; if, lastly, there was the express declaration, as we read in the Epistle to the Hebrews, that "by one offering he hath perfected for ever them that are sanctified," we can no longer feel this idea of Christ's sacrifice to be so very strange; for history has decided in its favor, and we are beginning to get in touch with it. His death had the value of an expiatory sacrifice, for otherwise it would not have had strength to penetrate into that inner world in which the blood-sacrifices originated; but it was not a sacrifice in the same sense as the others, or else it could not have put an end to them; it suppressed them by settling accounts with them. Nay, we may go further; the validity of all material sacrifices was destroyed by Christ's death. Wherever individual Christians or whole Churches have returned to them, it has been a relapse: the earliest Christians knew that the whole sacrificial system was thenceforth abolished, and if they asked for a reason, they pointed to Christ's death.

In the second place: any one who will look into history will find that the sufferings of the pure and the just are its saving element; that is to say, that it is not words, but deeds, and not deeds only but self-sacrificing deeds, and not only self-sacrificing deeds, but the surrender of life itself, that forms the turning point in every great advance in history. In this sense I believe that, however far we may stand from any *theories* about vicarious sacrifice, there are few of us after all who will mistake the truth and inner justice of such a description as we read in Isaiah 53: "Surely he hath borne our griefs and carried our sorrows." "Greater love hath no man than this, that a man lay down his life for his friends" — it is in this light that Jesus' death was regarded from the beginning. Wherever any great deed has been accomplished in history, the finer a man's moral feelings are, the more sensible will he be of vicarious suffering; the more he will bring that suffering into relation to himself. Did Luther in the monastery strive only for himself? — was it not for us all that he inwardly bled when he fought with the religion that was handed down to him? But it was by the cross of Jesus Christ that mankind gained such an experience of the power of purity and love true to death that they can never forget it, and that it signifies a new epoch in their history.

Finally, in the third place: no reflection of the "reason," no deliberation of the "intelligence," will ever be able to expunge from the moral ideas of mankind the conviction that injustice and sin deserve to be punished, and that everywhere that the just man suffers, an atonement is made which puts us to shame and purifies us. It is a conviction which is impenetrable, for it comes out of those depths in which we feel ourselves to be a unity, and out of the world which lies behind the world of phenomena. Mocked and denied as though it had long perished, this truth is indestructibly preserved in the moral experience of mankind. These are the ideas which from the beginning onwards have been roused by Christ's death, and have, as it were, played around it. Other ideas have been disengaged — ideas of less importance but, nevertheless, very efficacious at times — but these are the most powerful. They have taken shape in the firm conviction that by his death in suffering he did a definitive work; that he did it "for us." Were we to attempt to measure and register what he did, as was soon attempted, we should fall into dreadful paradoxes; but we can in our turn feel it for ourselves with the same freedom with which it was orginally felt. If we also consider that Jesus himself described his death as a service which he was rendering to many, and that by a solemn act he instituted a lasting remembrance of it — I see no reason to doubt the fact — we can understand how this death and the shame of the cross were bound to take the central place.

Jesus, however, was proclaimed as "the Lord" not only because he had died for sinners but because he was the risen and the living one. If the resurrection meant nothing but that a deceased body of flesh and blood came to life again, we should make short work of this tradition. But it is not so. The New Testament itself distinguishes between the Easter message of the empty grave and the appearances of Jesus on the one side, and the Easter faith on the other. Although the greatest value is attached to that message, we are to hold the Easter faith even in its absence. The story of Thomas is told for the exclusive purpose of impressing upon us that we must hold the Easter faith even without the Easter message: "Blessed are they that have not seen and yet have believed." The disciples on the road to Emmaus were blamed for not believing in the resurrection even though the Easter message had not yet reached them. The Lord is a Spirit, says Paul; and this carries with it the certainty of his resurrection. The Easter *message* tells us of that wonderful event in Joseph of Arimathæa's garden, which, however, no eye saw; it tells us of the empty grave into which a few women and disciples looked; of the appearance of the Lord in a transfigured form — so glorified that his own could not immediately recognize him; it soon begins to tell us, too, of what the risen one said and did. The reports became more and more complete, and more and more confident. But the Easter *faith* is the conviction that the crucified one gained a victory over death; that God is just and powerful; that he who is the firstborn among many brethren still lives. Paul based his Easter faith upon the certainty that "the second Adam" was from heaven, and upon his experience, on the way to Damascus, of God revealing his Son to him as still alive. God, he said, revealed him "in me"; but this inner revelation was coupled with "a vision" overwhelming as vision never was afterwards. Did the apostle know of the message about the empty grave? While there are theologians of note who doubt it, I think it probable; but we cannot be quite certain about it. Certain it is that what he and the disciples regarded as all-important was not the state in which the grave was found but Christ's appearances. But who of us can maintain that a clear account of these appearances can be constructed out of the stories told by Paul and the evangelists; and if that be impossible, and there is no tradition of single events which is quite trustworthy, how is the Easter faith to be based on them? Either we must decide to rest our belief on a foundation unstable and always exposed to fresh doubts, or else we must abandon this foundation altogether, and with it the miraculous appeal to our senses. But here, too, the images of the faith have their roots in truth and reality. Whatever may have happened at the grave and in the matter of the appearances, one thing is certain: *This grave was the birthplace of the indestructible belief that death is vanquished, that there is a life eternal.* It is useless to cite Plato; it is useless to point to the Persian religion, and the ideas and the literature of later Judaism. All that would have perished and has perished; but the certainty of the resurrection and of a life eternal which is bound up with the grave in Joseph's garden has not perished, and on the conviction that *Jesus lives* we still base those hopes of citizenship in an eternal city which make our earthly life worth living and tolerable. "He delivered them who through fear of death were all their lifetime subject to bondage," as the writer of the Epistle to the Hebrews confesses. That is the point. And although there be exceptions to its sway, wherever, despite all the weight of nature, there is a strong faith in the infinite value of the soul; wherever death has lost its terrors; wherever the sufferings of the present are measured against a future of glory, this feeling of life is bound up with the conviction that Jesus Christ has passed through death, that God has awakened him and raised him to life and glory. What else can we believe but that the earliest disciples also found the ultimate foundation of their faith in the living Lord to be the strength which had gone out from him? It was a life never to be destroyed which they felt to be going out from him; only for a brief span of time could his death stagger them; the strength of the Lord prevailed over everything; God did not give him over to death; he lives as the first-fruits of those who have fallen asleep. It is not by any speculative ideas of philosophy but by the vision of Jesus' life and death and by the feeling of his imperishable union with God that mankind, so far as it believes in these things, has attained to that certainty of eternal life for which it was meant, and which it dimly discerns — eternal life in time and beyond time. This feeling first established faith in the value of personal life.... Belief in the living Lord and in a life eternal is the *act* of the freedom which is born of God.

As the crucified and risen one Jesus was the Lord. While this confession of belief in him expressed a man's whole relation to him, it also afforded endless matter for thought and speculation. This conception of the "Lord" came to embrace the many-sided image of the Messiah and all the Old Testament prophecies of a similar kind. But as yet no ecclesiastical "doctrines" about him had been elaborated; everyone who acknowledged him as the Lord belonged to the community. . . .

Paul is the most luminous personality in the history of primitive Christianity, and yet opinions differ widely as to his true significance. Only a few years ago we had a leading Protestant theologian asserting that Paul's rabbinical theology led him to corrupt the Christian religion. Others, conversely, have called him the real founder of that religion. But in the opinion of the great majority of those who have studied him the true view is that he was the one who understood the master and continued his work. This opinion is borne out by the facts. Those who blame him for corrupting the Christian religion have never felt a single breath of his spirit, and judge him only by mere externals, such as clothes and book-learning; those who extol or criticize him as a founder of religion are forced to make him bear witness against himself on the main point, and acknowledge that the consciousness which bore him up and steeled him for his work was illusory and self-deceptive. As we cannot want to be wiser than history, which knows him only as Christ's missionary, and as his own words clearly attest what his aims were and what he was, we regard him as Christ's disciple, as the apostle who not only worked harder but also accomplished more than all the rest put together.

It was Paul who delivered the Christian religion from Judaism. We shall see how he did that if we consider the following points:

It was Paul who definitely conceived the gospel as the message of the redemption already effected and of salvation now present. He preached the crucified and risen Christ, who gave us access to God and therewith righteousness and peace.

It was he who confidently regarded the gospel as a new force abolishing the religion of the law.

It was he who perceived that religion in its new phase pertains to the individual and therefore to all individuals; and in this conviction, and with a full consciousness of what he was doing, he carried the gospel to the nations of the world and transferred it from Judaism to the ground occupied by Greece and Rome. Not only are Greeks and Jews to unite on the basis of the gospel, but the Jewish dispensation itself is now at an end. That the gospel was transplanted from the East, where in subsequent ages it was never able to thrive properly, to the West, is a fact which we owe to Paul.

It was he who placed the gospel in the great scheme of spirit and flesh, inner and outer existence, death and life; he, born a Jew and educated a pharisee, gave it a *language*, so that it became intelligible, not only to the Greeks but to all *men* generally, and united with the whole of the intellectual capital which had been amassed in previous ages.

These are the factors that go to make the apostle's greatness in the history of religion. On their inner connexion I cannot here enter in any detail. But, in regard to the first of them, I may remind you of the words of the most important historian of religion in our day. Wellhausen declares that "Paul's especial work was to transform the gospel of the kingdom into the gospel of Jesus Christ, so that the gospel is no longer the prophecy of the coming of the kingdom, but its actual fulfillment by Jesus Christ. In his view, accordingly, redemption from something in the future has become something which has already happened and is now present. He lays far more emphasis on faith than on hope; he anticipates the sense of future bliss in the present feeling of being God's son; he vanquishes death and already leads the new life on earth. He extols the strength which is made perfect in weakness; the grace of God is sufficient for him, and he knows that no power, present or future, can take him from his love, and that all things work together for good to them that love God." What knowledge, what confidence, what strength, was necessary to tear the new religion from its mother earth and plant it in an entirely new one! Islam, originating in Arabia, has remained the Arabian religion, no matter where it may have penetrated. Buddhism has at all times been at its purest in India. But this religion, born in Palestine, and confined by its founder to Jewish ground, in only a few years after his death was severed from that connexion. Paul put it in competition with the Israelitish religion: "Christ is the end of the law." Not only did it bear being thus rooted up and transplanted, but it showed that it was meant to be thus transplanted. It gave stay and support to the Roman empire and the whole world of western civilization. If, as Renan justly observes, anyone had told the Roman emperor in the first century that the little Jew who had come from Antioch as a missionary was his best collaborator, and would put the empire upon a stable basis, he would have been regarded as a madman, and yet he would have spoken nothing but the truth. Paul brought new forces to the Roman empire, and laid the foundations of western and Christian civilization. Alexander the Great's work has perished; Paul's has remained. But if we praise the man who, without being able to appeal to a single word of his master's, ventured upon the boldest enterprise, by the help of the spirit and with the letter against him, we must nonetheless pay the meed of honor to those personal disciples of Jesus who after a bitter internal struggle ultimately associated themselves with Paul's principles. That Peter did so we know for certain; of others we hear that they at least acknowledged their validity. It was, indeed, no insignificant circumstance that men in whose ears every word of their master's was still ringing, and in whose recollection the concrete features of his personality were still a vivid memory — that these faithful disciples should recognize a pronouncement to be true which in important points seemed to depart from the original message and portended the downfall of the religion of Israel. What was kernel here, and what was husk, history has itself showed with unmistakable plainness, and by the shortest process. Husk were the whole of the Jewish limitations attaching to Jesus' message; husk were also such definite statements as "I am not sent but unto the lost sheep of the house of Israel." In the strength of Christ's spirit the disciples broke through these barriers. It was his personal disciples — not, as we might expect, the second or third generation, when the immediate memory of the Lord had already paled — who stood the great test. That is the most remarkable fact of the apostolic age.

Without doing violence to the inner and essential features of the gospel — unconditional trust in God as the Father of Jesus Christ, confidence in the Lord, forgiveness of sins, certainty of eternal life, purity and brotherly fellowship — Paul transformed it into the universal religion, and laid the ground for the great Church. But whilst the original limitations fell away, new ones of necessity made their appearance; and they modified the simplicity and the power of a movement which was from within. Before concluding our survey of the apostolic age, we must direct attention to these modifications.

In the first place: the breach with the synagogue and the founding of entirely independent religious communities had well-marked results. Whilst the idea was firmly maintained that the community of Christ, the "Church," was something suprasensible and heavenly, because it came from within, there was also a conviction that the Church took visible shape in every separate community. As a complete breach had taken place, or no connexion been established, with the ancient communion, the formation of entirely new societies was logically invested with a special significance, and excited the liveliest interest. In his sayings and parables Jesus, careless of all externals, could devote himself solely to the all-important point; but *how and in what forms* the seed would grow was not a question which occupied his mind; he had the people of Israel

177

with their historical ordinances before him and was not thinking of external changes. But the connexion with this people was now severed, and no religious movement can remain in a *bodiless* condition. It must elaborate *forms* for common life and common public worship. Such forms, however, cannot be improvised; some of them take shape slowly out of concrete necessities; others are derived from the environment and from existing circumstances. It was in this way that the "Gentile" communities procured themselves an organism, a body. The forms which they developed were in part independent and gradual, and in part based upon the facts with which they had to deal.

But a special measure of value always attaches to forms. By being the means by which the community is kept together, *the value of that to which they minister is insensibly transferred to them*; or, at least, there is always a danger of this happening. One reason for this is that the observance of the forms can always be controlled or enforced, as the case may be; whilst for the inner life there is no control that cannot be evaded.

When the breach with the Jewish national communion had once taken place, there could be no doubt about the necessity for setting up a new community in opposition to it. The self-consciousness and strength of the Christian movement was displayed in the creation of a Church which knew itself to be the true Israel. But the founding of churches and "the Church" on earth brought an entirely new interest into the field; what came from within was joined by something that came from without; law, discipline, regulations for ritual and doctrine, were developed, and began to assert a position by a logic of their own. The measure of value applicable to religion itself no longer remained the only measure, and with a hundred invisible threads religion was insensibly worked into the net of history.

In the second place: we have already referred to the fact that it was above all in his Christology that Paul's significance as a teacher consisted. In his view — we see this as well by the way in which he illuminated the death on the cross and the resurrection, as by his equation, "the Lord is a Spirit" — the redemption is already accomplished and salvation a present power. "God hath reconciled us to himself through Jesus Christ"; "If any man be in Christ, he is a new creature"; "Who shall separate us from the love of God?" The absolute character of the Christian religion is thus made clear. But it may also be observed in this connexion that every attempt to formulate a theory has a logic of its own and dangers of its own. There was one danger which the apostle himself had to combat, that of men claiming to be redeemed without giving practical proof of the new life. In the case of Jesus' sayings no such danger could arise, but Paul's formulas were not similarly protected. That men are not to rely upon "redemption," forgiveness of sin, and justification, if the hatred of sin and the imitation of Christ be lacking, inevitably became in subsequent ages a standing theme with all earnest teachers. Who can fail to recognize that the doctrines of "objective redemption" have been the occasion of grievous temptations in the history of the Church, and for whole generations concealed the true meaning of religion? The conception of "redemption," which cannot be inserted in Jesus' teaching in this free and easy way at all, became a snare. No doubt it is true that Christianity is the religion of redemption; but the conception is a delicate one, and must never be taken out of the sphere of personal experience and inner reformation.

But here we are met by a second danger closely connected with the first. If redemption is to be traced to Christ's person and work, everything would seem to depend upon a right understanding of this person together with what he accomplished. The formation of a correct theory of and about Christ threatens to assume the position of chief importance, and to pervert the majesty and simplicity of the gospel. Here, again, the danger is of a kind such as cannot arise with Jesus' sayings. Even in John we read: "If ye love me, keep my commandments." But with the way in which Paul defined the theory of religion, the danger can certainly arise and did arise. No long period elapsed before it was taught in the Church that the all-important thing is to know how the person of Jesus was constituted, what sort of physical nature he had, and so on. Paul himself is far removed from this position — "Whoso calleth Christ Lord speaketh by the Holy Ghost" — but the way in which he ordered his religious conceptions, as the outcome of his speculative ideas, unmistakably exercised an influence in a wrong direction. That, however great the attraction which his way of ordering them may possess for the understanding, it is a perverse proceeding to make Christology the fundamental substance of the gospel, is shown by Christ's teaching, which is everywhere directed to the all-important point, and summarily confronts every man with his God. This does not affect Paul's right to epitomise the gospel in the message of Christ crucified, thus exhibiting God's power and God's wisdom, and in the love of Christ kindling the love of God. There are thousands today in whom the Christian faith is still propagated in the same manner, namely, through Christ. But to demand assent to a series of propositions about Christ's person is a different thing altogether.

There is, however, another point to be considered here. Under the influence of the messianic dogmas, and led by the impression which Christ made, Paul became the author of the speculative idea that not only was God in Christ, but that Christ himself was possessed of a peculiar nature of a heavenly kind. With the Jews, this was not a notion that necessarily shattered the framework of the messianic idea; but with the Greeks it inevitably set an entirely new theory in motion. Christ's *appearance* in itself, the entrance of a divine being into the world, came of necessity to rank as the chief fact, as itself *the real redemption*. Paul did not, indeed, himself look upon it in this light; for him the crucial facts are the death on the cross and the resurrection, and he regards Christ's entrance into the world from an ethical point of view and as an example for us to follow: "For our sakes he became poor"; he humbled himself and renounced the world. But this state of things could not last. The fact of redemption could not permanently occupy the second place; it was too large. But when moved into the first place it threatened the very existence of the gospel, by drawing away men's thoughts and interests in another direction. When we look at the history of dogma, who can deny that that was what happened? To what extent it happened we shall see in the following lectures.

In the third place: the new Church possessed a sacred book, the Old Testament. Paul, although he taught that the law had become of no avail, found a means of preserving the whole of the Old Testament. What a blessing to the Church this book has proved! As a book of edification, of consolation, of wisdom, of counsel, as a book of history, what an incomparable importance it has had for Christian life and apologetics! Which of the religions that Christianity encountered on Greek or Roman ground could boast of a similar book? Yet the possession of this book has not been an unqualified advantage to the Church. To begin with, there are many of its pages which exhibit a religion and a morality other than Christian. No matter how resolutely people tried to spiritualize it and give it an inner meaning by construing it in some special way, their efforts did not avail to get rid of the original sense in its entirety. There was always a danger of an inferior and obsolete principle forcing its way into Christianity through the Old Testament. This, indeed, was what actually occurred. Nor was it only in individual aspects that it occurred; the whole aim was changed. Moreover, on the new ground religion was intimately connected with a political power, namely, with nationality. How if people were seduced into again seeking such a connexion, not, indeed, with Judaism, but with a new nation, and not with ancient national laws, but with something of an analogous character? And when even a Paul here and there declared Old Testament laws to be still authoritative in spite of their having undergone an allegorical transformation, how could anyone restrain his successors from also proclaiming other laws, remodelled to suit the circumstances of the time, as valid ordinances of God? This brings us to the second point. Although whatever was drawn from the Old Testament by way of authoritative precept may have been inoffensive in substance, it was a menace to Christian freedom of both kinds. It threatened the freedom which comes from within, and also the freedom to form Church communities and to arrange for public worship and discipline.

I have tried to show that the limitations which surrounded the gospel did not cease with the severance of the tie binding it to Judaism, but that, on the contrary, new limits made their appearance. They arose, however, just at the very points upon which the necessary progress of things depended, or, as the case might be, where an inalienable possession like the Old Testament was in question. Here, again, then, we are reminded of the fact that, so far as history is concerned, as soon as we leave the sphere of pure inwardness, there is no progress, no achievement, no advantage of any sort, that has not its dark side, and does not bring its disadvantages with it. The apostle Paul complained that "we know in part." To a much greater degree is the same thing true of our actions and of everything connected with them. We have always to "pay the penalty" of acting, and not only take the evil consequences but also knowingly and with open eyes resolutely neglect one thing in order to gain another. Our purest and most sacred possessions, when they leave the inward realm and pass into the world of form and circumstance, are no exception to the rule that the very shape which they take in action also proves to be their limitation.

When the great apostle ended his life under Nero's axe in the year 64, he could say of himself what a short time before he had written to a faithful comrade: "I have finished my course; I have kept the faith." What missionary is there, what preacher, what man entrusted with the cure of souls, who can be compared with him, whether in the greatness of the task which he accomplished, or in the holy energy with which he carried it out? He worked with the most living of all messages, and kindled a fire; he cared for his people like a father and strove for the souls of others with all the forces of his own; at the same time he discharged the duties of the teacher, the schoolmaster, the organizer. When he sealed his work by his death, the Roman empire from Antioch as far as Rome, nay, as far as Spain, was planted with Christian communities. There were to be found in them few that were "mighty after the flesh" or of noble degree, and yet they were as "lights in the world," and on them the progress of the world's history rested. They had little "illumination," but they had acquired the faith in the living God and in a life eternal; they knew that the value of the human soul is infinite, and that its value is determined by relation to the invisible; they led a life of purity and brotherly fellowship, or at least strove after such a life. Bound together into a new people in Jesus Christ, their head, they were filled with the high consciousness that Jews and Greeks, Greeks and barbarians, would through them become one, and that the last and highest stage in the history of humanity had then been reached. (C: 152-189)

*

THE PRESENT STATE OF RESEARCH IN EARLY CHURCH HISTORY

This selection is an edited version of an address Harnack delivered in the summer of 1885 at a conference in Giessen. He was a member of the university-faculty there and had just completed the work on the first volume of his magnum opus, History of Dogma. *This overview was meant to show how he approached the research he had begun with the publication of the* History. *What becomes apparent in this selection is his "reforming" interest: the need to have theology present new formulations of faith for the people of his age.*

The translation was prepared by J. King in 1886 for publication in Contemporary Review, *August 1886; it can be found, in English, in Harnack's* Reden und Aufsätze, *vol. 2, pp. 219-35.*

If the present position of inquiry in the field of early Church history is to be understood, we must start with the science as it was thirty years ago. The Tübingen school, led by a great master, had examined with rare industry the Christian literature of the first two centuries, and believed that it had found a key which unlocked every problem. "Jewish Christianity," "Gentile Christianity" — these were the magic words which sufficed to explain the development of the Church up to the time of Irenæus. It was an immanent process, which, beginning with the appearance and preaching of Jesus Christ, branched into two opposite tendencies, the Petrine and the Pauline, and advanced through a cycle of antitheses and syntheses till it culminated in the Catholic Church. An echo of the assured conviction, that all problems are now solved, may be heard in the words uttered eleven years ago by a famous critic, that theology could now describe the rise of the ancient Catholic Church as clearly or distinctly as the growth of a plant. He who did not believe in the picture as Baur had painted it was almost sure to be written down as an "apologist," a man who attempted to hinder the progress of science. Many may still retain a lively recollection of those days, when in historical theology the words "Jewish Christianity," "Gentile Christianity," buzzed for ever about our ears, and beside them the philosophical notions of "Consciousness," "Image," "Idea," and "Reality." "It is the fate of the Idea in positing itself to posit itself in an infinitely manifold way" — so Schelling and Hegel had said, and so the ideas "posited themselves" in primitive Christianity, though in a manner less manifold than monotonous, till they posited themselves to rest in Catholicism.

I am far from disparaging the historical importance which belongs to the Tübingen school. Everything has been said which need be said, and the highest praise has been accorded when, we confess that the main problem, the rise of Catholicism, was first rightly defined by this school as a problem, that it was the first to attempt to draw with frank openness and tenacious energy a picture, which was possible, of the period in question, and that, following the only true method, it discovered at once the clearest and the surest point with which all inquiry must begin — Paul and Paulinism. But the possible picture which it sketched was not the real, and the key with which it attempted to solve all problems did not suffice even for the most simple. It is not my purpose to show how far the views of the Tübingen school with respect to the apostolic age were just, and how far they are still valid. They have indeed been compelled to undergo very large modifications. But as regards the development of the Church in the second century, it may safely be said that the hypotheses of the Tübingen school have proved themselves everywhere inadequate, nay erroneous, and are today held only by a very few scholars. Indeed, the critic who eleven years ago used the simile of the plant, confesses today that "science grows daily more chary of assertions touching early Christianity, and grows more so in the very proportion that she becomes richer in historical points of view."

"Richer in historical points of view" — in this gain, above all, is the advance beyond the Tübingen school founded. This will at once appear if we simply indicate the chief matters through knowledge of which this advance has been made.

I. The Tübingen school saw in Judaism, so far as it had significance for the earliest history of Christianity, but few differences of shade; they fondly emphasized its rigid monotheism and strict legalism, attending, in addition, only to the philosophical Judaism of Philo. But now we know that Judaism in the age of Christ and his apostles was a richly-composed and multiform picture; that it had many and very varied differences in its shades, which have become highly important for the history of the development of primitive Christianity. The Judaism of the dispersion, in distinction from the Palestinian, claims today our particular attention, and we know that it was in many ways both the prelude to Christianity and the bridge leading over to it.

II. The Tübingen school identified the standpoint of the original apostles with that of the rigidly legal and exclusive Jewish Christians. But now the great majority of critics are agreed on this point: to distinguish beside the Pauline two other standpoints — the Pharisaic Judæo-Christian, which was the more exclusive, and that of the "pillar-apostles," which was freer, and conceded in principle the gospel of Paul.

III. The Tübingen school identified Paulinism with Gentile Christianity. Now, however, we know — and this knowledge is of the highest importance — that Paulinism was a Judæo-Christian doctrine, really intelligible only to Jewish Christians, while the Gentile Christianity of the first and second centuries was an altogether original and independent view of the gospel, which agreed with the Pauline theology only in holding to the universalism of the salvation brought by Christ.

IV. The Tübingen school resolved all the antagonisms which are found in the Church of the second century back into the one great antithesis between Jewish and Gentile Christianity. But today it is recognized that Jewish Christianity was in the second century no more a factor in the development of the Church; that rather on the soil of Gentile Christianity quite new antitheses took form, and new questions, which had absolutely nothing to do with the problems at issue between Paul and the exclusive Jewish Christians, came to be discussed. The Tübingen school, in fact, did not acknowledge that a new element streamed into the Church after the controversies between Paul and the Judaizers; it meant from these controversies rather to explain all that followed. Today, on the contrary, we have come to see that even in the first century there streamed in a potent new element, the Greek spirit, the spirit of the ancient world.

V. The Tübingen school had, properly speaking, an eye for the history of the development of the Church so far as it was registered in images, conceptions, and dogmatic statements. Everything led finally to these, even the forms of worship and of polity. But today we have more truly learned that the Christian religion was, above everything, a new life and a new form of human society. New life creates new opinions; not only do new opinions create new life. Much more attention is therefore now directed to the social life, the public worship, the morality and the discipline of the early Christians, than was ever the case with the Tübingen school.

VI. The first question of the Tübingen school, in criticizing the writings of the New Testament, was always "genuine or counterfeit?" The first question which we now put is, whether these canonical books have been transmitted to us pure and without additions — i.e., whether they have not received, perhaps on their canonization, those superscriptions, author's name, etc., which we now read there. We know that the canonization of books, in and for itself, obscures their origin and true meaning; and we must therefore always ask, whether the obscuration has not been helped by other causes. Only after this question is answered may we propose the other, "genuine or counterfeit?" Many books which critics used to regard as forgeries, are no forgeries, but are only documents which have come to us falsely labelled.

If these points of difference be considered, it will be found that they all result from the fact that we are "richer in historical points of view." But to grow richer is to grow more cautious. So long as only a simple and meagre theory was employed, it was deemed permissible to cut out and ascribe to a later period all that could not be comprehended under the theory. But to have perceived the vast variety of the contemporaneous phenomena, is to have been taught caution. The immediate result of this was to restore with tolerable unanimity to the first century a series of writings for which before no place could be found there. Thus most critics now regard as genuine the Epistle to the Philippians and the two Epistles to the Thessalonians.

But why have we become so much "richer in historical points of view?" Three main causes may be specified. First, the emancipation of the science of history from the thraldom of the philosophical systems. After the complete death of ideas which characterized rationalism, the age of romanticism and philosophy was indeed a wholesome reaction; but it was still only a reaction, and as such it brought with it new limitations, which have been gradually overcome. We have become more realistic, and a historical temper has been formed. We have become more elastic, and have acquired the power to transplant ourselves into other times. Great historians — men like Ranke — have taught us this.

The second cause has been the union of ecclesiastical history with general history, the recognition that only by accurate knowledge of the soil on which the Church has grown can this growth be rightly understood. Every period and every people has only one history: the history of religion and of the Church is only a section of this one history, and only from the standpoint of the whole can the section be understood. Here let me mention a Church historian whose very great merits have not yet been sufficiently recognized — I mean Richard Rothe. It was Rothe, who in his lectures on Church History, showed that the rise and development of the ancient Catholic Church remains unintelligible unless studied throughout in relation to the ancient world; for he says: "The ancient world built up the Catholic Church on the foundation of the gospel, but in doing so it built itself bankrupt." What a store of historical knowledge is packed into that sentence! Only if it be carefully applied in all the branches of early Church history, will this history be really understood. Along with Rothe I mention another great scholar, whose "Vie de Jésus" has made his name no sweet sound — Renan. But let us not judge the six later volumes of his "Histoire des Origines du Christianisme" by his "Vie de Jésus." They contain quite as much solid research as broad and comprehensive views of history. When we compare this work with Baur's "Church History of the First Three Centuries," or with the first volume of Neander's "Church History," we are astonished at the progress which history has made by taking the living as alive, and by studying the soil upon which the tree of the Catholic Church grew. Beside Rothe and Renan stands a band of scholars who have, by bringing their chosen questions in ancient ecclesiastical into connexion with universal history, promoted in a remarkable way special branches of inquiry. I may name Von Engelhardt, Hatch, Heinrici, Overbeck, and De Rossi.

The third cause is the new discoveries which have enriched historical knowledge. We can say with gladness: in the region of ancient Church history we live once more in an age of discovery. That these discoveries have come to us more by accident than by well-directed search, awakens the hope that systematic research may have still happier results. When it has been possible to discover, only a few years ago, not perchance in Turkey or Africa, but in Italy, a hitherto unknown beautiful codex of the gospels, the Purpureus, dating from the sixth century; when Dr. von Gebhardt alone has within three years been able to find in Germany, France, and Italy, more than a dozen manuscripts, previously unknown, of Hermas, we may surely expect to be enriched by still undreamed-of treasures. The harvest truly is great, but the laborers are few. Alas! it was not hard to reckon the number of theologians able to seek after literary treasures, and appraise treasures already discovered. Here is a splendid opening for service!

The discoveries made in recent years in the field of Early Church History may be divided into four groups.

I. First, in the case of several very important works, which have hitherto reached us in partly corrupt and partly defective forms, we have obtained new and better manuscripts. This applies not only to the New Testament, and there notably to the discovery of the Sinaitic MS., but also to patristic literature. We read today the Epistle of Barnabas, the Pastor of Hermas, and other important documents, in far better manuscripts than existed thirty years ago. Our knowledge has thus become more certain, and often the new manuscripts have solved hard problems which owed their very existence to the old defective texts. Only the other day news came of a remarkable discovery — the fragment of a gospel written on a piece of papyrus not larger than the half of an ordinary visiting card. It was found in a bundle of more than a thousand very old papyri, brought from the Fayoum in Egypt, and now at Vienna. I cannot but agree with the editor, the Catholic scholar, Dr. Bickell, that in all probability we have here the fragment of a gospel which has contained a more original text than even our Matthew and Mark.

II. Secondly, from critical examination of their sources, original works, which had been lost, have been recovered from the books into which they had been elaborated. These are real discoveries. Thus from the many late works against Gnosticism, the older and more important, which had perished, have with no little certainty been approximately restored. Thus Krawutzky, some years before the "Teaching of the Twelve Apostles" had been discovered, reconstructed the first half of it from the seventh book of the Apostolic Constitutions, the so-called Apostolic Church Order, and the conclusion of the Epistle of Barnabas. Again, from a work belonging to the fifth century, hitherto judged insignificant, and accordingly overlooked, there has been recovered a fragment of the time of Hadrian — a dialogue between a Jew and a Christian.

III. The third group of discoveries is described by the inscriptions found in the catacombs at Rome. Thanks to the untiring labor and genius of De Rossi, new Christian inscriptions are ever coming to light from the debris of ancient Rome; hitherto unknown catacombs are being discovered, and the already known are being more thoroughly explored. What these discoveries teach is certainly nothing (in the strict sense of the word) new, while accurate dating is almost impossible. But as the relics of departed friends are more dear to us than any mere notice of them, and as from the lines of the original manuscript the spirit of the writer rises more distinctly before us than from the varied figures of the printed copy, so these old stones, inscriptions, and paintings have for us a quite unique worth. While, for example, we may know well enough that to the ancient Christian the sure hope of resurrection was the most treasured good, yet this knowledge grows strangely vivid when we enter those subterranean cemeteries of the ancient saints, and with our own eyes see how here everything breathes peace and joy, and how the certain hope of a glorious awakening rules over all. And, besides, many a detail emerges which enriches or confirms our historical knowledge; thus the uncovering of the vault of the old Roman bishops has proved highly important, and the discovery of the catacomb of Domitilla has shown that at the end of the first century there were not only Christians among the servants of the Emperor in the Palatine Palace — of such Paul had already spoken — but that Christianity had actually penetrated into the imperial family of the Flavii.

IV. But even the third group of discoveries is thrown into the background by the fourth and last group which I have to mention — viz., the discovery of entirely new, hitherto unknown, primitive Christian writings. Leaving on one side the less important of these, like the new Acts of the Martyrs of the second century — which, however, are not to be despised — I would specify four great discoveries of recent years: 1. The complete Epistles of Clement; 2. A large fragment of the lost "Apology" of Aristides; 3. The Diatessaron of Tatian; 4. "The Teaching of the Twelve Apostles."

*

After this survey of the discoveries of the last few years let us return to the point from which we started. I quoted above a sentence of Rothe, to which we may again refer: "The ancient world built up the Catholic Church on the foundation of the gospel, but in doing so it built itself bankrupt." This sentence, whose bearings Rothe himself had not fully perceived, is in fact the egg of Columbus. For long had it been customary to remark upon the great distance which divided the apostolic literature from Jewish Christianity on the one hand, and on the other from post-apostolic writings, no matter how different these were in relation to each other. Heinrich Thiersch has consequently supposed that at the end of the first century the Church, after a sort, fell, like our first parents. The Tübingen school sought so to explain the difference between the apostolic and post-apostolic literatures as to see in the latter the product of a compromise. It spoke of a modified Jewish Christianity and of a modified Paulinism; from these modifications, and from the consequent softening of the sharpness of the early antitheses, it believed that it was able to explain the varied riches of the later formations, as concerned not only doctrine, but also the constitution, discipline, and cultus of the Church. Where, for example, it found in the apostolic fathers and apologists an ethical mode of thought — Christianity conceived as the new law — it assumed the working of Jewish Christianity, which had given up merely circumcision and the ceremonial law; where it detected the formation of a fixed order of worship — elders, priests, and so forth — there it thought could not but be seen the continued influence of the synagogue shaping the growth of the early Catholic Church; conversely, where it found the universalism of the gospel impressed on these Fathers, but without the Pauline basis of justification by grace only, there it believed that a modified, and as it were bisected Paulinism, must be recognized. Nay, more, in movements as late as the Montanistic it tried to see the operation of Jewish Christianity, and, conversely, in Gnosticism, a perverted form of Paulinism. But this conception could be upheld only by doing violence to the facts, and reading into them a foreign meaning. About thirty years ago a reaction set in, led by the work of Albrecht Ritschl, "Die Entstehung der altkatholischen Kirche." In this work there are four determinative principles, which have since been clearly formulated, and have found acceptance, if not with all, yet with the majority of independent critics. These principles are as follows:

1. The divergence of the Christianity of the sub-apostolic from the Christianity of the apostolic age, is to be explained by the fact that the Gentile Christians either did not know or did not understand the Old Testament principles which the Jewish Christians possessed.

2. The Gentile Christians brought into Christianity the religious interests, hopes, and aspirations, which animated them, and could accept at first only some of the fundamental ideas of that gospel which rested on the Old Testament — those, viz., which they had to receive necessarily before all others — the belief in one God, the duty of holy living, the redemption from death through Jesus Christ the Son of God, the Judgment, and the Resurrection.

3. When we find among the Gentile Christians any peculiarities in doctrine, cultus, constitution, etc. — and such peculiarities occur from the very first — we must not, in order to their explanation, draw in the Pauline theology, still less that of the strict Jewish Christianity, but are to consider as factors — (a) certain fundamental thoughts in the gospel, (b) the letter of the certainly not understood Old Testament, which the Gentile Christians treasured as a collection of divine oracles, and (c) the state and constitution of the Græco-Roman world at the time of the first preaching of the gospel.

4. The resultant Catholicism which became fully formed in the third century, is, therefore, not to be understood either through Paulinism or through Jewish Christianity, or apprehended as a compromise between the two; but the Catholic Church is rather that form of Christianity in which every element of the ancient world has been successively assimilated, which Christianity could in any way take up into itself without utterly losing itself in the world.

If these principles are accepted, it follows that the problems which Church history proposes for inquiry are changed at one stroke; for it now becomes no longer possible, in the manner of the old historical schools, to limit ourselves to the written sources of the Christian religion. The historian must rather make his horizon wider, and get a view of the general history of the civilization, morals, and political organization of his period. He must study the earliest sub-apostolic writings with a view to seeing whether already, in their deviations from the oldest Palestinian tradition of the gospels, traces of that spirit of the ancient world, which we call Catholicism, are not to be found. It is remarkable that the earliest Protestant Church historians, Flacius and Gottfried Arnold, had a forecast of how the question really stood: they both, for example, called attention to the fact that the peculiar Christianity of Justin Martyr, in his deviation from Paul and Judæo-Christianity, is to be understood from his heathen antecedents; and both saw in the constitution which the Catholic Church elaborated for herself the effective action of the constitution of the Roman state; yet their conclusions on those two points, because still unverified, remained without any effect. The task set in this field for our modern historical science is to apply these principles to the four great problems of pre-Nicene Church history — that is, to the problems which relate to its literature, cultus, constitution, and doctrine. As concerns all these problems, it may be shown that the Catholic process of formation was nothing else than a building up of the ancient world on the ground of the gospel, and that in the heathen world old forms and thoughts died, just as they had been assimilated by Christianity.

It is of course impossible in the space of an article to bring forward all the evidences in proof of this position; inquiry on this method has only just begun, yet good work has already been accomplished — as regards the history of the literature, by Overbeck; of the cultus, by Rothe and Theodosius Harnack; of the constitution of the Church, by Rothe, Renan, and Hatch; of its doctrine, by M. von Engelhardt. But with reference to one problem, the history of the literature, a few remarks may be allowed. The history of Christian literature has been hitherto very unfruitfully treated, because it has been handled generally from the entirely inadequate point of view of the history of doctrine. There is perhaps no literature in the world which is still so little scientifically investigated as the patristic; and yet what high significance it has! It became, when it stepped into the place of the ancient heathen literature, like the maternal bosom for all the literatures of the Latin and Germanic peoples. But into the place of the ancient heathen literature it stepped only after it had appropriated all its forms and a portion of its spirit. Christian literature begins in the first century with quite peculiar forms, alien alike to the Greek and Roman; in particular it begins with the forms of the Apocalypse and the gospel. But as early as the fourth century it has made use of all the literary forms known to the ancient world — the scientific treatise, the dialogue, the commentary, the philosophical system, the elegant oration, the panegyric, the historical essay, the chronicle, the romance, the novel, the hymn, the ode, the didactic poem, etc., etc. Here, then, is the great question for the history of early Christian literature: How, in what order, and under what conditions did Christianity make itself the master of the old classical literary forms? In answering this question historical science has to show that Christianity at first stood in a relation of very deep distrust to these forms, that the so-called Gnosticism did indeed in the conflict for the gospel lay hold upon them, but that the Church still declined this prize. There is further to be shown how the Church, gradually indeed and cautiously, turned to the literature which was alien to her, and passed from her own earliest forms (the gospel, apocalypse, the prophetic oracle) to the forms of profane literature. The most important precaution taken by the Church was the formation of the Canon of the New Testament, which places before us a selection of the primitive Christian literature. After the Canon had been formed, and raised as a sacred collection above all other writings, the Church could well concede entrance to the profane literature, so far as it did not contradict the Canon. The profane or classical Church style began with the apologies; to them succeeded one style after another; and finally in the catechetical school of Alexandria almost all the forms of ancient literature were cultivated. The patristic literature is nothing else than the continuation of the ancient classical literature, but under the control of the two Testaments. The ancient heathen literature died out in the fourth and fifth centuries, so that at length nothing remained but the Catholic. But this, which had taken into itself every element in the ancient still retaining any vitality, had now fused into innermost union within itself the gospel and the spirit of Greek and Roman antiquity. Whatever the German people has received of spiritual good, the inheritance of antiquity and the inheritance of Christianity, they have received through the patristic literature. It appears at the first glance barren and without spirit; but when we think that it possessed spirit enough to found the mediæval literatures of all European peoples, we shall see that it must be due to our defective study and understanding if we find no spirit in it. Can there be a more important or interesting historical undertaking than to describe the development of Catholic literature, and to show how it gradually made all the forms of classical literature its own, how it thereby became rich and attractive, and how it has, like some creeping plant, so exhausted the heathen literature that the mighty tree it fed on could only die?

Precisely the same holds good of the cultus, the doctrine, and the organization of the Christian Church. Christianity has throughout sucked the marrow of the ancient world, and assimilated it; even dogma is nothing but the Christian faith nourished on ancient philosophy, and the whole of Catholicism is nothing else than the Christianity which has devoured the possessions of the Græco-Roman world. What an insight do we thus get into Catholicism! Whatever in the old world was still capable of life, noble and good, Christianity appropriated — of course with much that was bad and untrue — and placed all under the protection of the gospel. Out of this material she created for herself a body: thus did she preserve and save for the future whatever was worth saving from the culture and the ideas of the old world. To the young German peoples the Church came not only as the Society of the Preacher of Galilee, but also as the great impressive secular power which alone held sway over all the forces of civilization, literature, and law. It is indeed nothing else than the universal Roman empire itself, but in the most wonderful and beneficent metamorphosis, built upon the gospel as a kingdom of Jesus Christ: "*Christus vincit, Christus regnat, Christus trium-*

phat," Christ conquers, Christ reigns, Christ triumphs. The fittest and most suggestive criticism we can today pass on Catholicism is to conceive it as Christianity in the garb of the ancient world, covered with a mediæval overcoat: the Pope is the Roman Emperor, the archbishops and bishops are the old pro-consuls, the monks and priests are the Roman soldiery, the Mass is the old Græco-Roman mystery cultus, the system of doctrine is the Greek philosophy; and so on. The strength and greatness of the gospel has consisted in this, that it could ever attract to itself and preserve everything worthy of life which the ages possessed. Just through this power of assimilation and expansion the gospel has established its right to be the universal religion, and has proved itself the most conservative of forces upon the face of the earth, because securing endurance to everything worthy to endure.

But surely this great enrichment could not take place without the more definite ideas in the gospel becoming diminished and changed. A pure embodiment of the gospel was, under such conditions, not possible. What is the Reformation but the work of God which was to set the Church free again from that bondage which had bound it to the ancient world 1400 years? When Luther did away with the Mass, and restored the service of God in spirit and in truth; when he overthrew the whole Roman building of the system of the Church; when he wished, in opposition to the scholastic theology, to establish the Christian society again on the pure word of God — all may be expressed in the single formula, the Reformation is the return to the pure gospel. Only what is sacred shall be held sacred: the traditions of men, though they be most fair and most worthy, must be taken for what they are — viz., the ordinances of man.

But in recognizing all this let us not, as many polemical Protestants have done, condemn the old Catholicism and the whole development of the Church up to the Reformation. Everything has its time, and every step in the history of the Church was needed. If it was possible in Christ's own sense to follow him within the pale of Judaism and its law, without anything being annulled, it was quite as certainly possible in this sense to live according to the gospel within that ancient Catholic Church. It was God's providence that so guided the development of the Roman empire that it resulted in that wonderful covenant between Christianity and the ancient world which endured nearly 1500 years. When it had done its work, when the time was accomplished, the covenant was dissolved, and could be dissolved because the Church in her New Testament possessed scriptures which have nothing to do with that covenant, because they are older than it. There lies the abiding value of the New Testament. *(PSR: 219-235)*

*

WHAT IS CHRISTIANITY?

(Fifth Selection)

This, the longest selection from What Is Christianity?, *pp. 190-294, surveys the development of the Christian religion from the sub-apostolic age to what Harnack regards as the completion of the formation of dogma, Protestantism, to be precise, the formulation of the faith by Luther. (In his* Outline, *the introduction to which is part of this reader, he stated that the theological developments in Protestantism after Luther are no longer part of the history of dogma, but part of the history of Protestant theology.) The "rediscovery" of the gospel by the Reformer was, in Harnack's view, a return to the directness of Jesus' "simple gospel," although several problematic aspects had remained and had still to be overcome. That task was what theology now had to complete.*

This selection presents in a graphic way the sense of certainty Harnack had in speaking about religious phenomena that lay outside his own experience; this is one of the hallmarks of his sense of scholarship and of the liberalism which he represents.

The apostolic age now lies behind us. We have seen that in the course of it the gospel was detached from the mother-soil of Judaism and placed upon the broad field of the Græco-Roman empire. The apostle Paul was the chief agent in accomplishing this work, and in thereby giving Christianity its place in the history of the world. The new connexion which it thus received did not in itself denote any restricted activity; on the contrary, the Christian religion was intended to be realized in mankind, and mankind at that time meant the *orbis Romanus*. But the new connexion involved the development of new forms, and new forms also meant limitation and encumbrance. We shall see more closely how this was effected if we consider:

THE CHRISTIAN RELIGION IN ITS DEVELOPMENT
INTO CATHOLICISM

The gospel did not come into the world as a statutory religion, and therefore none of the forms in which it assumed intellectual and social

194

expression — not even the earliest — can be regarded as possessing a classical and permanent character. The historian must always keep this guiding idea before him when he undertakes to trace the course of the Christian religion through the centuries from the apostolic age downwards. As Christianity rises above all antitheses of the here and the beyond, life and death, work and the shunning of the world, reason and ecstasy, Hebraism and Hellenism, it can also exist under the most diverse conditions; just as it was originally amid the wreck of the Jewish religion that it developed its power. Not only can it so exist — it must do so, if it is to be the religion of the living and is itself to live. As a gospel it has only *one* aim — the finding of the living God, the finding of him by every individual as *his* God, and as the source of strength and joy and peace. How this aim is progressively realized through the centuries — whether with the co-efficients of Hebraism or Hellenism, of the shunning of the world or of civilization, of gnosticism or of agnosticism, of ecclesiastical institution or of perfectly free union, or by whatever other kinds of bark the core may be protected, the sap allowed to rise — is a matter that is of secondary moment, that is exposed to change, that belongs to the centuries, that comes with them and with them perishes.

Now the greatest transformation which the new religion ever experienced — almost greater even than that which gave rise to the Gentile Church and thrust the Palestinian communities into the background — falls in the second century of our era, and therefore in the period which we shall consider in the present lecture.

If we place ourselves at about the year 200, about a hundred or a hundred and twenty years after the apostolic age — not more than three or four generations had gone by since that age came to an end — what kind of spectacle does the Christian religion offer?

We see a great ecclesiastical and political community, and side by side with it numerous "sects" calling themselves Christian, but denied the name and bitterly opposed. That great ecclesiastical and political community presents itself as a league of individual communities spanning the empire from end to end. Although independent they are all constituted essentially alike, and interconnected by one and the same law of doctrine, and by fixed rules for the purposes of intercommunion. The law of doctrine seems at first sight to be of small scope, but all its tenets are of the widest significance; and together they embrace a profusion of metaphysical, cosmological, and historical problems, give them definite answers, and supply particulars of mankind's development from the creation up to its future form of existence. Jesus' injunctions for the conduct of life are not included in this law of doctrine; as the "rule of discipline" they were sharply distinguished from the "rule of faith." Each Church, however, also presents itself as an institution for public worship, where God is honored in conformity with a solemn ritual. The distinction between priests and laymen is already a well-marked characteristic of this institution; certain acts of divine worship can be performed only by the priest; his mediation is an absolute necessity. It is only by mediation that a man can approach God at all, by the mediation of right doctrine, right ordinance, and a sacred book. The living faith seems to be transformed into a creed to be believed; devotion to Christ, into Christology; the ardent hope for the coming of "the kingdom," into a doctrine of immortality and deification; prophecy, into technical exegesis and theological learning; the ministers of the Spirit, into clerics; the brothers, into laymen in a state of tutelage; miracles and miraculous cures disappear altogether, or else are priestly devices; fervent prayers become solemn hymns and litanies; the "Spirit" becomes law and compulsion. At the same time individual Christians are in full touch with the life of the world, and the burning question is, "In how much of this life may I take part without losing my position as a Christian?" This enormous transformation took place within a hundred and twenty years. The first thing which we have to determine is: How did that happen? next: Did the gospel succeed in holding its own amid this change, and how did it do so? . . .

There were, if I am not mistaken, three leading forces engaged in bringing about this great revolution, and effecting the organization of new forms. The first of these forces tallies with a universal law in the history of religion, for in every religious development we find it at work. When the second and third generations after the founding of a new religion have passed away; when hundreds, nay thousands, have become its adherents no longer through conversion but by the influences of tradition and of birth; when those who have laid hold upon the faith as great spoil are joined by crowds of others who wrap it round them like an outer garment, a revolution always occurs. The religion of strong feeling and of the heart passes into the religion of custom and therefore of form and of law. A new religion may be instituted with the greatest vigor, the utmost enthusiasm, and a tremendous amount of inner emotion; it may at the same time lay ever so much stress on spiritual freedom — where was all this ever more powerfully expressed than in Paul's teaching? — and yet, even though believers be forced to be celibates and only adults be received, the process of solidifying and codifying the religion is bound to follow. Its forms then at once stiffen; in the very process of stiffening they receive for the first time a real significance, and new forms are added. Not only do they acquire the value of laws and regulations, but they come to be insensibly regarded as though they contained within them the very substance of religion; nay, as though they were themselves that substance. This is the way in which people who do not feel religion to be a reality are compelled to regard it, for otherwise they would have nothing at all; and this is the way in which those who continue really to live in it are compelled to handle it, or else they would be unable to exercise any influence upon others. The former are not by any means necessarily hypocrites. Real religion, of course, is a closed book to them; its most important element has evaporated. But there are various points of view from which a man may still be able to appreciate religion without living in it. He may appreciate it as discharging the functions of morality, or of police; above all he may appreciate it on æsthetic grounds.... That is one of the ways in which a man can appreciate a religion without being an inward adherent of it; but there are many others, and, amongst them, some in which a nearer approach is made to its true substance. All of them, however, have this much in common, that any actual experience of religion is no longer felt, or felt only in an uncertain and intermittent way. Conversely, a high regard is paid to the outward shows and influences connected with it, and they are carefully maintained. Whatever finds expression in doctrines, regulations, ordinances and forms of public worship comes to be treated as the thing itself. This, then, is the first force at work in the transformation: *the original enthusiasm*, in the large sense of the word, *evaporates*, and the religion of law and form at once arises.

But not only did an original element evaporate in the course of the second century; another was introduced. Even had this youthful religion not severed the tie which bound it to Judaism, it would have been inevitably affected by the spirit and the civilization of that Græco-Roman world on whose soil it was permanently settled. But to what a much greater extent was it exposed to the influence of this spirit after being sharply severed from the Jewish religion and the Jewish nation. It hovered bodiless over the earth like a being of the air; bodiless and seeking a body. The spirit, no doubt, makes to itself its own body, but it does so by assimilating what is around it. The influx of Hellenism, of the Greek spirit, and the union of the gospel with it, form the greatest fact in the history of the Church in the second century, and when the fact was once established as a foundation it continued through the following centuries. In the influence of Hellenism on the Christian religion three stages may be distinguished.... The first stage of any real influx of definitely Greek thought and Greek life is to be fixed at about the year 130. It was then that the religious philosophy of Greece began to effect an entrance, and it went straight to the center of the new religion. It sought to get into inner touch with Christianity, and, conversely, Christianity itself held out a hand to this ally. We are speaking of Greek *philosophy*, as yet, there is no trace of mythology, Greek worship, and so on; all that was taken up into the Church, cautiously and under proper guarantees, was the great capital which philosophy had amassed since the days of Socrates. A century or so later, about the year 220 or 230, the second stage begins: Greek mysteries, and Greek civilization in the whole range of its development, exercise their influence on the Church, but not mythology and polytheism; these were still to come. Another century, however, had in its turn to elapse before Hellenism as a whole and in every phase of its development was established in the Church. Guarantees, of course, are not lacking here either, but for the most part they consist only in a change of label; the thing itself is taken over without alteration, and in the worship of the saints we see a regular Christian religion of a lower order arising. We are here concerned, however, not with the second and third stage, but only with that influx of the Greek spirit which was marked by the absorption of Greek philosophy and, particularly, of Platonism. Who can deny that elements here came together which stood in elective affinity? So much depth and delicacy of feeling, so much earnestness and dignity, and — above all — so strong a *monotheistic* piety were displayed in the religious ethics of the Greeks, acquired as it had been by hard toil on a basis of inner experience and metaphysical speculation, that the Christian religion could not pass this treasure by with indifference. There was much in it, indeed, which was defective and repellent; there was no personality visibly embodying its ethics as a living power; it still kept up a strange connexion with "demon-worship" and polytheism; but both as a whole and in its individual parts it was felt to contain a kindred element, and it was absorbed.

But besides the Greek ethics there was also a cosmological conception which the Church took over at this time, and which was destined in a few decades to attain a commanding position in its doctrinal system — *the logos*. Starting from an examination of the world and the life within, Greek thought had arrived at the conception of an *active central idea* — by what stages we need not here mention. This central idea represented the unity of the supreme principle of the world, of thought, and of ethics; but it also represented, at the same time, the divinity itself as a creative and active as distinguished from a quiescent power. The most important step that was ever taken in the domain of Christian doctrine was when the Christian apologists at the beginning of the second century drew the equation: the logos = Jesus Christ. Ancient teachers before them had also called Christ "the logos" among the many predicates which they ascribed to him; nay, one of them, John, had already formulated the proposition: "The logos is Jesus Christ." But with John this proposition had not become the basis of every speculative idea about Christ; with him, too, "the logos" was only a predicate. But now teachers came forward who previous to their conversion had been adherents of the platonico-stoical philosophy, and with whom the conception "logos" formed an inalienable part of a general philosophy of the world. They proclaimed that Jesus Christ was the logos incarnate, which had hitherto been revealed only in the great effects which it exercised. In the place of the entirely unintelligible conception "Messiah," an intelligible one was acquired at a stroke; Christology, tottering under the exuberance of its own affirmations, received a stable basis; Christ's significance for the world was established; his mysterious relation to God was explained; the cosmos, reason, and ethics, were comprehended as one. It was, indeed, a marvellous formula; and was not the way prepared for it, nay hastened, by the speculative ideas about the Messiah propounded by Paul and other ancient teachers? The knowledge that the divine in Christ must be conceived as the logos opened up a number of problems, and at the same time set them definite limits and gave them definite directives. Christ's unique character as opposed to all rivals appeared to be established in the simplest fashion, and yet the conception provided thought with so much liberty and free play that Christ could be regarded, as the need might arise, on the one side as operative deity itself, and on the other as still the first born among many brethren and as the first created of God.

What a proof it is of the impression which Christ's teaching created that Greek philosophers managed to identify him with the logos! For the assertion that the incarnation of the logos had taken place in an historical personage there had been no preparation. No philosophising Jew had ever thought of identifying the Messiah with the logos; no Philo, for instance, ever entertained the idea of such an equation! *It gave a metaphysical significance to an historical fact; it drew into the domain of cosmology and religious philosophy a person who had appeared in time and space;* but by so distinguishing one person it raised all history to the plane of the cosmical movement.

The identification of the logos with Christ was the determining factor in the fusion of Greek philosophy with the apostolic inheritance and led the more thoughtful Greeks to adopt the latter. Most of us regard this identification as inadmissible, because the way in which we conceive the world and ethics does not point to the existence of any logos at all. But a man must be blind not to see that for that age the appropriate formula for uniting the Christian religion with Greek thought was the logos. Nor is it difficult even today to attach a valid meaning to the conception. An unmixed blessing it has not been. To a much larger extent than the earlier speculative ideas about Christ it absorbed men's interest; it withdrew their minds from the simplicity of the gospel, and increasingly transformed it into a philosophy of religion. The proposition that the logos had appeared among men had an intoxicating effect, but the enthusiasm and transport which it produced in the soul did not lead with any certainty to the God whom Jesus Christ proclaimed.

The loss of an original element and the gain of a fresh one, namely, the Greek, are insufficient to explain the great change which the Christian religion experienced in the second century. We must bear in mind, thirdly, the great struggle which that religion was then carrying on within its own domain. Parallel with the slow influx of the element of Greek philosophy experiments were being made all along the line in the direction of what may be briefly called "acute Hellenization." While they offer us a most magnificent historical spectacle, in the period itself they were a terrible danger. More than any before it, the second century is the century of religious fusion, of theocracy. The problem was to bring Christianity into the realm of theocracy, as one element among others, although the chief. The "Hellenism" which made this endeavor had already attracted to itself all the mysteries, all the philosophy of Eastern worship, elements the most sublime and the most absurd, and by the never failing aid of philosophical, that is to say, of allegorical interpretation, had spun them all into a glittering web. It now fell upon — I cannot help so expressing it — the Christian religion. It was impressed by the sublime character of this religion; it did reverence to Jesus Christ as the Savior of the world; it offered to give up everything that it possessed — all the treasures of its civilization and its wisdom — to this message, if only the message would suffer them to stand. As though endowed with the right to rule, the message was to make its entry into a ready-made theory of the world and religion, and into mysteries already prepared for it. What a proof of the impression which this message made, and what a temptation! This "gnosticism" — such is the name which the movement has received — strong and active in the plenitude of its religious experiments, established itself under Christ's name, developed a vigorous and abiding feeling for many Christian ideas, sought to give shape to what was still shapeless, to settle accounts with what was externally incomplete, and to bring the whole stream of the Christian movement into its own channel. The majority of the faithful, led by their bishops, so far from yielding to these enticements, took up the struggle with them in the conviction that they masked a demonic temptation. But struggle in this case meant definition, that is to say, drawing a sharp line of demarcation around what was Christian and declaring everything heathen that would not keep within it. *The struggle with gnosticism compelled the Church to put its teaching, its worship, and its discipline, into fixed forms and ordinances, and to exclude everyone who would not yield them obedience.* In the conviction that it was everywhere only conserving and honoring what had been handed down, it never for a moment doubted that the obedience which it demanded was anything more than subjection to the divine will itself, and that in the doctrines with which it encountered the enemy it was exhibiting *the impress of religion itself.*

If by "Catholic" we mean the church of doctrine and of law, then the Catholic Church had its origin in the struggle with gnosticism. It had to pay a heavy price for the victory which kept that tendency at bay; we may almost say that the vanquished imposed their terms upon the victor. It kept dualism and the acute phase of Hellenism at bay; but by becoming a community with a fully worked out scheme of doctrine, and a definite form of public worship, it was of necessity compelled to take on forms analogous to those which it combated in the gnostics. To encounter our enemy's theses by setting up others one by one, is to change over to his ground. How much of its original freedom the Church sacrificed! It was now forced to say: You are no Christian, you cannot come into any relation with God at all, unless you have first of all acknowledged these doctrines, yielded obedience to these ordinances, and followed out definite forms of mediation. Nor was anyone to think a religious experience legitimate that had not been sanctioned by sound doctrine and approved by the priests. The Church found no other way and no other means of maintaining itself against gnosticism, and what was set up as a protection against enemies from without became the palladium, nay, the very foundation, within. This entire development, it is true, would probably have taken place apart from the struggle in question — the two elements which we first discussed would have produced it — but that it took place so rapidly and assumed so positive, nay, so draconian, a shape, was due to the fact that the struggle was one in which the very existence of the traditional religion was at stake. The superficial view that the personal ambition of certain individuals was at the bottom of the whole system of established ordinance and priesthood is absolutely untenable. The loss of the original, living element is by itself sufficient to explain the phenomena. *La médiocrité fonde l'autorité.* It is the man who knows religion only as usage and obedience that creates the priest, for the purpose of ridding himself of an essential part of the obligations which he feels by loading him with them. He also makes ordinances, for the semi-religious prefer an ordinance to a gospel.

We have endeavored to indicate the tendencies by which the great change was effected. It remains to answer the second question: Did the gospel hold its own amid the change, and, if so, how? That it entered upon an entirely new set of circumstances is already obvious; but we shall have to study them more closely. (C: 190-209)

*

No one can compare the internal state of Christendom at the beginning of the third century with the state in which it found itself a hundred and twenty years earlier without being moved by conflicting views and sentiments. Admiration for the vigorous achievement presented in the creation of the Catholic Church, and for the energy with which it extended its activity in all directions, is balanced by concern at the absence of those many elements of freedom and directness, united, however, by an inward bond, which the primitive age possessed. Although we are compelled gratefully to acknowledge that this Church repelled all attempts to let the Christian religion simply dissolve into contemporary thought, and protected itself against the acute phase of Hellenization, still we cannot shut our eyes to the fact that it had to pay a high price for maintaining its position. Let us determine a little more precisely what the alteration was which was effected in it, and on which we have already touched.

The first and most prominent change is the way in which freedom and independence in matters of religion is endangered. No one is to feel and count himself a Christian, that is to say, a child of God, who has not previously subjected his religious knowledge and experience to the controlling influence of the Church's creed. The "Spirit" is confined within the narrowest limits, and forbidden to work where and as it will. Nay, more; not only is the individual, except in special cases, to begin by being a minor and by obeying the Church; he is never to become of full age, that is to say, he is never to lose his dependence on doctrine, on the priest, on public worship, and on the "book." It was then that what we still specifically call the Catholic form of godliness, in contrast with evangelicalism, originated. A blow was dealt to the direct and immediate element in religion; and for any individual to restore it afresh for himself became a matter of extraordinary difficulty.

Secondly, although the acute phase of Hellenization was avoided, Christendom became more and more penetrated by the Greek and philosophical idea that true religion is first and foremost "doctrine," and doctrine, too, that is coextensive with the whole range of knowledge. That this faith of "slaves and old women" attracted to itself the entire philosophy of God and the world which the Greeks had formed, and undertook to recast that philosophy as though teaching it were part of its own substance, and unite it with the teaching of Jesus Christ, was certainly a proof of the inner power of the Christian religion; but the process involved, as a necessary consequence, a displacement of the fundamental religious interest, and the addition of an enormous burden. The question "What must I do to be saved?" which in Jesus Christ's and the apostles' day could still receive a very brief answer, now evoked a most diffuse one; and even though in view of the laymen shorter replies might still be provided, the laymen were insofar regarded as imperfect, and expected to observe a submissive attitude towards the learned. The Christian religion had already received that tendency to intellectualism which has clung to it ever since. But when thus presented as a huge and complex fabric, as a vast and difficult system of doctrine, not only is it encumbered, but its earnest character threatens to disappear. This character depends upon the emotional and gladdening element in it being kept directly accessible. The Christian religion is assuredly informed with the desire to come to terms with all knowledge and with intellectual life as a whole; but when achievements in this field — even presuming that they always accord with truth and reality — are held to be equally binding with the evangelical message, or even to be a necessary preliminary to it, mischief is done to the cause of religion. This mischief is already unmistakably present at the beginning of the third century.

Thirdly, the Church obtained a special, independent value as an *institution*; it became a *religious power*. Originally only a developed form of that community of brothers which furnished place and manner for God's common worship and a mysterious shadow of the heavenly Church, it now became, *as an institution*, an indispensable factor in religion. People were taught that in this institution Christ's Spirit had deposited everything that the individual man can need; that he is wholly bound to it, therefore, not only in love but also in faith; that it is there only that the Spirit works, and therefore there only that all gifts of grace are to be found. That the individual Christian who did not subordinate himself to the ecclesiastical institution relapsed, as a rule, into heathenism, and fell into false and evil doctrines or an immoral life, was, indeed, an actual fact. The effect of this, combined with the struggle against the gnostics, was that the institution, together with all its forms and arrangements, became more and more identified with the "bride of Christ," "the true Jerusalem," and so on, and accordingly was even itself proclaimed as the inviolable creation of God, and the fixed and unalterable abode of the Holy Ghost. Consistently with this, it began to announce that all its ordinances were equally sacred. How greatly religious liberty was thus encumbered I need not show.

Fourthly and lastly, the gospel was not proclaimed as the glad message with the same vigor in the second century as it had been in the first. The reasons for this are manifold: on the one hand personal experience of religion was not felt so strongly as Paul, or as the author of the fourth gospel, felt it; on the other, the prevalent eschatological expectations, which those teachers had restrained by their more profound teaching, remained in full sway. *Fear* and *hope* are more prominent in the Christianity of the second century than they are with Paul, and it is only in appearance that the former stands nearer to Jesus' sayings; for, as we saw, God's Fatherhood is the main article in Jesus' message. But, as Romans 8 proves, the knowledge of this truth is just what Paul embodied in his preaching of the faith. While the element of *fear* thus obtained a larger scope in the Christianity of the second century — this scope increased in proportion as the original buoyancy died down and conformity to the world extended — the ethical element became less free and more a matter of law and rigorism. In religion, rigorism always forms the obverse side of secularity. But as it appeared impossible to expect a rigoristic ethics of everyone, the distinction between a perfect and a sufficient morality already set in as an element in the growth of Catholicism. That the roots of this distinction go further back is a fact of which we need not here take account; it was only towards the end of the second century that the distinction became a fatal one. Born of necessity and erected into a virtue, it soon grew so important that the existence of Christianity as a Catholic Church came to depend upon it. The uniformity of the Christian ideal was thereby disturbed and a quantitative view of moral achievement suggested which is unknown to the gospel. The gospel does, no doubt, make a distinction between a strong and a weak faith, and greater and smaller moral achievements; but he that is least in the kingdom of God may be perfect in his kind.

These various tendencies together denote the essential changes which the Christian religion experienced up to the beginning of the third century, and by which it was modified. Did the gospel hold its own in spite of them, and how may that be shown? Well, we can cite a whole series of documents, which, so far as written words can attest inner and genuinely Christian life, bear very clear and impressive testimony that such life existed. Martyrdoms like those of Perpetua and Felicitas, or letters passing between communities, like those from Lyons to Asia Minor, exhibit the Christian faith and the strength and delicacy of moral sentiment with a splendor only paralleled in the days when the faith was founded; while of all that had been done in the external development of the Church they make no mention whatever. The way to God is found with certainty, and the simplicity of the life within does not appear to be disturbed or encumbered. . . . In this Old-Catholic Church the gospel, truly, was not as yet stifled!

Further, this Church still kept up the all-important idea that the Christian community must present itself as a society of brothers active in work, and it gave expression to this idea in a way that puts subsequent generations to shame.

This religion had, no doubt, already developed a husk and integument, to penetrate through to it and grasp the kernel had become more difficult; it had also lost much of its original life. But the gifts and the tasks which the gospel offered still remained in force, and the fabric which the Church had erected around them also served many a man as the means by which he attained to the thing itself.   (C: 210-217)

*

Greek Catholicism is characterized as a religion by two elements: by *traditionalism* and by *intellectualism.* According to traditionalism, the reverent preservation of the received inheritance, and the defence of it against all innovation, is not only an important duty, but is itself the practical proof of religion. That is an idea quite in harmony with antiquity and foreign to the gospel; for the gospel knows absolutely nothing of intercourse with God being bound up with reverence for tradition itself. But the second element, intellectualism, is also of Greek origin. The elaboration of the gospel into a vast philosophy of God and the world, in which every conceivable kind of material is handled; the conviction that because Christianity is the absolute religion it must give information on all questions of metaphysics, cosmology, and history; the view of revelation as a countless multitude of doctrines and explanations, all equally holy and important — this is Greek intellectualism. According to it, *knowledge* is the highest good, and spirit is spirit only insofar as it knows; everything that is of an æsthetical, ethical, and religious character must be converted into some form of knowledge, which human will and life will then with certainty obey. The development of the Christian faith into an all-embracing theosophy, and the identification of faith with theological knowledge, are proofs that the Christian religion on Greek soil entered the prescribed circle of the native religious philosophy and has remained there.

But in this vast philosophy of God and the world, which possesses an absolute value as the "substance of what has been revealed" and as "orthodox doctrine," there are two elements which radically distinguish it from Greek religious philosophy and invest it with an entirely original character. I do not mean the appeal which it makes to revelation — for to that the Neoplatonists also appealed — but the *idea of creation* and the doctrine of *the God-Man nature of the Savior.* They traverse the scheme of Greek religious philosophy at two critical points, and have therefore always been felt to be alien and intolerable by its genuine representatives.

The idea of creation we can deal with in a few words. It is undoubtedly an element which is as important as it is in thorough keeping with the gospel. It abolishes all intertwining of God and world, and gives expression to the power and actuality of the living God. Attempts were not wanting, it is true, among Christian thinkers on Greek soil — just because they were Greeks — to conceive the deity only as the uniform power operating in the fabric of the world, as the unity in diversity, and as its goal. Traces of this speculative idea are even still to be found in the Church doctrine; the idea of creation, however, triumphed, and therewith Christianity won a real victory.

The subject of the God-Man nature of the Savior is one on which it is much more difficult to arrive at a correct opinion. It is indubitably the central point in the whole dogmatic system of the Greek Church. It supplied the doctrine of the Trinity. In the Greek view these two doctrines together make up Christian teaching *in nuce*. When a Father of the Greek Church once said, as he did say: "The idea of the God-Man nature, the idea of God becoming a man, is what is new in the new, nay, is the only new thing under the sun," not only did he correctly represent the opinion of all his fellow-believers, but he also at the same time strikingly expressed their view that, while sound intelligence and earnest reflection yield all the other points of doctrine of themselves, this one lies beyond them. The theologians of the Greek Church are convinced that the only real distinction between the Christian creed and natural philosophy is that the former embraces the doctrine of the God-Man nature, including the Trinity. Side by side with this, the only other doctrine that can at most come in question is that of the idea of creation.

If that be so, it is of radical importance to obtain a correct view of the origin, meaning, and value of this doctrine. In its completed form it must look strange to anyone who comes to it straight from the evangelists. While no historical reflection can rid us of the impression that the whole fabric of ecclesiastical Christology is a thing absolutely outside the concrete personality of Jesus Christ, historical considerations nevertheless enable us not only to explain its origin but also even to justify, in a certain degree, the way in which it is formulated. Let us try to get a clear idea of the leading points.

We saw earlier how it came about that the Church teachers selected the conception of the logos in order to define Christ's nature and majesty. They found the conception of the "Messiah" quite unintelligible; it conveyed no meaning to them. As conceptions cannot be improvised, they had to choose between representing Christ as a deified man, that is to say, as a hero, or conceiving his nature after the pattern of one of the Greek gods, or identifying it with the logos. The first two possibilities had to be put aside, as they were "heathenish," or seemed to be so. There remained, therefore, the logos. Did it not readily admit of being combined with the conception of the Sonship, without leading to any objectionable theogonies? It involved, too, no menace to monotheism. But the formula had a logic of its own, and this logic led to results which were not absolutely free from suspicion. The conception of the logos was susceptible of very varied expression; in spite of its sublime meaning, it could be also so conceived as to permit of the bearer of the title not being by any means of a truly divine nature but possessing one that was only half divine.

The question as to the more exact definition of the nature of the logos-Christ could not have attained the enormous significance which it received in the Church, and might have been stilled by various speculative answers, if it had not been accompanied by the triumph of a very precise idea of the nature of redemption, which acted as a peremptory challenge. Among all the possible ideas on the subject of redemption — forgiveness of sins, release from the power of the demons, and so on — that idea came victoriously to the front in the Church in the third century which conceived of it as *redemption from death and therewith as elevation to the divine life, that is to say, as deification.* It is true that this conception found a safe starting-point in the gospel, and support in the Pauline theology; but in the form in which it was now developed it was foreign to both of them and conceived on Greek lines; *mortality is in itself reckoned as the greatest evil, and as the cause of all evil, while the greatest of blessings is to live for ever.* What a severely Greek idea this is we can see, in the first place, from the fact that redemption from death is presented, in a wholly realistic fashion, as a *pharmacological* process — the divine nature has to flow in and transform the mortal nature — and, in the second, from the way in which eternal life and deification were identified. But if actual interference in the constitution of human nature and its deification are involved, then *the redeemer must himself be God and must become man.* It is only on this condition that so marvellous a process can be imagined as actually taking place. Word, doctrine, individual deeds, are here of no avail — how can life be given to a stone, or a mortal made immortal, by preaching at them? Only when the divine itself bodily enters into mortality can mortality be transformed. It is not, however, the hero, but God himself alone, who possesses the divine, that is to say, eternal life, and so possesses it as to permit of his *giving it to others.* The logos, then, must be God himself, and he must have actually become man. With the satisfying of these two conditions, real, natural redemption, that is to say, the deification of humanity, is actually effected. These considerations enable us to understand the prodigious disputes over the nature of the logos-Christ which filled several centuries. . . . The doctrines of the identical nature of the three persons of the Trinity and of the God-Man nature of the redeemer are in strict accordance with the distinguishing notion of the redemption as a deification of man's nature by making him immortal. Without the help of the notion those formulas would never have been attained; but they also stand and fall with it. They prevailed, however, not because they were akin to the ideas of Greek philosophy, but because they were contrasted with them. Greek philosophy never ventured, and never aspired, to meet, in any similar way by "history" and speculative ideas, that wish for immortality which it so vividly entertained. To attribute any such interference with the cosmos to an *historical* personality and the manner in which it appeared, and to ascribe to that personality a transformation in what, given once for all, was in a state of eternal flux, must necessarily have seemed, to Greek philosophy, pure mythology and superstition. The "only new thing under the sun" must necessarily have appeared to it, and did appear, to be the worst kind of fable.

The Greek Church still entertains the conviction today that in these doctrines it possesses the essence of Christianity, regarded at once as a mystery and as a mystery that has been revealed. Criticism of this contention is not difficult. We must acknowledge that those doctrines powerfully contributed to keeping the Christian religion from dissolving into Greek religious philosophy; further, that they profoundly impress us with the absolute character of this religion; again, that they are in actual accordance with the Greek notion of redemption; lastly, that this very notion has *one* of its roots in the gospel. But beyond this we can acknowledge nothing; nay, it is to be observed (i) that the notion of the redemption as a deification of mortal nature is subchristian, because the moral element involved can at best be only tacked on to it; (ii) that the whole doctrine is inadmissible, because it has scarcely any connexion with the Jesus Christ of the gospel, and its formulas do not fit him; it is, therefore, not founded in truth; and (iii) that as it is connected with the real Christ only by uncertain threads, it leads us away from him; it does not keep his image alive, but, on the contrary, demands that this image should be apprehended solely in the light of alleged hypotheses about him expressed in theoretical propositions. That this substitution produces no very serious or destructive effects is principally owing to the fact that in spite of them the Church has not suppressed the gospels, and that their own innate power makes itself felt. It may also be conceded that the notion of God having become man does not everywhere produce the effect only of a bewildering mystery, but, on the contrary, is capable of leading to the pure and definite conviction that God was in Christ. We may admit, lastly, that the egoistic desire for immortal existence will, within the Christian sphere, experience a moral purification through the longing *to live with and in God*, and to remain inseparably bound to his love. But all these admissions cannot do away with the palpable fact that in Greek dogma we have a fatal connexion established between the desire of the ancients for immortal life and the Christian message. Nor can anyone deny that this connexion, implanted in Greek religious philosophy and the intellectualism which characterized it, has led to formulas which are incorrect, introduce a supposititious Christ in the place of the real one, and, besides, encourage the delusion that, if only a man possesses the right formula, he has the thing itself. Even though the Christological formula were the theologically right one — what a departure from the gospel is involved in maintaining that a man can have no relation with Jesus Christ, nay, that he is sinning against him and will be cast out, unless he first of all acknowledges that Christ was *one* person with two natures and two powers of will, one of them divine and one human. Such is the demand into which intellectualism has developed. Can such a system still find a place for the gospel story of the Syrophœnician woman or the centurion at Capernaum?

But with traditionalism and intellectualism a further element is associated, namely, ritualism. If religion is presented as a complex system of traditional doctrine, to which the few alone have any real access, the majority of believers cannot practice it at all except as ritual. Doctrine comes to be administered in stereotyped formulas accompanied by symbolic acts. Although no inner understanding of it is thus possible, it produces the feeling of something mysterious. The very deification which the future is expected to bring, and which in itself is something that can neither be described nor conceived, is now administered as though it were an earnest of what is to come, by means of ritual acts. An imaginative mood is excited, and disposes to its reception; and this excitement, when enhanced, is its seal.

Such are the feelings which move the members of the Greek Catholic Church. Intercourse with God is achieved through the cult of a mystery, and by means of hundreds of efficacious formulas small and great, signs, pictures, and consecrated acts, which, if punctiliously and submissively observed, communicate divine grace and prepare the Christian for eternal life. Doctrine as such is for the most part something unknown; if it appears at all, it is only in the form of liturgical aphorisms. For ninety-nine per cent of these Christians, religion exists only as a ceremonious ritual, in which it is externalized. But even for Christians of advanced intelligence all these ritual acts are absolutely necessary, for it is only in them that doctrine receives its correct application and obtains its due result.

There is no sadder spectacle than this transformation of the Christian religion from a worship of God in spirit and in truth into a worship of God in signs, formulas, and idols. To feel the whole pity of this development, we need not descend to such adherents of this form of Christendom as are religiously and intellectually in a state of complete abandonment, like the Copts and Abyssinians; the Syrians, Greeks, and Russians are, taken as a whole, only a little better. Where, however, can we find in Jesus' message even a trace of any injunction that a man is to submit to solemn ceremonies as though they were mysterious ministrations, to be punctilious in observing a ritual, to put up pictures, and to mumble maxims and formulas in a prescribed fashion? *It was to destroy this sort of religion that Jesus Christ suffered himself to be nailed to the cross,* and now we find it re-established under his name and authority! Not only has "mystagogy" stepped into a position side by side with the "mathesis," that is to say, the doctrine, which called it forth; but the truth is that "doctrine" — be its constitution what it may, it is still a spiritual principle — has disappeared, and ceremony dominates everything. This is what marks the relapse into the ancient form of the lowest class of religion. Over the vast area of Greek and oriental Christendom religion has been almost stifled by ritualism. It is not that religion has sacrificed one of its essential elements. No! it has entered an entirely different plane; it has descended to the level where religion may be described as a cult and nothing but a cult.   (*C:* 228-239)

*

THE CHRISTIAN RELIGION IN ROMAN CATHOLICISM

The Roman Church is the most comprehensive and the vastest, the most complicated and yet at the same time the most uniform structure which, as far as we know, history has produced. All the powers of the human mind and soul, and all the elemental forces at mankind's disposal, have had a hand in creating it. In its many-sided character and severe cohesion Roman Catholicism is far in advance of Greek. We ask, in turn:

What did the Roman Catholic Church achieve?

What are its characteristics?

What modifications has the gospel suffered in this Church, and how much of it has remained?

What did the Roman Catholic Church achieve? Well, in the first place, it educated the Romano-Germanic nations, and educated them in a sense other than that in which the Eastern Church educated the

Greeks, Slavs, and Orientals. However much their original nature, or primitive and historical circumstances, may have favored those nations and helped to promote their rise, the value of the services which the Church rendered is not thereby diminished. It brought Christian civilization to young nations, and brought it, not once only, so as to keep them at its first stage — no! it gave them something which was capable of exercising a progressive educational influence, and for a period of almost a thousand years it itself led the advance. Up to the fourteenth century it was a leader and a mother; it supplied the ideas, set the aims, and disengaged the forces. Up to the fourteenth century — thenceforward, as we may see, those whom it educated became independent, and struck out paths which it did not indicate, and on which it is neither willing nor able to follow them. But even so, however, during the period covered by the last six hundred years, it has not fallen so far behind as the Greek Church. With comparatively brief interruptions it has proved itself fully a match for the whole movement of politics and even in the movement of thought it still has an important share. The time, of course, is long past since it was a leader; on the contrary, it is now a drag; but, in view of the mistaken and precipitate elements in modern progress, the drag which it supplies is not always the reverse of a blessing.

In the second place, however, this Church upheld the idea of religious and ecclesiastical independence in Western Europe in the face of the tendencies, not lacking here either, towards State-omnipotence in the spiritual domain. In the Greek Church religion has become so intimately allied with nationality and the state that it has no room left for independent action. On Western ground it is otherwise; the religious element and the moral element bound up with it occupy an independent sphere and jealously guard it. This we owe in the main to the Roman Church.

These two facts embrace the most important piece of work which this Church achieved and in part still achieves. We have already indicated the bounds which must be set to the first. To the second also a sensible limitation attaches, and we shall see what it is as we proceed.

What are the characteristics of the Roman Church? This was our second question. Unless I am mistaken, the Church, complicated as it is, may be resolved into three chief elements. The first, *Catholicism*, it shares with the Greek Church. The second is the *Latin spirit* and the *Roman World-Empire* continuing in the Roman Church. The third is the spirit and religious fervor of *St. Augustine. . . .*

These three elements, the Catholic, the Latin in the sense of the

Roman World-Empire, and the Augustinian, constitute the peculiar character of the Roman Church.

So far as the first is concerned, you may recognize its importance by the fact that the Roman Church today receives every Greek Christian, nay, at once effects a "union" with every Greek ecclesiastical community, without more ado, as soon as the Pope is acknowledged and submission is made to his apostolic supremacy. Any other condition that may be exacted from the Greek Christians is of absolutely no moment; they are even allowed to retain divine worship in their mother tongue, and married priests. . . . The element which the Roman Church shares with the Greek must, then, be of significant and critical importance, when it is sufficient to make union possible on the condition that the papal supremacy is recognized. As a matter of fact, the main points characteristic of Greek Catholicism are all to be found in Roman as well, and are, on occasion, just as energetically maintained here as they are there. Traditionalism, orthodoxy, and ritualism play just the same part here as they do there, so far as "higher considerations" do not step in; and the same is true of monasticism also.

So far as "higher considerations" do not step in — here we have already passed to the examination of the second element, namely, the Latin spirit in the sense of the Roman world-dominion. In the Western half of Christendom the Latin spirit, the spirit of Rome, very soon effected certain distinct modifications in the general Catholic idea. As early as the beginning of the third century we see the thought emerging in the Latin Fathers that salvation, however effected and whatever its nature, is bestowed in the form of a contract under definite conditions, and only to the extent to which they are observed; in fixing these conditions the deity manifested its mercy and indulgence, but it guards their observance all the more jealously. Further, the whole contents of revelation are law, the Bible as well as tradition. Again, this tradition is attached to a class of officials and to their correct succession. The "mysteries," however, are "sacraments"; that is to say, on the one hand, they are binding acts; on the other, they contain definite gifts of grace in a carefully limited form and with a specific application. Again, the discipline of penance is a procedure laid down by law and akin to the process adopted in a civil action or a suit in defense of honor. Lastly, the Church is a *legal institution*; and it is so, not side by side with its function of preserving and distributing salvation, but it is a legal institution for the sake of this very function.

But it is in its constitution as a Church that it is a legal establishment.

We must briefly see how things stand in regard to this constitution, as its foundations are common to the Eastern and the Western Church. When the monarchical episcopate had developed, the Church began to approximate its constitution to state government. The system of uniting sees under a metropolitan who was, as a rule, the bishop of the provincial capital, corresponded with the distribution of the Empire into provinces. Above and beyond this, the ecclesiastical constitution in the East was developed a step further when it adapted itself to the division of the Empire introduced by Diocletian, by which large groups of provinces were united. Thus arose the constitution of the patriarchate, which was not, however, strictly enforced, and was in part counteracted by other considerations.

In the West no division into patriarchates came about; but on the other hand something else happened: in the fifth century the Western Roman Empire perished of internal weakness and through the inroads of the barbarians. What was left of what was Roman took refuge in the Roman Church — civilization, law, and orthodox faith as opposed to the Arian. The barbarian chiefs, however, did not venture to set themselves up as Roman Emperors, and enter the vacant shrine of the *imperium*; they founded empires of their own in the provinces. In these circumstances the Bishop of Rome appeared as the guardian of the past and the shield of the future. All over the provinces occupied by the barbarians, even in those which had previously maintained a defiant independence in the face of Rome, bishops and laity looked to him. Whatever Roman elements the barbarians and Arians left standing in the provinces — and they were not few — were ecclesiasticized and at the same time put under the protection of the Bishop of Rome, who was the chief person there after the Emperor's disappearance. But in Rome the episcopal throne was occupied in the fifth century by men who understood the signs of the times and utilized them to the full. *The Roman Church in this way privily pushed itself into the place of the Roman world-empire, of which it is the actual continuation;* the empire has not perished, but has only undergone a transformation. If we assert, and mean the assertion to hold good even of the present time, that the Roman Church is the old Roman empire consecrated by the gospel, that is no mere "clever remark," but the recognition of the true state of the matter historically, and the most appropriate and fruitful way of describing the character of this Church. It still governs the nations; its Popes rule like Trajan and Marcus Aurelius; Peter and Paul have taken the place of Romulus and Remus; the bishops and archbishops, of the proconsuls; the troops of priests and monks correspond to the legions; the Jesuits, to the imperial body-guard. The continued influence of the old empire and its institutions may be traced in detail, down to individual legal ordinances, nay, even in the very clothes. That is no Church like the evangelical communities, or the national Churches of the East; it is a political creation, and as imposing as a world-empire, because the continuation of the Roman empire. The Pope, who calls himself "King" and "Pontifex Maximus," is Cæsar's successor. The Church, which as early as the third and fourth century was entirely filled with the Roman spirit, has re-established in itself the Roman empire. . . . It is an *empire* that this priestly Cæsar rules, and to attack it with the armament of dogmatic polemics alone is to beat the air.

I cannot here show what immense results follow from the fact that the Catholic Church is the Roman empire. Let me mention only a few con-clusions which the Church itself draws. It is just as essential to this Church to exercise governmental power as to proclaim the gospel. The phrase "Christus vincit, Christus regnat, Christus triumphat," must be understood in a political sense. He rules on earth by the fact that his Rome-directed Church rules, and rules, too, by law and by force; that is to say, it employs all the means of which states avail themselves. Accor-dingly it recognizes no form of religious fervor which does not first of all submit to this papal Church, is approved by it, and remains in constant dependence upon it. This Church, then, teaches its "subjects" to say: "Though I understand all mysteries, and though I have all faith, and though I bestow all my goods to feed the poor, and though I give my body to be burned, and have not unity in love which alone floweth from unconditional obedience to the Church, it profiteth me nothing." Out-side the pale of the Church, all faith, all love, all the virtues, even martyr-doms, are of no value whatever. Naturally; for even an earthly state appreciates only those services which a man has rendered for its sake. But here the state identifies itself with the kingdom of Heaven, in other respects proceeding just like other states. From this fact you can your-selves deduce all the Church's claims; they follow without difficulty. Even the most exorbitant demand appears quite natural as soon as you only admit the truth of the two leading propositions: "The Roman Church is the kingdom of God," and "The Church must govern like an earthly state." It is not to be denied that Christian motives have also had a hand in this development — the desire to bring the Christian religion into a real connexion with life, and to make its influence felt in every situation that may arise, as well as anxiety for the salvation of individuals and of nations. How many earnest Catholic Christians there have been who had no other real desire than to establish Christ's rule on earth and build up his kingdom! But while there can be no doubt that their intention, and the energy with which they put their hands to the work, made them superior to the Greeks, there can be as little that it is a serious misunderstanding of Christ's and the apostles' injunctions to aim at establishing and building up the kingdom of God by political means. The only forces which this kingdom knows are religious and moral forces, and it rests on a basis of freedom. But when a Church comes forward with the claims of an earthly state, it is bound to make use of all the means at the disposal of that state, including, therefore, crafty diplomacy and force; for the earthly state, even a state governed by law, must on occasion become a state that acts contrary to law. The course of development which this Church has followed as an earthly state was, then, bound to lead logically to the absolute monarchy of the Pope and his infallibility; for in an earthly theocracy infallibility means, at bottom, nothing more than full sovereignty means in a secular state. That the Church has not shrunk from drawing this last conclusion is a proof of the extent to which the sacred element in it has become secularized.

(C: 245-256)

*

THE CHRISTIAN RELIGION IN PROTESTANTISM

Anyone who looks at the external condition of Protestantism, especially in Germany, may, at first sight, well exclaim: "What a miserable spectacle!" But no one can survey the history of Europe from the second century to the present time without being forced to the conclusion that in the whole course of this history the greatest movement and the one most pregnant with good was the Reformation in the sixteenth century; even the great change which took place at the transition to the nineteenth is inferior to it in importance. What do all our discoveries and inventions and our advances in outward civilization signify in comparison with the fact that today there are thirty millions of Germans, and many more millions of Christians outside Germany, who possess a religion without priests, without sacrifices, without "fragments" of grace, without ceremonies — a spiritual religion!

Protestantism must be understood, first and foremost, by the contrast which it offers to Catholicism, and here there is a double direction which any estimate of it must take, first as *Reformation* and secondly as

Revolution. It was a reformation in regard to the doctrine of salvation; a revolution in regard to the Church, its authority, and its apparatus. . . .

Protestantism was a *Reformation*, that is to say, a renewal, as regards the core of the matter, as regards religion, and consequently as regards the doctrine of salvation. That may be shown in the main in three points.

In the first place, religion was here brought back again to itself, insofar as the gospel and the corresponding religious experience were put into the foreground and freed of all alien accretions. Religion was taken out of the vast and monstrous fabric which had been previously called by its name — a fabric embracing the gospel and holy water, the priesthood of all believers and the Pope on his throne, Christ the Redeemer and St. Anne — and was *reduced* to its essential factors, to the Word of God and to faith. This truth was imposed as a *criterion* on everything that also claimed to be "religion" and to unite on terms of equality with those great factors. In the history of religions every really important reformation is always, first and foremost, *a critical reduction* to principles: for in the course of its historical development, religion, by adapting itself to circumstances, attracts to itself much alien matter, and produces, in conjunction with this, a number of hybrid and apocryphal elements, which it is necessarily compelled to place under the protection of what is sacred. If it is not to run wild from exuberance, or be choked by its own dry leaves, the reformer must come who purifies it and brings it back to itself. This critical reduction to principles Luther accomplished in the sixteenth century, by victoriously declaring that the Christian religion was given only in the Word of God and in the inward experience which accords with this Word.

In the second place, there was the definite way in which the "Word of God" and the "experience" of it were grasped. For Luther the "Word" did not mean Church doctrine; it did not even mean the Bible; it meant the message of the free grace of God in Christ which makes guilty and despairing men happy and blessed; and the "experience" was just the certainty of this grace. In the sense in which Luther took them, both can be embraced in one phrase: *the confident belief in a God of grace.* They put an end — such was his own experience, and such was what he taught — to all inner discord in a man; they overcome the burden of every ill; they destroy the sense of guilt; and, despite the imperfection of a man's own acts, they give him the certainty of being inseparably united with the holy God.

Nothing, he taught, is to be preached but the God of grace, with whom we are reconciled through Christ. Conversely, it is not a question of ecstasies and visions; no transports of feeling are necessary; it is *faith* that is to be aroused. Faith is to be the beginning, middle, and end of all religious fervor. In the correspondence of Word and faith "justification" is experienced, and hence justification holds the chief place in the Reformers' message; it means nothing less than the attainment of peace and freedom in God through Christ, dominion over the world, and an eternity within.

Lastly, the third feature of this renewal was the great transformation which *God's worship* now inevitably underwent, God's worship by the individual and by the community. Such worship — this was obvious — can and ought to be nothing but putting *faith* to practical proof. As Luther declared over and over again, "all that God asks of us is faith, and it is through faith alone that he is willing to treat with us." To let God be God, and to pay him honor by acknowledging and invoking him as Father — it is thus alone that a man can serve him. Every other path on which a man tries to approach him and honor him leads astray, and vain is the attempt to establish any other relation with him. What an enormous mass of anxious, hopeful, and hopeless effort was now done away with, and what a revolution in worship was effected! But all that is true of God's worship by the individual is true in exactly the same way of public worship. Here, too, it is only the Word of God and prayer which have any place. All else is to be banished; the community assembled for God's worship is to proclaim the message of God with praise and thanksgiving, and call upon his name. Anything that goes beyond this is not worship at all.

These three points embrace the chief elements in the Reformation. What they involved was a *renewal* of religion; for not only do they denote, albeit in a fashion of their own, a return to Christianity as it originally was, but they also existed themselves in Western Catholicism, although buried in a heap of rubbish.   (*C:* 268-272)

*

Protestantism was not only a Reformation but also a *revolution.* From the legal point of view the whole Church system against which Luther revolted could lay claim to full obedience. It had just as much legal validity in Western Europe as the laws of the state themselves. When Luther burnt the papal bull he undoubtedly performed a revolutionary act — revolutionary, not in the bad sense of a revolt against legal ordinance which is also moral ordinance as well, but certainly in the sense of a violent breach with a given legal condition. It was against this state of things that the new movement was directed, and it was to the following chief points that its protest in word and deed extended. Firstly: It protested against the entire hierarchical and priestly system in the Church, demanded that it should be abolished, and abolished it in favor of a common priesthood and an established order formed on the basis of the congregation. . . .

Secondly: It protested against all formal, external authority in religion; against the authority, therefore, of councils, priests, and the whole tradition of the Church. That alone is to be authority which shows itself to be such within and effects a deliverance; the thing itself, therefore, the gospel. Thus Luther also protested against the authority of the letter of the Bible; but this was a point on which neither he nor the rest of the Reformers were quite clear, and where they failed to draw the conclusions which their insight into fundamentals demanded.

Thirdly: It protested against all the traditional arrangements for public worship, all ritualism, and every sort of "holy work." As it neither knows nor tolerates, as we have seen, any specific form of worship, any material sacrifice and service to God, any mass and any works done for God and with a view to salvation, the whole traditional system of public worship, with its pomp, its holy and semi-holy articles, its gestures and processions, came to the ground. How much could be retained in the way of form for *æsthetic* or *educational* reasons was, in comparison with this, a question of entirely secondary importance.

Fourthly: It protested against sacramentalism. Baptism and the Lord's Supper it left standing, as institutions of the primitive Church, or, as it might be, of the Lord himself; but it desired that they should be regarded either as symbols and marks by which the Christian is known, or as acts deriving their value exclusively from that message of the forgiveness of sins which is bound up with them. All other sacraments it abolished, and with them the whole notion of God's grace and help being accessible in bits, and fused in some mysterious way with definite corporeal things. To sacramentalism it opposed the *Word*, and to the notion that grace was given by bits, the conviction that there is only one grace, namely, to possess *God himself* as the source of grace. It was not because Luther was so very enlightened that in his tract "On the Babylonian Captivity" he rejected the whole system of sacramentalism — he had enough superstition left in him to enable him to advance some very shocking contentions — but because he had had inner experience of the fact that where "grace" does not endow the soul with the living God himself it is an illusion. Hence for him the whole doctrine of sacramentalism was an infringement of God's majesty and an enslavement of the soul.

Fifthly: It protested against the double form of morality, and accordingly against the higher form; against the contention that it is particularly well-pleasing to God to make no use of the powers and gifts which are part of creation. The Reformers had a strong sense of the fact that the world passes away with the lusts thereof; we must certainly not represent Luther as the modern man cheerfully standing with his feet firmly planted on the earth; on the contrary, like the men of the Middle Ages he had a strong yearning to be rid of this world and to depart from the "vale of tears." But because he was convinced that we neither can nor ought to offer God anything but trust in him, he arrived, in regard to the Christian's position in the world, at quite different theses from those which were advanced by the grave monks of previous centuries. As fastings and ascetic practices had no value before God, and were of no advantage to one's fellowmen, and as God is the Creator of all things, the most useful thing that a man can do is to remain in the position in which God has placed him. This conviction gave Luther a cheerful and confident view of earthly ordinances, which contrasts with and actually got the upperhand of his inclination to turn his back upon the world.

He advanced the definite thesis that all positions in life — constituted authority, the married state, and so on, down to domestic service — existed by the will of God, and were therefore genuinely spiritual positions in which we are to serve God; a faithful maidservant stands higher, with him, than a contemplative monk. Christians are not to be always devising how they may find some new paths of their own, but to show patience and love of neighbor within the sphere of their given vocation. Out of this there grew up in his mind the notion that all worldly laws and spheres of activity have an independent title. It is not that they are to be merely tolerated, and have no right to exist until they receive it from the Church. No! they have rights of their own, and they form the vast domain in which the Christian is to give proof of his faith and love; nay, they are even to be respected in places which are as yet ignorant of God's revelation in the gospel.

It was thus that the same man who asked nothing of the world, so far as his own personal feelings were concerned, and whose soul was troubled only by thought for the Eternal, delivered mankind from the ban of asceticism. He was thereby really and truly the life and origin of a new epoch, and he gave it back a simple and unconstrained attitude towards the world, and a good conscience in all earthly labor.

This fruitful work fell to his share, not because he secularized religion, but because he took it so seriously and so profoundly that, while in his view it was to pervade all things, it was itself to be freed from everything external to it.   (C: 277-281)

*

The question has often been raised whether, and to what extent, the Reformation was a work of the *German* spirit. I cannot here go into this complicated problem. But this much seems to me to be certain, that while we cannot, indeed, connect Luther's momentous religious experiences with his nationality, the results positive as well as negative with which he invested them display the German; the German man and German history. From the time that the Germans endeavored to make themselves really at home in the religion handed down to them — this did not take place until the thirteenth century onwards — they were preparing the way for the Reformation. And just as Eastern Christianity is rightly called Greek, and the Christianity of the Middle Ages and of Western Europe is rightly called Roman, so the Christianity of the Reformation may be described as German, in spite of Calvin. For Calvin was Luther's pupil, and he made his influence most lastingly felt, not among the Latin nations but among the English, the Scots, and the Dutch. Through the Reformation the Germans mark a stage in the history of the universal Church. No similar statement can be made of the Slavs.

The recoil from asceticism, which as an ideal never penetrated the Germans to the same extent as other nations, and the protest against religion as external authority, are to be set down as well to the Pauline gospel as to the German spirit. Luther's warmth and heartiness in preaching, and his frankness in polemical utterance, were felt by the German nation to be an opening out of its own soul. . . .

But what was here achieved had its dark side as well. If we ask what the Reformation cost us, and to what extent it made its principles prevail, we shall see this dark side very clearly.

We get nothing from history without paying for it, and for a violent movement we have to pay double. What did the Reformation cost us? I will not speak of the fact that the unity of Western civilization was destroyed, since it was after all only over a part of Western Europe that the Reformation prevailed, for the freedom and many-sided character of the resulting development brought us a greater gain. But the neces-

221

sity of establishing the new Churches as *state-churches* was attended by serious disadvantages. The system of an ecclesiastical state is, of course, worse, and its adherents have truly no cause to praise it in contrast with the state-churches. But still the latter — which are not solely the outcome of the breach with ecclesiastical authority, but were already prepared for in the fifteenth century — have been the cause of much stunted growth. They have weakened the feeling of responsibility, and diminished the activity, of the evangelical communities; and, in addition, they have aroused the not unfounded suspicion that the Church is an institution set up by the state, and accordingly to be adjusted to the state. Much has happened, indeed, in the last few decades to check that suspicion by the greater independence which the Churches have obtained; but further progress in this direction is necessary, especially in regard to the freedom of individual communities. The connexion with the state must not be violently severed, for the Churches have derived much advantage from it; but steps must be taken to further the development upon which we have entered. If this results in multifarious organizations in the Church, it will do no harm; on the contrary, it will remind us, in a forcible way, that these forms are all arbitrary.

Further, Protestantism was forced by its opposition to Catholicism to lay exclusive emphasis on the inward character of religion, and upon "faith alone"; but to formulate one doctrine in sharp opposition to another is always a dangerous process. The man in the street is not sorry to hear that "good works" are unnecessary, nay, that they constitute a danger to the soul. Although Luther is not responsible for the convenient misunderstanding that ensued, the inevitable result was that in the reformed Churches in Germany from the very start there were accusations of moral laxity and a want of serious purpose in the sanctification of life. The saying "If ye love me, keep my commandments" was unwarrantably thrust into the background. Not until the pietistic movement arose was its central importance once more recognized. Up till then the pendulum of the conduct of life took a suspicious swing in the contrary direction, out of opposition to the Catholic "justification by works." But religion is not only a state of the heart; it is a deed as well; it is faith active in love and in the sanctification of life. This is a truth with which evangelical Christians must become much better acquainted, if they are not to be put to shame.

There is another point closely connected with what I have just mentioned. The Reformation abolished monasticism, and was bound to abolish it. It rightly affirmed that to take a vow of lifelong asceticism was

a piece of presumption; and it rightly considered that any worldly vocation, conscientiously followed in the sight of God, was equal to, nay, was
better than, being a monk. But something now happened which Luther
neither foresaw nor desired: "monasticism," of the kind that is conceivable and necessary in the evangelical sense of the word, disappeared
altogether. But every community stands in need of personalities living
exclusively for its ends. The Church, for instance, needs volunteers who
will abandon every other pursuit, renounce "the world," and devote
themselves entirely to the service of their neighbor; not because such a
vocation is "a higher one," but because it is a necessary one, and because
no Church can live without also giving rise to this desire. But in the
evangelical Churches the desire has been checked by the decided attitude which they have been compelled to adopt towards Catholicism. It
is a high price that we have paid; nor can the price be reduced by considering, on the other hand, how much simple and unaffected religious fervor has been kindled in home and family life. We may rejoice, however,
that in the past century a beginning has been made in the direction of
recouping this loss. In the institution of deaconesses and many cognate
phenomena the evangelical Churches are getting back what they once
ejected through their inability to recognize it in the form which it then
took. But it must undergo a much ampler and more varied development.

Not only had the Reformation to pay a high price; it was also
incapable of perceiving all the conclusions to which its new ideas led,
and of giving them pure effect. It is not that the work which it did was not
absolutely valid and permanent in every particular — how could that be,
and who could desire it to have been so? No! it remained stationary in its
development even at the point at which, to judge by the earnest foundation that was laid at the start, higher things might have been expected.
Various causes combined to produce this result. From the year 1526
onwards national Churches had to be founded at headlong speed on
evangelical lines; they were forced to be "rounded and complete" at a
time when much was still in a state of flux. Then again, a mistrust of the
left wing, of the "enthusiasts," induced the Churches to offer an energetic resistance to tendencies which they could have accompanied for a
good bit of their way. Luther's unwillingness to have anything to do with
them, nay, the manner in which he became suspicious of his own ideas
when they coincided with those of the "enthusiasts," was bitterly
avenged and came home to the evangelical Churches in the Age of
Enlightenment. Even at the risk of being reckoned among Luther's

detractors, we must go further. This genius had a faith as robust as Paul's, and thereby an immense power over the minds and hearts of men; but he was not abreast of the knowledge accessible even in his own time. The *naïve* age had gone by; it was an age of deep feeling, of progress, an age in which religion could not avoid contact with all the powers of mind. In this age it was his destiny to be forced to be not only a reformer but also an intellectual and spiritual leader and teacher. The way of looking at the world and at history he had to plan afresh for generations; for there was no one there to help him, and to no one else would people listen. But he had not all the resources of clear knowledge at his command. Lastly, he was always anxious to go back to the original, to the gospel itself, and, so far as it was possible to do it by intuition and inward experience, he did it; moreover, he made some admirable studies in history, and in many places broke victoriously through the serried lines of the traditional dogmas. But any trustworthy knowledge of the history of those dogmas was as yet an impossibility, and still less was any historical acquaintance with the New Testament and primitive Christianity attainable. It is marvellous how in spite of all this Luther possessed so much power of penetration and sound judgment. We have only to look at his introductions to the books of the New Testament, or at his treatise on "Churches and Councils." But there were countless problems of which he did not even know, to say nothing of being able to solve them; and so it was that he had no means of distinguishing between kernel and husk, between what was original and what was of alien growth. How can we be surprised, then, if in its doctrine, and in the view which it took of history, the Reformation was far from being a finished product; and that, where it perceived no problems, confusion in its own ideas was inevitable? It could not, like Pallas Athene, spring complete from Jupiter's head: as doctrine it could do no more than mark a *beginning*, and it had to reckon on future development. But by being rapidly formed into national Churches it came near to itself cutting short its further development for all time.

As regards the confusion and the checks which it brought upon itself, we must content ourselves with referring to a few leading points. Firstly, Luther would admit nothing but the gospel, nothing but what frees and binds the consciences of men, what everyone, down to the man-servant and the maid-servant, can understand. But then he not only took the old dogmas of the Trinity and the two natures as part of the gospel — he was not in a position to examine them historically — and even framed new ones, but he was absolutely incapable of making any sound distinction between "doctrine" and gospel; in this respect falling far behind Paul. The necessary result was that intellectualism was still in the ascendant; that a scholastic doctrine was again set up as necessary to salvation; and that two classes of Christians once more arose: those who understand the doctrine, and the minors who are dependent on the others' understanding of it.

Secondly, Luther was convinced that that alone is the "Word of God" whereby a man is inwardly born anew — the message of the free grace of God in Christ. At the highest levels to which he attained in his life he was free from every sort of bondage to the letter. What a capacity he had for distinguishing between Law and gospel, between Old and New Testament, nay, for distinguishing in the New Testament itself! All that he would recognize was the kernel of the matter, clearly revealed as it is in these books, and proving its power by its effect on the soul. But he did not make a clean sweep. In cases where he had found the letter important, he demanded submission to the "it is written"; and he demanded it peremptorily, without recollecting that, where other sayings of the Scriptures were concerned, he himself had declared the "it is written" to be of no binding force.

Thirdly, grace is the forgiveness of sins, and therefore the assurance of possessing a God of grace, and life, and salvation. How often Luther repeated this, always with the addition that what was efficacious here was the *Word* — that union of the soul with God in the trust and childlike reverence which God's Word inspires; it was a personal relation which was here involved. But the same man allowed himself to be inveigled into the most painful controversies about the means of grace, about communion and infant baptism. These were struggles in which he ran the risk of again exchanging his high conception of grace for the Catholic conception, as well as of sacrificing the fundamental idea that it is a purely spiritual possession that is in question, and that, compared with Word and faith, all else is of no importance. What he here bequeathed to his Church has become a legacy of woe.

Fourthly, the counter-Church which, as was inevitable, rapidly arose in opposition to the Roman Church, and under the pressure which that Church exercised, perceived, not without reason, that its truth and its title lay in the re-establishment of the gospel. But whilst the counter-Church privily identified the sum and substance of its doctrine with the gospel, the thought also stole in surreptitiously: *We*, that is to say, the particular Churches which had now sprung up, *are the true Church*. Luther, of course, was never able to forget that the true Church was the sacred community of the faithful; but still he had no clear ideas as to the relation between it and the visible new Church which had now arisen, and subsequent generations settled down more and more into the sad misunderstanding: We are the true Church *because we have the right "doctrine."* This misunderstanding, besides giving rise to evil results in self-infatuation and intolerance, still further strengthened that mischievous distinction between theologians and clergy on the one side, and the laity on the other, on which we have already dwelt. Not, perhaps, in theory, but certainly in practice, a double form of Christianity arose, just as in Catholicism; and in spite of the efforts of the pietistic movement, it still remains with us today. The theologian and the clergyman must defend the whole doctrine, and be orthodox; for the layman it suffices if he adheres to certain leading points and refrains from attacking the orthodox creed. A very well-known man, as I have been lately told, expressed the wish that a certain inconvenient theologian would go over to the philosophical faculty; "for then," he said, "instead of an unbelieving theologian we should have a believing philosopher." Here we have the logical outcome of the contention that in the evangelical Churches, too, doctrine is something laid down for all time, and that in spite of being generally binding it is a matter of so much difficulty that the laity need not be expected to defend it. But if we persist on this path, and other confusions become worse confounded and take firmer root, there is a risk of Protestantism becoming a sorry double of Catholicism. I say a sorry double, because there are two things which Protestantism will never obtain, namely, a pope and monastic priests. Neither the letter of the Bible nor any belief embodied in creeds can ever produce the unconditional authority which Catholics possess in the pope; and Protestantism cannot now return to the monastic priest. It retains its national Churches and its married clergy, neither of which looks very stately by the side of Catholicism, if competition with Catholicism is what the evangelical Churches desire.   (*C:* 282-294)

*

THE CONSTITUTION AND LAW OF THE CHURCH IN THE FIRST TWO CENTURIES

Harnack wrote the study from which this selection is taken in the year 1909, at a time when the question of constitutions and by-laws was much on his mind in relation to his work at the Royal Library; he knew first-hand what constitutions and laws needed to be in order to support and further the spirit of those who had called an institution into being. The first two centuries of the Christian Church were, therefore, a field of investigation of decisive importance to him since they would show what form Jesus' message and community were to take in the company of those who bore his name. The material, taken from pp. 1-5 and 166-72, was translated by F. L. Pogson from the German text, which was published in 1909, with the English version appearing in 1910, under the title given above.

INTRODUCTION

In no other department of Church history is the opposition between the ecclesiastical and the historical standpoint so great as in that dealing with the earliest constitution of the Church and the history of ecclesiastical law. According to Catholic doctrine Christ founded the Church, placed Peter at its head, associated with Peter a governing body of apostles, who were to be succeeded by the monarchical episcopate just as the primacy was to devolve upon the successors of Peter, and established the distinction between clergy and laity as fundamental. In addition, all the rest of the constitution of the Church as it exists today is carried back to Christ himself, and the only points about which there is a minor controversy are: how much he commanded directly during his earthly life; how much he ordained as the exalted Lord in the forty days of his intercourse with the disciples; how much the apostles added subsequently, led by his spirit; and what less important and alterable additions have been made in the course of the history of the Church. In any case he founded the Church as a visible kingdom, equipped with a vast jurisdiction, which has its root in the power of binding and loosing, and both pope and clergy derive their authority from him. He entrusted the Church with the right and duty of universal missionary activity, and thereby gave to her the ends of the earth for her possession, and he granted infallibility to her and to her decrees by promising that through his spirit he would be with her all the days. The Church is thus set over against the secular kingdoms of the present and the future as a kingdom of a unique kind, it is true, but yet as a kingdom in face of which the sovereign rights that still belong to the earthly kingdoms can have only the most restricted scope and in all "mixed cases" must yield to the decision of the Church.

But, according to the old Protestant doctrine also, the Church is a deliberate and direct foundation of Christ, and although the Catholic conception is radically corrected by the doctrine that the Church is

227

"a congregation of the faithful" based on the Word of God, yet — in Calvinism and parts of Lutheranism — considerable theocratic and clerical elements, although latent, are not entirely absent.

Both views have the whole historical development of the apostolic and post-apostolic age against them, and besides, they stand or fall with the question of the authenticity of a few New Testament passages (especially in the gospel of Matthew). If we put these aside — and by all the rules of historical criticism we are compelled to do so — then every direct external bond between Jesus and the "Church" and its developing orders is severed. There remains the inner spiritual bond, even if Jesus neither founded nor even intended the Church.[6] And naturally there also remains the fact that it was precisely his disciples and followers who founded the Church, and that he appointed twelve of them as propagators of his teaching and as future judges over the twelve tribes. But everything that actually came about did not arise from any previously conceived plan, but, under the given conditions of the period, grew automatically out of the brotherly association of men who had found God through Jesus, who therefore knew that they were ruled by the Spirit of God, and who, standing within the Jewish theocracy, believed in the realization of the theocratic ideal through Jesus, and for this end staked their lives. On one side these early disciples had had a spiritual experience of God; on the other side they were members of a definite historical organization, the Jewish theocracy — a tortuous double development was bound to be the result! For the seed sown, or rather the seed and the soil together, contained in germ not only a society of brethren embracing all mankind and living in the fear of God, but also the Church in the very form in which it has developed in Catholicism, and which the latter represents as primitive.   (*CL*: 1-5)

*

CONCLUSION

In the constitutional history of the Church of the first two centuries there are to be found, with the exception of the emperor, all the elements which played a part and took definite shape in the succeeding centuries. In fact these elements are not only there, but they are already operating. Here, too, it is not correct, with reference to the conflicts that have been waged over the operative factors in the early Christian organization, to insist upon mutually exclusive alternatives, but rather to recognize the co-operation of many factors, though this comprehensiveness should not obscure the fact that there *was* one fundamental and ever-active principle, which was innate in the religious consciousness of Christians, namely, the thought that the Church was the realization of the ideal expressed by the phrase "the people of God." This conception itself had two aspects, and therefore developed in two very closely connected directions, viz. a spiritual and a theocratic. In the former it was the charisma that inspired and moulded the development; in the latter the thought of the rule of God (God as all and in all). In this latter the formal element was derived from the connexion maintained with the organization of Judaism, existing both as a whole and as a system of synagogues. Originally, of course, this connexion was almost entirely severed, or at any rate very much obscured, owing to the prominence given to the charismatic element, but it soon reappeared more and more clearly — not through the influence of Jewish Christianity, still less through the direct influence of Judaism, but through the continued use of the Old Testament and the increasing need, similar to that which had been formerly felt by Judaism itself, for an ecclesiastical and religious organization here on earth.

In the development of the organization of Gentile Christianity, the heathen religious societies, the politico-religious organization of the empire, the municipal and provincial organization, and lastly, though perhaps only in certain localities, the organization of the philosophical schools: all these had, strictly speaking, only so much influence as they exercised unconsciously — an influence, too, of which the Gentile-Christian communities in their progressive development had not the least suspicion. The Churches (or in some cases particular circles in them) automatically imitated these organizations, or rather, compelled by necessity, directed their activities into the channels which already traversed the land, rejecting, however, in the process everything that savored of polytheism. We may thus certainly say, with some reservations, that the above-mentioned organizations had their share in the constitution of the Church; but yet it is misleading to assert that the Christian communities organized themselves on the model of heathen "religious societies" or of civic "corporations," much less on the model of "philosophical schools," for it should not be forgotten that the chief points of resemblance in external form which they had in common with the religious societies, philosophical schools, etc., sprang from the inner principle of the Christian societies themselves. It is most important always to see clearly, not only that the Christian religion had a specific principle of organization in the thought that the Church was the realization of the ideal expressed in the phrase "the people of God upon earth," but also that in the second century it has already drawn to itself so effectively all the elements which seemed necessary to complete the edifice that nothing more was wanting; in fact, it was purely a question of shaping a unified structure out of this abundance of materials. As regards the idea of a "right to legislate," this also (and indeed in the form of "divine right") was innate in the Church on the theocratic view, in however spiritual a form that view was held, as well as on the other view that the Church was the successor to the legislative rights of the ancient people of God, or indeed was this people in its final form. Legislation resulted (still always invested with a divine sanction) in consequence of the development of the charismata. This led to various forms of organization, for "charisma" and "law" do not exclude one another in this connexion; indeed, the charisma creates certain rights for itself. Finally the Church, when she began to become naturalized on earth and was compelled to regulate the natural social relations of her members, found herself unable simply to take over the public regulations already in force or to give them her adherence. Accordingly she increased the severity of the moral and social ordinances which she found already in existence and began, although comparatively late, to set up regulations of her own. These are in principle moral, but since in part they are made compulsory on the communities (marriage regulations, etc.), there arises an ecclesiastical law of a mixed character, *i.e.* a mixture of moral and legal elements and a confused compound of divine and secular law. Just for this reason the Church persistently felt and maintained that she stood above and beyond the secular legal system of the state.

All the elements of the later development of the constitution of the Church were present at the end of the second century, and indeed earlier. There was no subsequent emergence of new factors except that of the Christian emperor, nor was a revolution ever necessary to attain that which was to be won in the third, in the fourth and fifth, in the ninth and eleventh, in the sixteenth and nineteenth centuries. It was always possible to have recourse to something already present, which needed only to be brought to the front, to be "developed" and fixed by law. But very different "developments" were possible. In no period could the one which actually took place be accomplished without the abolition of some rights, and therefore without the invention of historical or legal fictions in order to veil the loss of these rights. Nothing, however, became more complicated — complication was a characteristic of the condition of things at the beginning. In reality, a continually increasing simplification was introduced. The external features of ecclesiastical organization appear indeed in a greater variety of forms, but in no century have the essential features of the Western Catholic constitution of the Church been simpler than in our own. A breach has been made by the Reformation, and by the Reformation only. Here, in relation to the organization, constitution, and law of the Church, the Reformation has cut more deeply into history and historical development than at any other point. It has not only destroyed in its own compass the medieval constitution of the Church, but it no longer possesses any connexion with the constitution of the Church of the first and second centuries. The Reformation, insofar as it is Lutheran, has fallen back on the only principle which it was admittedly able to prove from the oldest documents, and with which it goes to the root of the matter, namely, that the word of God must be proclaimed and that an office for this proclamation dare not be wanting. From the standpoint of this achievement of Luther's, in its positive and negative aspects, it is possible to answer with certainty the question, which is again so much debated at the present day, as to when the beginning of the modern period is to be placed. What post-Reformation movement, then, has been even approximately so successful as the Reformation? In history it is a question of deeds, or rather of ideas which become deeds and create new forms. Meanwhile the nations of Western Europe still live as Catholics or as Protestants. There is as yet no third course open. That they are one or the other is still at the present day far more important than the amount of philosophical and scientific enlightenment or the number of mechanical appliances which they possess. Luther has created this condition of things. In the meantime the nations are still waiting for a third kind of Church as the foundation of their higher life.   (*CL:* 166-172)

3

THE PRESENCE AND INFLUENCE OF THE "RELIGIOUS GENIUS" IN THE HISTORY OF CHRISTIANITY

"If you read Augustine's Confessions," *Harnack said in 1900, "you will acknowledge . . . it is the work of a genius who has felt God, the God of the Spirit, to be the be-all and the end-all of his life: who thirsts after him and desires nothing beside him. . . . he managed by what he wrote to go so straight to the souls of millions, to describe so precisely their inner condition, and so impressively and overpoweringly to put the consolation before them, that what he felt has been felt again and again. . . . It is by what he felt that they are kindled, and it is his thoughts that they think."[7] Later, when dealing with Luther, Harnack declared that "the same man who asked nothing of the world . . . delivered humankind from the ban of asceticism. He was thereby really and truly the life and origin of a new epoch."[8]*

The key to those men's genius was, for Harnack, their utter simplicity in depicting divine revelation. He was convinced that everyone understood what Augustine and Luther wanted to teach others about God and God's relation to us humans, for the substance of that teaching was simplicity itself. It was, not surprisingly, Harnack's own wish to present the nature of Christianity in as simple a way as possible. His biographer, daughter Agnes von Zahn-Harnack, cites his love for the expression Bildung ist wieder-gewonnene Naivität *(education/formation is naiveté regained).[9] Harnack sought to express what is so extraordinary in the language of the ordinary. His lectures strove to depict the religion he held to be, also, "naiveté regained" for himself, so that it would be so also for others. The positive echoes to the lectures lead one to think that what Harnack claimed for Augustine and Luther in terms of their impact on people's piety was being claimed for the impact Harnack's lectures had made. Harnack himself, of course, made no such claims for his work. What genius achieved was, through simplicity, synthesis and directness, to place people directly before the claim of Jesus on their lives and into the conviction of the goodness of God and of life.*

The two selections are almost contemporaneous to each other; the first grew out of Harnack's work on Augustine for his magnum opus: the History of Dogma, published between 1886 and 1890. The second selection comes from the climactic conclusion of that work.

THE CONFESSIONS OF ST. AUGUSTINE

The material of this selection was presented initially as a lecture and, when published, combined with another lecture on monasticism. The former was delivered in 1887, at the time when the second volume of History of Dogma, *which covered the span from the second century to Augustine, was about to be published. It is clear from everything Harnack wrote about this significant figure of the Church that he was profoundly touched by him and his piety. The lecture is almost a panegyric, full of admiration, if not veneration. The significant dimension to be noticed is the place Harnack assigns to persons such as Augustine (or Luther, as the next selection will show) in the development of the faith of others.*

The translation is that of E. E. Kellett and F. H. Marseille and was published in English in 1901. It is found in the book entitled Monasticism: Its Ideal and History and The Confessions of St. Augustine, *p. 119-71.*

During the period between the death of Constantine and the sack of Rome by the Vandals, that is, from about 340 A.D. to 450, took place the accumulation of the spiritual capital inherited from antiquity by the Middle Ages. Whether we look at religion and theology, or at science and politics, or at the leading ideas generally of the mediæval mind, everywhere we become conscious of the absolute dependence of these ideas on the intellectual acquisitions made by the Fathers of the Church in the century of migrations. These acquisitions, it is true, do not themselves bear the stamp of new production; rather are they entirely a selection from a much richer abundance of ideas and living forces.

When, in the reign of Constantine, the Church had gained the victory, her leaders sought to make themselves masters of all forms of spiritual life, and to subject everybody and everything to the dominion of the Church and her spirit. The great task, long since commenced, of fusing Christianity with the empire and with ancient culture, was finished with astonishing quickness. Now first was the union between the Christian religion and ancient philosophy completed. Through the favor of circumstances an active interchange between East and West, Rome and Greece, was again brought about. The Latin Church was equipped with a store of Greek philosophy immediately before the great severance between East and West. It would almost seem that the impending doom, the approaching night of barbarism, had been already foreboded. The firm building of the Church was completed in haste. Whatever in Greek philosophy seemed capable of use was drawn into the scheme of dogmatic teaching; the remainder was relegated to the rear as dangerous or as heretical, and thus gradually got rid of. The constitution of the Church was supplemented from the tried forms of the imperial constitution; the ecclesiastical canons followed the lines of Roman law. Public service was revised and its forms extended. Already whatever appeared imposing and venerable in the old heathen mysteries had been long imitated; but now the whole service became still more magnificent. Thus was formed that splendid pomp, that wonderful union of elevated thoughts with ceremonial forms, which even today makes the Catholic service so impressive. Art, again, was not forgotten: ancient tradition was made to yield up certain of its "motives" — few, but those highly significant and of high creative import — to which the Church lent the glamor of sanctity. Even the stores of ancient culture, and the literature of leisure, were prepared for the good of the coming centuries. The old heathen fables, heroic sagas, and novels were sifted and transformed into Christian Lives of Saints.

In every case the ascetic ideal of the Church formed the basis of these stories; though the contrast to the varied and sinful life in which this ideal was given its play, lent an especial charm to the old legends in their new form.

Thus everything borrowed from antiquity was made "Christian," and received, by its union with sanctity, the guarantee of permanence. The remnant of old culture, thus incorporated with the Church, was now able to defy the approaching storms and to serve the coming nations.

But it was after all a mere remnant, a poor selection from the capital of a falling world, protected by the authority of sanctity; not, indeed, lacking in inner unity, but as yet without progressive force or the power of growth.

In the Middle Ages, during more than seven centuries, if we disregard the fresh and youthful vigor contributed by the Germanic races, the West remained confined to the above possession; but, on the other hand, it owned a treasure of incomparable fulness, a man who lived at the end of the ancient time, and who projected his life over the centuries of the new — Augustine.

Between St. Paul the apostle and Luther the reformer, the Christian Church has possessed no one who could measure himself with Augustine; and in comprehensive influence no other is to be compared with him. We are right, both in the Middle Ages and today, to mark a distinction between the spirit of the East and that of the West; and we are right to observe in the latter a life and motion, the straining of mighty forces, high problems, and great aims. But, if so, the *Church* of the West at least owes this peculiarity of hers in no small degree to one man, Augustine. Along with the Church he served, he has moved through the centuries. We find him in the great mediæval theologians, including the greatest, Thomas Aquinas. His spirit sways the pietists and mystics of those ages: St. Bernard no less than Thomas à Kempis. It is he that inspires the ecclesiastical reformers — those of the Karling epoch as much as a Wyclif, a Hus, a Wesel and a Wessel: while, on the other hand, it is the same man that gives to the ambitious Popes the ideal of a theocratic state to be realized on earth.

All this, perhaps, may to us, today, seem somewhat foreign: our culture, it is said, springs from the Renaissance and the Reformation. True enough; but the spirit of Augustine ruled the beginnings of both. Upon Augustine, Petrarch and the great masters of the Renaissance formed themselves; and without him Luther is not to be understood. Augustine, the founder of Roman Catholicism, is at the same time the only Father of the Church from whom Luther received any effective teaching, or whom the humanists honored as a hero.

But Augustine has still closer points of contact with us than these. The religious language we speak, so familiar to us from songs, prayers, and books of devotion, bears the stamp of his mind. We speak, without knowing it, in his words; and it was he who first taught the deepest emotions how to find expression, and lent words to the eloquence of the heart. I am not here speaking of what is called the tongue of Zion. In this also he has his share, though to but a small degree. But it is the language of simple piety and of powerful Christian pathos; and further, that of our psychologists and pedagogues is still under his influence. Hundreds of great masters have since his time been given us; they have guided our thoughts, warmed our emotions, enriched our speech; but none has supplanted Augustine.

Finally, which is the main point, we find in his delineation of the essence of religion and of the deepest problems of morality, such striking depth and truth of observation, that we must still honor him as our master, and that his memory is still able in some measure, even today, to unite Protestant and Catholic.

I do not propose to set before you a complete picture of the activity and influence of this man. I prefer rather to portray him merely according to the work in which he has portrayed himself — the "Confessions" — the most characteristic of the many writings he has left us.

This work Augustine wrote in mature years — he was then forty-six — and twelve years after his baptism at Milan. He had already been for some time Bishop of Hippo in Northern Africa, when he felt impelled to give to himself and to the world, in the form of a confession to God, an account of his life down to his baptism, in order that, as he says, God might be praised. "He hath made us, but we had brought ourselves to destruction; He who made us, also hath made us anew." "I tell this to the whole race of man, howsoever few thereof may read my writing, in order that I and all who read this may think from how great a depth must man cry to God." At the end of his life, thirty years later, he looked back to this work. He calls it the one of his books which is read most fondly and most often. Some points in it, it is true, he himself censures; but, as a whole, in the presence of death itself, he marks it as a witness of the truth. It was not to be a mingling of *Dichtung and Wahrheit*;[10] but he meant, plainly and without reserve, to show in the book what he had been.

The significance of the "Confessions" is as great on the side of form as on that of content. Before all, they were a literary *achievement.* No poet, no philosopher before him undertook what he here performed; and I may add that almost a thousand years had to pass before a similar thing was done. It was the poets of the Renaissance, who formed themselves on Augustine, that first gained from his example the daring to depict themselves and to present their personality to the world. For what do the "Confessions" of Augustine contain? The portrait of a soul — not psychological disquisitions on the understanding, the will, and the emotions in man, not abstract investigations into the nature of the soul, not superficial reasonings and moralizing introspections like the Meditations of Marcus Aurelius, but the most exact portraiture of a distinct human personality, in his development from childhood to full age, with all his propensities, feelings, aims, mistakes; a portrait of a soul, in fact, drawn with a perfection of observation that leaves on one side the mechanical devices of psychology, and pursues the method of the physician and the physiologist.

Observation, indeed, is the strong point of Augustine. Because he observes, he is interested in everything that the professed philosopher disregards. He depicts the infant in the cradle and the naughtinesses of the child; and he passes reflections on the "innocence of child-hood." ... He observes the dominant educational system, how it reposes on fear and ambition. He is of opinion that we ought only to learn what is true, and that grammar is better than mythology, physics better than windy speculation. Next, he watches the busy doings of the adult: "The antics of children are called business in the grown-up." He appraises society, and finds that every man in it strives to obtain good things, and that malice is an aim in itself to no man; but he finds, on the other hand, that the man who does not set his heart on moral perfection, sinks step by step to lower ideals, and that we have a greater repugnance to the good and holy, the longer we live without goodness and holiness . . . What is *characteristic*, indeed, never escapes him. But, above all, he watches the most secret motions of his own heart; he tracks the dainty ripples and mighty upheavings of his own feelings. He knows every subterfuge and by-path by which man strives to escape from his God and his high destiny.

If we consider what was written elsewhere at the time, and the manner in which it was written, we are struck dumb with astonishment at the sight of this poetic delineation of truth, this unparalleled literary achievement. Stimulating influences were certainly not wanting. In the school of the Neoplatonists Augustine had learnt to flee the barren steppes of Aristotelian and Stoic psychology, and to fix his attention on mind and character, impulse and will. A great teacher — his own master, Ambrose of Milan — again, had introduced him to a new world of emotion and observation. But his "Confessions" are none the less entirely his own. No forerunner threatens the claim of this undertaking to originality. It has, indeed, been observed that there is a morbid strain in the book, that he has made a stage-play of his bleeding heart, and it is true that in many places he seems to us over-strained, unhealthy, or even false; but if we remember in what an age of depraved taste and lying rhetoric he wrote, we shall justly wonder that he has raised himself so high above the foibles of the time.

As the very conception of Augustine's book was new, so also was its execution and language. Not only is the force of his observation admirable, but equally so is the force of his diction. In the language of the "Confessions" there meets us an inexhaustibly rich individuality, dowered at once with the irresistible impulse and faculty to express what it feels. It was given to him to trace every motion of his heart in words, and above all, to lend speech to the pious mind and to intercourse with God. Of the power of sin and of the blessedness of the heart that hangs on God, he has been able so to speak that even today every tender conscience must understand his language. Before him, Paul and the psalmists alone had thus spoken; to their school Augustine, the pupil of the rhetoricians, went to learn: and thus arose the language of the "Confessions." Admirable, above all, is the use of sayings and ideas from Holy Writ. Through the position which he gives them, he lends to the most insignificant words something striking or moving. In that great literary art, the art of giving to a well-known saying the most effective setting, he has surpassed all others.

Wonderful also is his power of summing up the phenomena of life and the riddles of the soul in short maxims and antitheses, or in pregnant sentences and new connotations. "The dumb chatterers," "victorious garrulity," "the biter bit," "the betrayed betrayers," the "hopeful young man," the "fetters of our mortality," the "rich poverty," "ignominious glory," "hateful gibberish," "life of my life," and many similar images are either borrowed direct from Augustine, or can be traced back to him. But more important are his psychological descriptions and his maxims: — "That was my life — was it a life?" "I became to myself a great problem," "Man is a deep abyss," "Peace of mind is the sign of our secret unity," "Every man has only his one ego," "Every unordered spirit is its own punishment," "Every forbidden longing, by an unchangeable law, is followed by delusion," "You cannot do good without willing it, though what you do may in itself be good."

But he is much greater even than here in his connected descriptions. One example among hundreds must suffice. He pictures himself as wishing to rise to a vigorous Christian life, but held back by the lust of the world and by custom:

"Thus the burden of the world lay softly on me as on a dreamer, and the thoughts in which my senses turned towards Thee, my God, were like the efforts of those who would rouse themselves from sleep, but, overcome by the depth of slumber, ever sink back again. And when Thou calledst to me, 'Awake, thou that sleepest,' I would give thee no other answer than the words of delay and dream, 'Presently, but let me dream a little longer.' Yet the 'presently' had no end, and the 'yet a little longer' lengthened evermore."

Great as is his art, he never destroyed the uniformity of his style, which is from one fount, because dominated by a single rounded personality. It is a *person* that meets us in his language, and we feel that this person is everywhere richer than his expression. This is the key to the understanding of the enduring influence of Augustine. Life is kindled only upon life, one lover inflames the other: these are his own words, and we may apply them to himself. He was far greater than his writings, for he understood how by his writings to draw men into his life. And with all the tenderness of feeling, with all the constant melting into emotion and the lyricism of the style, there is yet a sublime repose throughout the work. The motto of the book — "Thou, Lord, hast made us after

238

Thine own image, and our heart cannot be at rest till it finds rest in Thee" — is at the same time the seal of the book and the keynote of its language. No fear, no bitterness thenceforward troubles the reader; and that though the book is a sketch of the history of distress and inner trouble. "Fear is the evil thing," says Augustine in one place; but he talks with God fearlessly as with a friend. He has not ceased to see riddles everywhere — in the course of the world, in man, in himself; but the riddles have ceased to oppress him, for he trusts that God in his wisdom has ordered all things. Mists of sorrow and of tears still surround him, but at heart he is free. The impression, then, that the book leaves, may be compared with the impression we receive when, after a dark and rainy day, the sun at length gains the victory, and a mild ray lightens the refreshed land.

But the wonderful form and the magical language of the book are not, after all, its most important characteristics. It is the content, the story he tells, that gives it its real value. As a record of facts, the book is poor indeed. It paints the life of a scholar who grew up under conditions then normal, who had not to contend with adverse fortune or want, who absorbs the manifold wisdom of his time, and accepts a public office in order at last, with scepticism and dissatisfaction, to hand himself over to a holy life of resignation, to theological science, and to the firm-based authority of the Church. It was a course of development such as not a few of Augustine's contemporaries passed through. No other outlet, indeed, was then possible to piety and a serious scientific mind. If we conceive the story of Augustine from this point of view, we can get rid of a widespread prejudice, for the existence of which, it is true, he is himself to some degree responsible.

In wide circles the "Confessions" are viewed as the portrait of a Prodigal Son, of a man who, after a wild and wasteful career, suddenly comes to himself and repents, or else as the picture of a heathen who, after a life of vice, is suddenly overcome by the truth of the Christian religion. No view can be more mistaken. Rather do the "Confessions" portray a man brought up from youth by a faithful mother in the Christian, that is, in the Catholic, faith; who yet, at the same time, from his youth, by the influence of his father and of the mode of culture into which he was plunged, received an impulse towards the highest *secular* aims. They depict a man on whose mind from childhood the name of Christ has been ineffaceably imprinted, but who, as soon as he is roused to independent thought, is informed by the impulse to seek *truth*. In this effort, like us all, he is held down by ambition, worldliness, and sensuality; but he struggles unceasingly against them. He wins, at last, the victory over self, but in doing so he sacrifices his freedom of purpose to the authority of the Church, because in the message of this Church he has experienced the power of breaking with the world and devoting himself to God.

In his external life this change presents itself as a breach with his past; and it is in this view that he has himself depicted it. To him there is here nothing but a contrast between the past and the present. But in his inner life, in spite of his own representations, everything appears to us a quite intelligible development. It is true — and we understand the reason — that he was unable to judge himself in any other way. No one who has passed from inner unrest to peace, from slavery to the world to freedom in God and dominion over himself, can possibly, in surveying the path he trod in the past, call it the way of truth. But others, both contemporary and later, may judge differently; and in this case such a judgment is made specially easy. For the man who here speaks to us is, against his will, compelled to give evidence that, even before his conversion, he strove unceasingly after truth and moral force; and, on the other hand, the numerous writings he produced immediately after his "break with the past," prove that that break was by no means so complete as the "Confessions" — written twelve years afterwards — would have us believe. Much of what only came to maturity in him during those twelve years, he has unconsciously transferred to the moment of conversion. At that time he was no ecclesiastical theologian. In spite of his resolve to submit himself to the Church, he was still living wholly in philosophical problems. The great break was limited entirely to worldly occupations and to his renunciation of the flesh; the interests that had hitherto occupied his mind it did not affect. Thus it is not hard to refute Augustine out of Augustine, and to show that he has in his "Confessions" antedated many a change of thought. Yet, at bottom, he was right. His life, essentially, had but two periods — one, that which he paints in the words, "In distraction I fell to pieces bit by bit, and lost myself in the many;" the other, that in which he found in God the strength and unity of his being.

The former of these periods lies before us in his "Confessions." These have been repeatedly compared with those of Rousseau and Hamann, but really belong to a totally different class. In spite of the most deep-seated differences, I can compare Augustine's book with no other except Goethe's "Faust." In the "Confessions" we meet a living Faust, whose end is, of course, not that of the Faust of the poem. There is much affinity between the two nevertheless. All those anguished revelations in the early scenes of "Faust," from the "Alas, I have explored philosophy," to the resolve on suicide ("Say thy firm farewell to the sun") appear in the "Confessions." With heart-stirring emphasis Augustine cries again and again, "O truth, how the very marrow of my soul sighs after thee!" How often, like Faust, does he complain that the "hot struggle of eternal study" has left him no wiser than before. How often does he compassionate his pupils that he, a drunken teacher, has given them the wine of error. How painfully, too, falls from his lips the confession — "And now, to feel that nothing can be known, this is a thought that burns into my heart." "Could dog, were I a dog, so live?" says Faust; and Augustine, with the most savage envy, envies the ragged but cheerful beggar. He too, "to magic, with severe and patient toil, has now applied, despairing of all other guide, that from some spirit he may hear deep truths, to others unrevealed, and mysteries from mankind sealed;" and in his soul, too, there rises the enticing question, "whether death, when it dissolves all feeling, dissolves and takes away all sorrows too."

Even the solution which Goethe gives to his poem, the way by which Faust attains release, is not quite without its parallel in Augustine. Faust, we read, is saved by heavenly love:

> "Upward rise to higher borders!
>   Ever grow, insensibly,
> As, by pure eternal orders,
>   God's high presence strengthens ye:
> Such the Spirit's sustentation,
>   With the freest ether blending;
> Love's eternal revelation
>   To Beatitude ascending."

And again:

> "As, up by self-impulsion driven,
>   The tree its weight suspends in air,
> To love, almighty love, 'tis given
>   All things to form, and all to bear."

All this is precisely in the spirit of Augustine; and the idea of the wonderful concluding scene of the second part of Faust rests on one of his conceptions, little as Goethe was conscious of the fact. It is unlikely that Goethe had any direct acquaintance with Augustine; he probably knew him only at secondhand. That in this world of illusion and error, love, *divine* love, alone is strength and truth; that this love alone, in fettering, frees and blesses — this is the fundamental thought of the "Confessions" and of most of Augustine's later works. The righteousness which avails with God is the love with which he fills us; and therefore the beginning of love, which is righteousness, is the beginning of blessedness, and perfected love is perfected blessedness. Such is the knowledge to which the struggling philosopher has attained, after seeking in vain elsewhere for rest and peace.

Nevertheless, there is a great gulf between the Faust of the poem and this Faust of reality. The former, in all his struggles, stands with a foot firmly planted on this earth. The God who has given him over for the time being to the devil, is not the good for the possession of which he strives; the inner battle with one's own weakness and sin is scarcely hinted at. To Augustine, on the contrary, the strife for truth is the strife for a supernatural good, for the holy and the high — in a word, for God. It is for this reason that the conclusion of Faust has about it an air of strangeness; we are in no degree prepared for this sudden turn. In Augustine the conclusion follows by an inner necessity. His wanderings prove to be the very paths along which he has been led directly to this aim — blessedness through divine love.

Let us, in a few touches, draw a picture of these paths. Interesting in themselves, they are further interesting because they are typical of the time. Augustine entered into the closest sympathy with all the great spiritual forces of his age. His personality became actually enlarged till it embraced that of the whole existing world; and his individual advance therefore shows us how that world passed from heathenism and philosophy into Catholicism.

Born at Tagasta, a country town of Northern Africa, Augustine showed as a boy good but not brilliant capacity. After he had studied in the school of his native town and at Madaura, his father with some difficulty found the means to have him educated at Carthage. This father was in the ordinary way respectable, but weak in character, and in his private life not free from reproach. He had no higher aim for his son than a career of worldly prosperity. He was himself a heathen; but his wife was a Christian — a relation not uncommon in the middle of the fourth century; it was the women who spread Christianity in the family. To his mother Augustine has raised a noble monument, not only in his "Confessions," but elsewhere in his works. He tells how she taught him to pray, and with what passion he drank in her lessons: often, he tells us, he fervently prayed to God that at school he might escape the ferule. Later in life he recalled how as a boy, in the delirium of fever, he cried out furiously for baptism; and, in all his wanderings, one relic of childhood remained with him never to be extinguished — reverence for Christ. Again and again in his "Confessions" he tells us that all wisdom left him unsatisfied that was not somehow connected with the name of Christ. Thus the recollections of youth became of the highest significance to the man.

Till the boy's seventeenth year imagination and youthful pleasure predominated in his mind. He had at first little taste for learning, although he mastered his lessons with ease. His only delight was to joke and play with his friends. To his mother's grief, also, he early fell into the sins of youth — sins which to his father and to society were no sins at all. At this time, in Carthage, one of Cicero's writings, the "Hortensius," came into his hands; and it is from this moment that he reckons the beginning of a new and higher effort. The "Hortensius" no longer exists; but we can clearly make out its spirit from the remaining works of the man: a high moral flight, a serious interest in the pursuit of truth, but on an uncertain foundation, stimulating rather than strengthening the principles; a book well adapted to wean a youthful mind from the wild life of a student to introspection and the study of the highest questions. And this it actually accomplished for Augustine; he severed himself henceforward from his boon companions, in order with absolute devotion to search for truth. But the book gave him no power over his sensual desires; and he soon found that he had outgrown a tuition which did not satisfy his understanding, left his religious feeling still hungry, and gave him no power of self-mastery. He had learned to know Cicero, the philosopher and moralist, and had become no better than before. But what Cicero did for him — leading him from an empty and trifling existence to serious self-examination and to the search for truth — moralists like Cicero did for the world of that time generally. Augustine remained, as the earliest books he wrote as a Catholic Christian prove, far more powerfully and permanently influenced than he is willing to allow. He now turned to Manichæism, a doctrine which then exercised a great attraction on the deeper spirits. Anyone who had gained some impressions from the contents of the Bible, but held the ecclesiastical interpretation of the Bible as a false one — especially if he could not surmount the stumbling-blocks of the Old Testament; anyone who was determined to cast aside leading-strings and examine things freely for himself; anyone who sought to know what inner principle holds the world together; anyone who strove from the physical to grasp the constitution of the spiritual world and the problem of evil — became in those days a Manichæan. Again, this sect, partly from necessity, partly by an inward impulse, surrounded itself like our freemasons with secrets, and formed at the same time a firm inner ring within the society of the age. Finally, its members exhibited a serious way of life; and the neophyte, in mounting step by step to ever higher and narrower circles, found himself at last in a company of saints and redeemers. Into this society Augustine entered, and to it he belonged for the nine years preceding this twenty-eighth year of his life. What attracted him to it was the fact that it allowed Christ a high rank, and yet assured to its disciples a reasonable solution of the riddle of the world. Hungry as he was, he flung himself greedily upon this spiritual nourishment. The doctrine that evil and good are alike physical forces — that the struggle in man's breast is only the continuation of the great struggle in nature between light and darkness, sun and cloud — struck him as profound and satisfactory. In place of a shallow ethic he found here a deep metaphysic. Nevertheless, after but a few years — he had meanwhile become a professor in Carthage — he began to have his doubts. It was the astrological knowledge, which he had sought along with the metaphysical, that first appeared to him as mere deception. Next, a deeper study of Aristotle sobered his view of the Manichæan physics. His clear intelligence began to perceive that the whole Manichæan wisdom reposed on a physical mythology. The inborn turn of his mind towards the experimental and real gained the victory as soon as it was reinforced by the influence of Aristotle, the great logician and natural scientist of the ancient world. It was he that led back Augustine, like so many before and after, to a calm and sober thinking. Of all fables, the Manichæan now seemed to him the worst, because absolutely nothing in the world of the actual corresponds to them. But the actual was his aim; and he made no secret of his rising doubts to his brethren in the society. At the time there was living in Rome a renowned Manichæan teacher, named Faustus. The friends who found themselves unable to solve the doubts of Augustine consoled him with the name of Faustus. Augustine allowed himself to be thus consoled for some time. At last, however, Faustus came in the flesh. The only section of the "Confessions" over which lies a breath of humor, is that in which is painted the belauded Faustus, the perfect drawing-room professor, who yet was honest enough to confess, when Augustine alone was by, his own ignorance. Thenceforward, in his heart of hearts, Augustine was done with Manichæism.

But what next? Aristotle, it is true, had brought emancipation; but he was able to give no hint upon the questions to which Augustine sought an answer. It was here that Augustine began again to draw near the Church. But the Church forbade free inquiry; she maintained the fables of the Old Testament; she proclaimed, as Augustine thought, a God with eyes and ears, and made him out to be the creator of evil. It was impossible that she should be the depositary of truth. Then, he decided, there can be no truth at all; we must doubt everything. To this view he now resigned his soul, and fortified it by the reading of sceptical philosophers. He sought for a ready-made truth, and yet was unwilling to stifle his restless longing for it. . . . But . . . he was unable to free himself from a connexion which he already regarded as immoral. Little as it contravened the social laws of the age, to him this relation caused a deep breach and cleavage in his personality. He saw himself severed from the good and holy, and from God; in spite of all his good resolutions, he saw himself entangled with the world and with sensuality; and, as he confesses later, he *would* not let himself be healed, because his sickness was dear to him. Yet, as in his serious contemporaries, pure moral feeling and artificiality even then were in him closely interwoven. A holy life appeared to him to be nothing but a life of most utter renunciation; and to lead such a life he was still without the strength. In these perplexities, and in the mood of a sceptic, he left Carthage in order to work in Rome as a professor of rhetoric. The Carthaginian students with their loose manners had given him a distaste for his native Africa. But in Rome also he had some bad experiences with his pupils, and accordingly but a few months passed before he took a public professorship at Milan. The Manichæans, with whom he still maintained constant relations, since "nothing better had as yet appeared," had secured him this post by their recommendations to the influential Symmachus.

Here in Milan the transformation was at last completed, slowly it is true, but with extraordinary transparency and dramatic sequence. Augustine recognized with growing clearness that man can gain a solid hold in the highest questions only by serious unintermitting self-discipline; and he was now to prove that man gains moral force by freely giving himself up to a personality far surpassing his own. In Milan he met Bishop Ambrose. Hitherto he had fallen in with no Catholic Christian capable of impressing him. Such a one he was now to know. If at first it was perhaps the kindliness and extraordinary eloquence of Ambrose that captivated him, it was soon the matter of the Bishop's sermons that drew his attention. He himself tells us in the "Confessions" that the highest service Ambrose did him was to remove the stumbling-blocks of the Old Testament. Certainly the Greek method of interpretation, of which Ambrose was an exponent, exerted a strong influence on Augustine as on every cultivated mind of the age. But the really dominating force in Ambrose was the personality that lay behind his words. It was here that Augustine broke openly with Manichæism. If truth is to be found anywhere, it must be in the Church; to this acknowledgment he was brought by the influence of the great Bishop. The picture of Christ which his mother had been the first to show him, rose again before his soul, and he never afterwards lost it.

But Ambrose had no time to trouble himself about a man who, though he would willingly have believed, was nothing but a sceptic; and even yet there remained a fundamental stumbling-block to be removed. Augustine could not bring himself to believe that there can be an active spiritual being without material substance. The *spiritual* conception of God and the idealistic view of the world seemed to him unprovable, impossible. But while he thus struggled in vain for certainty, his despair at finding himself still a slave to the world and sense, and unable to attain the mastery over himself, was much deeper than before. Fear of his judge and fear of death lay like a dead-weight on his soul. He thirsted for *strength*. . . . What *essentially* he was already seeking in his theoretical and practical doubts was but one thing — intercourse with the living God, who frees us from sin. But God did not appear to him, and he did not find him.

Help came to him from an unexpected quarter. He was reading some writings of the neoplatonic school — a school in which Greek philosophy spoke its last word, and uttered its last testament. . . . In neoplatonism she taught that we must follow the authority of revelation, and that there is only *one* reality, God, and only *one* aim, to mount up to him; that evil is nothing but separation from God, and the world of sense only an unreal appearance; that we can only attain to God by self-discipline and self-restraint, by contemplation ever rising from lower to higher spheres, and finally by an indescribable intoxication, an "ecstasy," in which God himself embraces the soul and sends his light upon her.

The neoplatonic philosophy had more and more renounced the "dry light" of science; it had thrown itself into the arms of revelation, in order to raise men above themselves. This, the last product of the proud Greek mind, did not disdain even Christian writings in its desire to learn from them. St. John's gospel was read and highly valued in neoplatonic circles. It was in this philosophy that Augustine now steeped himself; it was this that solved for him his theoretical riddles and doubts; it was this that drew him out of scepticism and subjugated him for ever. The reality of spiritual values, the spiritual conception of God, became for him now a certainty. The keen criticism which he formerly had applied to the theoretical groundwork of philosophical systems here failed him. Scepticism had dulled his critical faculty; or rather — he sought above all for guidance to the blessed life, and for an authority which might guarantee to him the living God. That there existed a philosophy on to which he could fasten what his soul longed for, was to him important before all else. Neoplatonism became to him, as to many before and after, a pathway to the Church; by its means he acquired confidence in the fundamental ideas of the ecclesiastical theology of the time. It is remarkable how speedily, how imperceptibly he passed from neoplatonism to the recognition of the Bible in its entirety and of the Catholic doctrine; or rather, how he came to see neoplatonism as true, but not as the whole truth. There was wanting to it, above all, *one* item — the recognition of redemption through the incarnate God, and thereby the right way to truth. These philosophers, said he, see the promised land like Moses, but they know not how to enter in and possess it. This he fancied that he now knew: by the subjection of the understanding to Christ. But Christ, as he had learnt from Ambrose, is only where the Church is. We must therefore *believe*, and believe what the Church believes. Augustine in his "Confessions" allows us no doubt that the *decision* to submit ourselves to authority is the condition of the attainment of the truth. This decision he made, and thus became a Catholic Christian. In this inner transformation the causes are wonderfully linked together — the neoplatonic influence, the enduring impression of the person of Christ, strengthened by the perusal of Paul's Epistles, and the grand authority of the Church.

He was now a Catholic Christian by conviction and will; but he himself describes his state of mind in the words: "Thus I had found the pearl of great price, but I still hesitated to sell all I had; I delighted in the law of God after the inward man, but I found another law in my members." No theory, no doctrine, could here avail him: only overpowering personal impressions could subject him or carry him away. And such impressions arrived. First, it was the news of a famous heathen orator in Rome, who had suddenly renounced a brilliant career and publicly professed himself a Catholic; a report that stirred him to his depths. Then, a few days later, a fellow-countryman, happening to visit him, told him an

event that had recently taken place in Trèves. A few young imperial officials had gone a walk in the gardens on the city-walls, and there fallen
upon the hut of a hermit. In the hut they found a book, the Life of St.
Antony. One of them began to read it; and the book exerted such a fasci-
nation upon them that they forthwith resolved to leave all and follow
Antony. The narrator told this story with flaming enthusiasm; he had
himself been present and a witness of the sudden transformation. He
did not see what an impression his tale made on his listener. A fearful
struggle arose in Augustine's mind: "Where do we allow ourselves to
drift? Why is this? The unlearned take the kingdom of heaven by force,
and we with our heartless learning still wallow in flesh and blood!" In
the conflict of his feelings, no longer master of himself, he flung into the
garden. The thought of that which he was to renounce struggled in him
with the might of a new life. He fainted; and only awoke to consciousness as he heard in a neighboring house a child's voice, probably in play,
repeating again and again the words, "Take and read, take and read."
He hurried back to the house, and, remembering the story of St. Antony,
opened his Bible. His eye fell on the passage in Romans, "Not in rioting
and drunkenness, not in chambering and wantonness, not in strife and
envying; but put ye on the Lord Jesus Christ, and make not provision for
the flesh, to fulfil the lusts thereof." "I would not read further, nor was
there need; for as I finished the passage there immediately streamed
into my heart the light of peaceful certainty, and all the darkness of inde-
cision vanished away." At this moment he broke with his past: he felt in
himself the power to renounce the sinful habit, and to lead a new and
holy life in union with his God. This he vowed to do, and kept his vow.

A proof that it was an *inner* transformation which he had undergone
lies in the fact that while he thenceforward renounced his wife and his
public occupation as an evil, he in no degree for the present gave up his
studies or the circle of his interests. So far from it, that he removed with
his friends and his mother to an estate near Milan, in order there to
devote himself undisturbed to philosophy and to serious intercourse
with his companions, and to pursue his philosophical speculations as
he had pursued them hitherto. His ideal and that of his friends was not
St. Antony, but a society of wise men, as conceived by Cicero, Plotinus,
and Porphyry. No obtrusive Church dogmas as yet disturbed the philosophical dialogues of the friends; but their minds were ruled by a sure
belief in the living God; and in place of the old uncertainties about the
starting-point and aim of all knowledge of truth, they now lived in the
assurance given by the revelation of God in Christ and by the authority

of the Church. The question whether happiness is secured by the search for truth or by the possession of truth, was mooted by Augustine in the circle of these friends, and decided in favor of the latter hypothesis. He resolved to pursue his unceasing investigations further; but the last and highest truth he *sought* no more, convinced that he had found it in subjection to the authority of God as proclaimed by the Church. . . .

Two things are henceforward inseparably interwoven in Augustine's life and thought. On the one side he speaks in a new fashion — but on the lines of the Church — of God and divine things. From the experience of his heart he witnesses of sin and guilt, repentance and faith, God's power and God's love. In place of a sterile morality he sets up a living piety, life in God through Christ. To this life he summons the *individual*; he shows him how poor and wretched he is, with all his knowledge and all his virtue, so long as he is not penetrated by the love of God. He shows him that the natural man is swayed by selfishness, that selfishness is slavery and guilt, and that every man is by nature a link in an infinite chain of sin. But he also teaches him that God is greater than our heart, that the love of God as revealed in Christ is stronger than our natural impulses, and that freedom is the blessed necessity of what is good. Wherever in the following millennium and later the struggle has arisen against a mechanical piety, self-righteousness, or jejune morality, there the spirit of Augustine has been at work. But, at the same time, no one before Augustine has, in so decided and open a fashion, established Christianity on the authority of the Church, or confused with the authority of institutions the *living* authority of saintly persons, who engender a life like their own.

The forces which were inseparably conjoined in his own experiences and life have continued to affect the Church through his influence; his significance in the formation of Catholic ecclesiasticism and in the rule of the Church is no less than his *critical* significance, or than the power given him to arouse *individual* piety and *personal* Christianity.

The solution of this problem I shall not here attempt; it must suffice to observe that fundamentally it is by no means astonishing. Religion and the faith dependent on authority, different as they are, are severed by a narrow partition; and, where faith is imagined as first of all a matter of knowledge, the partition vanishes entirely. At this point Luther stepped in and undertook to establish the Christian on a foundation from which he must view the authority of institutions, and monasticism, as a degenerate form of belief.

But every age has received from God its content, and every spirit its measure. Augustine's limits are at the same time his strength and the conditions of his activity. Within his limitations, in the forty-three years of his Catholic life, he raised himself to a personality whose sublimity and humility are amazing to us. A stream of truthfulness, kindness, and benevolence, and on the other hand of living ideas and deep conceptions, runs through his writings, by means of which he became the great teacher of the West. True, he was left behind at the Reformation, though that very Reformation he helped to call into existence; and his religious view of the world failed to hold its ground against the scientific knowledge to which we have since Leibnitz attained. True, Catholicism strove to stifle his still surviving influence at the Council of Trent, in the contest with Jansenism, and by the Vatican decrees. But he is, in spite of all, no dead force; what he has been to the Church of Christ will not vanish, and even to the Romish Church he will leave no rest.

From Easter 387 to Easter 1887 fifteen hundred years have passed since Augustine was baptized and started on the service of the Church. No one has celebrated the day; no monument has been set up to the teacher of the Church. But he has the noblest of all memorials: his name stands written in imperishable characters on the leaves of Western history from the days of the great migrations to our own.   (*CA:* 119-171)

*

HISTORY OF DOGMA

In this selection from the final volume of History of Dogma *(pp. 168-274), Harnack describes the theological work of Luther as the completion of the Church's dogmatic development. It comes to completion because Luther, in returning to the Scriptures, takes up again the inwardness and higher dimensions of Jesus' gospel while, at the same time, trying to reduce the significance of "tradition": councils, creeds, canon laws, etc., in and for the faith of the believer. But it is more Luther himself, the man, whom Harnack wants to portray; he is exemplary of the kind of life to which Jesus called us, for which he came and lived among us: the life of the good, of the higher values, the life free from legalism and ecclesial authority. As a man who lived the life of true Christianity, the time-conditioned aspects of his witness notwithstanding, Luther is one with whose legacy our minds may meld perfectly in their search for goodness, truth and beauty.*

The translation is that of N. Buchanan; it was first published in 1900 from the German edition which had appeared first in 1890.

THE ISSUES OF DOGMA IN PROTESTANTISM

Introduction

... Post-Tridentine Catholicism and Socinianism are in many respects *modern* phenomena; but this is not true of them when we deal with their *religious kernel*; they are rather the further conclusions of *mediæval* Christianity. *The Reformation on the other hand, as represented in the Christianity of Luther, is in many respects an Old Catholic, or even a mediæval phenomenon, while if it be judged of in view of its religious kernel, this cannot be asserted of it, it being rather a restoration of Pauline Christianity in the spirit of a new age.*[11]

In making this statement there is assigned to the Reformation (the Christianity of Luther) its position in history, while at the same time its relation to dogma is determined. From here also we can see why the Reformation cannot be estimated simply by the results which it achieved for itself during the two first generations of its existence. How can any one deny, then, that Catholicism, after it had roused itself to become a counter-Reformation, and that Socinianism stood, for more than a century, in a closer relation to the new age than Lutheran Protestantism did? They worked in alliance with all the culturing influences of the period; and poets, humanists, men of learning, discoverers, kings, and statesmen, soon felt where their proper place was if they were nothing else than scholars and statesmen. At the cradle of the Reformation, certainly, it was not sung that it would one day lag behind the times. It was rather greeted at its birth with the joyful acclamations of the nation, encircled with the shouts of humanists and patriots. But this its *more immediate* future was already foreshadowed in him from whom alone its future was to be expected — namely, in Luther. It is not the furthest possible advance beyond the average of an age that makes the truly great man, but the power with which he can awaken a new life in existing society.[12]

What is at least a very one-sided and abstract view of Luther is taken, when we honor in him the man of the new time, the hero of an aspiring age, or the creator of the modern spirit. If we wish to contemplate such heroes, we must turn to Erasmus and his associates, or to men like Denck, Franck, Servede, and Bruno. In the periphery of his existence Luther was an Old Catholic, a mediæval phenomenon. For a period, certainly — it was only for a few years — it seemed as if this spirit would attract to itself and mould into a wonderful unity all that at the time had living vigor in it, as if to him as to no one before the power had been given to make his personality the spiritual center of the nation and to summon his century into the lists, armed with every weapon.

Yet that was only a splendid episode, which for the time being came rapidly to an end. Certainly those years from 1519 till about 1523 were the most beautiful years of the Reformation, and it was a wonderful providential arrangement that all that was to be achieved, the whole task of the future, was taken in hand forthwith by Luther himself and was close on being accomplished by him. Still, this rich spring-time was followed by no abundant summer. In those years Luther was lifted above himself, and seemed to transcend the limits of his peculiar individuality — he was *the* Reformation, inasmuch as he summed up in himself what was at once implied in the return to Pauline Christianity and in the founding of a new age. At that time the alliance also was concluded between Protestantism and Germany. It is true, no doubt, that evangelical Christianity has been given to mankind, and, on the other hand, that the German spirit is even today far from having surrendered itself yet to Protestantism; nevertheless, Protestantism and Germany are inseparably connected. As the Reformation saved the German empire in the sixteenth century, so it still continues always to be its strongest force, its permanently working principle and its highest aim.

But it is given to no man to accomplish everything, and every one whose work is lasting and who does not merely blaze forth like a meteor, must retire within the limits appointed to his nature. Luther also retired within those peculiar to him. Those limits were not merely slight integuments, as some would have us believe, so that for his having become narrowed we should have to throw the whole blame on Melanchthon and the Epigones with their want of understanding; Luther felt them to be with other things the roots of his power, and in this character allowed them to have their effect.

But when the problem is contemplated of giving a picture of this peculiar individuality of Luther, and reckoning up as it were the sum of his existence, it must be said that no one as yet has perfectly fulfilled this task. A representation of Luther can only be given when he is allowed himself to speak and to express himself in every line of his spiritual constitution: this Luther can be *reproduced within us in sympathetic feeling*, so far as this is possible for more limited spirits; but the attempt to analyze seems to involve us in insoluble contradictions. Yet the attempt must be made, if the complicated and in part confused legacy he has left behind is to be rightly understood, and if we are to master the problem that is forced upon those coming after him by his appearing in an age in many respects foreign to him.

He was only in *one* thing great and powerful, captivating and irresistible, the master of his age, marching victoriously ahead of the history of a thousand years with the view of inducing his generation to relinquish the paths that were being followed and to choose paths that were new — *he was only great in the re-discovered knowledge of God which he derived from the gospel, i.e., from Christ.* What had once been *one* of the motives in building up dogma, but had become unrecognizable in dogma, what had thereafter, from the time of Augustine on through the Middle Ages, accompanied dogma, vague in its expression, and with a vaguely recognized title, namely, the living faith in the God who in Christ addresses to the poor soul the words: "I am thy salvation" ("Salus tua ego sum"), the firm assurance that God is the Being on whom one can place reliance — that was the message of Luther to Christendom.[13]

For what he restored was nothing less than the religious way of understanding the gospel, the sovereign right of religion in religion. In the development that had preceded him there had not been merely the making a mistake here and there; there had been a betrayal of religion to its enemies and to its friends. Luther spoke himself of a Babylonian captivity, and he was right in seeing this captivity both in the domination of an earthly, self-seeking ecclesiasticism over religion, and in the clinging around religion of a moralism that crushed its life. It may be remarked here at once, that he did not with equal distinctness perceive the deplorableness of that captivity into which religion had been brought by the Old Catholic theology. That was not merely because his historic horizon extended only to about the time of the origin of the Papal Church — what lay beyond blending for him at many points into the golden line of the New Testament — *but above all because dogma, the historic legacy of the period between the second and seventh centuries, was no longer the more immediate source from which there had flowed the wrong conditions he had to contend with in the present.* In his day the old dogma was a thing lying dead. No one vitalized it for faith. When Luther therefore attacked the errors of theology, he directed himself almost exclusively against the *Schoolmen* and the mediæval Aristotle. When he rated and ridiculed reason, it was these people as a rule whom he had in view; when he severed the baleful bond between religious doctrine and philosophy, he was turning his weapons against the Jesuits. In combating theology he combated the theology of the Middle Ages, and even this he combated only insofar as it ignored the honor of God and of Christ, the rights of God and the wrong done by the creature. Keeping out of view his controversy with the Anabaptists, he knew of no other controversy with reason than the controversy with self-righteousness, and with the shifts of the man who makes use even of religion to escape from his God.

What a wonderful linking together of things! The same man who delivered the gospel of Jesus Christ from ecclesiasticism and moralism *strengthened its authority in the forms of the Old Catholic theology, nay, was the first to impart again to these forms meaning and importance for faith, after they had for long centuries remained inoperative.* From the time of Athanasius there had been no theologian who had given so much living power for faith to the doctrine of the Godhead of Christ as Luther did; since the time of Cyril no teacher had arisen in the Church for whom the mystery of the union of the two natures in Christ was so full of comfort as for Luther — "I have a better provider than all angels are: He lies in the cradle, and hangs on the breast of a virgin, but sits, nevertheless, at the right hand of God, the almighty Father;" no mystic philosopher of antiquity spoke with greater conviction and delight than Luther of the sacred nourishment in the eucharist. The German Reformer restored life to the formulæ of Greek Christianity; he gave them back to faith. It is to be attributed to him that till the present day these formulæ are in Protestantism a living power for faith — yes, *only* in Protestantism. Here there is a living in them, a defending or contesting of them; but even those contesting them understand how to estimate their relative title. In the Catholic Churches they are a lifeless possession.

There is certainly injustice done to the "entire Luther" when this side of his significance as a Reformer — which to his own mind was knit in an indissoluble unity with the evangelical side — is dropped out of view or under-estimated. *Luther was the restorer of the old dogma.* He forced the interests of this on the teaching of his time, thereby also compelling it to desert the lines of the Humanist, Franciscan and political Christianity: the Humanist and Franciscan age was obliged to interest itself in what was most foreign to it — *in the gospel and the old theology.*[14]

Indeed we may go a step further: Luther would at any moment have defended with fullest conviction the opening words of the Athanasian Creed: "Whosoever will be saved, before all things it is necessary that he hold the Catholic faith." Not only does the Confession of Augsburg ratify the old dogma in its first article, the Smalcaldic Articles also begin with it: "regarding these articles there is no controversy between us and our opponents since we confess them on both sides"; and if in the immediately succeeding article "on the office and work of Jesus Christ" it is then stated: "To depart from this article, or to condone or permit anything against it, is not possible for any of the pious," the article is not meant to be raised by an addition of the kind above those formerly named: the former were regarded by Luther so much as settled matters that he did not think of such a remark regarding them as being at all necessary. Of this also there can be no doubt — that the gospel was for him "saving *doctrine, doctrine* of the gospel," which certainly included the old dogmas; the attempt to represent the matter otherwise has in my opinion been a failure: the gospel is sacred *doctrine*, contained in the Word of God, the purpose of which is to be learned, and to which there must be subjection.[15]

How is it to be explained that in an age which had thrown dogma into the background, and in which the spirit of science and of criticism had grown so much stronger that it was already combated from the various sides, Luther appeared as a defender of dogma and restored it to life again? To this question more than *one* answer can be given; one has been already stated: Luther fought against the abuses and errors of the *Middle Ages*. This answer can be still further expanded; Luther never contended against wrong theories and doctrines as such, but only against such theories and doctrines as *manifestly* did serious injury to the purity of the gospel, and to its comforting power. The statement of this carries with it the other thing — namely, that there was no alliance between him and the bright-visioned spirits whose aim was to amend theology, and thereby to introduce a truer knowledge of the world and its causes. There was entirely wanting to him the irrepressible impulse of the thinker that urges him to secure theoretic clearness: nay, he had an instinctive dislike for, and an inborn mistrust of every spirit who, guided simply by knowledge, boldly corrected errors. Any one who thinks that here again he can at the present day be a defender of the "entire Luther," either does not know the man, or throws himself open to the suspicion that for him the *truth* of knowledge is a matter of small importance. That was the most palpable limitation in the spiritual nature of the Reformer — that he neither fully made his own the elements of culture which his age offered, nor perceived the lawfulness and obligation of free investigation, nor knew how to measure the force of the critical objections against the "doctrine" that were then already asserting themselves. There may seem to be something paltry, or even indeed presumptuous in this remark; for Luther has indemnified us for this defect, not only by being a Reformer, but by the inexhaustible richness of his personality. What a wealth this personality included! How it possessed, too, in *heroic shape* all we have just found wanting at the time — a richness of original intuition which outweighed all the "elements of culture" in which it lacked, a certainty and boldness of vision which was more than "free investigation," a power to lay hold upon the untrue, to conserve what could stand the test, as compared with which all "critical objections" appear pointless and feeble; above all, a wonderful faculty for giving expression to strong feeling and true thought, for being really a *speaker*, and for persuading by means of the word as no prophet had done before! Yet all these powerful qualities were still incapable of securing for the coming generation a pure culture, because in Luther's own case they were not produced by the impulse to know things as they are. Certainly he had greater things to do than to correct science and promote general culture in the full breadth of its development; and we may be devoutly thankful that we have had experience of such a man, who made all his activity subservient to the knowledge of the living God. But it is pure Romanticism and self-delusion when one devoutly admires the limitations of Luther's special individuality as being the best thing in him, and it is something worse than Romanticism and self-delusion when what was allowed in a hero, who did not reflect, but did what he *was obliged to do*, is raised to a general law for an age which, when it frankly and without hesitation applies itself to know the truth, likewise does what it is under obligation to do. And then — who really ventures to restore again the "entire Luther," with the coarseness of his mediæval superstition, the flat contradictions of his theology, the remarkable logic of his arguments, the mistakes of his exegesis and the unfairness and barbarisms of his polemic? Shall we forget, then, all that has been learned by us, but that was unknown to Luther — the requisite conditions of a true knowledge that is determined only by the matter dealt with, the relativity of historic judgment, the proportion of things and the better understanding of the New Testament? Is it not the case that the more strictly Christianity is conceived of as *spiritual* religion, the greater is its demand that it shall be in accord with the whole life of our spirit, and can it be honestly said that this accord is secured by the Christianity of Luther?

Yet it was not only his defective theoretic interest that led Luther to stop short before the old dogma, nor was it only his vague knowledge and imperfect understanding of the old Catholic period; *the old dogma itself, rather, joined hands with the new conception of the gospel which he enunciated.*[16] Here also, therefore, as everywhere, he was *not regulated merely by external authorities;* the inward agreement, rather, which he thought he found between his faith and that dogma prevented him becoming uncertain about the latter. In "faith" he sought only the honor of God and Christ; that was also done by the old formulæ of faith. In "faith" he would hear nothing of law, work, achievement and merit; the formulæ of faith were silent regarding these. For him the forgiveness of sins, as creating a holy Church and securing life and peace, was the main part of religion; he found these things holding a commanding place in the old formulæ. Jesus Christ was apprehended by him as the mirror of the fatherly heart of God, and therefore as God, and he would know of no other comforter save God himself, as he appeared in Christ and as he works through the Holy Spirit; the old formulæ of faith bore witness to the Father, Son and Spirit, to the *one* God, who is a Triunity, and said nothing of Mary, the saints, and other helpers of the needy. His soul lived by faith in the God who has come as near to us in earthly form as brother to brother; the old formulæ of faith testified to this by their doctrine of the two natures in Christ. Like Paul he armed himself against the assaults of the devil, the world and sin with the assurance that Christ by his death has vanquished the powers of darkness and cancelled guilt, and that he sits now as the exalted Lord at the right hand of God; the old formulæ of faith bore witness to the death on the cross, the resurrection and exaltation of Christ. While, under the rubbish-heaps of the Middle Ages, he rediscovered the old faith of Paul in the New Testament, he discovered this faith also in the old dogma: the Church possessed it, confessed it daily, but no longer paid regard to it, knew no longer what it had imported into the mutterings of its priests, and thus in the midst of its possessions forgot what it possessed. *Over against this Church*, why should he not honor, along with the New Testament, the old dogma which witnessed to the Word of God! And in *one* very important respect he was certainly entirely in the right — this old dogma was really an expression of *the religion of ancient times: that which those times maintained together with this, and by means of which they delimited dogma, was not introduced into dogma itself.* Only in the Middle Ages did law, merit and achievement find a place among the doctrines of faith and in worship. As compared with the mediæval, the Old Catholic Church had impressed on it more of a *religious* character; in its faith and in its worship it confessed what God has done, and what he will do, through Christ.

But was he not altogether right? Was there not really the most beautiful harmony between his faith and the old dogma? This is still asserted at the present day, and an appeal is made in support of it to the apparently strongest witness — to Luther himself, who had no other idea in his mind. According to this view, the shaping of dogma in the ancient

257

Church, down to the sixth and seventh centuries, was "sound"; the only thing lacking to it was justification by faith. This supplement was added by Luther, while at the same time he purified — or cancelled — the false development of the Middle Ages. Over and above this there is a talk about a "reconstruction," a "remodelling" of dogma, that was undertaken by Luther; but there is difficulty in explaining what such terms are intended to mean: additions and subtractions are not equivalent to reconstruction. Hence the terms are not employed seriously; they suggest rather the admission that Luther's notion of faith in some way modified dogma as a whole. How that took place there is, of course, difficulty in stating, for the moulding of dogma in the ancient Church was "sound." From this point of view the whole development of Protestantism from the end of the seventeenth century till the present day must necessarily appear a mistaken development, nay, an apostasy. It is a pity, only, that almost all thinking Protestants have apostatized, and, for the most part, differ from each other only according to the clearness and honesty with which they admit their apostasy.

We have to inquire whether or not Luther's conception of faith, *i.e.*, what admittedly constituted his importance as a Reformer, postulates the old dogma, and therefore, also, is most intimately united with it.

With this in view, we shall first gather together the most important propositions in which he set forth *his Christianity*. Then we shall adduce the most decisive *critical* propositions which he himself stated as conclusions from his religious conception of the gospel. On the basis of these investigations it will then appear whether, and to what extent, the general attitude which Luther assumed towards the old dogma was free from contradictions. If this can be determined, the final question will arise, whether it is still possible for the Church of the present day to take up the same attitude.

The Christianity of Luther

In the cell of his convent Luther fought out the spiritual battle, the fruit of which was to be the new and yet old evangelical knowledge. Inward unrest, anxiety about his salvation, had driven him into the convent. He had gone there in order that — in a genuinely Catholic way — he might, through multiplied good works, propitiate the strict Judge, and "get for himself a gracious God." But while he used all the means the mediæval Church offered him, his temptations and miseries became more intense. He felt as if he was contending with all the powers of darkness, and as if, instead of being in the society of angels in the convent, he was among devils. When in after days at the height of his active career depression came upon him, all that was required in order to regain strength was to remember these convent horrors.[17] In the system of sacraments and performances to which he subjected himself he failed to find the assurance of peace which he sought for, and which only the possession of God could bestow. He wished to base his life for time and for eternity upon a rock (the mystic's fluctuation between rapture and fear he had no experience of, for he was too strict with himself), but all supports that were recommended to him fell to pieces in his hands, and the ground trembled beneath his feet. He believed he was carrying on a conflict with himself and his sin; but he was in reality contending against the religion of his Church: the very thing that was intended to be to him a source of comfort became known to him as a ground of terror. Amid such distress there was disclosed to him — slowly and under faithful counsel — from the buried-up ecclesiastical confession of faith ("I believe in the forgiveness of sins"), and therefore also from Holy Scripture (Psalms, Epistles of Paul, especially the Epistle to the Romans), what the truth and power of the gospel are. In addition to this, Augustine's faith-conception of the first and last things, and especially his doctrine of "the righteousness which God gives," were for him in an increasing degree guiding stars.[18] But how much more firmly he grasped the essence of the matter.[19] What he here learned, what he laid hold of as *the one thing,* was *the revelation of the God of grace in the gospel, i.e.,* in the incarnated, crucified, and risen Christ. The same experience which Paul had undergone in his day was passed through by Luther, and although in its beginning it was not in his case so stormy and sudden as in the case of the apostle,[20] yet he, too, learned from this experience *that it is God who gives faith:* "When it pleased God to reveal His Son in me." In Luther's development down to the year 1517, there was an entire absence of all dramatic and romantic elements: that is perhaps the most wonderful thing in this wonderful character, and is the seal of its inward greatness. From mysticism, to which he owed much, and the speculations of which he not unfrequently followed in connexion with particular questions, he was separated by the entirely unmystical conviction that trust in God "on account of Christ" is the real content of religion, which nothing transcends, and the limitations of which can be removed by no speculation. Trust in the "truth" of God and in the work of Christ formed for him a unity, and he knew no other way of approaching the Being who rules heaven and earth than by the cross of Christ.

That, however, which he had experienced, and which, with ever-increasing clearness, he now learned to state, was, in comparison with the manifold things which his Church offered as religion, above everything else an immense *reduction*, an emancipating *simplification*. In this respect he resembled Athanasius — with whom in general he had the most noteworthy affinity — and was very unlike Augustine, who never controlled the inexhaustible riches of his spirit, and who stimulated, therefore, rather than built up. *That reduction meant nothing else than the restoration of religion*: seeking God and finding God. Out of a complex system of expiations, good deeds and comfortings, of strict statutes and uncertain apportionments of grace, out of magic and of blind obedience, he led religion forth and gave it a strenuously concentrated form. The Christian religion is living assurance of the living God, who has revealed himself and opened his heart in Christ — nothing else. Objectively, it is Jesus Christ, his person and work; subjectively, it is faith ("faith is our life"); its content, however, is the God of grace, and therefore the forgiveness of sins, which includes adoption and blessedness. For Luther, the whole of religion was contained within this circle. The living God — not a philosophical or mystical abstraction — the God manifest, certain, the God of grace, accessible to every Christian. Unwavering trust of the heart in him who has given himself to us in Christ as our Father, personal assurance of faith, because Christ with his work undertakes our cause — this became for him the entire sum of religion. Rising above all anxieties and terrors, above all ascetic devices, above all directions of theology, above all interventions of hierarchy and sacraments, he ventured to lay hold of God himself in Christ, and in this act of his faith, which he recognized as God's work, his whole being obtained stability and firmness, nay, even a personal certainty and joy, such as no mediæval man had ever possessed.[21]

From perceiving that "with force of arms we nothing can," he derived the utmost freedom and force; for he now knew the power which imparts to the life of steadfastness and peace; he knew it, and called it by its name. *Faith* — that meant for him no longer adherence to an incalculable sum of Church doctrines or historical facts; it was no opinion and no action, no act of initiation upon which something greater follows; it was the certainty of forgiveness of sins, and therefore also the personal and continuous surrender to God as the Father of Jesus Christ, which transforms and renews the whole man.[22]

That was his confession of faith: faith is a living, busy, *active* thing, a sure confidence, which makes a man joyous and happy towards God and all creatures,[23] which, like a good tree, yields without fail good fruit, and which is ever ready to serve everyone and to suffer all things. In spite of all evil, and in spite of sin and guilt, the life of a Christian is hid in God. That was the ground-thought of his life. As included within this, the other thought was discovered and experienced by him — the thought of the *freedom* of a Christian man. This freedom was not for him an empty emancipation, or a licence for every kind of subjectivity; for him freedom was dominion over the world, in the assurance that if God be for us, no one can be against us; for him that soul was free from all human laws, which has recognized in the fear of God and in love for and trust in him its supreme law and the motive principle of its life. He had learned, certainly, from the old mystics; but he had found what they sought for. Not unfrequently they remained imprisoned in sublime feelings; they seldom attained to a lasting sense of peace; while at one time their feeling of freedom rose to oneness with God, at another time their feeling of dependence deepened into psychical self-annihilation. On Luther's part there was a struggle issuing in active piety, and in an abiding assurance of peace. He vindicated the rights of the individual in the first instance for himself; freedom of conscience was for him a personal experience. But for him the free conscience was a conscience inwardly bound, and by individual right he understood the sacred duty of trusting courageously to God, and of rendering to one's neighbor the service of independent and unselfish love.

Of trusting courageously to God — because he feared nothing, and because, in his certainty of God, his soul overflowed with joy: "It is impossible for one who hopes in God not to rejoice; even if the world falls to wreck, he will be overwhelmed undismayed under the ruins." Thus he became the Reformer, because through his joyous faith he became a hero. If even in science knowledge is not enough, if the highest things are achieved only where there is courage, how should it be otherwise in religion? What Christian faith is, revealed itself to the Germans in Luther's person. What he presented to view was not new doctrine, but an experience, described at one time in words strongly original, at another time in the language of the Psalms and of Paul, sometimes in that of Augustine, and sometimes even in the cumbrous propositions of the scholastic theology. The critical application of his faith to the state of things existing at the time, to the Church as it was, Luther never desired; it was forced upon him because his opponents observed much sooner than himself the critical force of what he declared.

In Luther's view of faith there was implied his view of the *Church*. For him the Church was the community of the saints, *i.e.*, of believers, whom the Holy Spirit has called, enlightened and sanctified through the Word of God, who are continually being built up by means of the gospel in the true faith, who look forward confidently and joyfully to the glorious future of the sons of God, and meanwhile serve one another in love, each in the position in which God has placed him. That is his whole creed regarding the Church — the community of believers (saints), invisible, but recognizable by the preaching of the Word.[24] It is rich and great; and yet what a reduction even this creed is found to contain when it is compared with what the mediæval Church taught, or at least assumed, regarding itself and the work assigned to it! Luther's creed was entirely the product of his religious faith, and it rests on the following closely united principles, to the truth of which he constantly adhered. *First,* that the Church has its basis in the Word of God; *second,* that this Word of God is the preaching of the revelation of God in Christ, as being that which creates faith; *third,* that accordingly the Church has no other field than that of faith, but that within this field it is for every individual the mother in whose bosom he attains to faith; *fourth,* that because religion is nothing but faith, therefore neither special performances, nor any special province, whether it be public worship, or a selected mode of life, nor obedience to ecclesiastical injunctions, though these may be salutary, can be the sphere in which the Church and the individual give proof of their faith, but that the Christian must exhibit his faith in neighborly service within the natural relationships of life, because they alone are not arbitrarily chosen but *provided,* and must be accepted therefore as representing the order of God.

With the first principle Luther assumed an antagonistic attitude towards the received doctrine both of tradition and of the power belonging to the bishops and the Pope. He saw that previous to his time, the question as to *what is Christian and what the Church is* had been determined in a way quite arbitrary and therefore also uncertain. He accordingly turned back to the sources of religion, to Holy Scripture, and in particular to the New Testament. The Church has its basis in something fixed, something given, which has never been wanting to it — in this he distinguished himself from the "enthusiasts" — but this thing that is given is not a secret science of the priesthood, nor is it a dreary mass of statutes under the protection of the holy, still less papal absolutism; but it is something which every simple-minded Christian can discern and make proof of: it is *the Word of God as dealt with by the pure understanding.* This thesis required the unprejudiced ascertainment of the really literal sense of Holy Scripture. All arbitrary exposition determined by authority was put an end to. As a rule Luther was in earnest in complying with this demand, so far as his vision carried him. He could not, certainly, divine how far it was to lead. Yet his methodical principles of "interpretation," his respect for language, laid the foundation for scripture-science.

The second principle distinguishes Luther both from the theologians and from the ascetics and sectaries of the Middle Ages. In thinking of the Word of God they thought of the letter, of the inculcated doctrines, and the miscellaneous promises of Holy Scripture; he thought of what formed the core. If he speaks of this core as being "the gospel according to the pure understanding," "the pure gospel," "the pure Word of God," "the promises of God," but, above all, as being "Jesus Christ," all these expressions as understood by him are identical. The Word of God which he constantly had in his mind, was the testimony of Jesus Christ, who is the Savior of souls. As faith has only to do with the living God and Christ, so also the authority for faith and for the Church is only the *effectual* Word of God, as the Christ who is *preached*.[25] Accordingly the Church doctrine also is nothing but the statement of the gospel, as it has created and holds together the Christian community, the sum of the "consolations offered in Christ."

But if the Church has its basis simply in these "consolations" and in the faith that answers to them, it can have no other sphere and no other form than those which the Word of God and faith give to it. Everything else must fall away as disturbing, or as at least unessential. In this way the third principle is obtained. The conception of the Church is greatly reduced as compared with the mediæval conception, but it has thereby gained in inner force, and has been given back to faith. Only the believer sees and knows the holy Christian community; for it is only he who perceives and understands the Word of God; he *believes* in this Church, and knows that *through* it he has attained to faith, because the Holy Spirit has called him through the *preached* Word.[26]

Finally, the fourth principle had, outwardly, the most far-reaching consequences; if everything depends upon faith, both for the individual and for the Church, if it is God's will to transact with men only through faith, if faith alone is acceptable to him, there can be no special fields and forms of piety and no specific pious ways of life as distinct from other ways. From this it followed that the demonstration and practical exercise of faith had to be within the great institutions of human life that have their origin in God (in marriage, family, state, and calling). But all that was included in worship now appeared also in quite a different light. If it is an established fact, that man has neither power nor right to do anything in the way of influencing God, if the mere thought of moving God to alter his feeling means the death of true piety, if the entire relation between God and man is determined by the believing spirit, *i.e.*, by firmly established trust in God, humility and unceasing prayer, if, finally, all ceremonies are worthless, there can no longer be exercises which in a special sense can be described as "worship of God."[27] There is only *one* direct worship of God, which is faith; beyond this there is the rule that cannot be infringed, that God must be served in love for one's neighbor. Neither mystic contemplation nor an ascetic mode of life is embraced in the gospel.

The inherent right of the natural order of life was for Luther as little an independent ideal as was freedom from the law of the letter. Like every earnest Christian he was eschatologically determined, and looked forward to the day when the world will pass away with its pleasure, its misery, *and its institutions.* Within it the devil in bodily form continues to ply his daring and seductive devices; therefore there can be no real improvement of it. Even in one of his most powerful treatises, "On the freedom of a Christian man," he is far from making the religious man, the man of faith, feel at home in and be contented with this world, and far from saying to him that he must find his satisfaction and ideal in building up the kingdom of God on earth by ministering love. No, the Christian awaits in faith the glorious appearing of the kingdom of Christ, in which his own dominion over all things shall be made manifest; meanwhile, during this epoch of time, he *must* be a servant in love and bear the burden of his calling. Yet whether we are disposed to regard this view of Luther as a limitation or as the most correct expression of the matter, it is certain *that he transformed, as no Christian had done before him since the age of the apostles, the ideal of religious perfection,* and that at the same time it fell to him to transform also the *moral* ideal, although it was only on the religious side that he was able firmly to establish what was new. If we will make clear to ourselves the significance of Luther, his breach with the past, we must keep his new ideal of the Christian life and Christian perfection as much in view as his doctrine of faith, from which that ideal originated, and his freedom from the law of the letter and of Church doctrine and Church authority. What an extraordinary reduction is represented also by Luther's new ideal! That which was hitherto least observed under the accumulation of fine-spun and complicated ideals — lowly and assured confidence in God's Fatherly providence and faithfulness in one's calling (in neighborly service) — he made the chief matter; nay, he raised it to the position of the sole ideal! That which the mediæval period declared to be something preliminary, knowledge of God as Lord and Father and faith in his guardianship, he declared to be the main part of practical Christianity: *those only who belong to Christ have a God*; all others have him not, nay, know him not. That which the mediæval age looked upon with mistrust, worldly calling and daily duty, was regarded by him as the true sphere of the life that is well-pleasing to God. The effects were immeasurable; for at *one* stroke religion was now released from connexion with all that was foreign to it and the independent right belonging to the spheres of the natural life was recognized. Over the great structure of things which we call the Middle Ages, over this chaos of unstable and inter-blended forms, there brooded the spirit of faith, which had discerned its own nature and therefore its limits. Under its breath everything that had a right freely to assert itself began to struggle forth into independent development. Through his thinking out, proclaiming, and applying the gospel, everything else was to fall to the Reformer. He had no other aim than to teach the world what the nature of religion is; but through his seeing the most important province in its distinctive character, the rights of all others also were to be vindicated; *science* no longer stands under the ban of ecclesiastical authority, but must investigate its object in a secular, *i.e.*, in a "pure" way; the *state* is no longer the disastrous combination of compulsion and need, so constructed as to lean for support on the Church, but is the sovereign order of public social life, while the home is its root; *law* is no longer an undefinable thing lying midway between the power of the stronger and the virtue of the Christian, but is the independent norm of intercourse, guarded by the civil authorities, and a divinely ordained power, withdrawn from the influences of the Church; marriage is no longer a kind of ecclesiastical concession to the weak, but is the union of the sexes, instituted by God, free from all ecclesiastical guardianship, and the school of the highest morality; *care for the poor and active charity* are no longer a one-sided pursuit carried on with a view to securing one's own salvation, but are the free service of one's neighbor, which sees in the real giving of help its ultimate aim and its only reward. But above all this — *the civil calling*, the simple activity amidst family and dependents, in business and in office, is no longer viewed with suspicion, as an occupation withdrawing the thoughts from heaven, but is the true spiritual province, the field in which proof is to be given of one's trust in God, one's humility and prayerfulness — that is, of the Christian character that is rooted in faith.

These are the fundamental features of Luther's Christianity. Any one who takes his stand here and becomes absorbed in Luther's conception of faith, will at once find difficulty in holding the view that, in spite of all this, Luther only supplemented the old "sound" dogma by adding one, or one or two, doctrines. He will be inclined rather to trust here the Catholic judgment, according to which Luther overthrew the system of doctrine of the ancient and mediæval Church and only retained portions of the ruins. At the same time it must not be denied that the steps towards constructing on principle a new ideal of life were not developed by critical force to the point of clearness. For this the time was not yet ripe. In an age when life still continued every day to be threatened by a thousand forms of distress, when nature was a dreaded, mysterious power, when legal order meant unrighteous force, when terrible maladies of all kinds abounded, and in a certain sense no one was sure of his life — in such a time there was necessarily no rising beyond the thought that the most important earthly function of religion is to give comfort amidst the world's misery. Assuagement of the pain of sin, mitigation of the evil of the world — this Augustinian mood remained the prevalent one, and assuredly it is neither possible nor intended that this mood should ever disappear. But the task that is set to Christian faith today is no apocryphal one because it has not on its side a tradition of Church history. It must be able to take a powerful part in the moulding of personality, in the productive development of the dominion over nature, in the interpenetrating of the spiritual life with the spirit, and to prove its indispensableness in these directions, otherwise it will become the possession of a sect, in disregard of whom the great course of our history will pass on its way. . . .   (*HD:* 168-195)

*

Concluding Observations

In the preceding sections an attempt has been made to state as clearly as possible Luther's attitude towards the Catholic tradition and the old dogma. Our task has not been to describe Luther's theology in the whole breadth of its development. The more difficult problem had to be solved of bringing out the significance of Luther — and thereby of the Reformation — within the *history of dogma.* It has been shown, I hope, that Luther (the Reformation) represents an issue of the history of dogma as much as, in other ways, Post-Tridentine Catholicism and

Socinianism. It has been shown *that the new view of the gospel taken by Luther forms a complete whole, and that the elements of the old which he retained are not in accord with this whole, nay, that at all points at which he allowed what was Catholic to remain, he at the same time himself indicated the main features of a new structure.*

This complete whole, however, which he outlined with a firm hand, rises superior, not merely to this or that particular dogma, *but to dogmatic Christianity in its entirety.* Christianity is something else than a sum of traditional doctrines. Christianity is not Biblical theology, nor is it the doctrine of the Councils; but it is the *spirit* which the Father of Jesus Christ awakens in hearts through the gospel. All authorities which support dogma are abolished; how then can dogma maintain itself as infallible *doctrine*; but what, again, is a dogma without infallibility? Christian doctrine establishes its right only for faith; what share, then, can philosophy still have in it? but what, again, are dogma and dogmatic Christianity without philosophy? Of course one can appeal here to Luther against Luther, yet only in the same way in which one can raise up Augustine to reply to Augustine, and in the same way in which every genius can easily be made away with when a rope to despatch him has been twisted out of his imperfections and out of what he shared with his age. The history of dogma comes to a close with Luther. Any one who lets Luther be Luther, and regards his main positions as *the valuable possession* of the evangelical Church — who does not merely tolerate them, that is to say, under stress of circumstances — has the lofty title and the strict obligation to conclude the history of dogma with him.[28]

(*HD:* 267-8)

*

The gospel entered into the world, not as a doctrine, but as a joyful message and as a power of the Spirit of God, originally in the forms of Judaism. It stripped off these forms with amazing rapidity, and united and amalgamated itself with Greek science, the Roman empire and ancient culture, developing, as a counterpoise to this, renunciation of the world and the striving after supernatural life, after deification. All this was summed up in the old dogma and in dogmatic Christianity. Augustine reduced the value of this dogmatic structure, made it subservient to a purer and more living conception of religion, but yet finally left it standing so far as its foundations and aim were concerned. Under his direction there began in the Middle Ages, from the 11th century, an astonishing course of labor; the retrograde steps are to a large extent only apparent, or at least counter-balanced by great steps of progress. But no satisfying goal is reached; side by side with dogma, and partly in opposition to it, exists a practical piety and religious self-criticism, which points at the same time forwards and backwards — to the gospel, but ever the more threatens to vanish amid unrest and languor. An appallingly powerful ecclesiasticism is taking shape, which has already long held in its possession the stolid and indifferent, and takes control of the means whereby the restless may be soothed and the weary gathered in. Dogma assumes a rigid aspect; it is elastic only in the hands of political priests; and it is seen to have degenerated into sophistry; faith takes its flight from it, and leaves the old structure to the guardians of the Church. Then appeared Luther, to restore the "doctrine," on which no one any longer had an inward reliance. But the doctrine which he restored was the gospel as a glad message and *as a power of God.* That this was what it was, he also pronounced to be the chief, nay the only, principle of theology. What the gospel is must be ascertained from Holy Scripture; the power of God cannot be construed by thought, it must be experienced; the *faith* in God as the Father of Jesus Christ, which answers to this power, cannot be enticed forth by reason or authority; it must become a part of one's life; all that is not born of faith is alien to the Christian religion and therefore also to Christian theology — all philosophy, as well as all asceticism. Matthew 11:27 is the basis of faith and of theology. In giving effect to these thoughts, Luther, the most conservative of men, shattered the ancient Church and set a goal to the history of dogma. That history has found its goal in a return to the gospel. He did not in this way hand over something complete and finished to Christendom but set before it a problem, to be developed out of many encumbering surroundings, to be continuously dealt with in connexion with the entire life of the spirit and with the social condition of mankind, but to be solved only in faith itself. Christendom must constantly go on to learn, that even in religion the simplest thing is the most difficult, and that everything that is a burden upon religion quenches its seriousness ("a Christian man's business is not to talk grandly about dogmas, but to be always doing arduous and great things in fellowship with God": Zwingli). Therefore the goal of all Christian work, even of all theological work, can only be this — to discern ever more distinctly the simplicity and the seriousness of the gospel, in order to become ever purer and stronger in *spirit*, and ever more loving and brotherly in *action.*

(*HD:* 272-4)

4

THE RELIGIOUS-SOCIAL IMPERATIVE IN THE GOSPEL AND CHURCH

For much of his remarkably active life as a scholar and academician, Harnack was much involved in the Evangelical Social Congress, of which, in 1890, he was co-founder. At one time he was its President (1903 to 1912). It strove to place the public discussion concerning social issues on a foundation of exact knowledge and objectivity.[29] In his endeavors related to the Congress, Harnack manifested again his steadfast convictions about the methods and certainties of the scholarly enterprise, about Wissenschaft. *Under his influence, the manner of discerning the "social gospel" gave little room, if any, to the approach of those who, guided by Marx and Religious Socialism, read the Bible and proposed social actions which we would today call informed by a political theology. One sees here again a sharp feature of the theological liberalism represented by Harnack, namely the repudiation of approaches seen to be "partisan." His own work and stature assured what was held to be objectivity. The issue is not whether or not such liberalism was capable of dealing effectively with social issues; the issue is the question what theological foundations and conclusions does a liberal theology provide for the tasks of social welfare and how it integrates that welfare into its foundational reflections.*

The two selections chosen here are of a piece; Harnack's turn-of-the-century "state of the art" lectures add some nuances to the more expanded treatment of 1894, nuances in line with the main aim of providing a comprehensive and cohesive understanding of the Christian religion.

ESSAYS ON THE SOCIAL GOSPEL

Harnack was sure that the priceless message of Christianity about the higher life of humankind was not only to be heard *in the context of modern society but also to be* acted out *for that society's benefit. This is the reason for his extensive and personal Christian engagement. The width of Christian practice of which he spoke becomes apparent in two major publications on the social imperative of the gospel:* The Evangelical-Social Task as Seen in the Light of Church-History, *delivered initially as a lecture in 1894, and* The Moral and Social Significance of Modern Education,

269

published in 1902. The former is presented here; it was one of the joint projects Harnack undertook with Wilhelm Herrmann.

The German text of the two men's essays appeared in 1894, was trans-lated by G. M. Craik and published in English in 1907 in the volume Essays on the Social Gospel, *pp. 3-91.*

INTRODUCTORY

In the year 1694, H. A. Francke was profoundly moved by the saying of the apostle Paul: "God is able to make all grace abound toward you; that ye, always having all sufficiency in all things, may abound to every good work." The words henceforth never lost their hold over him, but became the source and impulse of his activity. The origin of very much that has since been done in our country in the name of Christian charity may be dated from that time, and the bold confidence expressed in the apostle's words has led to the accomplishment of projects that at one time appeared impossible.

And now, after two hundred years, there is again especial need of that same confidence. It is not that we belong, as did Francke, to a Church in which the duty of Christian charity is neglected, but that the nature of that duty itself has clearly changed, and is now so new and so vast that all our old methods appear inadequate. It seems to be no longer a problem with which individuals can deal, and the principal object of this Congress is to take counsel together, with a view to right action. While particular points require to be discussed on the lines appropriate to each, it is essential to have the whole question set clearly before us, to see plainly what it is we are aiming at, and examine the means at our disposal. We are not, however, now concerned with the problem of social questions in general, but with the duty of the Church and the Christian community.

Such a duty is obvious if we are to apply the gospel to present circumstances, and I can easily understand the radical tendency of some who would exclude all remoter matters. It is true that historical retrospect is not always free from danger. A good steersman must look ahead, not behind; and a backward glance over the past may check bold action, and see impossibilities where really it is only a question of difficulties. Furthermore, history can never throw light on the path that lies before us. Among the members of this Congress, however, there will be no doubt that the social mission of the Church today can be determined only by the help of history, not merely because this is a guide to the shallows and reefs to be avoided, but still more because the different churches in all their aspects, including that of charitable societies, are, in their gradual growth, historic institutions. Unless we are prepared to undervalue all the experience gained in the course of history, we must make up our minds to preserve the links between the present and the past.

Before proceeding to deal with the problem itself, I must call attention to a fact that may well inspire us with hope and gladness. Throughout the whole civilized world questions are now being discussed concerning economic arrangements and the relations between capital and labor; this is in itself proof that much social work has already been accomplished. It is not long since culture, rights and human dignity were the monopoly of some few thousands amongst all the inhabitants of Europe, while the great masses of people lived dreary lives under tyrannous oppression, possessing neither rights nor education, their whole existence being one long misery. Today, on the contrary — at least in our own country, and among many other kindred nations — all citizens are equal in the eyes of the law; all enjoy the same legal protection; slavery and serfdom are things of the past; a fair amount of knowledge and education are within the reach of all; and labor is respected. Liberty, equality and fraternity are in many ways no mere empty words, but the real framework of our individual and social life, the pillars of the building we are raising. All this has been accomplished in the lifetime of a few generations, and it is absurd to question the fact of progress, amidst improvements so obvious and immense.

Yet the retort is frequently made: What in practice have this liberty, this equality, this fraternity proved to be? Have we not been deceived by them in the past? Do they not, on the one hand, threaten us with the rule of ignorance and folly, and, on the other hand, are they not mere catchwords, deprived of real meaning by the dependence of labor upon that capital which it does not itself possess? The truth — say these pessimists — is that the old oppression still prevails — in a different cloak, it may be, but, for all that, in an aggravated form; the worst kind of servitude is rife; legal equality, besides being imperilled by the existence of capital, is at best but a negative good; and education for the masses is a mere possibility, of which they cannot avail themselves! Nominally we are all equal; but in reality a minority lives as before at the expense of a vast majority, whose members are still consumed by cares, and find the rights they have won to be in part but a niggardly instalment of their dues, and at the same time a mockery of their helpless condition.

Those who argue thus are not wholly wrong, but they are not right. The above-mentioned blessings, in which all are supposed to share, may indeed be, and to some extent really are, mere delusions. But just try to remove them now, or even to imagine that they do not exist! They are great and lasting possessions, won with effort, and none the less valuable because not all-sufficient. Blessings they still would be, even though at the present time they should result in intensifying economic difficulties. Retrogression is no longer possible for us; and shame upon those who desire it! Let us rather rejoice in having already achieved much that, a few generations ago, seemed but an empty dream.

I must now, after these introductory remarks, ask you to follow me in a historical retrospect. Before entering upon this, however, it is necessary to consider the underlying historical question of the general attitude of the gospel towards social arrangements. We shall then glance at the successive epochs of ecclesiastical history, and finally endeavor to answer the question, What is the social mission of the Church of today?

(*SG:* 3-8)

*

GENERAL ATTITUDE OF THE GOSPEL
TOWARDS SOCIAL ARRANGEMENTS

The gospel is the glad tidings of benefits that pass not away. In it are the powers of eternal life; it is concerned with repentance and faith, with regeneration and a new life; its end is redemption, not social improvement. Therefore it aims at raising the individual to a standpoint far above the conflicts between earthly success and earthly distress, between riches and poverty, lordship and service. This has been its meaning to earnest Christians of all ages, and those who are unable to appreciate this idea, fail to appreciate the gospel itself. The indifference to all earthly affairs, which proceeds from the conviction that we possess life eternal, is an essential feature of Christianity. It is the result of a twofold mental attitude, which may be summed up in the following words: "Fear not, be not anxious; the very hairs of your head are all numbered;" and "Love not the world, neither the things that are in the world." In accordance with these two precepts two principles arise. One may be called the tranquil, quietistic principle, and the other, the radical; the former impels men to acquiesce, with faith and resignation, in the whole course of the world, whatever it may be, or, however it may develop, while the latter urges them to renounce the world, and live for something new. In the gospel itself, then, a problem is thus presented, for it is obvious that between the tranquil and the radical principles there is a

272

possibility of conflicts. Indeed, the radical principle, where it predominates to the exclusion of the other, allows of further subdivision according as it finds expression in one of two ways — either in complete renunciation of the world, or in the attempt to do away with all the existing ordinances of the world, as being all impregnated by sin, combined with an endeavor to establish a new order of world. History will show us how, through directing one-sided attention to one or other of these principles, instead of harmonising the two, Christians have evaded the difficulty.

But the same gospel which preaches a holy indifference to earthly things, embraces yet another principle: "Love thy neighbor as thyself." This spirit of love likewise is to be a guiding rule of the character built up by the gospel. Accordingly Christianity originally took the form of a free brotherhood — a form essential to its very nature, for, after trust in God, the very essence of religion is brotherly love. In addition, then, to the quietistic and radical principles we have a third — the social, active principle. I give it this name of a social active principle, because the gospel nowhere teaches that our relations to the brethren should be characterized by a holy indifference. Such indifference expresses rather what the individual soul should feel towards the world with all its weal and woe. Whenever it is question of one's neighbor, the gospel will not hear of this indifference, but, on the contrary, preaches always love and mercy. Further, the gospel regards as absolutely inseparable the temporal and spiritual needs of the brethren. It draws no fine distinctions between body and soul; sickness is always sickness, and want is want. Thus, "I was an hungered, and ye gave me meat: I was thirsty, and ye gave me drink." Again, when it is a question of giving signs to prove that the promises of God have now been fulfilled, it is said: "The blind see, the lame walk — . . . and to the poor the gospel is preached;" while in the gospel of the Hebrews we read in the story of the rich young man: "Behold many of thy brethren, sons of Abraham, are clad with dung, dying with hunger, and thy house is full of much goods, and there goeth out therefrom nought at all unto them." Thus, in the simplest and most emphatic terms possible, Christians are urged to help the needy and the miserable with all the strength of love. But it is to the rich that the most earnest exhortation is addressed. While it is assumed that wealth tends to make its possessors hard-hearted and worldly, they are warned that their perilous possessions impose upon them the highest responsibility.

A new spectacle was presented to the world: religion hitherto had either clung to what was earthly, adapting itself readily to things as it found them, or else built in the clouds, and set itself up in opposition to everything; but now it had a new duty — to scorn earthly want and misery, and earthly prosperity alike, and yet to relieve distress of every kind; to raise its head to heaven in the courage of its faith, and yet with heart and hand and voice to labor for the brethren upon earth. The task thus set them has never been wholly abandoned by Christians, who consequently, have held fast the conviction that no economic system can oppose to the mission of Christianity a really insuperable obstacle, while, on the other hand, no economic system can ever release it from its duties.

But does not the gospel contain much more than this? Does it not include definite teaching on the subject of temporal welfare, and a definite social and economic programme? So indeed men have believed, both in the early ages of Christianity, in the Middle Ages, and at the present time; and yet the belief is wrong. Undoubtedly the gospel contains definite teaching concerning temporal good, but none that could be summed up in the form of national economic laws, and consequently no economic program. Only if the gospel or the New Testament be regarded as a legal code, can social and political laws be found in it; but we have no right to regard it thus, and any attempt to do so will speedily end in failure. It is unauthorized, because our faith is the religion of liberty, and its duties are specially imposed upon you, and upon me, and upon every age, as an individual problem for each to solve. And it must needs end in failure, because no self-consistent economic precepts can possibly be derived from the New Testament. Are we, in accordance with the story of the rich young man, to sell all that we have? Or are we, at least, not to lay up treasures for ourselves? Or are we, as taught by the apostle Paul, to turn to profit every gift, wealth and property included, but so as to convert them into instruments of service? May a Christian never settle vexed questions of inheritance? Is it right for him to make large outlay only, as in the gospel story, on ointments; or is this always justifiable? May he, or may he not, keep money in a strong-box? "Labor, working with your hands the thing which is good, that you may have to give to him that needeth": that surely is the gist of the matter, and firm resistance must be offered to all attempts to read into the gospel any other social ideal than this: "You are accountable to God for all the gifts you have received, and so for your possessions also; you are bound to use them in the service of your neighbor." Anything in the gospel that seems to point in any other direction is merely apparent contradiction, or is relevant only to some particular case, or results from the undeveloped economic conditions and special historical circumstances of the time in which the gospel arose. An age in which capital was almost always hoarded in a useless way, as a dead thing, cannot be compared with an age in which it is the greatest economic power; and an age which believed the end of the world to be approaching is not to be compared with one which recognizes as sacred the duty of working for the future.

But conversely, it does not at all follow from the lack of economic precepts in the gospel, that the matter is one which does not concern a Christian. On the contrary, where he clearly perceives that any economic condition has become a source of distress to his neighbor, he is bound to seek for a remedy, for he is a disciple of the Savior. If a man falls into the water, one may help him by simply pulling him out; but if any one is imprisoned in a burning house, the exits being fast closed, the only way to help him is to effect a change in the circumstances: that is to say, to extinguish the fire. The question whether such an act belongs to Christian economics, or is simply and solely Christian, or should rather be called humane, may be left to those who delight in argument. Love knows that it is always bound to help in such a way as to render real assistance.

The Church has from the first availed itself of three means of helping the brethren and relieving misery and want; and the same three methods are still at its command. The first of these consists in rousing the individual conscience, in such a way as to awaken strong, regenerate, self-sacrificing personalities. This is the all-important thing; but the means to such an end vary; as the Lord's method of teaching shows, it may either begin within, and work outwards, or it may penetrate from without to the inmost being. But the vital point is that there should be a Christ-like personality, and that in every action the power of love from one person to another should operate, and make itself felt. The kingdom of God must be built upon the foundation, not of institutions, but of individuals in whom God dwells and who are glad to live for their fellow men.

The second method consists in converting every congregation of individuals into a community full of active charity, and bound together by brotherly love; for without such a bond all effort is sporadic. This fellowship was strongest in the early days of the Church, and the consciousness that Christianity cannot exist upon earth in any other form never altogether passed away, although, as we shall see, it became enfeebled.

Then there is still the third line of action. Religion is not independent in its growth; even if it takes refuge in solitude, it must enter into some relation with the arrangements of the world as it finds them, and it cannot regard with indifference the nature of these ordinances. It was, indeed, at a time when extortion and violence were common, and slavery and tyrannical oppression prevailed, that the apostles instructed the faithful to "take no anxious thought." But at the same time they at once began to exert their influence against so much of the existing order of things as was in fact disorder and sin. Christians were urged so to walk that their example should both make others ashamed and incite them to imitation. Only a few decades later, representatives of Christianity were presenting petitions to the emperors and the governors of provinces, and addressing written appeals to society, demanding the abolition of gross and flagrant abuses and outrages. But, as far as I can see, the limit of their interference was clearly defined: it did not occur to them to propose economic improvements, or to attack fixed institutions, such as slavery. What they demanded was the suppression of such sin and shame as could not but be recognized as sins and scandals even by a Greek or Roman conscience. They were convinced that the divine image in man cannot be destroyed by oppression and suffering of any kind (never was there an age of less sentimentality with regard to want and misery than the early days of Christianity); but that it is effaced by uncleanness and sensuality, and that therefore conditions which plainly tended in that direction — for example, a tolerated and privileged unchastity, secret murder, exposing of children, and wholesale prostitution — are altogether intolerable.

This brings us to a most important point. At the present time Christianity is being reproached with never, at any time in its history, having taken the lead in economic reforms. Even if the facts were in accordance with this sweeping statement, it would be no real reproach, in view of the distinctive character of the Christian religion.

It is enough if religion prepares men's minds for great economic changes and revolutions; if it foresees the new moral duties which these impose; if it knows how to adapt itself to them, and perceives the right moment at which to step in with its forces, and do its work. A religion which aims at saving the soul and transforming the inner man, and which regards a change in outward circumstances as but a small matter in comparison with the power of evil, can only follow in the wake of earthly changes and exercise an after-influence; it is not qualified to lead the way in economic developments.

To be sure, that is not the conclusion of the whole matter. It is undeniable that the greatest danger of Churches once established has always been lest they should become in a bad sense conservative and indolent, and should hide this indolence under cover of very lofty conceptions of their creed. Instead of helping their poor brother, they preach to him that "pious indifference" with which individuals should regard their own earthly fortunes. Even in the days when the Epistle of St. James was written, Christians would say to a destitute brother: "God help you!" — and yet give him nothing. The other-worldly aspect of religion was exploited to such an extent that love in this world was forgotten, or, in other words, the present world was not forgotten, but love was.

It is no mere coincidence that from the very beginning this perverted quietism has always had as its counterpart the tendency which I have called radicalism. If indifference towards all earthly matters is to take the place of love in determining our relations with our neighbors, there is at least as much justification for radicalism as for quietism. Therefore let all earthly possessions be forsaken, divided equally, or held in common! The fantastic idea, derived from antiquity, of communism in matters economic, has always clung to the Church like a shadow, faint at one time, at another more distinct. Combined with thoughts of complete renunciation of this world, or with material hopes of another world, it seemed to offer the best solution to the problem of the evangelical-social mission of the Church, and at the same time declared war against indolent indifference. The idea, though naïvely conceived, and never really carried out, or capable of being carried out, was valuable in so far as it stirred up easy-going Christians, called attention to faults in the prevailing economic order, and modified obstinate ideas of individual ownership; but the merits were outweighed by the disadvantages of the movement. Wherever it attempted to practise its theories — indeed, wherever it was able to gain a hearing at all — the result was to make men blind to the duties nearest at hand and within their powers; it always undervalued the simple, personal acts of charity in the interests of its own institutions, supposed to be capable of overcoming all evil, and eventually it degenerated into the opposite of its own ideals, its "heaven upon earth" becoming a degradation of religion. Moreover, in those ages of the Church in which the communistic theory was most common, religion was most selfish. For the strongest motive that impelled towards communism was scarcely ever brotherly love; it was at one time a desire to escape from the world, incompatible with concern for one's

277

fellow men; at another time, a longing for earthly welfare, encouraged by the self-deluding belief that heaven could be established upon earth.

(*SG:* 9-21)

*

THE SOCIAL MISSION OF THE CHURCH OF TODAY

It may be said that the social mission of the Church today is both new in kind and of greater urgency than in the past: not because poverty and distress have increased — for that is, to say the least, not capable of proof; nor because the Church is more negligent than before in works of charity — quite the reverse is true; nor yet because self-sacrificing and trained workers are less numerous than hitherto — on the contrary, they have never been so numerous as now. In what sense, then, can the Church's task today be called new and more urgent than in the past? Well, to begin with, history proves that new and urgent duties never come to light during the dark days of declining movements. In the dreariness and distress that then prevail, all available energy must be exerted to hold fast at least the things that remain. It is only in a progressive age that the obligation to new and higher action can be felt; and so at the present time it is just the progress we have already made that thrusts new tasks upon us. In indicating briefly the various lines along which we have advanced, I hope to say nothing with which you will not all agree.

First, we have no longer to do with classes in a state of tutelage, but, though in some respects they may still be powerless, all have equal recognition, and a certain measure of education now belongs to all. I need not enter in further detail into this matter, in which the immense progress of the last century is clearly shown. It is only in small sequestered districts, or under special circumstances, that it is still possible for the relief of the poor to take the form of patriarchal care or patronage by the upper classes of those beneath them. Now that all classes have dealings with each other on the footing of legal equality, a similar freedom of intercourse on equal terms, whether friendly or the reverse has become more and more general in all the relations of life — a condition towards which the spread of education and equality of political rights have been largely conducive. This only serves to heighten the contrast between wealth and the lack of it, as represented by capital and labor, opposed to each other as though they were impersonal forces; and to render more intolerable a state of affairs in which whole classes of the population, after enjoying a good education and acquiring thereby a genuine taste

278

for the blessings of culture, must yet spend their lives in such straitened circumstances that they are able to appropriate but few of those blessings, and are, moreover, liable to be ruined by the slightest economic disturbance.

Secondly, conscience is more alive, and there is a keener sense of duty than before with regard to the welfare of all the members of society; that is an unmistakable advance, of such cogency as to compel people to take part in it outwardly, even if they do not really do so in their hearts. Moreover, we have learned to regard poverty and distress as a serious social danger, in a sense very different from that formerly thought of, while at the same time we have become aware that no thorough reform can be effected except by preventive means. The obligation arising from the recognition of these facts is an entirely new one, such as no past generation ever felt. In coping with it, the study of sociology and economics is found to resemble that of therapeutics, where attention is more and more being concentrated upon hygiene, the science of preventive measures.

Thirdly, everything today is dominated by the mighty power of an economic system embracing the whole world; nothing can escape it; its influence is felt on the remotest village handicraft; it alters or does away with existing conditions, and threatens with insecurity the economic existence of whole industries. No wonder that it also affects the organization of the Church; to mention one point alone, congregational life is endangered by those facilities for migration which follow naturally upon the improved means of communication throughout the world. Both in the great cities, and outside their bounds, there is a vast nomadic population — a class of people in whom, as every page of history shows, it is very difficult to maintain a high standard of morality and religion.

In the fourth place, we are face to face, no longer with merely naïve ideas of communism, but with socialistic systems of considerable economic development, founded on a materialistic view of life. These systems and these views are gaining ground among the nations, and already crowds of people are definitely and deliberately giving up, not only membership in the Church, but also the Christian faith, and Christian ethics, so that materialism, theoretical and practical, is becoming a power in public life. But even this development can by no means be regarded simply from the point of view which condemns it as "desertion" or "backsliding." Before talking of desertion, we must prove that there was, to begin with, real membership in a corporate body. But large numbers, who are now termed "deserters," never did lay claim to living membership, and it is only from having been so long disguised that this fact now appears the more striking and appalling. Such make-believe is, to be sure, under certain circumstances a restraining and humanizing influence, and one may therefore regret the disillusionment. All the same, it is a step in advance when one theory of existence is straightforwardly confronted with another. Besides, there are even worse things than deliberate materialism, namely, absolute indifference or calculating selfishness, endeavoring to get what advantage it can for itself from all theories of existence at once, and hating every conviction that threatens to destroy its own comfort and impose duties upon it.

These are the principal factors which go to make up the existing situation, and they must be kept in view while seeking for an answer to the question: What is the special social mission of the Church today? There are two mistaken notions which I surely no longer require to correct, namely, that it is the duty of the Church to disentangle these difficulties, and that it is in possession of a sovereign remedy for all ills. The Roman Catholic Church does indeed sometimes seem to imply that it holds such a secret panacea, and is only waiting for the nations to swallow it; but it does not seriously mean it. As a Christian Church, it, too, cannot eventually disregard the fact that the peace promised by the gospel is a peace which the world cannot give, and that the improvement of economic conditions is not the duty of religion. Therefore, when we are speaking of the social mission of the Church — of our Evangelical Church — our object must simply be to settle what form, under present circumstances, this task must assume, a task always one and the same in its fundamental nature, but differing much from time to time in its characteristic forms. So, too, the means at its disposal never really change, but the use to be made of them varies with the period.

Above all it must be remembered that the chief task of the Church is still the preaching of the gospel, that is to say, the message of redemption and of eternal life. Christianity as a religion would be at an end if this truth were obscured, and the gospel were to be changed into a social manifesto, whether for the sake of gaining popularity, or owing to excessive zeal for reform. More than that; none dare ultimately expect more for himself from the message of the Church than a firm, consolatory faith, able to triumph over all the troubles of life. "What shall it profit a man, if he shall gain the whole world, and lose his own soul?" This conviction and the glad tidings of Jesus Christ the Redeemer constitute the essence of the gospel, from which is developed that view of life — that is to say, that way of thinking of the soul and the body, life and death, happiness and unhappiness, riches and poverty — which is the truth, and therefore makes men free. But the power that lies in every definite theory of existence is proved at the present day by the socialistic movement. At one of our last Congresses it was eloquently demonstrated that it is just to such a clear theory of life that the social-democratic movement owes its strength. Its thousands of adherents do not want merely bread; they know full well they do not live by bread alone; they want an answer to all the questions of the universe and of life, and for that — for their faith — they are ready to make sacrifices. For that very reason, the work of the Church is easier at the present time than at any period in the past, since never before were so many men filled with such longing as today for firm and consistent convictions. In spite of social divisions and apparent disintegration, there is an all-penetrating force which binds men together with close ties of spiritual fellowship, namely, thought and speech. And the strongest expression of thought will prevail. Men are ready today to give anything for a conviction that is real conviction — for a belief that really is believed in. Men are not so base that they can find satisfaction in the gratification and the service of their individual existence; they require convictions as to the meaning of life. But the demand is for a faith in which there is real faith; and to provide this, constitutes the mission of the Church — its task both new and old. It has to proclaim to the present generation the living God and life eternal. It has to testify of the redeeming Lord, whose person still wins reverence and love even from those who are most alienated. Zealously and earnestly it must teach that sin is the ruin of mankind and the strongest root of all misery; and must preach that truth both fully and freely, in an intelligible form, so expressed that all may understand. When that is done, the main part of its social mission will already be fulfilled. But in order to be able to do so, it must ally itself with all real knowledge and with truth of every kind, or else it will bring discredit on the message it proclaims. It is true that one ray of gospel light is often sufficient to illumine the heart, and make a man free; and the lowliest servant of Jesus Christ may prove a true savior to his neighbor; but in the great battle of intellects, where one theory of the universe is opposed to another, the victory can only remain with that interpretation which is a complete whole, and can prove itself true and strong in every way.

I said that none dare ultimately expect more for himself from the message of the Church than a firm, consolatory faith, able to triumph over the troubles of life. The emphasis here is on the words "for himself"; it is a very different matter with regard to other people. Historical retrospect shows us that it is an essential part of Christianity to weld the individual members of a congregation into a brotherhood full of active life, and then to knit such congregations together into a great association of willing helpers, and that when in course of time congregational life collapsed, this meant a serious loss to the Church. In the early days of Christianity active philanthropy was one of the most persuasive methods of propaganda, and Jesus Christ himself preached the gospel while he went about doing good. If sin is at the root of misery, misery and error in turn produce fresh sin and shame. Therefore war must be waged upon misery; but to win the day two things are essential — personal influence from man to man, and the growth of genuine congregational life. Of the first of these there is no need to speak at length. We all know that in the end it is only personal love that really counts. Institutions and charitable organizations touch but the fringe of the matter; only that which proceeds from the heart and addresses itself to the heart is of real moment as weighed in the balance of eternity. In helping one's neighbor, one must set oneself neither above nor beneath him but beside him. Brothers, not patrons, we are called to be; and in answering this call, Christian charity finds its scope and proper work — a work the more necessary the more the relations between the classes assume an impersonal form owing to the development in our midst of our modern economic order.

With regard to the second point, it is certain that where there are no close congregational ties, all effort remains isolated. We should therefore be grateful to those who are now once more calling attention to the fact that ever since the Reformation our Church has been called upon to build up real congregations, and so to revive a vigorous corporate life. The following objection is often heard: "It is too late for that now; organization of that sort is no longer possible; neither is it compatible with the bureaucratic constitution of our Church, nor yet can living congregations be formed from the kind of Christianity professed by the masses and the state." To be sure such a task is hard enough, but we need not yet despair of its fulfilment. If we really had to abandon it, I do not know where we could turn for help, for the service of the congregation is one that no public institutions can perform, and for which neither their social work nor their coercive measures are any adequate substitute. We have much to be thankful for in the survival of the congregation, even in a defective form; and it would be a fatal error to despise what remains to us, and search for other ideals of organization. As every one knows and feels, these congregations are in their original intention communities in which all distinctions of high and low, rich and poor, are swept away, and class differences count for nothing; in fact, just such institutions as we have special need of at the present time. Therefore we must do all in our power to build them up, and give them life, and then patiently wait to see whether their existence will not lead to the gradual transformation or abandonment of state-government in our ecclesiastical polity. Next to the preaching of the gospel, the reconstruction of congregational life is the chief evangelical-social task now before the Church. The pusillanimous, who regard with despair the fulfilment of this task, on the ground that existing conditions would never allow of such an organization, would do well to consider the example set by the social-democratic movement. It has succeeded in creating and maintaining, among a migratory population, and in face of obstacles of every kind, an organization closely knit, operative alike in the cities and the provinces, both national and international. Why could we not do the like? Because, it will be said, that movement is essentially concerned with one class, and with a common interest serving as a link between its members. But have not we, too, a common interest, and have not we a message which unites the different classes in a spiritual union? If our congregations neither are nor become what they ought to be, it is not the fault of circumstances, but of lack of faith and love.

It is, indeed, certain that we can no longer draw people into congregations whose sole end is divine service, and that such congregations are necessarily without real efficacy. But the early Church furnishes a pattern of what true congregational life should be, and the lines along which charitable work in the Church has developed during the last century point in the same direction. It is no empty dream that, in the history of Christianity, there have been congregations — capable of supervision, well ordered, bound together by close ties — in which, next to divine service, active charity was the central point — in which, rather, service to God and active charity were merged in one. And dare we say that for us that is unattainable? Nay, rather we must keep it clearly before us, as the goal towards which we constantly aspire. For this reason all great works of Christian charity must not only be fostered and extended, but also made more and more congregational in their organization. Where one congregation is too small to do by itself all that is required, several must join together so as to form eventually a strong local association. The church-building must also be an assembly-hall for the community, or, better still, there must be an assembly-hall in addition to the Church, and people should meet together, not only to hear sermons, but also to take counsel about benevolent work of every sort. A true Christian sense of honor must be aroused, allowing none to call himself a Christian unless he is ready to come forward in person to minister to the distressed and help the needy; and, besides this, there should be professional trained deacons and deaconesses at work in every parish. Not one of the destitute should any longer be able to say that nobody cares for him. The present age is one that delights in utopias — dangerous toys with which it is only too ready to play. This idea is not utopian, but can be realized. Upon its realization, and the consequent triumph over indolence, avarice, and selfish love of ease, depends, not indeed the actual existence of our Church — for it has many supports, and might possibly hold out for a very long time — but at all events the existence of a really evangelical Christianity, and the claim of our Church to appeal to the hearts of the people.

At the same time, our opponents are right in saying that the formation of such congregations is a task demanding time, and that the present conditions of public life necessitate action of another and more immediate kind. Can and should the Church — I am referring to the organized Church — do anything more than preach the gospel, and revive congregational life? This is a most important question, and we have to answer it. Some — and the majority — reply most decidedly in the negative, and they explain their reason for doing so in very different ways. Others answer it in the affirmative, but generally not without qualification; or else they evade it by the reply that, whatever the Church may do or leave undone, individual Christians are bound to carry the gospel into public life and bring it to bear upon current conditions.

We need not here discuss the duties of individuals, but there seems to me to be no question that since our Church still holds a great and influential place in the state, and in the life of the nation, it is bound to make use of this position for the advancement of evangelical social ideals, and accordingly to seek the most opportune ways of making its voice heard. Otherwise it will always be suspected of being merely an accommodating tool in the hands of an "aristocratic government," and will incur the blame of allowing an ever-widening breach to divide Christian ideals from the social ordinances of public life. Even in the days when it was numerically weak, the early Church raised its voice against abuses in the state. We saw that the Church of the empire, as it became after the reign of Constantine, was faithful to its obligations, and exerted its influence to bring about the suppression of moral evils. In the Middle

Ages, too, the Popes opposed tyranny and violence, as well as open immorality, and they do not to this day forego their claim to pronounce judgment upon important ethical and social questions. It is, indeed, on this very point that the difference is so marked between Roman Catholicism and Protestantism. To the former the "Church" means simply the hierarchical institution, with which, consequently, all responsibility rests, whereas, according to Protestantism, the spirit of Christianity is not confined to any organized ecclesiastical body, but is to be found also in the mundane pursuits and ordinances of Christendom. Therefore Protestants believe that if the government or other secular authority exercises its power rightly, it will be at one with the ethical ideals of Christianity, and accordingly, the ordering of temporal affairs may safely be left in its hands. But this in no way debars the Church from raising its voice in protest against moral and social evils, and from influencing both public opinion and the conduct of matters of national interest. It becomes, indeed, its duty so to do, if the state shows itself negligent or callous. Within the last thirty years our churches have become better able to express their opinions. But to what purpose have they this voice — in congregational representation, district, provincial and general synods, ecclesiastical courts and high consistories — if not to testify in the parish, in the city, in the province, in the whole country, on questions of moral and social welfare, and to declare: "This is right; that is wrong"? Are they to deal only with church rates, church formularies, and unimportant details? This may satisfy people for a time, but in the long run it will prove intolerable, and must soon excite feelings of pity or worse towards the organization of the Church as a whole; for its vast apparatus has a right to exist only if it renders real service to the whole body — not by words, but by evangelical-social work, work in which every order must perform its own share.

But the more stress is laid upon this, the more need there is to define the limits within which the Church must confine its activity — bounds that do not include economic questions. It has nothing to do with such practical questions of social-economics as the nationalization of private property and enterprise, land-tenure reforms, restriction of the legal hours of work, price-regulations, taxation, and insurance; for in order to settle these matters, such technical knowledge is required as is altogether outside the province of the Church, and if it were to meddle with them at all it would be led into a secularization of the worst description. But it is its duty to interfere in public conditions wherever it finds that serious moral evils are being tolerated. Can it be right for the Church, as it were, to shrug its shoulders and pass prostitution by in silence, as the priest did the man who had fallen among thieves? Is it enough to collect money for penitentiaries, leaving it to particular Christian associations to fight against the evil? Is the Church not bound to set its face against duelling? Dare it, again, keep silence when it sees a state of things destructive of the sanctity of marriage, and of family life, and devoid of the most elementary conditions of morality? Dare it look calmly on while the weak are trodden under foot, and none lends a helping hand to people in distress? Dare it hear, without rebuking it, language which, in the name of Christianity, destroys the peace of the land and sows scorn and hatred broadcast? Is it really only a bureaucratic institution, or is it not its duty, as an established Church, to preserve peace, both civil and international, to draw together rich and poor, and to help to break down mischievous class-prejudices? There will, it is true, be found plenty to reply that the Church has enough to do if it preaches the word of God and administers the sacraments. But the same answer was made to the demand that it should undertake foreign and home missions. To that suggestion, too, the Church at first was deaf, asserting that such an undertaking formed no part of its office; but it has since come to see that by not attending to these matters it is neglecting its duties. There would at first sight seem to be more weight in the objection that the representatives of the Church have no power to enforce their decisions on questions such as those I have mentioned; and that, owing to the peculiar composition of ecclesiastical gatherings, there is a risk of proposals being put forward without regard to their practicability, and therefore coming to nothing, as well as of meddling and interference in matters with which the Church has no concern. Such apprehensions are not unfounded, but the anticipation of mistakes in carrying it out is no adequate reason for opposing a course of action in itself necessary and good. Church assemblies will learn to measure their strength and to recognize their field of work only by practice in that work; and the well-defined and special relation in which the German Evangelical Churches stand to the state is sufficient guarantee against too ambitious schemes.

I have so far tried to indicate the social mission of the Church, but, besides this, there are many important tasks which Christians cannot regard with indifference, although their accomplishment lies outside the actual scope of the Church. Purely economic questions must admittedly be estimated and decided only from an economic standpoint; but there are many which affect vitally the moral conditions of the people.

Therefore the Church must not obstruct the discussion of such questions amongst its members — as, for instance, at these Evangelical-Social Congresses — for it is to the interest of the whole Church that warm-hearted, clear-sighted Christians should so study the subject as to be able to distinguish those efforts at reform which are full of promise for the future from such as are merely visionary, and to point out the nature and extent of their connexion with moral questions. They should be ready to make sacrifices for social progress on sound lines. It cannot, indeed, be denied that the whole history of the Church shows that when warm-hearted Christians take up economic questions, they tend to favor radical projects. For their demands bearing on political economy they are wont to claim the support of the gospel, and they endeavor to construct from it a socialistic programme. It must be admitted that we are even now threatened by this danger. Even Protestantism is not free from the danger that some day a second Arnold of Brescia may appear in its midst, Patarenes again arise, and clerical students of political economy attempt, in the name of the gospel, to prescribe to others, as with legal force, the attitude which, if they are to retain the name of Christians, they must assume towards social questions. There is certainly an element of danger in that coquetting with the social-democratic movement which may already be noticed in certain quarters. As long as the leaders and journals of that party inculcate a life devoid of religion, of duties, of sacrifice and of resignation, what can we have in common with their conception of life as a whole? It is, again, a more than questionable procedure to prejudge and condemn "the rich" and whole classes of the nation, and dream that it will be possible by beginning at the bottom to construct by degrees an entirely new Christian commonwealth. As yet, indeed, these are only fragmentary and passing indications of what might happen in the future. There is as yet no one among us who does not believe that only such claims ought to be put before any individual in the name of the gospel as are addressed to his conscience, his free choice and his love; and it is still clearly felt that the gospel is concerned with supplying other than temporal needs; but things have their own logic, and those who have sown the wind will reap the whirlwind.

This warning is, however, not intended to dissuade either evangelical Christians as such, or clergy and theologians generally, from occupying themselves with economic and social questions, and forming their own opinions upon them. On the contrary, Christianity ought to stand aloof from no common experience of life and the world, and it should be open to the consideration of all great questions. Thus for centuries its connexion was of the closest with philosophy, and especially with metaphysics, in which all the intellectual life of the time was summed up. No one was then an educated Christian who was not also a philosopher. In like manner, history and social questions occupy a prominent place in the intellectual life of today, and those who wish to participate in this life cannot afford to neglect them.

But, above all, it is the want and misery of our fellow countrymen that act like a goad, urging us on to study and investigate the construction of the social organism, to examine which of its ills are inevitable, and which may be remedied by a spirit of self-sacrifice and energy. The magnitude and importance of this task make everything else that we have to do on and for this earth seem small. How can we as Christians leave this work undone, and how, if, through our selfishness, indolence and sloth, our position becomes ever more difficult and critical, can we be surprised when we find ourselves overwhelmed with radical proposals from those who think differently from ourselves?

A few words in conclusion. The signs of the times seem to point to further development of the socialistic principle of state administration of public and economic affairs. There are many who hail this tendency with unmixed delight, but I cannot number myself unreservedly among them. We have certainly reason to rejoice when sources of poverty and want are stopped, and misery is obviated. But we must not forget that every fresh regulation of this kind acts also as a check upon free development, and so compels us to devise new ways and means whereby conditions necessary for the training of free and independent personalities may be maintained. If it were all to end in legalized slavery; if, hemmed in from childhood by coercive measures, we were to lose all individual character, what a disaster that would be!

Three great tasks have been committed to our charge, as duties not only towards ourselves, but towards future generations. These are the defence of the evangelical faith, the prevention, as far as in us lies, of distress among our fellow men, and the encouragement of education and culture. In the heat of economic conflict, and amidst rival schemes for allaying it, the last of these is apt to be forgotten; and yet moral and economic ruin would follow speedily upon the decline of culture. But the successful pursuit of education depends upon certain fixed conditions, which cannot be changed in an arbitrary manner, and by which, therefore the nature and scope of all social and economic work must in part be determined.

Education can no more be brought within the bounds of one unbending system than truth, from which it draws its breath, can be reduced to one dead level. But the Evangelical Church would be false to its own nature were it to renounce its alliance with truth and education, no longer making it its aim to train up free and independent Christians. This too is a great evangelical social work, and we have good reason to attend to it, since powers hostile to education stand in strong array against us.

Evangelical faith, a heart sensitive to the wants of others, and a mind open to truth and the treasures of the intellect — these are the powers on which our Church and nation rest. If we are but true to them, we shall realize more and more the truth of the promise expressed in your brave hymn of faith:

> "Now is there peace unceasing;
> All strife is at an end."

(SG: 66-91)

*

WHAT IS CHRISTIANITY?

(Sixth Selection)

On pp. 88-116 of this text, Harnack depicts, in the context of developing a picture of the newly emerging religion, the "social question" of Christianity. He is convinced that the gospel of Jesus is not a social or political entity but, rather, something about "eternity in the midst of time," as he was to put it elsewhere. But so that it may find acceptance in time, Christians need to act in this world in accordance with the commandments of Jesus and be the servants of all. Jesus did not give those commandments any specificity in terms of his own time's needs; had he done so his message would not have been timeless, would not have been able to appeal to our souls or our higher life.

THE GOSPEL AND THE POOR, OR THE SOCIAL QUESTION

Here we encounter different views prevalent at the present moment, or, to be more exact, two views, which are mutually opposed. We are told, on the one hand, that the gospel was in the main a great social message to the poor, and that everything else in it is of secondary importance — mere contemporary wrapping, ancient tradition, or new forms supplied by the first generations of Christians. Jesus, they say, was a great social reformer, who aimed at relieving the lower classes from the wretched condition in which they were languishing; he set up a social program which embraced the equality of all men, relief from economical distress, and deliverance from misery and oppression. It is only so, they add, that he can be understood, and therefore so he was; or perhaps — so he was, because it is only so that we can understand him. For years books and pamphlets have been written dealing with the gospel in this sense; well-meant performances which aim at thus providing Jesus with a defence and a recommendation. But amongst those who take the gospel to be an essentially social message there are also some who draw the opposite conclusion. By trying to prove that Jesus' message was wholly directed to bringing about an economical reform, they declare the gospel to be an entirely utopian and useless program; the view, they say, which Jesus took of the world was gentle, but also weak; coming himself from the lower and oppressed classes, he shared the suspicion entertained by small people of the great and the rich; he abhorred all profitable trade and business; he failed to understand the necessity of acquiring wealth; and accordingly he shaped his programme so as to disseminate pauper-ism in the "world" — to him the world was Palestine — and then, by way of contrast with the misery on earth, to build up a kingdom in heaven; a program unrealizable in itself, and offensive to men of energy. This, or something like this, is the view held by another section of those who identify the gospel with a social message.

Opposed to this group of persons, united in the way in which they look at the gospel but divided in their opinions in regard to it, there is another group upon whom it makes quite a different impression. They assert that as for any direct interest on Jesus' part in the economical and social conditions of his age; nay, further, as for any rudimentary interest in economical questions in general, it is only read into the gospel, and that with economical questions the gospel has absolutely nothing to do. Jesus, they say, certainly borrowed illustrations and examples from the domain of economics, and took a personal interest in the poor, the sick, and the miserable, but his purely religious teaching and his saving activity were in no way directed to any improvement in their earthly position: to say that his objects and intentions were of a social character is to secularize them. Nay, there are not a few among us who think him, like themselves, a "conservative," who respected all these existing social differences and ordinances as "divinely ordained."

The voices which make themselves heard here are, as you will observe, very different, and the different points of view are defined with zeal and pertinacity. Now, if we are to try to find the position which corresponds to the facts, there is, first of all, a brief remark to be made on the age in which Jesus lived. Our knowledge of the social conditions in Palestine in his age and for some considerable time previously does not go very far; but there are certain leading features of it which we can establish, and two things more particularly which we can assert.

The governing classes, to which, above all, the pharisees, and also the priests, belonged — the latter partly in alliance with the temporal rulers — had little feeling for the needs of the people. The condition of those classes may not have been much worse than it generally is at all times and in all nations, but it was bad. Moreover, there was here the additional circumstance that mercy and sympathy with the poor had been put into the background by devotion to public worship and to the cult of "righteousness." Oppression and tyranny on the part of the rich had long become a standing and inexhaustible theme with the psalmists and with all men of any warm feelings. Jesus, too, could not have spoken of the rich as he did speak, unless they had grossly neglected their duties.

In the poor and oppressed classes, in the huge mass of want and evil, amongst the multitude of people for whom the word "misery" is often only another expression for the word "life," nay, is life itself — in this multitude there were groups of people at that time, as we can surely see, who, with fervent and steadfast hope, were hanging upon the promises and consoling words of their God, waiting in humility and patience for the day when their deliverance was to come. Often too poor to pay even for the barest advantages and privileges of public worship, oppressed, thrust aside, and unjustly treated, they could not raise their eyes to the temple; but they looked to the God of Israel, and fervent prayers went up to him: "Watchman, what of the night?" Thus their hearts were opened to God and ready to receive him, and in many of the psalms, and in the later Jewish literature which was akin to them, the word "poor" directly denotes those who have their hearts open and are waiting for the consolation of Israel. Jesus found this usage of speech in existence and adopted it. Therefore when we come across the expression "the poor" in the gospels we must not think, without further ceremony, of the poor in the economic sense. As a matter of fact, poverty in the economic sense coincided to a large extent in those days with religious humility and an openness of the heart towards God, in contrast with the elevated "practice of virtue" of the pharisees and its routine observance in "righteousness." But if this were the prevailing condition of affairs, then it is clear that our modern categories of "poor" and "rich" cannot be unreservedly transferred to that age. Yet we must not forget that in those days the economical sense was also, as a rule, included in the word "poor." We shall, therefore, have to examine the direction in which a distinction can be made, or perhaps to ask, whether it is possible to fix the inner sense of Jesus' words in spite of the peculiar difficulty attaching to the conception of "poverty." We can have some confidence, however, that we shall not have to remain in obscurity on this point; for in its fundamental features the gospel also throws a bright light upon the field covered by this question. (*C:* 88-92)

*

In considering the social question we must put aside all those sayings of Jesus which obviously refer to the poor in the spiritual sense. These include, for instance, the first beatitude, whether we accept it in the form in which it appears in Luke or in Matthew. The beatitudes associated with it make it clear that Jesus was thinking of the poor whose hearts were inwardly open towards God. But, as we have no time to go through all the sayings separately, we must content ourselves with some leading considerations in order to establish the most important points.

Jesus regarded the possession of worldly goods as a grave danger for the soul, as hardening the heart, entangling us in earthly cares, and seducing us into a vulgar life of pleasure. "A rich man shall hardly enter the kingdom of heaven."

The contention that Jesus desired, so to speak, to bring about a general condition of poverty and distress, in order that he might afterwards make it the basis of his kingdom of heaven — a contention which we encounter in different forms — is erroneous. The very opposite is the case. Want he called want, and evil he called evil. Far from showing them any favor, he made the greatest and strongest efforts to combat and destroy them. In this sense, too, his whole activity was a saving activity, that is to say, a struggle against evil and against want. Nay, we might almost think that he over-estimated the depressing load of poverty and affliction; that he occupied himself too much with it; and that, taking the moral bearings of life as a whole, he attributed too great an importance to those forces of sympathy and mercy which are expected to counteract this state of things. But neither, of course, would this view be correct. He knows of a power which he thinks still worse than want and misery, namely, sin; and he knows of a force still more emancipating than mercy, namely, forgiveness. His discourses and actions leave no doubt upon this point. It is certain, therefore, that Jesus never and nowhere wished to keep up poverty and misery, but, on the contrary, he combated them himself and bid others combat them. The Christians who in the course of the Church's history were for countenancing mendicancy and recommending universal pauperization, or sentimentally coquetted with misery and distress, cannot with any show of reason appeal to him. Upon those, however, who were anxious to devote their whole lives to the preaching of the gospel and the ministry of the Word — he did not ask this of everyone, but regarded it as a special calling from God and a special gift — upon them he enjoined the renunciation of all that they had, that is to say, all worldly goods. Yet that does not mean that he relegated them to a life of beggary. On the contrary, they were to be certain that they would find their bread and their means of livelihood. What he meant by that we learn from a saying of his which was accidentally omitted from the gospels, but has been handed down to us by the apostle Paul. In the ninth chapter of his first epistle to the Corinthians he writes: "The Lord hath ordained that they which preach the gospel should live of the gospel." An absence of worldly possessions he required of the ministers of the Word, that is, of the missionaries, in order that they might live entirely for their calling. But he did not mean that they were to beg. This is a Franciscan misconception which is perhaps suggested by Jesus' words but carries us away from his meaning.

In this connexion allow me to digress for a moment from our object. Those members of the Christian churches who have become professional evangelists or ministers of the Word in their parishes have not, as a rule, found it necessary to follow the Lord's injunction to dispossess themselves of their worldly goods. So far as priests or pastors, as the case may be, and not missionaries, are concerned, it may be said with some justice that the injunction does not refer to them; for it presupposes that a man has undertaken the office of *propagating* the gospel. It may be said, further, that the Lord's injunctions, over and above those relating to the commandment of love, must not be made into inviolable laws, as otherwise Christian liberty will be impaired, and the high privilege of the Christian religion to adapt its shape to the course of history, free from all constraint, will be prejudiced. But still it may be asked whether it would not have been an extraordinary gain to Christianity if those who are called to be its ministers — the missionaries and pastors, had followed the Lord's rules. At the very least, it ought to be a strict principle with them to concern themselves with property and worldly goods only so far as will prevent them being a burden to others, and beyond that to renounce them. I entertain no doubt that the time will come when the world will tolerate a life of luxury among those who are charged with the care of souls as little as it tolerates priestly government. Our feelings in this respect are becoming finer, and that is an advantage. It will no longer be thought fitting, in the higher sense of the word, for anyone to preach resignation and contentment to the poor, who is well off himself, and zealously concerned for the increase of his property. A healthy man may well offer consolation to the sick; but how shall a man of property convince those who have none that worldly goods are of no value? The Lord's injunction that the minister of the Word is to divest himself of worldly possessions will still come to be honored in the history of his communion.

Jesus laid down no social program for the suppression of poverty and distress, if by program we mean a set of definitely prescribed regulations. With economical conditions and contemporary circumstances he did not interfere. Had he become entangled in them; had he given laws which were ever so salutary for Palestine, what would have been gained by it? They would have served the needs of a day, and tomorrow would have been antiquated; to the gospel they would have been a burden and a source of confusion. We must be careful not to exceed the limits set to such injunctions as "Give to him that asketh thee" and others of a similar kind. They must be understood in connexion with the time and the situation. They refer to the immediate wants of the applicant, which were satisfied with a piece of bread, a drink of water, an article of clothing to cover his nakedness. We must remember that in the gospel we are in the East, and in circumstances which from an economical point of view are somewhat undeveloped. Jesus was no social reformer. He could say on occasion, "The poor ye have always with you," and thereby, it seems, indicate that the conditions would undergo no essential change. He refused to be a judge between contending heirs, and a thousand problems of economics and social life he would have just as resolutely put aside as the unreasonable demand that he would settle a question of inheritance. Yet again and again people have ventured to deduce some concrete social program from the gospel. Even evangelical theologians have made the attempt, and are still making it — an endeavor hopeless in itself and full of danger, but absolutely bewildering and intolerable when people try to "fill up the gaps" — and they are many — to be found in the gospel with regulations and programs drawn from the Old Testament.

No religion, not even Buddhism, ever went to work with such an energetic social message, and so strongly identified itself with that message as we see to be the case in the gospel. How so? Because the words "Love thy neighbor as thyself" were spoken in deep earnest; because with these words Jesus turned a light upon all the concrete relations of life, upon the world of hunger, poverty and misery; because, lastly, he uttered them as a religious, nay, as *the* religious maxim. Let me remind you once more of the parable of the Last Judgment, where the whole question of a man's worth and destiny is made dependent on whether he has practised the love of his neighbor; let me remind you of the other parable of the rich man and poor Lazarus. I should like to cite another story, too, which is little known, because it occurs in this wording not in our four gospels but in the gospel of the Hebrews. The story of the rich young man is there handed down as follows: "A rich man said to the Lord: Master, what good must I do that I may have life? He answered him: Man, keep the law and the prophets. The other answered: That have I done. He said to him: Go sell all thy possessions and distribute them to the poor, and come and follow me. Then the rich man began to scratch his head, and the speech did not please him. And the Lord said to him: How canst thou say: I have kept the law and the prophets, as it is written in the law, Love thy neighbor as thyself? Behold, many of thy brethren, sons of Abraham, lie in dirty rags and die of hunger, and thy house is full of many goods, and nothing comes out of it to them." You observe how Jesus felt the material wants of the poor, and how he deduced a remedy for such distress from the commandment: "Love thy neighbor as thyself." People ought not to speak of loving their neighbors if they can allow men beside them to starve and die in misery. It is not only that the gospel preaches solidarity and the helping of others; it is in this message that its real import consists. In this sense it is profoundly socialistic, just as it is also profoundly individualistic, because it establishes the infinite and independent value of every human soul. Its tendency to union and brotherliness is not so much an accidental phenomenon in its history as the essential feature of its character. The gospel aims at founding a community among men as wide as human life itself and as deep as human need. As has been truly said, its object is to transform the socialism which rests on the basis of conflicting interests into the socialism which rests on the consciousness of a spiritual unity. In this sense its social message can never be outbid. In the course of the ages people's opinions as to what constitutes "an existence worthy of a man" have, thank God, become much changed and improved. But Jesus, too, knew of this way of measuring things. Did he not once refer, almost bitterly, to his own position: "The foxes have holes, and the birds of the air have nests: but the Son of Man hath no where to lay his head"? A dwelling, sufficient daily bread, cleanliness — all these needs he touched upon, and their satisfaction he held to be necessary, and a condition of earthly life. If a man cannot procure them for himself, others are to step in and do it for him. There can be no doubt, therefore, that if Jesus were with us today he would side with those who are making great efforts to relieve the hard lot of the poor and procure them better conditions of life. The fallacious principle of the free play of forces, of the "live and let live" principle — a better name for it would be the "live and let die" — is entirely opposed to the gospel. And it is not as our servants, but as our brothers, that we are to help the poor.

Lastly, our riches do not belong to us alone. The gospel has prescribed no regulations as to how we are to use them, but it leaves us in no doubt that we are to regard ourselves not as owners but as administrators in the service of our neighbor. Nay, it almost looks as if Jesus contemplated the possibility of a union among men in which wealth, as private property in the strict sense of the word, was non-existent. Here, however, we touch upon a question which is not easy to decide, and which, perhaps, ought not to be raised at all, because Jesus' eschatological ideas and his particular horizon enter into it. Nor is it a question that we need raise. It is the disposition which Jesus kindled in his disciples towards poverty and want that is all-important.

The gospel is a social message, solemn and over-powering in its force; it is the proclamation of solidarity and brotherliness, in favor of the poor. But the message is bound up with the recognition of the infinite value of the human soul, and is contained in what Jesus said about the kingdom of God. We may also assert that it is an essential part of what he there said. But laws or ordinances or injunctions bidding us forcibly alter the conditions of the age in which we may happen to be living are not to be found in the gospel.   (*C:* 93-101)

*

We were occupied with the relation of the gospel to law and legal ordinance. We saw that Jesus was convinced that God does, and will do, justice. We saw, further, that he demanded of his disciples that they should be able to renounce their rights. In giving expression to this demand, far from having all the circumstances of his own time in mind, still less the more complex conditions of a later age, he has one and one only present

296

to his soul, namely, the relation of every man to the kingdom of God. Because a man is to sell all that he has in order to buy the pearl of great price, so he must also be able to abandon his earthly rights and subordinate everything to that highest relation. But in connexion with this message of his, Jesus opens up to us the prospect of a union among men, which is held together not by any legal ordinance, but by the rule of love, and where a man conquers his enemy by gentleness. It is a high and glorious ideal, and we have received it from the very foundation of our religion. It ought to float before our eyes as the goal and guiding star of our historical development. Whether mankind will ever attain to it, who can say? But we can and ought to approximate to it, and in these days — otherwise than two or three hundred years ago — we feel a moral obligation in this direction. Those of us who possess more delicate and therefore more prophetic perceptions no longer regard the kingdom of love and peace as a mere utopia.

But for this very reason there are many among us today upon whom a very serious and difficult question presses with redoubled force. We see a whole class struggling for its rights; or, rather, we see it struggling to extend and increase its rights. Is that compatible with the Christian temper? Does not the gospel forbid such a struggle? Have we not been told that we are to renounce the rights we have, to say nothing of trying to get more? Must we, then, as Christians, recall the laboring classes from the struggle for their rights, and exhort them only to patience and submission?

The problem with which we have here to do is also stated more or less in the form of an accusation against Christianity. Earnest men in political circles of a socialistic tendency, who would gladly be guided by Jesus Christ, complain that in this matter the gospel leaves them in the lurch. They say that it imposes restraint upon aspirations which with a clear conscience they feel to be justified; that in requiring absolute meekness and submission it disarms everyone who wants to fight; that it narcotises, as it were, all real energy. Some say this with pain and regret, others with satisfaction. The latter assert that they always knew that the gospel was not for the healthy and the strong, but for the broken-down; that it knows, and wants to know, nothing of the fact that life, and especially modern life, is a struggle, a struggle for one's own rights. What answer are we to give them?

My own opinion is that these statements and complaints are made by people who have never yet clearly realized with what it is that the gospel has to do, and who rashly and improperly connect it with earthly things.

The gospel makes its appeal to the inner man, who, whether he is well or wounded, in a happy position or a miserable, obliged to spend his earthly life fighting or quietly maintaining what he has won, always remains the same. "My kingdom is not of this world;" it is no earthly kingdom that the gospel establishes. These words not only exclude such a political theocracy as the Pope aims at setting up and all worldly dominion; they have a much wider range. Negatively they forbid all direct and formal interference of religion in worldly affairs. Positively what the gospel says is this: Whoever you may be, and whatever your position, whether bondman or free, whether fighting or at rest — your real task in life is always the same. There is only *one* relation and *one* idea which you must not violate, and in the face of which all others are only transient wrappings and vain show: to be a child of God and a citizen of his kingdom, and to exercise love. How you are to maintain yourself in this life on earth, and in what way you are to serve your neighbor, is left to you and your own liberty of action. This is what the apostle Paul understood by the gospel, and I do not believe that he misunderstood it. Then let us fight, let us struggle, let us get justice for the oppressed, let us order the circumstances of the world as we with a clear conscience can, and as we may think best for our neighbor; but do not let us expect the gospel to afford us any direct help; let us make no selfish demands for ourselves; and let us not forget that the world passes away, not only with the lusts thereof, but also with its regulations and its goods! Once more be it said: the gospel knows only one goal, one idea; and it demands of a man that he shall never put them aside. If the exhortation to renounce takes, in a harsh and onesided way, a foremost place in Jesus' words, we must be careful to keep before our eyes the paramount and exclusive claims of the relation to God and the idea of love. The gospel is above all questions of mundane development; it is concerned not with material things but with the souls of men.   (*C:* 113-116)

5

THE PERSONAL FAITH OF THE THEOLOGIAN

Three and a half decades lie between the first and the last selections of this section, a period of profound experience and anguish for Harnack, his nation, his academy, his Weltanschauung and faith. One senses a personal faith in him of deep rootedness and resilience but not shut off to the realities of human existence.

Harnack had been vigorously assailed for his stance in the Apostoli-kumsstreit, *the upheaval in the Protestant churches in Germany over his support of Pastor Schrempf's decision to abandon the recitation of the Apostles' Creed in public worship. Harnack's tone in that document has all the marks of one really sure of and secure in his views. By the time we come to his Christmas sermon of 1928 the tone is doxological, no longer open to be taken as provocation. Instead, there is an awed praise of the One who in mercy still calls on a people who had shaken the world with a war, who still heralds peace to humankind. Here, as in the public lecture on Christ as Savior, which coincides in time with Harnack's lectures on Christianity, his personal devotion to "the God and Father of our Lord Jesus Christ" is apparent as is his sense of being claimed by Christ's Gospel into witness and action.*

When Harnack was laid to rest in Berlin, his tombstone bore the simple words of an ancient prayer, which expressed symbolically his own simple, yet firm faith: Veni, Creator Spiritus, *Come, Creator Spirit.*[30]

THE APOSTLES' CREED: AN HISTORICAL ACCOUNT WITH AN INTRODUCTION AND POSTSCRIPT

The publication of this selection was occasioned by an event not of Harnack's making or planning, but the substance of that event was close to his heart: the veracity of the confession of Christ on the part of modern confessing individuals. He had pleaded for modern creedal affirmations to be developed by the churches with which the traditional creed of Christian orthodoxy could be replaced in the public worship of God. He had already completed an historical examination of the Apostles' Creed; when a number of his students came to him for counsel in relation to the Church's dismissal of a minister from his duties as a result of having acted in the "spirit" of Harnack's views on the matter — Harnack had nothing to do at all with that minister's actions — he used the occasion to compose the theses which make up this selection.

The pamphlet which combined the longer historical study and these theses, first appeared in Germany in 1892; the theses themselves had already been published separately in Christliche Welt *on August 18th that year. They may be found now in the anthology* Reden und Aufsätze, vol. 1, *text translated by T. B. Saunders; it was published in 1901 as a pamphlet entitled* The Apostles' Creed. *It does not, however, include the theses which make up the selection to follow; that translation was prepared by the editor.*

In the wake of the case against Pastor Schrempf[31] a delegation of students met with Professor Harnack in Berlin a few weeks ago to discuss whether they and other Prussian students of theology should send a petition to the highest council of the Evangelical Church requesting that the so-called Apostles' Creed be stricken from the declaration of commitment demanded of clergy and removed from use in services of worship. Professor Harnack gave his answer in his seminar on recent church-history and sent the following reply to the members of the delegation.

The question has been put as follows: does it seem advisable for students of theology to petition the Superior Council of the Evangelical Church to do away with The Apostles' Creed?

(1) I share with the inquirers the view that it would become the Evangelical Church to put a short confession in place of, or next to, the Apostles' Creed in which the understanding of the gospel gained in and since the Reformation is expressed more clearly and with greater certainty. This would eliminate the offence which that Creed in its formulation causes to many sincere and true Christians, both lay and ordained.

(2) Together with the inquirers I regard the case against Schrempf as a good, yes even compelling, reason to rekindle the issue regarding the validity and use of the Apostles' Creed in the Evangelical Churches; one should not be deterred from pursuing the matter by the high probability of failure in this endeavor at the present time. I am of the opinion that there is no more serious and burning task before the general synods of the Evangelical Churches than to raise the question of creeds freely and courageously.

(3) It is ill advised in this undertaking to lead with the slogan: Let us get rid of the Apostles' Creed! Such a phrase would only turn into a wea-

pon in the hands of the enemies of Christianity, would do injustice to the high religious value and venerable age of that Creed; it would, in addition, be tantamount to raping those Christians who find their faith expressed fully and without offence in it. Finally such a phrase would not be in accord with the manner in which the Churches of the Reformation have related themselves to the confessions of faith of the past and need to do so still until they receive the power for a new act of reformation or a new reformatory personality in their midst.

(4) Therefore, the aim of whatever is to be done at this time can only be either to remove the Apostles' Creed from liturgical usage or to grant congregations the option of not using it. A third option would be to replace it with another evangelical confession of faith.

(5) Anyone of those options has a chance of succeeding only if it were possible actually to formulate and produce a short confession of faith which might replace, or be put next to, the Apostles' Creed and if it is superior to the old Creed in form and power. What holds true for the life of a state holds even more true in the Church: negate only by building up! Every other activity bodes evil; mere wishfulness for a new confession achieves nothing, no matter how well intentioned or seriously articulated it is.

(6) Acceptance of the Apostles' Creed in its literal form is not the touchstone of Christian and theological maturity; on the contrary, a Christian who has grown mature in the understanding of the gospel and church-history cannot avoid being offended by several statements of the Apostles' Creed. But one should equally expect mature and informed theologians to have sufficient historical perception to inquire about the high value and extensive truth-content of the Creed as well as to establish a positive relation to its basic idea, permitting them thereby to see in it an ancient testimony to their own faith.

(7) Such a positive relation cannot be extended, however, to each individual statement in its literal wording. Still, three things need to be remembered here: (a) the Evangelical Church itself does not stick to the exact, original wording of each of this symbol's statements ("the communion of saints"); (b) one of the statements contradicts St. Paul's teachings ("the resurrection of the flesh") and may, given the basic principles of the Evangelical Church, not be kept in its literal form; (c) not one of the individual facts to which Christians give their assent are brute facts but assertions of a confession of faith on account of the invisible connexions and values which faith perceives in them.

(8) There is one statement in this Creed, however, to which the re-

flections just given do not apply: "conceived by the power of the Holy Spirit and born of the Virgin Mary." Something is asserted here as a fact which to many believing Christians is unbelievable and which, were it to be reinterpreted in continuity with the customary reinterpretation of the Church, would have to be turned into its opposite. Here arises, in other words, a real distress for all sincere Christians who are to make use of this Creed as an expression of their faith without being able to inform themselves of the truth of this assertion. The simplest solution seems to be that those who do not accept this assertion should not become, or remain, members of the clergy and that lay people in a similar situation should leave the Church which holds on to the Apostles' Creed. Indeed, one ought seriously to counsel those who, for reasons of conscience, are compelled to act this way not to go against their conscience, for to do that is horrible. Yet, the situation is not such that people's conscientiousness has to be made a general law. A religious community cannot exist, if the possibility of upholding and participating in the inner life of the community into which one was born were to be denied for the sake of a single statement which does not even occupy the center of Christianity. How could one possibly create institutions of doctrine and worship which reflect in all aspects the convictions of everyone and cause offence to no one? And is one to think that those institutions do in actual fact agree to all changes immediately in Christian understanding, including the tried and true ones? It is not a matter of unconscientiousness but, rather, one of tenable and moral justification to remain in the Church, even as one of its teachers, when one takes offence at this or other assertions. It is morally justified to remain only when the theologians involved (a) are in agreement with the Church's basic principles, (b) when they may count on understanding, even if it takes the form of opposition, and do not need to suppress their divergence, and (c) where they work for the alleviation of the distress mentioned earlier within the limits which their profession sets. It is distress, indeed, because, on the one hand, they are not obliged on account of their divergence to withold their gifts from their churches which are not churches of law while, on the other hand, they are obliged to do all they can to end the distress. Only in this way can those theologians keep a good conscience. But this kind of work will vary according to people's professions and abilities. Only very few will, upon examination, find in themselves the proper and uncommon energy which a public agitation like this demands. And often loud acts of agitation have produced the opposite effect.

(9) I can give a negative answer only to the question whether future clergy who, currently, are still students of theology have the right, given their future profession, to participate in a movement which seeks to abolish the Apostles' Creed. I do so for the following reasons: (a) the phrase "abolish the Apostles' Creed!", as already mentioned, is a mistake; (b) even if the set task is kept within the limits referred to, students should, in my view, not make public declarations in issues such as this one; (c) to deal with this special issue requires a Christian and scholarly maturity which students will have attained to at best only at the end of their studies. But agitative actions inevitably draw the young and youngest students into their domain and, thus, become a highly questionable and worrisome spectacle which causes many a conscience to be confused and, soon, to be painfully remorseful.

I do respect the intent and desire from which the question was put to me in the first place. I would like to give the inquirers two tips by means of which they, if they follow them, might reach more appropriately and with more certainty what it is that they desire. The first is to study with diligence and firmness the history of dogma and of the creeds so that true understanding may be had of the original meaning of confessions and of how that meaning changed in history, for often such changes produced entirely new meanings. This will allow access to seemingly or, in fact genuinely, different understandings as well as the possibility of discerning the truth they contain. The second is to establish firmness in the convictions gained at university, the religious convictions particularly which differ from what is called or what is true tradition so that, once having entered upon one's vocation, those firmly held convictions will not be swept away in a short while or laid aside with a broken heart. The actions of agitators will not bring this about, least of all when undertaken by people not yet quite mature. But when all faithfully and firmly hold on to the ideals gained during their years of study then, surely, a golden age will arise for the Church of Jesus and the constraints which must be borne now will pass away.

*

CHRIST AS SAVIOR

Written and delivered as a public lecture in 1899, this selection parallels Harnack's reflections on Christ as redeemer in his lectures on the nature of Christianity. For him the issue was to delineate clearly what salvation and to be saved meant in relation to Jesus Christ as well as to support the claim that in Christ salvation is to be found. Clearly, to view Christ the person as savior is what Harnack rejects; he favors the doing of what Christ said as being salvific. We are saved, he would say, by being raised above our state of nature-existence to a level of spirituality on which the good and true are at one with a moral consciousness that is informed by Jesus. Harnack's personal faith in Jesus comes to view here as faith in the veracity of what Jesus taught to someone of higher insight and sensitivity.

The translation was prepared by the editor from the German text, published in 1911 in Aus Wissenschaft und Leben, *vol. 2, republished in* Ausgewählte Reden und Aufsätze, *pp. 137-48.*

The Christian religion has two foci: holiness and forgiveness. Its simplest expression is the confession of the almighty, holy God as Father. This confession, however, includes a commitment to and the strength for a godly life because of the certainty of forgiveness which is contained in it.

Christianity is the religion of salvation, for it is the religion of forgiveness. The petition: "Forgive us our trespasses" corresponds to the firm conviction that God really does forgive sins. When Luther wrote in his shorter catechism the words: "Where there is forgiveness of sins, there is also life and blessedness," he was not the first to combine forgiveness and blessed life. It was Jesus himself who, in the story which is paradigmatic for the whole gospel: the parable of the prodigal son, showed that the right of sonship is at one with forgiveness. The prodigal receives part of all the father has; in forgiveness he found salvation and blessedness.

Yet when we look at present-day Christianity, it would appear that faith in salvation has lost its certainty, indeed, the longing and hope for it seem all but extinguished. Thousands who hold belief in God or adhere to a Christian ethic seem to want to know nothing about salvation. For them this thought is powerless or without meaning, nothing more than historical tradition of a lost piety or, at best, the origin of a passing sentiment. To connect the concept of salvation with the person of Jesus appears to them like an impossibility. They rest content with a Christianity without Christ and without salvation. For that reason, they strongly disagree with the Church's teaching about Christ as savior or else quietly push it aside.

The reasons for such a negative position are varied. Some claim that they feel no need at all for salvation while others cannot agree that salvation is possible. Still others see something weak and feminine in this teaching which does not fit in with a serious, masculine ethic. And then there are those who do experience the need and the possibility of salvation but go on to claim that their relationship with Jesus is an illusion. How can someone who lived 1800 years ago be the savior of the present? they ask. Nearly all of them are governed by what they call "the modern world-view"; it no longer permits one to hold thoughts of salvation, for psychology has given us a new picture of humanity and research into the origins of morality has altered our view of evil and sin. In addition, historical scholarship, it is said, has given us a historical Christ instead of a heavenly one, and critical philosophy has set sharp boundary lines to what is knowable and what is actual: where does there remain room for salvation and for a savior?

But has the matter itself been indeed shaken? The forms in which earlier times experienced and expressed themselves about salvation and a savior are, for those who think clearly, partly destroyed; but what about the essence? Does not a major part of religious faith lie in that essence, and can such faith ever deny the power it has been given to stand fast even against attack? "And if you uproot me to the very roots, I will still bloom again," proclaims a triumphal old saying; "Humanity always moves forward, and the human always remains the same," said Goethe once. This recognition of the sameness of things human, even though it undeniably contains something depressing, is nevertheless elevating. Humans remain the same not only in that which is lowly and ordinary but also in those higher strivings which lead them forth above mere earthly existence. Augustine's words: "Lord, you have made us for yourself and our hearts are restless until they find rest in you" will find echo in human hearts as long as humans live on earth. The good news of salvation and of the savior will, in the same manner, never be lost either.

In what follows several arguments are to be stated which justify Christian faith in salvation. It is not my task to represent any particular position; rather, I will recall certain facts.

(1) Those who maintain that they experience no need for salvation either deceive themselves or they are considering only a particular form of it. I do not mean the common desire to better one's own situation, to escape certain restrictions and to free oneself from burdens but, instead, that deeper feeling, the longing to be set free from the ordinary course of life and to succeed to a higher and more profound existence. We need only open our eyes to be faced by a multitude of saviors, offering themselves and promising salvation to a yearning humanity. There are also demonic saviors: intoxication and intemperance. Even science and art promise liberation to their disciples. There are those who

expect their salvation from writers, poets and philosophers and who proclaim that through them they have found the road to freedom. The world is full of prophets, masters and saviors, even though few are called such today. That which never allows saviors to disappear and die, which always awakens them anew, is a noble longing. Everywhere in more elevated humanity there exists the desire to raise oneself above the stream of ordinary action and suffering; one does not wish to sink into and disappear in it. To be free from the service to transitory nature: who is there in whom this wish, be it ever so weak and obscured, does not live?

(2) Yet, this longing for salvation, as expressed among us, can be more clearly stated still. Wherever the Christian religion settled and even if a faint glimmer only was perceived of it, the recognition that innocence and purity are of highest value and that guilt was the greatest evil took hold. To be pure and to have inner peace: that is the longing of all longings. Just speak the right word to people, find the way into their soul, and you will find that this longing has not died out in anyone, this longing to be free from sin, to have noble thoughts and a pure heart. It is not true that the great majority of human beings have so sunk into ordinary, sensuous and self-seeking activity that they have lost not only the pure and sacred itself but also the feeling and longing for it. It is equally untrue that any science or knowledge of the world can kill this feeling. Certainly, one must concede that modern developments have increased the danger of undervaluing the inner life and of dissolving the value of our moral stirrings by the analysis of their origins. But this success can only be temporary. It makes no difference how we arrived today at our moral sensitivities, whether at one time we were this or that, whether we had freedom or not, we do experience such sensitivity now in relation to good and evil and, no matter by virtue of what theory, make demands on ourselves and others in actual practice which presuppose freedom and responsibility. And we value that which unfolds on this high level as the real life to which the physical life should be subordinate. What meaning is there in showing the butterfly that it once was a caterpillar and could only crawl? It is now a butterfly lifted high above those things which once prevailed over it. Through stages of evolution humankind has experienced metamorphoses of a higher nature. When they began no one can say, for their origins lie hidden on the other side of recorded history; but their results lie before us. Humans have become law-making and recreative beings and freedom, the freedom for the good, corresponds to this, their nature. We can recognize one of the last phases of this development historically, namely the time of the Israelite prophets

and that of Socrates and Plato. Their days lie within the sphere of the Græco-Roman world and are fulfilled in Christ and his disciples. They have all given us a new meaning and a new life, which we experience not only as an external obligation but also as the unveiling of our true nature and as an achievable goal.

Viewed from without, human history seems to have changed little, indeed. It is still filled with secret and open warfare, with the spilling of blood and with the struggle for earthly possessions. And yet, something new has joined in. Every eye that is open can see it and the unbiased historian has to affirm it. The deepest theme of personal life and the true theme of world-history is the struggle of faith with unfaith, the struggle concerning God and salvation. The individual and humankind, supported by the power of the ethical and the godly, struggle to be free from serving the transitory and to establish a realm of love: the realm of God. Modern historians would like to convince us that this is an illusion, that the theme of world-history is still simply the struggle for enough food and a place at the table. They are wrong. If challenged, thousands upon thousands today would, for the sake of the ethical ideal, renounce all earthly goods, yes, even their own lives. Challenge is given and people do it. Daily such sacrifices are quietly being made in the certainty that life is not the highest of goods. This certainty need not be the result of reflection; even the ethical, the life with God, can work with the gentle force of a natural law.

(3) If that is so, then we are in the sphere to which salvation belongs. In the highest sense salvation can only be the power which helps us lead a pure and holy life, a life with God, the power that fills us with the conviction that we are here not about an illusion but with the assurance that we shall gain life when we lose it.

It follows, therefore, that for us salvation can not be had as something "objective," something which takes place apart from or outside of personality. The greatest of events may have occurred on earth or between heaven and earth, they are worthless for us if they do not become our experience. They become our experience only through contemplation or faith. Something else follows now: if we are to become liberated from the world and become citizens of a realm beyond this world, that is to say, win new life, then it is clear that nothing earthly can bring about salvation, that God only can be the savior. It has always been experienced thus whenever real salvation was sought. The prophets and psalmists knew it in no other way; they looked for no human savior, they looked for God. "As the hart pants for fresh water, so pants my soul, Lord, for you."

"If I have you only, I ask for nothing else in heaven and on earth; even though my body and soul wither away, you, Lord, are my heart's comfort and my portion." Up to our time all who desired true salvation wished for nothing other than that God might arise in them, would come to them, poor and unworthy as they might feel themselves; they asked God for the forgiveness of their sins, for a pure heart and an untroubled spirit.

(4) It seems, therefore, that a human savior is an impossibility. Not only does it seem so, it is so. Only God is savior. A secret bond binds each human to God and only when this bond is experienced personally — "speak, Lord, for your servant hears" — can one be saved. And yet, Christianity names Jesus of Nazareth its savior. How is such a contradiction to be resolved?

There are people in whom the religious predisposition is so strong that they are able to find God virtually without help from others and to live in God. However, the history of religion shows that such people are rare and that the large majority of our species do not experience religion in the way they do. The prophets saw and heard God, felt God present and in that experience found the clearest proof of the existence and reality of God. History of religion shows furthermore that they experienced a very powerful impulse, indeed, a most compelling command, to declare what they had experienced, to proclaim God to their sisters and brothers and to enlarge for them their weak knowledge of God. Their sermons were not in vain. In this aspect it is as it is in art: we all have certain artistic tendencies, but only with the help of artists are they developed, otherwise they atrophy. But even an artist is often in need of another artist and a prophet anoints another prophet. This is an order of history, one of its linkages. Freedom, independence and the higher life are seldom merely natural gifts; they are the result of dependence and education.

The most significant stage in the history of religion occurred when people no longer sought God in the beams of the sun, in storm, or in paradoxical phenomena in the course of the world, but in the words of holy people such as the prophets. Only then did religion become a definite part of the inner life and was connected to morality. People did not lose the awe with which they beheld the deity in the workings of creation, but they looked to the God who spoke through the prophets with yet greater awe, for he was revealed through their spirit and word. Now people learned that genuine revelation of God can take place only in humans, for God is the Holy One. Holiness can not reveal itself through nature. Therefore, one harkened to the prophets and, as a result, conceded to them an exceptional place. One sensed that without them one would have remained imprisoned in ignorance and unending bondage. By believing the prophets and following them a portion of what they had experienced passed over into the souls of those who heard them. In this sense already they were saviors, for God, the Holy One and the savior, had become known to the people. For it was not their own fire which now burned in their souls, rather, they were the torches which God had lighted. These torches set the glimmering wicks afire.

(5) Jesus Christ was a prophet. Whoever wishes to approach him must begin with this observation concerning his person and work. Whoever is unprepared to understand the prophets and their task in history can also not understand Jesus Christ. However, Christianity not only calls him a prophet but also differentiates him from all other prophets in that it acknowledges him to be the savior and, in looking back to him, wants to know nothing more of any other savior either before or after him. How is such an acknowledgment to be understood and justified?

The simplest way seems to be to call upon the testimony of Jesus about himself. It is beyond dispute that he made a distinction between himself and all the prophets and that he claimed a unique place for himself. Those appeals alone would remain unimpressive were they not supported by the proof that he was justified in such testimony. Blind submission has no ethical value.

Jesus Christ was a prophet, but he was the last of them. Those who came after were either weak or false prophets or they confessed that they had received grace upon grace from his abundance. We are not, for that reason, justified in naming as prophets the great men of God who followed him: Paul, the fourth evangelist, Augustine, Francis, Luther and the others.

Jesus Christ was a prophet. But while the other prophets gathered only a small circle around themselves, he was the prophet for many peoples and an age that has seen no end.

Jesus Christ was a prophet. But while the other prophets had only an imperfect knowledge of God and mutually corrected one another, he brought perfect knowledge of God in that he proclaimed God as the holy, omnipotent father and, therefore, as gracious love.

Jesus Christ was a prophet. But while with the earlier prophets knowledge and deed were often at odds or incongruent with each other, even the penetrating glance of hatred failed to uncover any disunity between what he taught and what he did. His meat was to do the will of his Father in heaven.

These are historical facts and on account of them it is right and true not to judge Jesus as a prophet like the others. We are obliged to lift him out of their band, not to place him simply at its head but to place him above them. He called himself "the Son of God" and we understand that he had the right so to name himself. He taught his disciples to know the Father and he led them to him. And still today his gospel leads people out of self-seeking and worldly pleasures, out of fear of God and godlessness to a life with God the savior. It is because they have heard his voice that they say "I will arise and go to my father."

(6) But that is not all yet. Indeed, those who have experienced what has just been described are disciples of Christ and no one may deny them that name. However, the confession of the earliest Christians still includes more. In the first place, Christ is named by them as the reconciler, as the one who died for our sins. Secondly, they teach that he is the living one, that he lives in believers, fulfilling, leading and guiding them.

I will not belabor the last point; I will say that it is no paradox or mere postulation but a fact that he, who is prophet, guide and Lord, takes possession of those who are his in their inward being. However, that which lies behind this fact, that which is expressed by the confession: "Christ lives in me," the conviction concerning the eternal life of Christ, of his power and majesty, is the secret of faith which defies all explanation.

The first point needs more precision still. Christ died for our sins? Christ has reconciled us to God? What? Did God demand a reconciliation? Is God not love? Does God, who forgives sins, demand indemnity? Does the father in the parable of the prodigal son require satisfaction before he forgives his son? Does it not say of the tax-collector who prayed: "God, be merciful to me, a sinner" that he "returned home justified?" Of course, it is true. God is love. He has always been love and forever remains love. In what else does the comfort of the gospel consist but in that it reveals God to us as eternal love? Away with the thought that God turned from hate to love or that any sort of sacrifice or payment had to be made to him so that humanity might be forgiven and loved! Still, such an acknowledgment does not settle the matter completely.

There is an inviolable law which compels the godless and contentious either to deny God or fear and flee from him as the angry judge. That is the actual and strongest punishment for sin, for the separation from God; for there is no other sin. This punishment either drains the heart of everything lofty and holy or it turns belief in God into a torturous agony. Often it does both and the soul flounders between nothingness and unfocused feelings of an utterly unforgivable guilt or crippling pressure. This condition is unnatural and false, and yet, it is neither perverse or false, because it is the normal consequence of a self-willed and false orientation. How can it be overcome? How can people be set free from it? Certainly not by means of "self-made salvation," but only by means of a power that sets free from the outside what had been buried and breathes life into the never wholly extinguished striving for what is above. And deeds, not words can be effective here or, rather, words which are also deeds. When the Holy One stoops to sinners and lives and walks with them, when he does not consider them too insignificant but calls them sisters and brothers, demanding of them nothing except that they accept his presence among them, when he serves them and dies for them, then they believe once again in the Holy, for they have actually experienced it. And then also dissolves the fear of the rigor of his judgment. People then experience the Holy as mercy and learn that there is something mightier than nature, something mightier indeed than judgment, namely all-powerful love.

The life, word and death of Jesus need to be put into this context. *For thus it achieved its aims and thus it still achieves it.* He creates the assurance that forgiving love is a fact, the highest revelation of all higher life, and that this love is greater than punishing judgment, that, therefore, this judgment no longer is to be seen as the final word of the higher life. They who believe this are reconciled, reconciled to God; for it is not God who is in need of reconciliation, it is humans who need to be led back to God. The reconciler, however, is Christ, for he redeems humans from the law of sin into which they had fallen, the law either to deny God or to think of him as a terrible judge. How does Christ save? Only in that his word, life and death, that is, he himself, becomes an experience of the soul which through this experience, is freed from the power of the law of sin, freed from this unnatural law of nature.

That is the basic form of Christian faith concerning reconciliation and the reconciler. I do not wish to assert that every Christian must be conscious that this is what she/he believes, still less do I wish to maintain that this is all to be said about God's ways. What is very clear and what must have become so to every Christian in its significance is that Christ did not call the just to himself but sinners and those who yearned for justice but still feared it. This, too, history teaches: the most profound and mature Christians conceived of Jesus not as a prophet but as the savior and reconciler. Indeed, even more: they were not content with seeing reconciliation merely in his words and his life's work; they considered his suffering and death, too, to be substitutionary. How could they do otherwise? When they, the sinners, knew themselves set free from the judgment of justice and saw him, the Holy One, suffer and die, how should they not acknowledge that he suffered what they should have? Confronted with the cross no other feeling and judgment is possible. In this feeling and judgment the decisive has come to full expression. In relation to this matter, every calculating speculation must stray into uncertainty and groundlessness, for we can not venture beyond the bounds of the righteous. Awe, too, disappears when all-powerful love is probed concerning its right and method. It is manifest to us always as a fact only and lies on the boundary of that which reason comprehends. The cross of Christ, like every cross which stands in the service of brothers and sisters, like merciful love itself, is a holy secret, hidden from the wise and knowledgeable, but is the power and the wisdom of God.

*

WHAT IS CHRISTIANITY?

(Seventh Selection)

These words are the concluding sentences from Harnack's 1899/1900 lecture course; in a manner of speaking, they are a sage's admonition, given on the pinnacle of his power. To come to grasp that the one whom Jesus addressed in the language of defenseless intimacy as "my father" is also the "father" of every human being and is to be trusted with that same intimacy is, according to Harnack, to have the faith which comprises the true nature of Christianity.

Our knowledge of the world has undergone enormous changes — every century since the Reformation marks an advance, the most important being those in the last two; but, looked at from a religious and ethical point of view, the forces and principles of the Reformation have not been outrun or rendered obsolete. We need only grasp them in their purity and courageously apply them, and modern ideas will not put any *new* difficulties in their way. The real difficulties in the way of the religion of the gospel remain the old ones. In face of them we can "prove" nothing, for our proofs are only variations of our convictions. ...

It is religion, the love of God and neighbor, which gives life a meaning; knowledge cannot do it. Let me, if you please, speak of my own experience, as one who for thirty years has taken an earnest interest in these things. Pure knowledge is a glorious thing, and woe to the man who holds it light or blunts his sense for it. But to the question, whence, whither, and to what purpose, it gives an answer today as little as it did two or three thousand years ago. It does, indeed, instruct us in facts; it detects inconsistencies; it links phenomena; it corrects the deceptions of sense and idea. But where and how the curve of the world and the curve of our own life begin — that curve of which it shows us only a section — and whither this curve leads, knowledge does not tell us. But if with a steady will we affirm the forces and the standards which on the summits of our inner life shine out as our highest good, nay, as our real self; if we are earnest and courageous enough to accept them as the great reality and direct our lives by them; and if we then look at the course of mankind's history, follow its upward development, and search, in strenuous and patient service, for the communion of minds in it, we shall not faint in weariness and despair, but become certain of God, of the God whom Jesus Christ called his Father, and who is also our Father. (C: 299-301)

*

CHRISTMAS

It was Harnack's second to last Christmas: 1928. He had been invited to preach on the occasion of this high holiday, but not at a local congregation. In a way, this sermon sums up much of his work and faith: careful historical analysis of texts, exegesis in the manner of liberalism, the warmth of the celebration of a news that heralds "higher values": peace and good will, and a reflection on his and his nation's recent experience in which the longing for freedom from war and terror are expressed as powerfully as they are here. There is, too, the German Harnack who thinks in terms of "national" strengths and weaknesses, the man of European civilization and culture to whom heroic forces are still a value.

The text was published in German for the first time in the posthumously edited anthology Aus der Werkstatt des Vollendeten *in 1930 and republished in* Ausgewählte Reden und Aufsätze, *pp. 166-71. The translation was prepared by the editor.*

We should give praise that each year a day returns on which peace and joy are proclaimed, on which hearts and hands open to practice love,

313

and which radiates with its brilliance into the difficult darkness of our days. And the ardent wish fills every heart that none will be left out, none will be forgotten at the feast.

The Christmas celebration has its roots in the Christmas stories and, therefore, one should consider them in these days. We are indebted exclusively to two evangelists, the Jew Matthew and the Greek Luke, for these stories, as they will soon have been told, sung and painted for two thousand years, for the tales added later have enjoyed only minimal dispersion. Of the two evangelists it is Luke who bears the palm, even though Matthew has surely given us a masterful work in the story of the Magi from the East. He does not, however, equal Luke's marvellous story-telling skills. With good cause the early tradition called Luke "the painter." He was not a painter; rather, according to the testimony of his friend Paul, the Apostle, he was a physician. Still, his eye and hand were those of a great painter. What he told were not myths, though perhaps such do occasionally slip in, but rather legends, not created by him but taken from what had been already transmitted to him. But the manner of reception, the retelling of them in those magnificent yet simple pictures, their interconnectedness one with the other and their nuancing: all that is Luke's very own work. Greek artistic sense is wedded here to the deepest of Jewish-Christian piety, Greek openness to the world to the seclusion of a narrow Israelite circle, awaiting consolation and exaltation. From those connexions evolved pictures whose power of attraction for shape and content has survived every change in world history.

Of the many Christmas and childhood stories which Luke tells, the principal one, namely the actual birth story, is also the most artistically perfect one. One cannot help asking every time one reads this story anew whether the author was himself aware of all the splendid and suggestive things which grip and uplift us in his portrayal or whether his hand was guided as that of an unknowing observer. Who is to decide?

"An order went out from Caesar Augustus" — he begins with these words and immediately we are placed in the middle of world events and we hear the celebrated name of those times: Augustus, the Prince of Peace.

"When Quirinius was governor in Syria" — we are taken from Rome to the East, to that huge province where the interchange among many religions and two cultures was most lively.

"Joseph and Mary arose and went from Nazareth in Galilee to Bethlehem in Judaea, the city of David" — first Galilee, half-heathen and of little significance, then the narrow scene of a village in Judaea,

314

but over this area hovers the name of King David which encompasses the memories and hopes of all Israel!

Augustus and David: is it possible to heighten the readers' expectations any more? Is it possible to express more strongly that what is now to be told has meaning within the history of the world? But what does in fact follow is, in the first instance, the telling of a quite unimpressive story of a birth, a birth not even inside a house, but in the stable of an inn: the royal child lying in a manger! And more of the paltry: we are directed out into the fields in the dark, to shepherds pasturing their flocks by night. The descent can go no deeper: from Augustus to the shepherds! But then the heavens open, the marvellous news is proclaimed first of all to the poorest, news that holds true for all people: "Fear not." "Today is born to you a savior." "Peace among those with whom God is well-pleased." That is the lofty solid triad of the gospel message; at its height the word: "Fear not." Augustine, one of the Church-Fathers, once said that were all the evil removed from the world, but the fear of evil allowed to remain, nothing of the miserable condition of humankind would have changed. He was right. That which enslaves us is fear. And the only thing able to free us from it is trust. But it must be an absolute trust, otherwise it does not help. The more strongly the relativity and unreliability of all this earth's things touch our souls the clearer it also becomes that either we sink into pessimism or we dare to believe in God. "A mighty stronghold is our God." For the only ones able to live joyfully and work confidently are they who trust the course of the world and the meaning of their lives despite all apparent contradictions. That, however, means to believe in God and, at the same time, to be freed of all fear.

"Today is born to you a savior." The words "savior" and "salvation" seem to be forgotten words today, as if stricken from the current vocabulary. In Luke's time it was not so. Everyone was looking for saviors. Yet today also I dare to ask: have there ever been humans who never longed for salvation, have there ever been insightful humans who, looking back over their lives, did not have to acknowledge that for what they had become they were, indeed, indebted in large measure to "saviors," that is to say, to people they respected and who had brought them freedom and had helped them to the heights? Not only prophets awaken others, for, in the regular course of events also, purer and higher lives are kindled only by a more powerful flame which, in the end, is the fire of God. It is said that all things are from God, through God, and to God and we try to think this lofty thought. That every power which frees us from ourselves and lifts us above the world comes from God is also something we experience ourselves. The earliest Church already taught that a Christian should be a Christ for others. It did so because it had recognized the savior of the world in the one born in Bethlehem, the first born among many who draw on God's abundant grace. It is clear that the task of the world's savior is far from complete and even the wide expansion of the Christian Church is no measure and sure means of the completion of that task. And yet, no one of insight can maintain that the sweep of the world's history has proven the preaching of the savior of the world to be false, or that the biblical proclamation must make way for a deeper piety and higher ethic.

And the third part of the Christmas message: "Peace!" The saying which is, in fact, the actual festive proclamation of the festival should probably be translated as follows:

> Praise God in heaven and on earth,
> Peace to those humans with whom God is well pleased.

> [Preis in der Höhe sei Gott und auf Erden,
> Friede bei den Menschen seines Wohlgefallens.]

But this difference in translation matters little. The principal meaning remains the same: to God praise, to humans peace!

Peace: inwardly and outwardly, for home and family, for commerce and trade, for the nation and the whole world, for life and death: there is nothing more precious than peace, and if we attend to the voices of the peoples, their teachers, prophets and poets, we see that it is peace which they all uphold and fervently desire. But if we look more closely, we see also that this fervent desire is not the same as the clear insight as to what makes for perfect peace and, still less, as to how one succeeds in reaching it. We hear much more confused voices and half-true assertions: "War is the father of all things and of all progress." "If you want peace, prepare for war." "Lengthy peace enervates people." "Lively, lovely war." And others of the kind. But humankind has finally been freed from such unclarity, freed by means of the frightful experience of the World War. Indeed, this freedom is the only positive and blessed consequence, if humankind is prepared to acknowledge and accept it. The World War has taught us what war is and what it will be in even more fearful ways. We did not know what war was before but in teaching us this lesson, the War has also taught us what peace is.

War is the battle of everyone against everyone in the literal sense: all men, women and children; war is the suspension of all ethical rules, the surrender of all moral values; war is the campaign of slander and lies throughout the entire earth; war is hunger, the destruction of culture, chaos and annihilation. The World War has also taught us how war comes about: no previous summons to hate is necessary, no conspiracy of malice, no plunderous avarice, but "only" unrestrained nationalism, unrestrained pride and thoughtless indiscretion. From this follows with commanding clarity also what peace is and how it is to be attained. Peace is no uneasy balance of power, so easily upset by very little pressure; rather, peace is a genuine protective union in friendship among peoples, created and guarded by the mobilization of all moral powers. It is available only at such a high price. The word: "Am I my brother's keeper?" must disappear from the interchange of peoples just as much as the other: "my country — right or wrong"; go must the illusion that, properly understood, self-interest, if not too sharply employed, suffices to achieve peace. Complete recognition of the uniqueness and rights of the other, brotherly attitudes and genuine friendship — all these are needed; a union of peoples as all-inclusive as life itself: only these strong forces can prevent the revival of the danger of war. It is crystal clear today that the highest moral values and commands are the elementary, necessary prerequisites of peace, namely justice, love of neighbor near and far, the reign of good made real in the human community.

That this wonderful knowledge is addressed to us, even though it be forced on us, and that, therefore, our time has been given the task of bringing it into concrete being, should fill us with great joy. The previous century was given the tasks of eliminating slavery and improving the lot of workers and important tasks they were. But how much greater and more important is ours: to make the message of peace become reality on earth. Even to herald this task is the beginning of peace, and we can joyfully testify from the experience of the past year that a real beginning has been made. Thanks to our political leaders and to the enlightened statesmen in both hemispheres! We know only too well that progress here will be slow and that we are faced with a demanding struggle with the veiled economic and political egoism of the people; even the tasks of the previous century are far from being complete, but the right way is known. Clearly, knowledge alone will not do; repentance, strong moral exertion, courage to sacrifice, a new education and a new spirit are needed. But never before has bitter necessity of life so come to the aid of moral necessity as today since the Great War. One must not fear, however, that "pacifism" will undermine national strength and uniqueness, for it requires the exertion of the best heroic forces and must, therefore, serve to perfect national identity.

Let us celebrate Christmas and enter the new year with confidence. "Peace on earth": it must be ours! "We must at last prevail."

SELECTED BIBLIOGRAPHY

I

The definitive listing of Harnack's writings, listing 1611 titles, is: Friedrich Smend, *Verzeichnis der Schriften Adolf von Harnacks*; Leipzig: J. C. Hinrichs Verlag, 1927, augmented in 1931.

The seven volumes of speeches and addresses bring together an enormous sum of Harnack's lectures, addresses, sermons, talks etc., only a few of which have been translated into English.

Reden und Aufsätze, 2 vols.; Giessen: Alfred Töpelmann, 1906.

Aus Wissenschaft und Leben, 2 vols.; Giessen: Alfred Töpelmann, 1911.

Aus Friedens-und Kriegsarbeit; Giessen: Alfred Töpelmann, 1916.

Erforschtes und Erlebtes; Giessen: Alfred Töpelmann, 1923.

Aus der Werkstatt des Vollendeten; Giessen: Alfred Töpelmann, 1930.

A small selection from these volumes was published under the title:

Ausgewählte Reden und Aufsätze, Agnes von Zahn-Harnack and Axel von Harnack, eds.; Berlin: Walter de Gruyter & Co., 1951.

Other important works not translated into English are:

Die Entstehung der christlichen Theologie und des kirchlichen Dogmas; Gotha: Klotz Verlag, 1927.

Marcion, das Evangelium vom fremden Gott; Leipzig: J. C. Hinrichs Verlag, 1921.

The excellent biography:

Agnes von Zahn-Harnack, *Adolf von Harnack*; Berlin: Walter de Gruyter & Co., 1951.

II

HARNACK'S WORKS IN ENGLISH TRANSLATION

The Acts of the Apostles, J. R. Wilkinson, tr.; New York: G. P. Putnam's Sons, 1909.

The Apostles' Creed, Thomas Bailey Saunders, ed. and tr.; London: A. & C. Black, 1901.

Bible Reading in the Early Church, J. R. Wilkinson, tr.; New York: G. P. Putnam's Sons, 1912.

Christianity and History, Thomas Bailey Saunders, tr.; London: A. & C. Black, 1896.

The Constitution and Law of the Church in the First Two Centuries, H. D. A. Major, ed., F. L. Pogson, tr.; New York: G. P. Putnam's Sons, 1910.

Essays on the Social Gospel, with Wilhelm Herrmann, M. A. Canney, ed., G. M. Craik, tr.; New York: G. P. Putnam's Sons, 1907.

History of Dogma, 7 vols, Neil Buchanan, tr.; London: Williams and Norgate, 1896-9.

Militia Christi. The Christian Religion and the Military in the First Three Centuries, David McInnes Gracie, tr.; Philadelphia: Fortress Press, 1981.

The Mission and Expansion of Christianity in the First Three Centuries, J. Moffatt, ed. and tr.; New York: Harper and Row, Publishers, 1962.

Monasticism: Its Ideals and History and The Confessions of St. Augustine, E. E. Kellett and F. H. Marseille, trs.; London: William and Norgate, 1901.

New Testament Studies, 6 vols., W. D. Morrison, ed., J. R. Wilkinson, tr.; New York: G. P. Putnam's Sons, 1908-25.

Outlines of the History of Dogma, Edwin Knox Mitchell, tr.; Boston: Beacon Press, 1957.

Thoughts on the Present Position of Protestantism, Thomas Bailey Saunders, tr.; London: A. & C. Black, 1899.

What is Christianity?, Thomas Bailey Saunders, tr.; New York: Harper and Row Publishers, 1957.

III

SECONDARY LITERATURE IN ENGLISH

Cremer, Hermann, *A Reply to Harnack on the Essence of Christianity,* Bernhard Pick, tr.; New York: Funk and Wagnalls Co., 1903.

Garvie, A. E., *The Ritschlian Theology;* Edinburgh: T. and T. Clark, 1899.

Glick, G. Wayne, *The Reality of Christianity. A Study of Adolf von Harnack as Historian and Theologian;* New York: Harper and Row Publishers, 1967.

Hirsch, E. Felix, "The Scholar as Librarian. To the Memory of Adolf von Harnack", in *The Library Quarterly,* vol. IX (1939), pp. 299-320.

Mackintosh, H. R., *Types of Modern Theology;* London: Nisbet & Co., 1937.

Pauck, Wilhelm, *Harnack and Troeltsch. Two Historical Theologians;* New York: Oxford University Press, 1968.

Pauck, Wilhelm, "The Significance of Adolf von Harnack among Church Historians", in *Union Theological Seminary Quarterly Review,* Special Issue, (Jan. 1954), pp. 13-24.

Rumscheidt, H. Martin, *Revelation and Theology. An Analysis of the Barth-Harnack Correspondence of 1923;* Edinburgh: Scottish Academic Press, 1972.

NOTES TO THE INTRODUCTION

[1] Agnes von Zahn-Harnack, *Adolf von Harnack*; Berlin: Walter de Gruyter & Co., 1936, 2nd ed. 1951, p. 1 (Cited as AZH).

[2] In 1912 Chamberlain published a monograph on Goethe; the book drew the two men together in a remarkable friendship — Harnack read each chapter closely and, after every reading, wrote a letter to Chamberlain which, in itself, became a mini-dissertation on the poet. In one of those letters he wrote: "Goethe raised the people of good will, who know how to listen, to a higher level and protected them permanently from falling back into dull-mindedness, anarchy and despondency; you have not only tried to capture *this* Goethe but have truly succeeded and accomplished more than any biographer before you. . . . [I have the marvellous feeling] of being led by the hand of one whose psychological and realistic portraiture only sets in where that of others comes to an end and who not only knows the bounds from which we must flee but also sees the land clearly where we are to make our abode." — Chamberlain was ecstatic about Harnack's reactions; he wrote one day in response to the latest praise: "Never has anyone given to me so richly, spontaneously, extensively and with so divinatory an instinct for that which the worker longs for at the moment in which, after years of struggle for insight and for its formulation, the abyss of the end, of completion, the abyss of the merciless black and white opens up before him, and he waits for what he really *needs* but, in my experience, rarely ever receives. . . . I was able to convey to my publishers the strict prohibition against sending me any other reviews. Your reviews are unrepeatable; should someone be found, a rare person, who is as rich as you, he will not be as generous as you, so generous, that I could only repeat the beggars' "God bless you," for it is not possible to thank someone for something like this, unless one became sentimental, which neither of us likes to be." (AZH 273-4)

[3] Cited in Karl Hammer, *Deutsche Kriegstheologie 1870-1918*; Munich: Kösel Verlag, 1971, p. 203.

[4] Cited in Wilfried Härle, "Der Aufruf der 93 Intellektuellen und Karl Barths Bruch mit der liberalen Theologie," in *Zeitschrift für Theologie und Kirche*, vol. 72, (1975), pp. 209-10.

[5] Adolf von Harnack, *Marcion, das Evangelium vom fremden Gott*, 2nd edn.; Leipzig: J. C. Hinrichs Verlag, 1924, pp. 214-5.

[6] *Ibid.*; p. 217.

[7] Karl Barth, "Liberal Theology: Some Alternatives," in *Hibbert Journal*, vol. lix, No. 3, (April 1961), pp. 213-5.

[8] This discussion is treated more extensively in Martin Rumscheidt, *Revelation and Theology. An Analysis of the Barth-Harnack Correspondence of 1923*; Edinburgh: Scottish Academic Press, 1972, pp. 171-88.

[9] Karl Barth, "Reformation als Entscheidung," in *Der Götze wackelt*, Karl Kupisch, ed.; Berlin: Käthe Vogt Verlag, 1961, p. 77.

[10] *Ibid.*; pp. 82-3.

[11] Karl Barth, *Final Testimonies*, Eberhard Busch, ed., Geoffrey W. Bromiley, tr.; Grand Rapids: Wm. B. Eerdmans Publishing Co., 1977, p. 37.

[12] Trutz Rendtorff, "Adolf von Harnack," in *Tendenzen der Theologie im 20. Jahrhundert. — Eine Geschichte in Porträts*, H. J. Schultz, ed.; Stuttgart: Kreuz Verlag, 1966, p. 45.

[13] See below, p. 57.

[14] Adolf von Harnack, *What Is Christianity?*; New York: Harper and Brothers Publishers, 1957, p. 69.

[15] *Ibid.*; pp. 47-8.

[16] Rendtorff, *Op. Cit.*; p. 46.

[17] *Ibid.*; p. 46.

NOTES TO SELECTED TEXTS

[1] Herostrates, an Ephesian, so desired notoriety that he set fire to the temple of Artemis in Ephesus on the night when Alexander the Great was born.

[2] The word *Parabeln* carries a somewhat negative tone here. It does not convey what the word actually used for parables in the NT, *Gleichnis*, does. *Parabeln* is used here in the sense of "tale" as in: fishermen tell tales of their exploits.

[3] It is helpful to compare the Harnack-Barth correspondence of 1923 and this study to see how specific Harnack's reflections are in relation to Karl Barth.

[4] Earlier in the lectures Harnack had stated what he meant by "charismatic" theology. "Whenever a higher religion develops a theology, it is usually a theology in a two-fold form: a theology from within and one from without. The former presents the ideational content of religion from the point of view of the faithful and relies on the inner power of persuasion of the content to uphold the truth. Theologians of this kind know that their theology is charismatic theology. . . . The latter considers religion to be a part of the circle comprising all objects of cognition and judges its veracity on the basis of generally valid historical, psychological and theoretical principles of knowledge." *Die Entstehung der christlichen Theologie* . . . , p. 54.

[5] A few years earlier Harnack had aroused a stormy controversy in the churches with his assertion about the need to have the Old Testament removed from the canon of sacred scripture; see above, p. 29.

[6] Harnack adds this footnote to that sentence: "The Church is younger and older than Jesus. It existed in a certain sense long before him. It was founded by the prophets, in the first place within Israel, but even at that time it pointed beyond itself. All subsequent developments are changes of form. It came into being at the moment when a society was formed within Israel characterized by universalism, which strove to ride out of the darkness into light, from the popular and legalistic religion to the religion of the Spirit, and saw itself led to a higher stage of humanity, at which God and His holy moral law reign supreme." p. 4.

[7] *What Is Christianity?*; pp. 258-60.

[8] *Ibid.*; p. 281. Cf also above p. 220.

[9] *AZH*; p. 184.

[10] The fictive and the true; the reference is to one of Goethe's major works. (ed. note.)

[11] "In the spirit of a new age" — this also means that primitive Christianity was not copied, nay, that there was a passing beyond its lines at important points.

[12] The complement to this observation is to be found in the beautiful words Dilthey has applied to Luther: "Nowhere as yet has history spoken in favor of the ideal of a morality without religion. New active forces of will, so far as we observe, have always arisen in conjunction with ideas about the unseen. But the fruitful novelty within this domain always arises from the historical connexion itself, on the basis of the religiousness of a departing age, just as one condition of life emerges from another. For it is only when dissatisfaction arises for the genuinely religious man from the innermost and deepest religious and moral experience within the existing union, on the basis of the altered state of consciousness, that an impulse and direction are given for the new. So it was also with Luther."

[13] At lofty moments of his life Luther spoke like a prophet and evangelist. All inter-mediate conceptions and intermediary persons were transcended: "Your worshipful Highness the Elector knows, or if he does not know, let it be hereby declared to him, that I have the gospel, not from men, but only from heaven through our Lord Jesus Christ, so that I might very well have gloried in being, and written myself down as, a servant and evangelist, which I mean henceforward to do." Such self-consciousness almost awakens misgivings, but it must not be overlooked that it is united with the greatest humility before God; it did not arise suddenly, much less in a visionary way, but it slowly developed itself from dealing with Scripture and the religious possessions of the Church; it only makes its appearance, finally, in connexion with the spirit, "If God is for us, who can be against us?" and does not intrude into the empirical ecclesiastical sphere to dictate laws there. It must be recognized, therefore, as the genuine expression of religious freedom, of the kind described by Clement of Alexandria as the temper of the true Christian, and of the kind which the mystics of all ages have sought in their own way to reach. But we search in vain throughout the whole of church history for men who could write such letters as that one to the Elector, and for writings like those composed by Luther in Coburg. I can very well understand how Catholic critics should find in those letters an "insane arrogance." There really remains only the alternative that we pass this judgment upon Luther, or that we acknowledge that there belonged to him a special significance in the history of the Chris-tian religion.

[14] There is, in my opinion, no difference to be found in Luther at different periods. What he wrote (1541) in his pamphlet *Wider Hans Worst* in full agreement with the mediæval view of the "Twelve Articles" he could have written twenty years earlier: "No one can deny that we hold, believe, sing, and confess all things that correspond with the Apostles' symbol, the old faith of the old Church, that we make nothing new therein, nor add anything thereto, and in this way we belong to the old Church and are one with it. . . . If anyone believes and holds what the old Church did, he is of the old Church."

[15] One of the strongest passages is to be found in the *Kurzes Bekenntnis vom heiligen Abendmahl*: "Therefore, there must be a believing of everything, pure and simple, whole and entire, or a believing of nothing"; (he refers to his doctrine of the Eucharist).

[16] It has also been pointed out, that from the time of Justinian the old dogma introduced the book of civil law, that the legal protection which it promised was extended only to orthodoxy, and that, accordingly, every attack on the Trinity and Christology was at that time necessarily regarded as anarchism and threatened with the heaviest penalties. This is certainly correct, but I cannot discover that Luther ever thought of the serious conse-quences that would have followed for himself and his followers from opposition to the old dogma. So far as I see, he never went so far as to feel concerned about this, seeing that he adhered to the old dogma without wavering. Had the case been otherwise, he would cer-tainly have shown the courage that was exhibited by Servede. The same thing, unless I am mistaken, cannot be said of Calvin and Melanchthon. As to the latter, it was *also* anxious reflection about matters of ecclesiastical and civil polity that led him to avoid those whose attitude towards the old dogma was open to suspicion; and Calvin can scarcely be freed from the reproach that he would have taken a different attitude towards the old dogma, and would have treated the Antitrinitarians otherwise, if he had been less political.

[17] See his "Brief Answer to Duke George's latest book," and one of its most charac-teristic passages: "And after I had made the profession I was congratulated by the Prior, convent, and Father-confessor on the ground of being now an innocent child, returning pure from baptism. And certainly I could most willingly have rejoiced in the glorious fact

that I was such an excellent man, who by his own works (so that was the popular view in spite of all the dogmatic warnings against it), without Christ's blood, had made himself so beautiful and holy, and that so easily too, and in such a short time. But although I readily listened to such sweet praise and splendid language about my own deeds, and let myself be taken for a wonderworker, who in such an easygoing way could make himself holy and could devour death and the devil to boot, etc., nevertheless, there was no power in it all to sustain me. For when even a small temptation came from death or sin I succumbed, and found there was neither baptism nor monkery that could help me; thus I had now long lost Christ and his baptism. I was then the most miserable man on earth; day and night there was nothing but wailing and despair, so that no one could keep me under restraint. . . . God be praised that I did not sweat myself to death, otherwise I should have been long ago in the depths of hell with my monk's baptism. For what I knew of Christ was nothing more than that he was a stern judge, from whom I would have fled, and yet could not escape."

[18] Especially also Augustine's doctrine of the entire incapacity of fallen man for the good, and accordingly also his predestination doctrine (see the information Luther gives of himself from the year 1516 to the year 1517).

[19] For Augustine there is ultimately in the salvation which grace bestows something dark, indescribable, mysteriously communicated; Luther sees it in the forgiveness of sin — that is, the God of grace himself; and he substitutes therefore for a mysterious and transforming communication the revelation of the living God and *fides*.

[20] The way in which Luther gave expression to his faith during the first period shows us plainly that he learned not only from Augustine but also from the mediæval mystics (from Bernard onwards). The linking together of surrender to God with surrender to Christ is for the first time apparent in them; for Augustine it was much more vague. In this sense Luther's faith stands in a distinct historic line; yet the originality and force of his experience as a believer is not thereby detracted from. Even in the domain of religion there is no *generatio aequivoca.*

[21] The fullest, most distinct, and truest account of Luther's *religion* is to be found in Herrmann's book, . . . , *The Communion of the Christian with God; A discussion in agreement with the view of Luther,* 3rd ed., 1896. Dilthey also makes the excellent remarks . . . : "The justification of which the mediæval man had inward experience was the descending of an objective stream of forces upon the believer from the transcendental world, through the Incarnation, in the channels of the ecclesiastical institutions, priestly consecration, sacraments, confession, and works; *it was something that took place in connexion with a supersensible regime.* The justification by faith of which Luther was inwardly aware was the personal experience of the believer standing in the continuous line of Christian fellowship, by whom assurance of the grace of God is experienced *in the taking place of a personal faith,* an experience derived from the appropriation of the work of Christ that is brought about by the *personal election* of grace." What Dilthey adds is correct: "If it necessarily resulted from this that there was a change in the conscious attitude towards dogma and in the basing of faith thereon, *this change did not touch the matter of the old ecclesiastical dogma.*"

[22] Compare the exposition of the 2nd Main Article in the manual for prayer: "Here it is to be observed that there are two kinds of believing: first, a believing about God, which means that I believe what is said of God is true. This faith is rather a form of knowledge or observation than a faith. There is, secondly, a believing in God, which means that I put my trust in him, give myself up to thinking that I transact with him, and believe without any doubt that he will be and do to me according to the things said of him. Such faith, which

throws itself on God, whether in life or in death, alone makes a Christian man."
  [23] Preface to the Epistle to the Romans . . . : "Faith is a divine work in us, through which we are changed and regenerated by God. . . . O, it is a living, busy, active, powerful thing faith, so that it is impossible for it not to do us good continually. Neither does it ask whether good works are to be done, but before one asks it has done them, and is doing them always. *But anyone who does not do such works is an unbelieving man,* gropes and looks about him for faith and good works, and knows neither what faith is and what good works are. . . . Faith is a living, deliberate confidence in the grace of God, so certain that for it it could die a thousand deaths. And such confidence and knowledge of divine grace makes joyous, intrepid, and cheerful towards God and all creation."
  [24] One easily sees that this definition has an Augustinian basis, and that it is modified by the determinative position given the factors "word" and "faith."
  [25] Here, according to Luther's view, *office* also has its place in the Church; it is the "ministerium" in word and sacrament, instituted in the Church (not the individual congregation) with a view to leading the individual to faith. The creator of this office is, of course, God, not the Church, much less the individual congregation, and it has its field simply in the administration of the means of grace with a view to the establishment and maintenance of faith.
  [26] See the *Kirchenpostille,* Sermon for the Second day of Christmas . . . : "The Christian Church keeps all words of God in its heart, and revolves them, maintains their connexion with one another and with Scripture. Therefore anyone who is to find Christ must first find the Church. How would one know where Christ is and faith in him is, unless he knew where his believers are? And whoever wishes to know something about Christ must not trust to himself, nor by the help of his own reason build a bridge of his own to heaven, but must go to the Church, must visit it and make inquiry. Now the Church is not wood and stone, but the company of people who believe in Christ; with these he must keep in connexion, and see how those believe, live, and teach who assuredly have Christ among them. For outside of the Christian Church there is no truth, no Christ, no blessedness."
  [27] The whole Reformation of Luther may be described as a Reformation of "divine worship," of divine worship on the part of the individual and on the part of the whole community.
  [28] In the treatment of the history of dogma from a universal historical point of view Zwingli may be left out of account. Anything good that was said by him as the Reformer, in the way of criticizing the hierarchy and with regard to the fundamental nature of the new piety, is to be found in him as it is to be found in Luther, and his arriving at greater clearness regarding it he owed it to Luther. The points in which he diverged from Luther belong to the history of Protestant theology. There were many particulars which he understood how to express more lucidly than Luther, and many negations of the traditional were more definitely shaped by him. But he was not less doctrinaire than Luther; he had that quality rather in a higher degree; and he did not always make a beneficial use, for the system of faith, of his fine Humanistic perceptions. Calvin, again, is, as a theologian, an Epigone of Luther.
  [29] Friedrich Wilhelm Kantzenbach, "Harnack, Adolf von," in *Theologische Realenzyklopädie,* vol. 14; Berlin: Walter de Gruyter, 1985, p. 453.
  [30] Kantzenbach, *Op. Cit.,* p. 454.
  [31] Pastor Schrempf was a minister in Württemberg who, after a long internal conflict, decided in 1891 to delete the repetition of the Apostles' Creed from his baptismal services. The regional consistory at first had a neighboring clergy perform the baptisms of

his congregation and, then, removed him from office. He continued the struggle to remain a parish minister but left the Church 18 years later.

INDEX OF NAMES

Strauss, David Friedrich 100, 170
Strauss, Richard 32
Tertullian, Quintus Septimus 28
Thurneysen, Eduard 95
Tiersch, Carl 13
Tiersch, Heinrich 189
Tolstoi, Leo 78
Valentinus 123

Wellhausen, Julius 135, 176
Wesel, Johann von 235
Wessel, Johann (Gansfort) 235
Wilhelm II, Emperor 21, 22
Wyclif, John 235
Zwingli, Huldrych 96, 104, 268, 326

INDEX OF SUBJECTS